Holy Ambition:

RHETORIC, COURTSHIP, AND DEVOTION IN THE SERMONS OF JOHN DONNE

➤━◆➤━○━◁◆━┤━◄

Brent Nelson

MEDIEVAL AND RENAISSANCE
TEXTS AND STUDIES

VOLUME 284

Holy Ambition:

RHETORIC, COURTSHIP, AND DEVOTION IN THE SERMONS OF JOHN DONNE

> ⊱━⋆⊙⋆━⊰

Brent Nelson

Arizona Center for Medieval and Renaissance Studies
Tempe, Arizona
2005

BV
4253
.N37
2005

Library of Congress Cataloging-in-Publication Data

Nelson, Brent, 1966–
   Holy ambition : rhetoric, courtship, and devotion in the sermons of
John Donne / by Brent Nelson.
        p. cm. — (Medieval Rennaissance texts and studies ; v. 284)
   Includes bibliographical references.
   ISBN 0-86698-327-9 (alk. paper)
   1. Sermons, English—17th century. 2. Donne, John, 1572-1631.
3. Courtship—Religious aspects—Christianity. I. Title. II. Series.
   BV4253.N37 2005
   251'.0092—dc22   2005004745

This book is made to last.
It is set in Adobe Garamond, smythe-sewn,
and printed on acid-free paper to library specifications.

Printed in the United States of America

For Melanie, Elias, and Jesse

For thou hast created us for thyself, and our heart cannot be quieted till it may find repose in thee.
                                                        — St. Augustine[1]

---

[1] *St. Augustine's Confessions,* trans. William Watts, vol. 1 (Cambridge, MS: Harvard University Press, 1912): I.i.1.

~· Contents ·~

~· List of Figures ·~

~ List of Abbreviations ~

Works by Kenneth Burke

~ *Acknowledgments* ~

I am grateful to the Social Sciences and Humanities Research Council of Canada for funding this research and to the University of Saskatchewan Office of the Vice President (Research) for funding to prepare the manuscript for publication. The following graciously granted permission to reprint the illustrations in this book: Beinecke Rare Book and Manuscript Library at Yale University; Huntington Library; University of Glasgow Library; University of Waterloo Library; Newberry Library; University of Edinburgh Library; Regents of the University of California Press; and William E. Engel.

Above all, I am grateful to a host of individuals who have enabled me and the work published in this book. While an undergraduate at the University of Waterloo, I was introduced to John Donne by Roman Dubinski, a consummate teacher who taught me much about Donne and his age. Similarly, John North exemplified for me the teacher-scholar and has been a much valued friend and supporter. I began an academic career in large part owing to the encouragement of these men. I first began thinking about the *topos* of courtship in Brenda Cantar's graduate course on court(ier)ship in Sidney and Spenser, also at the University of Waterloo. At the University of Toronto I was fortunate to work with a thesis committee that was perfectly suited to this combination of scholarly interests: Greig Henderson and Michael Dixon were expertly equipped to help me sort through the intersections between Burke, rhetoric, and religious devotion; Douglas Chambers provided more of the same and also led me to begin making connections through avenues of early modern literature and culture that are still taking me in new and interesting directions. Anyone working on Donne's sermons is indebted to the work of Jeanne Shami, and I am doubly so for her criticism of the earliest form of this work as a doctoral dissertation. One of the press's external readers of my manuscript provided many more helpful suggestions for revision, and my diligent and thorough editor at MRTS, Leslie MacCoull, made many recommendations that improved the text and enriched my footnotes. For less formal conversations that helped to shape my thinking on these and related ideas that matter to me, I thank Dana Brown, Bill Bunn, Colby Grypiuk, Steve Habermehl, Nick Cradock-Henry and Sean Davidson; and to the fellowship at Lincoln Road (formerly Lakeshore), many thanks for blessing me and my family through all our years in Waterloo. Finally, I owe everything to Mel and the boys for enriching my life and saving me from my work.

Introduction

TO HIS CONTEMPORARIES JOHN DONNE, Dean of St. Paul's Cathedral in London, was remarkable not so much for his theology or his politics as for his eloquence as a preacher. Of course, as a preacher Donne needed to be theologically informed and politically astute, and he was; but Donne's chief achievement as a preacher was his ability to compose and deliver powerful sermons that would move his audience to greater devotion, and this, above all, he did with distinction. This study aims to provide some insight into Donne's effectiveness as a composer of sermons, focusing on his resourcefulness, particularly his ability to derive from his own culture diverse material that he could use in persuading his congregation toward a life of religious devotion.

Much recent study of Donne's sermons has focused on the first two aspects of Donne's career as preacher: his politics and his theology. The most important work, by Jeanne Shami and others, has elaborated the socio-political considerations that influenced Donne's preaching. The emerging picture is of a preacher who delicately balanced personal conscience regarding his spiritual duty with the external demands of political authority.[1] The present study also approaches Donne's sermons as cultural

---

[1] John N. Wall Jr. and Terry Bunce Burgin, for example, show that in his St. Paul's Cross sermon on 5 November 1622, Donne responded to King James's *Directions to Preachers* (which restricted political commentary in sermons) by conspicuously avoiding the "lurid anti-Catholic invective" that came to typify the occasion ("'This sermon...upon the Gun-powder day': The Book of Homilies of 1547 and Donne's Sermon in Commemoration of Guy Fawkes' Day, 1622," *SAR* 49.2 [1984]: 19–30, 23). Yet Jeanne Shami, in her comparison of the Royal Manuscript of Donne's 1622 Gunpowder Plot sermon with the 1649 published version, concludes that "Donne is concerned with

artifacts, inextricably involved with the conditions and circumstances in which they were produced, but it treats these cultural conditions not simply as limitations on Donne's freedom as a preacher, but rather as part of the rhetorical resources that Donne found available to him in early seventeenth-century England. The particular circumstances of Donne's sermons and his responsiveness to these conditions must continue to be of interest to Donne scholars, but this should not be our end, for it was not his end. Donne was ever mindful of his public function as Dean of St. Paul's, but he was equally alert to his duty as a shepherd of individual souls.

Often an emphasis on the politics of a sermon obscures the more interesting matter (from a literary point of view) of the means by which it seeks to move an audience to action. While Peter McCullough's documentation of the growing concern over Queen Anne's apparent recusancy, for example, helps to clarify a potential purpose for the sermon Donne delivered to her at Denmark House in 1617, this emphasis displaces the chief point of rhetorical interest: how does Donne endeavour to move her toward reconciliation with the state church, specifically, and toward devotion generally?[2] In another instance, Gale H. Carrithers, Jr. and James D. Hardy, Jr. glean passages from the sermons to derive a composite picture of Donne's attitude toward political-spiritual relations, a potentially rhetorical issue. Carrithers and Hardy describe Donne's oblique criticism of royal prerogative, noting that Donne routinely emphasizes the primacy of the *civitas dei* here on earth while asserting the ephemerality of the *civitas terrena*. They

authorized means of criticism, but that in 1622 he was wary of criticizing the King as openly as he did in the revised version" (*John Donne's 1622 Gunpowder Plot Sermon* [Pittsburgh: Duquesne University Press, 1996]: 36). She notes that notwithstanding Donne's general willingness to admonish political authorities, his sense of decorum caused him to temper his message according to the current political climate (29–36). In *John Donne and Conformity in Crisis in the Late Jacobean Pulpit* (Cambridge: D. S. Brewer, 2003), an extensive study of the political constraints imposed on preachers in the 1620's, Shami documents Donne's negotiation of the tension between the authority of the King and his sense of duty as a preacher of the Word. See also Jeanne Shami, "Kings and Desperate Men: John Donne Preaches at Court," *JDJ* 6 (1987): 9–23; Shami, "'The Stars in their Order Fought Against Sisera': John Donne and the Pulpit Crisis of 1622," *JDJ* 14 (1995): 1–58; Nancy E. Wright, "The *Figura* of the Martyr in John Donne's Sermons," *ELH* 56 (1989): 293–309; Meg Lota Brown, "'Though it be not according to the Law': Donne's Politics and the Sermon on Esther," *JDJ* 11 (1992): 71–84; Paul W. Harland, "Donne's Political Intervention in the Parliament of 1629," *JDJ* 11 (1992): 21–37.

2 Peter E. McCullough, "Preaching to a Court Papist? Donne's Sermon Before Queen Anne, December 1917," JDJ 14 (1995): 59–81; idem, *Sermons at Court: Politics and Religion in Elizabethan and Jacobean Preaching* (Cambridge: Cambridge University Press, 1998), 169–82.

note that Donne thereby advocates a heavenly perspective regarding matters of this world, but they do not clarify how Donne's handling of mundane matters (the journey of this life) contributes rhetorically to this reorientation of perspective. They, like so many before them, have "excerpted from the sermons" while asserting that these bits and pieces are nonetheless "representative" of Donne's thoughts on the relation between temporal and spiritual authority.[3] But the picture that emerges is a rather reductive one of *contemptus mundi*. Carrithers and Hardy's initial focus on Donne's political manoeuvring obscures the full rhetorical impact of Donne's strategic use of temporal-spiritual relations. The present study aims rather to show that Donne uses the concerns and desires of this life, political and otherwise, not simply as negative *exempla* of an improper motivation, but as goads to induce an analogous desire that is an extension and dialectical purification of these mundane reflections of a greater good.

Similarly, there has been some good recent work done on Donne's theology, but it has largely neglected one of the most important concerns determining Donne's handling of theology and biblical exegesis: his rhetorical purpose for his audience. In *The Theology of John Donne* Jeffrey Johnson elaborates the communal emphasis in Donne's doctrine of the Trinity, which shaped Donne's vision of the church. Johnson shows that community is an important element in the message of Donne's sermons, but he does not consider important implications of community in the strategies by which Donne appeals to his audience.[4] In *Gender and the Sacred Self in John Donne* Elizabeth M. A. Hodgson attempts to locate in the sermons Donne's "strategic adoption" of variously gendered identities in constructing his "spiritual identity," but these strategies are applied not to his audience as a preacher, but rather toward himself and his self-presentation. That is, the emphasis is again dislocated from rhetoric in an attempt to uncover Donne's ideas about gender, spirituality, and himself.[5] The same is true in other studies on Donne's ideas. While Geoffrey Bullough ("Donne the Man of Law") and Coburn Freer ("John Donne and Elizabethan Economic Theory"), for example, demonstrate Donne's adept-

---

[3] Gale H. Carrithers, Jr. and James D. Hardy, Jr., "Love, Power, Dust Royall, Gavelkinde: Donne's Politics," *JDJ* 11 (1992): 39–58, 54.

[4] Jeffrey Johnson, *The Theology of John Donne* (Woodbridge, Engl.: D. S. Brewer, 1999).

[5] Elizabeth M. A. Hodgson, *Gender and the Sacred Self in John Donne* (Newark, DE: University of Delaware Press, 1999).

ness in matters of law and economics respectively, they stop short of notic-
ing the rhetorical use Donne makes of them in the sermons.

Neglect of rhetorical issues can lead to misguided conclusions about
Donne's personal theology. Lori Anne Ferrell's examination of Donne's pastoral theology, for example, would benefit from consideration of the potential rhetorical motives behind his apparent anti-Calvinism.[6] Ferrell quotes
from Donne's sermon on the rich young ruler of Matthew 19:

> When he enquired of Christ after salvation, Christ doth not say,
> There is no salvation for thee, thou Viper, thou Hypocrite, thou
> Pharisee, I have locked an iron doore of predestination between
> salvation and thee; when he enquired of him, what he should do
> to be sure of heaven, Christ doth not say, There is no such art, no
> such way, no such assurance here; but you must look into the eter-
> nall decree of Election first, and see whether that stand for you or
> no: But Christ teaches him the true method of this art: for, when
> he sayes to him, *Why callest thou me good? There is none good but
> God,* he only directs him in the way to that end, which he did
> indeed, or pretended to seek (*Sermons,* 6:11.224–234).[7]

In the third partition, Donne goes on to elaborate the "method of this art"
that he names here: "a faire method leads him to the true end; Good ends,
and by good wayes, consummate goodnesse" (245–246). Donne's concern
is not the end (one's status in death) but the process that leads to that end
(the present life).

This final partition, the focus of the sermon, is not about predestination *per se* but rather about the distance between God's goodness and
human apprehension of it, of which the young ruler is an *exemplum.* In these
passages, then, Donne seeks not to deny the doctrine of predestination (a
predetermined essence), but rather to induce a desire for assurance in this
present life. Thus, midway through the final partition, Donne makes his
application to his audience:

> That therefore thou maist begin thy heaven here, put thy self in
> the sight of God, put God in thy sight, in every particular action.

---

[6] Lori Anne Ferrell, "Donne and his Master's Voice, 1615-1625," *JDJ* 11 (1992): 59-70.

[7] Donne, *The Sermons of John Donne,* eds. and intro. George R. Potter and Evelyn M.
Simpson, 10 vols. (Berkeley: University of California Press, 1953-1962). References to
Donne's sermons will be provided in-text, according to volume, sermon number, and
line(s).

We cannot come to the body of the Sun, but we can use the light of the Sun many waies: we cannot come to God himself here, but yet here we can see him by many manifestations (463–467).

One's status among the elect, like the sun itself, cannot be apprehended, owing to human limitations. Donne therefore counsels that his congregation look for "manifestations" of their status in their "every particular action," so that their present life will lead them in the way of God, toward their desired end. The spectre of predestination is not refuted, but rather incorporated into Donne's rhetorical strategy for directing his congregation to seek God. Donne's concern is not to be theologically precise so much as to move his congregation in devotion. Ferrell correctly attributes Donne's handling of this matter to pastoral motives, but she need not therefore conclude that Donne "eschews the doctrine of election as too arbitrary to produce anything but despair."[8] Elsewhere Donne clearly does not deny or avoid this doctrine. To summarize in the language of courtship (this sermon, incidentally, is loaded with courtship *topoi*), Donne in this sermon uses the potential for despair at one's indeterminate status among the elect to set the conditions of estrangement which will goad his audience in a courtship of assurance in a present life of devotion in their everyday actions. Moreover, where Ferrell finds in Donne's sermons a clear anti-Calvinist sentiment, Daniel Doerksen finds Calvinist sympathy.[9] We are on much safer ground, indeed more fertile ground, when we look for the rhetorical motives of the preacher rather than for his absolute theological position.

As a number of critics have noted, Donne's ideas are difficult to pin down, leading some critics, such as Theresa M. Di Pasquale in *Literature and Sacrament*, to describe Donne's doctrine as ambivalent and equivocal.[10] I will argue that Donne's expressed ideas on theology, politics, and any other subject he broaches, are very much determined by his resourcefulness as a preacher as he adapts his material to the purposes and demands of his present rhetorical occasion.[11] One should be wary of looking for bald state-

---

[8] Ferrell, "Donne and his Master's Voice," 62.

[9] Daniel Doerksen, *Conforming to the Word: Herbert, Donne, and the English Church before Laud* (Lewisburg, PA: Bucknell University Press, 1997), 23.

[10] Theresa M. DiPasquale, *Literature and Sacrament: The Sacred and the Secular in John Donne* (Pittsburgh, PA: Duquesne University Press, 1999). DiPasquale discusses the sermons only as a context for her study of Donne's poetry.

[11] In this study I focus on Donne's resourcefulness in adapting material from his own culture. Similar work needs to be done on his use of Patristic sources, especially his adap-

ments of belief or commitment from Donne on many of these issues, especially when they are used as material in such a highly rhetorical context as a
sermon. There is no need to conceive of a model of "two Donnes," as P. M.
Oliver recently has done, following John Carey's depiction of a Donne who
was fundamentally confused about his beliefs and commitments.[12] This
depiction *may* be true (I don't think it is); but it is *certainly* true that many
of Donne's apparent inconsistencies can be attributed to his adeptness as a
rhetorician in shaping his material, whatever material was at hand, to his
present needs. Bruce Henricksen rightly contends that in the sermons
"Donne reserves the right to make rhetorical reference to a body of knowledge without committing himself to it."[13] This is in keeping with Aristotle's
famous definition of rhetoric as "the faculty of observing in any given case
the available means of persuasion."[14] Or as the rhetorician John Smith puts
it, "*Rhetorique* is a faculty by which we understand what will serve our turn
concerning any subject to win belief in the hearer."[15] I would suggest this
includes theology. Donne of course never allows himself to expound heresy,
but he does take considerable latitude in his configuring of orthodox doctrine. This is not to say that Donne was not doctrinally committed, but
rather that in the sermons at least his primary commitment was to persuade
his congregation to respond in devotion to God. Donne was ever a pastor-
preacher, not a polemicist nor even a theologian. Not that he altogether
excludes doctrinal controversy from his sermons; rather, as I demonstrate
in chapter 5, he employs controversy not as an end in itself, but as a rhetorical means to a devotional end. Similarly, when Donne touches on
courtship issues and themes, he is not merely expressing his own desires
(though he may be doing that too), but visiting a *topos* for material that he

---

tion of them for rhetorical purposes. See P. G. Stanwood, "Donne's Reinvention of the
Fathers: Sacred Truths Spiritually Expressed," in *Sacred and Profane: Secular and
Devotional Interplay in Early Modern British Literature*, eds. Helen Wilcox et al.
(Amsterdam: VU University Press, 1996), 195–201, and Frank Kermode, "John
Donne," in *Renaissance Essays* (New York: Viking Press, 1971), 116–48, esp.141–42.

[12] P. M. Oliver, *Donne's Religious Writing* (London: Longman, 1997); John Carey, *John
Donne: Life, Mind, Art* (New York: Oxford University Press, 1981).

[13] Bruce Henricksen, "The Unity of Reason and Faith in Donne's Sermons," *PLL* 11
(1975): 18–30, here 29.

[14] Aristotle, *The Rhetoric and the Poetics of Aristotle*, intro. P. J. Corbett, trans. W. Rhys
Roberts and Ingram Bywater (New York: Modern Library, 1954), 24 (1.2, 1355b
26–27).

[15] John Smith, *The Mystery of Rhetoric Unveiled* (1657), 1, B1.

finds to be useful for persuading an audience that is inclined to think and feel along those lines.

Kenneth Burke, a twentieth-century rhetorical theorist, proves useful on this point. Specifically, his notions of rhetoric and courtship help to clarify this relationship between culture and rhetoric. Burke is especially fitting in this context, not only because his theory of courtship draws heavily on Renaissance culture, but also because his model of rhetoric fits well with the purpose and function of Donne's sermons. In one of his many formulations of the term, Burke defines rhetoric as *"the use of language as a symbolic means of inducing cooperation in beings that by nature respond to symbols."*[16] Joan Webber similarly describes Donne's sermons as not simply symbolic but themselves symbols.[17] I would add that a Donne sermon is not only a symbol but also, to borrow a term from Burke, symbolic action. To Burke (working on the premise that all people are naturally guilty), all poetry acts as a symbolic mode of "purification" and as an "expiatory strategy."[18] While such a statement may be idiosyncratically Burkeian in application to poetry, it applies quite naturally and universally to the Christian idea of a sermon. No matter how the purpose of a sermon might be formulated — to admonish the sinful, to encourage the saints, to comfort the sorrowful —, its general function is purgative-redemptive. To restate Burke for my purposes, a sermon is a rhetoric of rebirth, a ritual of cure which enables the preacher to purge his congregation's guilt and forge their new identity in Christ. Burke's methods, then, should be unnecessary in analyzing sermons, where these characteristics are generic and presumably laid bare. But although Donne frequently acknowledges a curative and purifying purpose in preaching, and though his sermons are replete with curative and purificatory imagery, *how* a given sermon effects this purpose is not so clear. The "how" of the sermon brings us to the realm of rhetoric.

---

[16] *RM*, 43 (emphasis in original).

[17] Joan Webber, *Contrary Music* (Madison: University of Wisconsin Press, 1963; repr. Westport, CT: Greenwood Press, 1986), 152, 181. Thomas F. Merrill describes Donne's sense of the sermon as a dynamic, sacramental act: "John Donne and the Word of God," *NM* 69 (1968): 597–616. See also Gale H. Carrithers Jr., *Donne at Sermons* (Albany: State University of New York Press, 1972) on the dramatic, "existential" quality of Donne's sermons.

[18] William H. Rueckert, *Kenneth Burke and the Drama of Human Relations*, 2nd ed. (Berkeley: University of California Press, 1982), 66. In the early stages of my research, Rueckert's book along with Greig Henderson's *Kenneth Burke: Literature and Language as Symbolic Action* (Athens, GA: University of Georgia Press, 1988) were invaluable in informing my thinking about Burke.

If purification accounts for Donne's overall purpose for his sermons, Burke's notion of courtship helps to conceptualize Donne's rhetorical (and symbolic) means for achieving this objective. While a great deal has been written on the social phenomenon of courtship in the Renaissance, there has been very little said about its relationship to literary modes of persuasion outside overt courtship applications.[19] A notable exception is Michael C. Schoenfeldt's study of George Herbert's blending of secular and sacred modes of reverence to encode his approaches to God. Specifically, Schoenfeldt finds that Herbert uses courtship strategies in his devotional poetry to explore his own submission and resistance to God's authority; at the same time, by transporting courtly relations into the context of *The Temple*, Herbert is able to criticize the power structure of the Renaissance court.[20] My interest is rather in Donne's application of courtship strategies to his audience in his attempt to persuade them in their relationship with God. It would accomplish little simply to establish that Donne was familiar with and employed courtship tropes in his sermons. What is more interesting is that Donne mines the wealth of this resource for rhetorical purposes. We know that Donne was learned in various fields of culture, such as law, economics, and science. Francis R. Johnson, for example, finds that Donne was abreast of current scientific discoveries; but more importantly, Johnson notes that Donne alludes sometimes to old theories, sometimes to new, "depending upon his poetic purpose."[21] In the same way, Donne makes use of a wide range of cultural material, including courtship, in his sermons and adapts it according to his rhetorical needs.

♣ Kenneth Burke and the rhetoric of courtship

For Burke, the principle of courtship functions as a commonplace, almost *the* commonplace which we invariably revisit each time we mean to persuade. Motives of courtship emerge whenever estrangement is perceived between different kinds of beings. From this perception of difference

---

[19] The two most important recent studies are Frank Whigham, *Ambition and Privilege* (Berkeley: University of California Press, 1984) and Catherine Bates, *The Rhetoric of Courtship in Elizabethan Language and Literature* (Cambridge: Cambridge University Press, 1992).

[20] Michael C. Schoenfeldt, *Prayer and Power: George Herbert and Renaissance Courtship* (Chicago and London: University of Chicago Press, 1991).

[21] Francis R. Johnson, *Astronomical Thought in Renaissance England* (Baltimore: Johns Hopkins University Press, 1937; repr. New York: Octagon, 1968), 243.

derives an attendant sense of mystery, "a radiance due to their place in the social order," which ensures this distance between the two parties.[22] Social distance invariably motivates attempts to bridge these conditions of estrangement, usually (but not always) attempts by those lower in the given hierarchy of being. Hence Burke's definition in *A Rhetoric of Motives*: "By the 'principle of courtship' in rhetoric we mean the use of suasive devices for the transcending of social estrangement."[23] Indeed, courtship is tantamount to rhetoric, which Burke similarly defines a few pages later as "the mode of appeal essential for bridging the conditions of estrangement 'natural' to society as we know it."[24]

Social estrangements (or any relation of difference) and the courtship dynamic which ensues are always hierarchically conceived. The difference between the haves and the have-nots in any given hierarchy produces in the subject a desire to mount within that hierarchy. According to Burke these hierarchical arrangements are basic to human society, such that the "human animal" is continually goaded by the spirit of hierarchy — or in the postmodern idiom, "[t]he world is always already hierarchized for us, but it can be re-hierarchized."[25] That is, because there is always difference (between employer and employee, between male and female, between this generation and that), there is no question of ridding ourselves of hierarchies, only of promoting new ones or reconfiguring old ones.

These hierarchies arrange values according to governing principles or "ultimate terms," alternately referred to by Burke as "god-terms." For example, at the apex of the Renaissance social hierarchy is the king. Similarly, God occupies the ultimate place in the spiritual order, as does the beloved Lady in the erotic. At each stage of ascent in a given hierarchy, the subject gains another measure of identification with its "ultimate term." In presenting oneself as a spurned would-be lover, one asserts a certain connection with the beloved, even if it simply means placing oneself in a courtship process which logically, if not actually, finds its fulfilment in union with the beloved. This bridging principle of courtship, then, functions as an identi-

---

22 *RM*, 210, n.
23 *RM*, 208.
24 *RM*, 211–12.
25 Robert Wess, *Kenneth Burke: Rhetoric, Subjectivity, Postmodernism* (Cambridge: Cambridge University Press, 1996), 127. Also see Ross Wolin, *The Rhetorical Imagination of Kenneth Burke* (Columbia, SC: University of South Carolina Press, 2001), 196–98.

fication strategy of appealing to some common ground on which the estranged parties can meet. "Identification," says Burke, "is compensatory to division. If men were not apart from one another, there would be no need for the rhetorician to proclaim their unity."[26]

If courtship, as we have seen, so thoroughly characterizes rhetoric, so does identification. In fact, under Burke's rubric of rhetoric there is a great deal of cross-fertilization between his concepts of courtship and identification, such that rhetoric is defined sometimes in terms of one and sometimes in terms of the other. "As for the relation between 'identification' and 'persuasion'," says Burke,

> we might well keep it in mind that a speaker persuades an audience by the use of stylistic identifications; his act of persuasion may be for the purpose of causing the audience to identify itself with the speaker's interests; and the speaker draws on identification of interests to establish rapport between himself and his audience.[27]

Identification is a richly ambiguous term in Burke, sometimes broadly signifying a relationship of close association or, as above, a rapport between two parties. Yet identification, especially in relation to courtship strategies, implies an assertion of one's identity. In its strictest sense, it signifies a union, a consubstantiality or sharing of substance between two parties, or in some cases, of two ideas or "charts" of reality.[28] The importance of this coincidence of courtship and identification will become clear in connection with the ways in which Donne defines and constructs his audience's motives. For now it is enough to note the overtly Christian resonance of Burke's ideas which make them so amenable to Donne's rhetorical situation, the aim of which is to bring his congregation into conformity or identification with Christ.

Rhetorically, courtship functions on the basis of similitude. As Michael Dixon puts it, "[b]ecause erotic, social, and transcendent courtship structures are thus both formally and functionally analogous, any one of them

---

[26] *RM*, 22.

[27] *RM*, 46.

[28] "Chart" is Burke's term for a poem's "realistic sizing-up of situations that is sometimes explicit, sometimes implicit" (*PLF*, 6). Or as Greig Henderson paraphrases Burke, "[t]he chart component involves the poem's relationship to an objective situation" (*Literature and Language*, 29). I am extending the term to apply to the version of reality to which a rhetorical utterance seeks to win its audience.

may stand surrogate for the others."[29] To illustrate this versatile paradigm of courtship, Burke uses Baldassare Castiglione's *The Book of the Courtier*, a source that would have been familiar to Donne.[30] Castiglione's courtiers, concerned with matters of love, status, and religion, exemplify the semantic borrowing that emerged in the Renaissance between the origins of the verb *to court*, meaning to be at court, and the new and closely associated sense of *to woo*. In her analysis of the semantic transformation of the verb *to court*, Catherine Bates confirms that the sexual sense of the term derived from the social sense of "being at court," or "behaving like a courtier."[31]

As the monarchical court of Renaissance Europe increasingly became the centralized source of cultural activity, the semantic field of *to court* grew accordingly to include various analogous modes of courtship. The often-intersecting motives at court resulted in an ambiguity by which one kind of courting could have cross-application to courtship of another sort. This intersection of motives was not limited to the aristocracy but also applied equally to the emerging middle class of seventeenth-century England. In Bates's words, "the word used to describe particular kinds of aristocratic behavior came, through similarity of sense, to apply to the bourgeois orthodoxy of love and marriage."[32] As Bates demonstrates, "[Elizabethan] courtship is ... semantically confusing as well as narratively and politically

---

[29] Michael F. N. Dixon, *The Polliticke Courtier* (Montreal and Kingston: McGill-Queen's University Press, 1996), 11. Dixon's introduction provides an excellent brief summary of Burkeian courtship in relation to early modern England. Burke concludes from his reading of the ostensibly erotic narrative of *Venus and Adonis* that "[t]he vocabularies of social and sexual courtship are so readily interchangeable, not because one is a mere 'substitute' for the other, but because sexual courtship is intrinsically fused with the motives of social hierarchy" (*RM*, 217). Donne would be less inclined to place the social cause in a privileged position. In fact, I will argue that for Donne the three orders are indeed consubstantial, that to court within one is to court within the others, if only one brings them to a proper orientation; however, the spiritual order of motives is always primary for Donne.

[30] Donne, who so self-consciously fashioned himself as a courtier, as his Lothian portrait attests, would certainly have known *The Book of the Courtier*. Peter DeSa Wiggins describes four strategies or "codes" that Donne derived from Castiglione's *Courtier* and used to maintain critical detachment in his poetry while at the same time advancing his own political interests: *Donne, Castiglione, and the Poetry of Courtliness* (Bloomington: Indiana University Press, 2000).

[31] Catherine Bates, "'Of Court it seemes': A Semantic Analysis of *Courtship* and *To Court*," *JMRS* 20 (1990): 21–57. For a fuller development of courtship as a political practice see Bates's prologue and chaps. 1–2 in eadem, *The Rhetoric of Courtship*. For more social theory on Elizabethan courtship see Whigham, *Ambition and Privilege*.

[32] Bates, "'Of court,'" 25.

potent."[33] My concern here, as will become apparent in application to Donne, is with the former potency, with the way in which the broadening sense of courtship provided Donne a flexible discursive and affective structure that would be recognizable and applicable to his congregation's motives.

In Castiglione, courtship even more broadly includes any means of self-presentation designed to impress or appeal to an audience at court according to their class distinction or sexual difference. The ambiguity arising from the etymology and usage of *to court* allows for analogous modes of courtship where one may stand-in as a surrogate for another. To paraphrase Burke, one principle can be talked about in two different orders of vocabulary. In Books I to III of Castiglione's *Book of the Courtier*, discussion moves comfortably between courtships that are social (between fellow courtiers and between courtier and sovereign) and those that are sexual, and the appropriate strategies for advancing in each. More importantly for my purposes, in Book IV Cardinal Bembo conforms political and erotic motives to the ultimate end of courting the divine. His grand Platonic discourse dialectically refines and rarefies sensual beauty into its pure idea "whereupon the soul is kindled by the desire to partake of the heavenly nature, so that with images of burning, and mounting, and coupling, we end on a prayer to 'the father of true pleasures, of grace, peace, lowliness, and good will'."[34] Political desire is easily translatable into erotic desire, and each can be seen as a stylization of spiritual desire. In this way, says Burke,

> [Castiglione's] work might thus make precise our understanding of the purely dialectical motives (ultimate verbal motives) behind the rhetorical convertibility between terms for social hierarchy and terms for theologic hierarchy. Here is a source of 'mystery' grounded in the very perfection of formal thinking, with worldly and transcendent 'reverence' each drawing sustenance from the other.[35]

Courtship, in other words, is a translating of the language of desire that is based on the formal operation of dialectical purification through hierarchy.[36] Burke thus posits three basic modes of courtship — sexual, social, and tran-

---

[33] Bates, *Rhetoric*, 4.
[34] *RM*, 231. Cf. Plato's *Symposium* 211A–212A and *Phaedrus* 250D–256E.
[35] *RM*, 232–33.
[36] *Translatio*, which was another word for metaphor, is an appropriate figure here.

scendent — deriving from three respective types of estrangement formalized into corresponding hierarchies: those which occur between the sexes, between persons of differing social status, and between God and humankind. This analogy of courtships becomes a resourceful *topos* in Renaissance literature where the poet draws from social and transcendent hierarchies to serve erotic courtships, and *vice versa*. In the reign of Elizabeth, which continued into Donne's thirty-first year, the ultimate object of erotic courtship (supremely eligible and un-requiting as she was) happily coincided with the apex of England's political hierarchy, inspiring the richest courtship poetry in the English language.[37] As Francis Bacon wrote in his *in memoriam* of the Queen, "she allowed herself to be wooed and courted, and even to have love made to her; and liked it."[38]

Burke's paradigm of courtship accords well with the culture of early modern England, which was in the midst of a gradual shift from a medieval to a modern social structure that enabled increasing opportunity for social mobility.[39] Elizabethan England was a place where such social climbers and upstarts as Sir Walter Ralegh (whose motto *amore et virtute*[40] seems to typify his precarious rise to the Queen's favour) began to meet with encourag-

---

[37] An obvious example is *The Faerie Qveene*, where Spenser uses erotic and transcendent language to court a political identification with Queen Elizabeth, whom he addresses in his proem as a dread and glorious goddess and characterizes in the poem itself both as the transcendently powerful Faerie Queene herself, Gloriana, and as the transcendently beautiful goddess Belphoebe. Catherine Bates, in *The Rhetoric of Courtship*, supplies a great deal of material on such Elizabethan courtiers, including Leicester, Essex, and Lyly, as well as Sidney and Spenser. A similar courtship relationship emerged in the golden age of devotional verse when, as Arthur Marotti argues, King James's support of devotional writing resulted in its use as a language of courtship: "Donne as Social Exile and Jacobean Courtier," in *Critical Essays on John Donne*, ed. idem (New York: G. K. Hall, 1994), 77–102, here 78.

[38] Bacon, *In felicem memoriam Elizabethæ*, trans. James Spedding, in *The Works of Francis Bacon*, eds. James Spedding et al., 14 vols. (London: Longman, 1868; repr. Stuttgart: Friedrich Frommann Verlag Gunther Holzboog, 1963), 6:317 (translating "...et amoris nomine se celebrari, extolli, sinebat, volebat..." [302]). Bates quotes this passage in "Of Court it seemes," 55.

[39] See Whigham, *Ambition and Privilege*, 6–12 and *passim*. Whigham summarizes Lawrence Stone on this "century of mobility" from 1540–1640, which peaked around 1610. He notes that with this increase in mobility came an increase in aspirations (*Ambition and Privilege*, 14). Whigham provides a great deal of useful historical information which supports many of Burke's notions of courtship, especially as derived from Castiglione. For Stone's statistical data and fuller analysis see "Social Mobility in England, 1500–1700," *P&P* 33 (1966): 16–55.

[40] "By love and courage." Ralegh's own sense of the need for courage is communicated in the legendary story (if it is not true it should be) of his writing in a window, for the Queen to see, "Fain would I climb, but I fear to fall" (Walter Oakeshott, *The Queen and the Poet* [New York: Barnes & Noble, 1961], 22; see also 21–35, *passim*).

ing success. But Burke seeks an even broader extension of the courtship principle beyond the political, covering a wide range of motives and relationships:

> The hierarchic principle of courtship sets a pattern of communi-
> cation between 'lower' and 'higher' classes (or kinds). This can be
> universalized in terms of a climbing from body to soul, from senses
> through reason to understanding, from worldly to the angelic to
> God, from woman to beauty in general to transcendent desire for
> Absolute union. Or the communication may be between merely
> 'different' kinds, where the relative grading is not established by
> general agreement.[41]

Motives of hierarchy can thus have a noetic application, informing structures of thought as well as social relations. Burke draws on Plato's dialectical method in the dialogues to demonstrate how ideas become arranged in
a graded series ordered in relation to an ultimate term. Conceived according to the Platonic scheme, courtship can be broadened to include any
order that is organized in relation to an ultimate object of desire, either
material (Helen of Troy) or conceptual (honour). Michael Dixon describes
the common conception of Platonic dialectic as a triad or cone with

> a wide base consisting of undifferentiated alternative answers to a
> specific question as data (What is Good? What is Love? What is
> Beauty? What is Virtue? What is Justice?), narrowing inductively
> through a series of ordered abstractions to a single principle of
> principles at the apex (Good, Beauty, Justice, or any other
> absolute, abstract 'Idea') from which, in turn, all objects partaking
> of such an abstraction could be deduced. None of the original
> answers is adequate but no answer is eliminated from the struc-
> ture: rather all are positioned in an ordered series, a 'grammar' of
> alternatives, each situated according to criteria of order determined
> by the principle of principles that necessarily transcends any indi-
> vidual answer.[42]

If one courts honour as an ultimate term, all considerations will find their
place according to the degree to which they conduce to notions of honour.
This realignment causes the subject to be more "pure" in relation to the

---

[41] *RM*, 231–32.
[42] Dixon, *The Polliticke Courtier*, 11–12.

ultimate term. In identifying this courtship *topos*, then, we should be on the look-out for situations hierarchically conceived which connote a process of purification *vis à vis* an ascendant object of desire.

In taking a Burkeian perspective I hope to redress two omissions in existing rhetorical criticism of Donne's sermons. For the most part, rhetorical studies of the sermons have been concerned with *elocutio* (commonly taken to be his "style"), addressing his use of imagery, figures, and grammatical structure.[43] Consequently, most of these have taken Donne's sermons piecemeal rather than considering a sermon as a rhetorical whole, a second omission in rhetorical studies of Donne's sermons.[44] The present study is chiefly concerned with strategies that work throughout the larger structures of a given sermon. I give particular emphasis to Donne's *inventio* as it relates to Kenneth Burke's notions of courtship, for it is the principle of *inventio* (the basic generating idea) that governs both the rhetor's selection of material and his manner of handling that material within the other offices of rhetoric, particularly *dispositio* (arrangement) and *elocutio* (verbal style). I also emphasize the sermons' structure, for it is through the movement of its *dispositio*, in concord with its principle of *inventio*, that the sermon involves its reader in the act of purification.

❧ Donne's resources of invention

Before turning more fully to the courtship *topos*, I would like to give a brief account of Donne's *inventio* (the finding, deriving, and developing of one's matter) in more traditional terms. There are numerous excellent studies of pulpit rhetoric throughout the ages, and especially of the Renaissance; but

---

[43] To take only the book-length studies, Evelyn M. Simpson's cursory treatment of Donne's rhetoric deals only with style (*A Study of the Prose Works of John Donne*, 2nd ed. [Oxford: Clarendon Press, 1948], 255–66). William R. Mueller in *John Donne: Preacher* (Oxford: Oxford University Press, 1962) reduces Donne's rhetoric to style, although he includes (separate from his section entitled "Rhetoric") a short section on structure (89–99); Winfried Schleiner is wholly concerned with *elocutio*, discussing Donne's exegesis (which, I argue, is fundamentally an activity of *inventio*) only as a means of establishing the decorum of Donne's imagery (*The Imagery of John Donne's Sermons* [Providence: Brown University Press, 1970]).

[44] Studies based on the assumption that *elocutio* is the essence of Donne's rhetoric have tended also to take Donne's sermons in bits and pieces. Conversely, studies on Donne's *inventio* and *dispositio* are more inclined to treat the sermons as rhetorically-whole units (for example: Jerome S. Dees, "Logic and Paradox in the Structure of Donne's Sermons," *SCR* 4 [1987]: 78–92; and William J. J. Rooney, "John Donne's 'Second Prebend Sermon' — A Stylistic Analysis," *Seventeenth-Century Prose*, ed. Stanley E. Fish [New York: Oxford University Press, 1971], 375–87).

again, *elocutio* is their chief occupation.[45] My primary concern is in the ways in which the first two offices of rhetoric, *inventio* and *dispositio*, along with *elocutio*, overlap.[46] A sensitive reading of Donne's sermons and of rhetorical thought contemporary to him illustrates the difficulty of dividing these offices in his rhetorical strategies. Rosemond Tuve, for example, has demonstrated the close relationship between *elocutio* and *inventio* in the discursive function (*logos*) of metaphysical imagery.[47] This relationship was well known in the seventeenth century. Alexander Richardson, a contemporary of Donne's, observes that "tropes do arise from the arguments in Logick; so that they do not only set a lustre or resplendency upon the word used, but also shew the argument [*inventio*] from whence it is drawn."[48] Similarly, for Erasmus, *copia* involves both "[r]ichness of expression" (*elocutio*) and "[r]ichness of subject-matter" (*inventio*) such that "[i]t might be thought that these two aspects are so interconnected in reality that one cannot easily separate one from the other, and that they interact so closely that any distinction between them belongs to theory rather than practice."[49]

---

[45] James J. Murphy provides a brief but excellent survey of the history of Christian preaching from Jesus to the middle ages in *Rhetoric in the Middle Ages* (Berkeley: University of California Press, 1974), chap. 6. The standard historical work on English Renaissance preaching is still W. Fraser Mitchell's *English Pulpit Oratory from Andrewes to Tillotson* (New York: Russell & Russell, 1962). The two most recent studies have been on style: Peter Auksi, *Christian Plain Style* (Montreal and Kingston: McGill-Queen's University Press, 1995) and Debora Shuger, *Sacred Rhetoric* (Princeton: Princeton University Press, 1988). For a brief introduction to rhetoric that emphasizes invention see Marion Trousdale, "Rhetoric," in *A Companion to English Renaissance Literature and Culture*, ed. Michael Hattaway (London: Blackwell, 2000), 624–633.

[46] Throughout this book I use the Latin terms for the offices of rhetoric and the parts of an oration and the Greek for the figures of *elocutio* and the modes of proof (*logos, pathos, ethos*). I devote less attention to the remaining offices of rhetoric. As to Donne's *pronuntiatio* (delivery), our only data come from Donne's contemporary reputation, which consistently represents him as powerful in his delivery (see Robert L. Hickey, "Donne's Delivery," *TSL* 9 [1964]: 39–47). *Memoria* (memory), the remaining office of rhetoric, traditionally pertained to the rhetor's memorization of his material, rather than to his consideration of his audience's memory, so that again we must rely on the testimony of Donne's contemporaries. Izaak Walton testifies to Donne's ability in memorizing his material (*The Lives of John Donne etc.* [London: Oxford University Press, 1927], 67).

[47] Rosemond Tuve, *Elizabethan and Metaphysical Imagery* (Chicago: University of Chicago Press, 1947).

[48] Alexander Richardson, "Rhetorical Notes," 34, [D1v], included with separate pagination in *The Logicians School-Master*, 2nd ed. (1657). According to Samuel Thomson, the publisher of this volume, Richardson's lecture notes, on which this text is based, were circulating in manuscript since the 1590s ([A3v]).

[49] Erasmus, *De Copia*, in *The Collected Works of Erasmus*, ed. Craig R. Thompson, vol. 24 (Toronto: University of Toronto Press, 1978), 301.

Throughout this book I emphasize the way in which *dispositio* and *elocutio* derive from and serve one of Donne's salient principles of *inventio*: courtship. I also demonstrate how the courtship *topos* combines rhetorical proofs of *pathos* and *logos* in particular, but *ethos* as well. Moreover, Donne's sermons demonstrate that in pulpit rhetoric, *inventio* and exegesis are almost identical.[50] For the preacher, *inventio* first and foremost involves amplifying a text in response to the rhetorical situation at hand. Grammar, rhetoric, and logic, as well as other fields of secular learning, were first applied to aid the preacher in understanding the biblical text, from which he derived his principal matter. Accordingly, Scripture is Donne's chief source of invention, providing "direct proofes" and "undeniable arguments" (logic) suitable for disputation, as well as "similitudinary, and comparative reasons" (rhetoric) suitable for devotional purposes (3:5.364-388). It is almost exclusively the latter, rhetorical methods and purpose that concern Donne in the sermons.

Some of Donne's readings of Scripture might strike a modern exegete as strange. One cause of his interpretive liberties is his sense of rhetorical-devotional need. Augustine's understanding of biblical interpretation affords Donne tremendous rhetorical freedom and sets the conditions for the methods of *inventio* I describe here. In giving the principle of charity first place in his rules governing exegesis, Augustine sets a precedent for accommodating interpretation to the benefit of an intended audience. He exemplifies this consideration in his reading of *Canticles* 4:2, "Your teeth are like a flock of shorn ewes ascending from the pool, all of which give birth to twins, and there is not a sterile animal among them." Augustine rather liberally takes this as a similitude of the saints of the church "tearing men away from their errors and transferring them into its body, breaking down their rawness by biting and chewing" so that these men might leave their

---

[50] In *De Doctrina Christiana*, St. Augustine first describes exegesis as "the process of discovery" (*inveniendi*) (*De Doctrina Christiana*, ed. and trans. R. P. H. Green [Oxford: Clarendon, 1995], 9.1. See John Monfasani, "The *De Doctrina* and Renaissance Rhetoric," in *Reading Wisdom: The De Doctrina Christiana of Augustine in the Middle Ages*, ed. Edward D. English, Notre Dame Conferences in Medieval Studies 6 (Notre Dame, IN: University of Notre Dame Press, 1995), 172–188. Niels Hemmingsen demonstrates this close identification between *inventio* and *exegesis* in *The Preacher*, trans. John Horsfall (1574), which he begins with grammatical, logical, and rhetorical methods for "dividing" Scripture, a term that resonates with both rhetorical and exegetical connotations (see 2 Timothy 2:15). J. W. Blench somewhat simplistically reduces *inventio* to Scriptural interpretation in *Preaching in England in the Late Fifteenth and Sixteenth Centuries* (New York: Barnes & Noble, 1964), chap. 1.

burdens as they ascend from the pool of baptism and produce the holy fruit of love.[51] Augustine interprets the passage this way for the delight the image would bring his auditory and the benefit they would therefore receive from the passage. Thus Dennis B. Quinn appropriately describes Donne's rules for a "right exposition of Scripture" as essentially Augustinian: that it adhere to "The glory of God, the analogie of faith, the exaltation of devotion, the extension of charity" (9:3.130-131).[52]

Donne makes a similar statement in a sermon preached at St. Paul's Cathedral on Easter Sunday, 1624, where he notes that some biblical passages need to be read figuratively in order to account for the literal sense. His present text on the "first resurrection" (Revelation 20:6) is one such instance. The resurrection signified here is not a literal bodily resurrection, but a "spiritual" resurrection. With Augustine in mind, Donne notes that in such cases a few guidelines of interpretation should be followed: "that it destroy not the literall sense, that it violate not the analogy of faith, that it advance devotion" (6:2.51-53). The last point is a rhetorical issue — how to *move* an audience to devout action — and the criterion Donne most rigorously follows.[53] Here the advancement of devotion is offered as a limitation to the liberties one can take with a text. But later, Donne makes devotion a cause for his manner of amplifying the text. In outlining the fourth point of his *divisio*, Donne notes that the occasion of the sermon, Easter Sunday,

> invites me to propose a fourth sense, or rather use of the words; not indeed as an exposition of the words, but as a convenient exaltation of our devotion; which is, that this first Resurrection should be the first fruits of the dead; The first Rising, is the first Riser, Christ Jesus (79-83).

In other words, rhetorical considerations are a strong determinant in Donne's handling of his text.

As a corollary to the traditional characterization of *inventio* as "finding" matter, preachers expressed the idea of exegesis as an "opening" of Scripture.

---

[51] *De Doctrina Christiana*, 2.11–12.
[52] Dennis B. Quinn, "Donne's Christian Eloquence," in *Seventeenth-Century Prose*, ed. Fish, 362. Donne also refers to the first and third criteria in 5:13.761–763.
[53] See also 8:14.82 and 9:8.10–19.

The preacher, says Donne, dilates the text in making a sermon (5:1.767).[54] Donne's *inventio*, then, derives first of all from his sense of the fecundity of Scripture.[55] He begins a sermon at St. Paul's by saying, with reference to his text, that

> THESE ARE such words, as if we were to consider the *words onely*, might make a *Grammar* Lecture, and a *Logick* Lecture, and a *Rhetorick* and *Ethick*, a *Philosophy* Lecture too; And of these foure Elements might a better Sermon then you are like to heare now, be well made. Indeed they are words of a large, of an extensive comprehension (8:12.1–6).

Notwithstanding his *humilitas*, Donne goes on to expound "not onely the *powerfulnesse* of the matter, but the *sweetnesse* and elegancy of *the words* of the Word of God in generall," before proceeding to dilate copiously his present text throughout the balance of the sermon (9–10). Later in the same sermon, he speaks of "the largenesse and *extention* of the words" in his text (124).[56] But to uncover the fullness of the text, suggests Donne, one needs the aid of the humane arts.

As John S. Chamberlin demonstrates, Donne makes full use of the arts of discourse (grammar, logic, and rhetoric) in inventing matter.[57] As a consequence of the close identification between *inventio* and exegesis, much of

---

[54] See also 7:13.73. William Perkins talks about the "Opening of the text" by means of the analytical tools of the arts, but what Perkins "finds" is only one sense with many levels of application (*The Arte of Prophecying* [1607], 26, [C2v]; 30, [C4v]). Similarly, Robert Cawdrey describes the use of similitudes for "opening" the grounds of Christian religion (*A Treasury or Store-house of Similies* [1600], [A2v], n. p.).

[55] Some of this sense derives from his typological and allegorical methods of interpretation. W. D. Robertson describes both St. Augustine's use of allegorical and typological interpretation and the plenitude of meaning they afford, as well as the transmission of these methods through the middle ages into the seventeenth century ("Introduction," *On Christian Doctrine* [New York: Macmillan, 1958], xi–xiii). See David Dawson, "Figure, Allegory," and James J. O'Donnell, "*De Doctrina Christiana*," in *Augustine Through the Ages*, ed. Allan D. Fitzgerald (Grand Rapids: Eerdmans, 1999), 365–68, 278–80 respectively. Schleiner describes Donne's use of the allegorical method (163–200, esp. 185ff). On typology see P. G. Stanwood and Heather Ross Asals, eds., *John Donne and the Theology of Language* (Columbia: University of Missouri Press, 1986), 179–82. Dennis Quinn discusses both typological and allegorical exegesis in "John Donne's Principles of Biblical Exegesis," *JEGP* 61 (1962): 313–29.

[56] Elsewhere he speaks of "the fecundity" of the words of Scripture (6:6.266–267). In 7:12.1–30, Donne likens his text and his preaching upon it to the miracle of the loaves and fishes which are miraculously multiplied.

[57] John S. Chamberlin, *Increase and Multiply* (Chapel Hill: University of North Carolina Press, 1976).

Donne's matter is grammatically derived.[58] His usual method is to attend closely to the words of the text, typically using Latin to extend the connotations of the English translation (with which he begins), and sometimes drawing in Greek and Hebrew words, either from the original text or from the Septuagint, to gloss his English and Latin. This polyglot method enables Donne to extend further the range of meaning and applicability of his text.[59] Although he does not always name them, Donne often employs the logical *topoi*, most commonly cause and effect.[60] And he frequently takes note of logical relations in grammatical connectors, in the "for"s and "therefore"s of the text.[61] One dialectical topic to which I will devote considerable attention is that of similarity, or similitude; another is the topic "of the name," which Donne frequently uses both as a means of textual analysis and of constructing his audience's sense of identity.[62] Donne also makes use of rhetorical *topoi*. He expounds the topics "of ease" and "of difficulty" in describing the Creation and Moses's depiction of it (9:1.1–60). Two topics which figure prominently in courtship strategies are the topics "of profit" and "of the good."[63] A cursory survey of Donne's methods of dividing his text, however, will demonstrate that his favourite analytical tool is the circumstances (who, what, when, where, how, and why), commonly known

---

[58] In this method, Donne had much more in common with Lancelot Andrewes (although Donne was not his equal as a linguist) than with the Puritan preachers.

[59] On Donne's methods for multiplying the sense of his text see Chamberlin, *Increase and Multiply*, 118–36. Good examples of this method can be found in 10:5 and 1:1, which I look at in chaps. 3 and 4 respectively.

[60] Chamberlin mentions Donne's familiarity with the topical means of invention (113–15). Walter Ong describes Donne's preaching as "'topical' in that it used the topics or places as if they were resonant with sentences or sayings"; this in contrast to the advocates of the plain style (*Ramus: Method, and the Decay of Dialogue* [Cambridge, MA: Harvard University Press, 1958], 284). Work still remains to be done on Donne's use of the particular resources of logic, or dialectic. Joan Webber, for example, takes no notice of Donne's use of analytical *topoi* in her categorization of Donne's nine basic methods of *divisio* (*Contrary Music*, 165). Webber rather de-emphasizes Donne's use of logic, characterizing his style as an eschewing of logical strictures (chap. 2). My chief source on the topical methods of invention is Douglas Chambers, "Lancelot Andrewes and the Topical Structure of Thought" (Ph.D. diss., Princeton University, 1968).

[61] See 4:12.1–24 and *passim*, 5:12.198–210, and 9:8.458 for examples. Stanwood and Asals comment on this practice of deriving logical relations from grammar and provide several examples (*Theology of Language*, 69–124). This principle of *inventio* is germane to *Deaths Duell*, which I discuss in detail in chap. 6.

[62] On Donne's use of names see Chamberlin (*Increase and Multiply*, 107–8) and Stanwood and Asals (*Theology of Language*, 179–82).

[63] On the topic "of the good" see 7:13.533–539. In 6:5.70–79, Donne employs three *topoi* in developing the third part of his *divisio*: of necessity, of difficulty, and of possibility.

as Aphthonius's topics of narration.[64] Donne's *divisiones* often begin with the "who," with the emphasis then falling upon issues related to the "what" — the action(s) of the person(s) in the text. Dividing John 10:10, Donne finds three parts: who ("The Shepheard and the sheep"); what (his coming, with emphasis on his new manner in coming); and why (his purpose in coming) (9:5.78–98).[65]

A full account of Donne's analytical tools of *inventio* is outside the scope of this study. Perhaps the best way to illustrate briefly the importance of these traditional methods in the sermons is to provide an example where Donne combines these analytical *topoi*. Donne begins a sermon on Christ's healing of the man sick with palsy (Matthew 9:2) with two circumstances: the occasion (when) and the act (what). He further analyzes the "when" as an indication of Christ's mercy ("Christ did it When he saw") to which Donne gives the logical distinctions of both cause and effect: "it is the effect and it is the cause too, there is no cause of his mercy, but his mercy" (10:2.19–20). He further divides the act (the "what") by noting that Jesus names (a topic of logic) the man "with that gracious appellation, *Fili, Son*" (23), and then by noting the manner ("how") of this healing with a generic distinction within the statement "*Thy sins are forgiven thee*" (30, 40–1). It is both a "Catechisme" and a correction: Jesus "catechises this patient" and "rectifie[s] the by-standers" (30–41). Donne further delineates each verbal act with recourse to the *topoi* of time (31), quality (35), cause (37), and manner (43–47). After all this, he concludes his complex *divisio* with an *apologia*: "And into fewer particulars then these, this pregnant and abundant Text is not easily contracted" (47-48).

It is evident, then, that Donne's arrangement as reflected in his *divisio* arises naturally from his methods of exegesis.[66] As to the larger *dispositio* of the sermons, Donne's typical method ostensibly follows the basic order of a classical oration, almost always including an *exordium* and *divisio*, a point-by-point elaboration (including the equivalent to *confirmatio* and sometimes *refutatio*), and a *peroratio*, as well as digressions along the way. This is largely the method recommended by St. Augustine in Book 4 of *De Doctrina Christiana*. J. W. Blench refers to this method as "the 'modern

---

[64] Aphthonius, *Progymnasmata* (London, 1572), 16b, [B8v]; cf. Richard Rainolde's adaptation of the same in *The Foundation of Rhetoric* (1563), [C4v].

[65] Other examples are 1:5.72–87; 5:16.60–81, 355–362; 8:8.118; 9:10.1–38; 10:2.2–3.

[66] On the relationship between analysis and arrangement see Jerome S. Dees, "Logic and Paradox in the Structure of Donne's Sermons," *SCR* 4.2 (1987): 70–92.

style' approximating to the classical form," which, he says, was used by the majority of Elizabethan preachers.[67] But within this basic structure, Donne uses a variety of organizational principles, including at times the doctrine-use method popular among Puritans.[68] Preaching on the great multitude at the resurrection, Donne first divides his text (Revelation 7:9) according to two predicaments: the *quantity* of those saved and the glorious *quality* of those saved (6:7.38–40). But in the transition between the first partition and the second, Donne recasts his arrangement in terms that are recognizable as the doctrine-use method. Here he reviews the first point — the "communicablenesse" of God signified by the large quantity of souls that are saved — in relation to God's goodness and grace "in the generall"; this is the general doctrine of the text (307–308). Then he proceeds in the second point to "a more speciall manner intimated" in the text; this is the use of the doctrine applied to the individual soul — the "seale" or "contract" between God and man (309–312). Another related principle of arrangement is the familiar Ramist method of moving from the general to the particular. This is a favourite strategy of Donne's, and one which often bears resemblance to the doctrine-use method (cf. 6:8.13–28, 153–156 and 7:10.63–98). In a sermon at Whitehall in 1626, Donne finds in the first half of his text of John 14:2 a "particular Doctrine," and in the second half a "generall Rule" (7:4.35, 37); but in the sermon he follows "the order of nature," beginning with the general and moving to the particular (39). In another sermon he combines a structure based on the circumstances of the text with this two-part structure of general and particular (5:1.32-67). There are a great many other principles of arrangement in Donne's sermons. I emphasize these to underscore the point that Donne draws his rhetorical resources from whatever quarter serves his turn, even from the Puritans.

While the traditional and homiletic resources of the arts of discourse are everywhere evident in Donne's sermons, equally necessary to his *inventio* are his methods of accommodating the needs of his all-too-human audi-

---

[67] Blench, *Preaching in England*, 102.

[68] Richard Bernard (*Faithfvll Shepherd*) specifies application as a separate element in a sermon's *dispositio*, whereas Perkins (*Arte of Prophecying*) and William Ames (*The Marrow of Theology* [*Medulla theologiæ*], trans. John D. Eusden [Durham, NC: Labyrinth Press, 1983]) include application as an aspect of use. When Donne evokes this method, he does so in terms of doctrine and application. See also 2:6.23–62 and 4:11.58–68, 542–549. Webber cites only 8:8 as falling within this category of arrangement (*Contrary Music*, 165).

ence, as he understood them.[69] As important as exegesis is to Donne's sermons, the most striking feature of his *inventio* is his infusing of the message of Scripture with his audience's common experience in the world outside the church walls. Much of Donne's interpretation of Scripture, in fact, bears the marks of his and his congregation's cultural experience. This socio-cultural resource of *inventio* is set down in the rhetorics of Donne's time. Richard Bernard prescribes the use of secular learning — including "Physicks, Mathematicks, Metaphysicks, Ethicks, Politicks, Oeconomicks, History, and Military Discipline" — as aids in extracting matter from Scripture: "The knowledge wherof are as so many lights to see into a Text by, both to find out and to lay open such variety of matter, as lye couched in the words."[70] Consistent with the notion of "finding" matter in the text, these various fields of learning do not add to Scripture, but rather throw into relief the matter already present. In the same context, Bernard notes the biblical authors' own use of the natural and social worlds of experience as sources for their many similitudes. He adds, "Who knoweth not, that hath read any thing in the Bible, that similitudes are fetcht from almost all things in Heauen aboue, in earth below." Although he does not specifically have preaching in mind, Thomas Blount compiles a similar list of fields from which to cull metaphors. He includes natural philosophy, husbandry, politics and government, navigation, the military profession, and medicine as appropriate sources of learning for drawing out "expressions ... to please the learned in severall kinds."[71]

Donne also turns to such cultural fields for drawing out similitudes to the Christian experience. More precisely, he employs various culturally-

---

[69] I use "audience" to include Donne's congregation at the sermon's oral delivery as well his reader of the printed text. The issue of audience is problematical in a study of Donne's sermons owing to the fact that their published form is not exactly the same as their original form as delivered orally. William Gifford nonetheless argues that the average Donne sermon in print is of a length that can be comfortably delivered in the standard one-hour span, and that Donne's sermon notes could very well have been quite extensive; he therefore concludes that we can be quite confident that each sermon is substantially the sermon Donne preached ("Time and Place in Donne's Sermons," *PMLA* 82.5 [1967]: 388–91). More recently, Jeanne Shami has brought to light an authorial manuscript of Donne's 1622 Gunpowder Plot sermon which provides an instance of a sermon that was written in full soon after its delivery and that is substantially the same as the printed text. Shami also addresses issues of transmission (*Gunpowder Plot Sermon*, 35–36). My strategy of concentrating on Donne's *inventio* and *dispositio*, the larger structures of the sermon, somewhat mitigates this problem.

[70] Richard Bernard, *The Faithfull Shepherd*, 3rd ed. (1621), 41, C11.

[71] Thomas Blount, *The Academy of Eloquence* (1654), 3, B2.

derived courtship structures to win his congregation's assent regarding devotional matters. Although Obadiah Walker wrote his manual on oratory some thirty years after Donne's death, he prescribes the very aspect of *inventio* I am describing here:

> In all our Proofs we have recourse to, either things of sense; or common received Axioms, and Truths, or Laws, and Customes, or the Concessions of our Adversary, or of our Auditors. Neither is it needful to ascend to the ultimate Causes of every thing, but to stay our Probation at our Auditors grants.[72]

Similarly, Donne handles the ultimate causes of spiritual matters with recourse to those cultural experiences and values which his audience will readily grant. Courtship, then, functions as a commonplace as outlined by Walker, or what Donne calls "*Testimonia ab homine,* Testimonies that passe like currant money, from man to man, obvious to every man, suspicious to none" (4:8.314–316). More precisely, courtship fits the category of a rhetorical topic of *inventio* as described by Boethius in *De topicis differentiis.* A topic, says Boethius, is a foundation of argument that is known *per se* and is universally accepted.[73]

Although Donne carefully tailored his sermons to the needs of his audience, his sermons are not easily grouped along traditional *ad clerum* / *ad populum* lines. In fact, Donne's most frequent audiences all had in common an involvement in the world of affairs (be it at court or in the marketplace), and it is to this aspect of his audience that his sermons consistently speak. Donne was a learned preacher, both in the arts and in worldly affairs, and he used his learning to full advantage. At court and at Lincoln's Inn, Donne preached to an audience that was similarly educated. And the same could be said for a large portion of his congregation at St. Paul's and

---

[72] Obadiah Walker, *Some instrvctions concerning the Art of oratory* (1659), 9, B5.

[73] Boethius, *Boethius's De topicis differentiis,* trans. Eleonore Stump (Ithaca: Cornell University Press, 1978), 46. This is Boethius's first class of topics, which he describes as a "maximal proposition." Similarly, courtship is easily associable with such rhetorical topics as "of profit," a common topic in Leonard Cox's *The Arte or Crafte of Rhethoryke* (1530) for both demonstrative and deliberative purposes. Courtship also meets Aristotle's qualification that a general or "common" topic be universally applicable, for humankind, says Burke, is by nature a classifying animal which invariably organizes its world into hierarchies which in turn constantly give rise to courtship strategies (*The Art of Rhetoric,* trans. H. C. Lawson-Tancred [New York: Penguin, 1991], 183-85 [subsequent references are to this edition]; Burke, *PLF,* 15-16).

St. Dunstan's, both parishes in the heart of London which included a diversity of people. The challenge of preaching to a mixed audience was not an easy one. George Parfitt argues that Donne made few concessions to the common folk in his mixed audience at St. Paul's, but rather aimed to dazzle them with his learning and rhetoric as a means of identifying himself with the socio-political establishment.[74] On the contrary, there is plenty in Donne's sermons to speak to the common person; at both St. Paul's and St. Dunstan's, Donne had to satisfy the merchant and labourer as well as the learned man about town. Such pulpit rhetoricians as Richard Bernard recognized the difficulties of addressing a mixed audience; there is no reason to assume that Donne was insensitive to this issue.[75] Donne expresses an awareness of audience in his handling of the Sermon on the Mount, a sermon that he characterizes as at once *ad clerum* and *ad populum*, concluding that "Both must be done; we must preach in the Mountaine, and preach in the plaine too; preach to the learned, and preach to the simple too; preach to the Court, and preach to the Country too" (7:13.207–210). But he goes on to add that neither audience should grumble if they perceive that the preacher sometimes preaches to the other (210–222). Donne clearly aimed a great number of his allusions at the learned, but he equally appealed to such common experiences as love, death, sickness, finances, and career. These, as much as Donne's learned discourse in economics and politics, serve the purposes I describe in this book.

Donne routinely draws on recognizable social discourse to codify spiritual issues in terms with which his congregation could readily identify, yet he does not, as one might expect, limit his legal and political discourse to court or to Lincoln's Inn, nor his mercantile discourse to St. Paul's or St. Dunstan's. All three socio-political fields of reference, and many more, are used for a variety of audiences. Two of the sermons I discuss in detail draw heavily on juridical references, yet neither was preached at Lincoln's Inn, but rather at court, where one might nonetheless expect an interest in legal issues; however, many of Donne's sermons at St. Paul's also draw on matters of jurispru-

---

[74] George Parfitt, *John Donne: A Literary Life* (New York: St. Martin's Press, 1989), 119.

[75] Bernard, in a sermon entitled *The Shepherds Practise*, appended with continuous pagination to *The Faithfull Shepherd*. On Donne's sensitivity to his mixed audiences, see Sister M. Geraldine Thompson, "'Writs Canonicall': The High Word and the Humble in the Sermons of John Donne," in *Familiar Colloquy*, ed. Patricia Bruckmann (Toronto: Oberon Press, 1978), 55–67, here 58–59, 64.

dence.[76] In short, it seems Donne saw the interests of his various audiences as different not in kind but in degree.

The argument of this book, in brief, is that Donne found in courtship effective means for structuring and guiding his audience's thoughts and feelings about their life in this world and its relation to the next. The first chapter introduces the cultural commonplace of courtship and draws out a number of features or sub-*topoi* of this broader *topos* from several sites that would have been widely accessible to much of Donne's audience. The purpose here is to demonstrate the riches that were available to Donne in this cultural resource and the relevance of the same to his congregation's experience. The second chapter uses this cultural frame of reference to show how Donne finds and selects his material along courtship lines in drawing on such related social discourses as law, commerce, and patronage. Having set out Donne's method of *inventio* with respect to courtship, I then demonstrate in the third chapter how this principle of invention also determines the manner in which he arranges his material, both conceptually and materially, in the *dispositio* of his sermon. Here I also introduce two other Burkeian notions that are relevant to courtship: his notions of form and "temporizing of essence." These features, I argue, are central to the curative function Donne so commonly attributes to his sermons. In each of the remaining three chapters, I devote my attention to a single sermon, further developing these Burkeian ideas to demonstrate how courtship strategies can apply to such diverse material as the social discourse of prodigality (chap. 4) and death (chaps. 5 and 6) and how they can account for a great deal of the rhetorical activity of a whole sermon. These sermons draw less overtly from matters of courtship than do many others, and for this very reason they help to emphasize that it is in the deep structures of *inventio* and *dispositio* that the courtship *topos*, and hence Donne's sermons, achieve much of their effect. The conclusion of this study regarding the eloquence of Donne's sermons (the task of any rhetorical criticism) is based on this common strategy of courtship: the force of Donne's sermons is largely attributable to his ability to infuse his audience's consideration of spiritual matters with their experience of desire in the workaday world of affairs and to draw on these socially inscribed desires to induce a similar motivation to "court" the divine.

---

[76] And as Wilfrid Prest notes, students at the Inns of Court were not necessarily interested in law *per se*: *The Inns of Court under Elizabeth I and the Early Stuarts, 1590–1640* (Totowa, NJ: Rowman and Littlefield, 1972), 21–32.

CHAPTER ONE

The Courtship Topos

But [man] has relations with his fellow man, closer infinitely
than with any of the things around him, and to many a man
far plainer than his relations with God. Now the nearer is
plainer that he may step on it, and rise to the higher, till then
the less plain.

— George MacDonald[77]

IN LITERATURE, IF NOT IN ACTUAL PRACTICE, JOHN DONNE was a
master of courtship, both sexual and political. In his poetry, and especially
in his sermons, Donne draws on a wide range of culturally defined desire-
quests, or courtships, in configuring human motives. In the Ovidian elegy
"Loves Progress," he uses the metaphor of seafaring exploration to describe
the motivational power of his beloved's "Centrique part" (36), the speaker's
object of desire:

> Who ever loves, if he do not propose
> The right true end of love, he's one that goes
> To sea for nothing but to make him sick (1–3).[78]

Courtship is an activity that is governed by a desired end, and which has
parallel expressions in all manner of human endeavour. The question is,
what is the proper end? The speaker aims to avoid this deliberation by the

---

[77] *Unspoken Sermons: Third Series*, new ed. (London: Longmans, 1891), 72.

[78] References to Donne's poems will be to John Shawcross's edition, unless otherwise noted, and will
be referred to parenthetically in the text according to line number (New York: Doubleday, 1967).

cumulative force of his analogy (lines 37–72) which instead argues the necessity of pursuing his predetermined goal.

This same question of the proper end of desire is at issue in Donne's *aubades*, where the lover seeks to persuade the beloved against succumbing to other calls to devotion signalled by a new day of activity. On the morning after love-making, the speaker in "The good-morrow" replaces the cartographer's and astronomer's objects of pursuit (earth and moon respectively) with a different globe, their own perfect (and thus symbolically circular) love emblematized by their reflections in each other's eyes. Significantly he expresses this desire in language that figures the lovers as merchant explorers: "Let us possesse one world, each hath one, and is one" (14). At a time of day that signals the encroachment of vocational pursuits, the speaker presses instead for a continuation of love. A similar anxiety is felt in "The Sunne Rising," where other objects of desire, symbolized by mercantile images of East Indian spice and West Indian gold, so much rival the speaker's courtship of his beloved that he must denigrate all "honor" and "wealth" in relation to her (24). Yet it is clear that in the end the motion of the sun, manifested in the pursuits of schoolboys, apprentices, and court huntsmen, is finally an irresistible force that must draw the speaker from his beloved if only for the day. The closing couplet in "Breake of day" expresses the similarity of these rival courtships: "He which hath businesse, and makes love, doth doe / Such wrong, as when a maryed man doth wooe" (17–18). In the modern idiom, this adulterer is "married" to his work.

Donne explains the nature of desire in his somewhat cynical description of the sex act in "Farewell to love," a poem about the transitory nature of sexual gratification. Here Donne makes the general observation that

> ...when
> Things not yet knowne are coveted by men,
> Our desires give them fashion, and so
> As they waxe lesser, fall, as they sise,[79] grow (7–10).

The growing and shrinking of the phallus is emblematic of all desire, which heightens in anticipation of a remote object, but declines once the object has been achieved and the "mystery" — likened to the transcendence of the divine in lines 1–6 — subsequently has been dispelled. It is the mystery and allure of "things not yet knowne" and unattained that produces desire.

---

[79] "Sise," or "size" is used here as a verbal synonym for "rise" which Theodore Redpath glosses as "get larger, swell" (*The Songs and Sonets of John Donne*, ed. Theodore Redpath, 2nd ed. [London: Methuen, 1983], 150, n.10). British Library, Stowe MS 961, has the variant "rise" (Redpath, *Songs and Sonets*, 148, n.10).

Courtship is the means of connecting with these remote objects of desire. Donne demonstrates the agility of the courtship metaphor in a verse epistle to the Countess of Bedford, itself a gesture of courtship. Here Donne depicts this well-known patron of poets, whom he desires to meet, as a transcendent divinity and himself as the devout soul.[80] He begins with *hyperbole*: "Reason is our Soules left hand, Faith her right, / By these wee reach divinity, that's you" (2–3). He goes on to say that he has faith, but needs reason also to enable him to explain his faith, so he studies those whose love for the Countess grew by reason of "the blessings of [her] light" (3). This "light" refers to her teaching by example, but as the developing image makes clear, it also refers to her patronage.[81] In the third stanza, Donne further specifies the Countess as a Calvinist god(dess). Here he says his first approach to understanding this deity is to study her saints, her friends (and presumably her beneficiaries) "whom [her] election glorifies" (10). By the logic of analogy, he too needs to be elected. Donne equivocates between Calvinist and Roman Catholic paradigms (election vs. the mediation of the saints), but he does so not out of theological indecision, but to draw out the full courtship potential of his imagery. In courtly circles one approaches a patron through his or her satellites, as Donne well knew; repeatedly in his personal letters he asks his friends to speak well of him to their patrons.[82] As Donne says in line 11 of this poem, he also studies her "accesses" (her giving of favour) and "restraints" (her withholding of it).[83] In stanzas 4 to 8 he finds that Bedford transcends the limits of reason, and so he must rely on faith after all — on his own declaration of his implicit belief in her glory. By the end of the poem, Donne has abandoned his divinity conceit and has replaced Bedford in her creaturely role, albeit exemplary. She is "Gods masterpeece, and so / His Factor for our loves" (33–34). She has become for her beneficiaries a means of courting God, an *exemplum* who is a causative agent ("factor") of their love of the divine.[84] But as Joan Faust

---

[80] As Barbara L. DeStefano describes, Donne uses the fact that he had never met the Countess as an opportunity to develop the analogy of humankind's means for knowing God: "Evolution of Extravagant Praise in Donne's Verse Epistles," *SP* 81 (1984): 75–93, here 88–89.

[81] W. Milgate sees in this poem a developing image of the Countess as a tutelary angel (*The Satires, Epigrams and Verse Letters*, ed. W. Milgate [Oxford: Clarendon Press, 1967], 253–55).

[82] Grierson suggests Donne may have been recommended to Lady Bedford by his friend Sir Henry Goodyer, who was attached to her household (*Poems*, ed. Herbert J. C. Grierson, vol. 2 [Oxford: Oxford University Press, 1912], 153). In a letter to Goodyer written three months after becoming Dean of St. Paul's, Donne concludes, "You forget me absolutely and intirely, whensoever you forget me to that noble Countesse [Bedford]" (*Letters to Severall Persons of Honour*, ed. Charles Edmund Merrill, Jr. [New York: Sturgis & Walton, 1910], 152, 299n.).

[83] Milgate, *Satires, Epigrams and Verse Letters*, 254, n. l.10.

[84] Shawcross, ed., *Complete Poetry*, 222, n. 34.

notes, throughout the poem Donne's religious language carries social and political associations, such that when he refers in the closing lines to her returning "home" (generally taken to mean heaven) to do him some good, he could also ambiguously mean her return to court to secure him a position there.[85]

Donne also understands that his devout motives and approaches toward God are not easily dissociated from his worldly ambition as a courtier. In his Holy Sonnet "Oh, to vex me, contraryes meete in one," the speaker rues his inconstant devotion to God in an analogy of sexual courtship: "As humorous is my contritione / As my prophane Love, and as soone forgott" (5–6). The analogy continues with a likeness that is as much courtly as amatory as the speaker laments, "I durst not view heaven yesterday; and to day / In prayers, and flattering speaches I court God" (9–10). Rather than pretending such a clear division between the profane and the sacred exists, Donne the preacher similarly looks for ways to harmonize his and his congregation's worldly motives with the higher calling of God upon their lives — and not only to harmonize them, but to employ these worldly courtships to induce an analogous desire for God. Robert Whalen finds a similar conjunction of sacred and profane, temporal and eternal, in Donne's handling of sacramentalism as a literary *topos*. Whalen elaborates Donne's incarnational poetics as characterized by an identification of sacred and profane experience whereby Donne "forces a recognition of the immanence of divinity in the world."[86] This same intersection of motives becomes a powerful rhetorical *topos* for Donne as he seeks to persuade his congregation to court God in a life of religious devotion. Donne's congregation, too, understands these structures of desire, which makes them rhetorically rich resources for inventing sermonic matter.

☙ God's courtier

Over forty years after Donne's death, John Milton's nephew, Edward Phillips, would describe Donne the poet as a gallant who accomplished himself in "the politer kind of Learning" and who "moderately enjoy'd the pleasures of the Town, and frequented good Company, to which the sharpness of his Wit, and gayety of Fancy, tender'd him not a little grateful."[87]

---

[85] Joan Faust, "John Donne's Verse Letters to the Countess of Bedford: Mediators in a Poet-Patroness Relationship," *JDJ* 12.1, 2 (1993): 79-99, here 87-89.

[86] Robert Whalen, *The Poetry of Immanence: Sacrament in Donne and Herbert* (Toronto: University of Toronto Press, 2002), 36, also 21–5, 31–2, and *passim*.

[87] Phillips, *Theatrum Poetarum* (1675), 106–7, [2E5v]–2E6, in the second part of the volume subtitled *Eminent Poets Among the Moderns*.

The young Donne sounds rather like an exemplar of the courtier Phillips aims to fashion in his courtesy handbook, *The Mysteries of Love & Eloquence* (1658).[88] Phillips goes on to describe Donne the preacher as a man with similar energies but a new direction: "as of an Eminent Poet he became a much more Eminent Preacher, so he rather improved then relinquisht his Poetical Fancy; only converting it from human and worldly to Divine and Heavenly subjects."[89] Phillips, a known plagiarist, can be taken as somewhat representative in his description of Donne.[90] An earlier contributor to this reputation was Donne's friend and elegist John Chudleigh.

Chudleigh, whom Izaak Walton describes as "a frequent hearer of [Donne's] Sermons," thoroughly characterizes Donne as both a poet and preacher of courtship.[91] Chudleigh begins by reminding poets and informing preachers too of the legacy Donne has left them. Then he elaborates the relation between these two offices of Donne's:

He kept his loves, but not his objects; wit
Hee did not banish, but transplanted it,
Taught it his place and use, and brought it home
To Pietie, which it doth best become;
He shew'd us how for sinnes we ought to sigh,
And how to sing Christs Epithalamy:
The Altars had his fires, and there hee spoke
Incense of loves, and fansies holy smoake:
Religion thus enrich'd, the people train'd,
And God from dull vice had the fashion gain'd (13–22).[92]

These modes of courtship remained in the preacher, but their objects were replaced. Donne did not reject old loves (desires) but reoriented them, subsuming them all to the highest object of desire. While at first this may seem like the same old Jack Donne/Dean Donne dichotomy, Chudleigh places

---

[88] The book is aimed to equip young gallants in "the Deportments of the most accomplisht Persons, the mode of their Courtly Entertainments, Treatments of their Ladies at Balls, their accustom'd Sports, Drolles and Fancies" etc. (Phillips, *The Mysteries of Love & Eloquence* [1658], t. p.)

[89] *Theatrum Poetarum*, part 2, 107, 2E6.

[90] For a brief but useful general survey of Donne's reputation as a preacher see Jeanne Shami, "Introduction: Reading Donne's Sermons," *JDJ* 11.1, 2 (1992): 1–20, here 3–4.

[91] Walton echoes Chudleigh's assessment in describing Donne's "sacred Art and Courtship" (*Lives*, 49). Sidney Godolphin's description in his elegy on Donne, which I discuss in chap. 3, is also significant to the courtship paradigm that I am about to develop here (see esp. lines 11-20).

[92] From Herbert Grierson's edition of the *Poems* (1:394–95); Shawcross omits Chudleigh's elegy.

his emphasis on the transformation of the audience rather than of the poet-preacher. Donne taught *us* the true cause of the lover's sigh and the epithal-amian song, "training" his congregants in a new courtship. In other words, Chudleigh is commenting on Donne's rhetoric, rather than his person. Chudleigh continues, still referring to the effect of love's desire in "us," Donne's audience:

> The first effects sprung in the giddy minde
> Of flashy youth, and thirst of woman-kinde,
> By colours lead, and drawne to a pursuit,
> Now once againe by beautie of the fruit,
> As if their longings too must set us free,
> And tempt us now to the commanded tree (23–28).

Donne's brilliance as a preacher was in his ability to incite a similar desire in his congregation by rendering godliness desirable. Moreover, the organic metaphor expressing the traditional identification between the tree of life and the tree of Christ's crucifixion emphasizes a continuity from the roots of lust to the mature fruit not of a forbidden tree conducing to bondage to sin, but to a "commanded" tree of life resulting in freedom. Chudleigh thus par-adoxically speaks of Donne as a seducer of souls:

> Tell me, had ever pleasure such a dresse,
> Have you knowne crimes so shap'd? or lovelinesse
> Such as his lips did cloth religion in?
> Had not reproofe a beauty passing sinne?
> Corrupted nature sorrow'd when she stood
> So neare the danger of becomming good,
> And wish'd our so inconstant eares exempt
> From piety that had such power to tempt:
> Did not his sacred flattery beguile
> Man to amendment? (29–38).

Chudleigh laments the sad consequence of the Fall that we should require such an allurement, that "man grew well / Through the same frailtie [i.e. lust, ambiguously for women and for power] by which he fell" (39–40). The effective preacher must work by inducing a new courtship, by trans-lating our lusts into holy desire:

> Who treats with us must our affections move
> To th'good we flie by those sweets which we love,

Must seeke our palats, and with their delight
To gaine our deeds, must bribe our appetite.
These traines he knew, and laying nets to save,
Temptingly sugred all the health hee gave (53–58).

The preacher (presumably) must train our appetite by first appealing to our taste and then by expanding and refining our palate.

In the following pages I will build upon the argument first laid down by Chudleigh in his poem: that courtship was the dominant and consistent rhetorical mode to which Donne turned again and again, not only in his poems, but in his sermons as well. The burden of this study, however, is not simply to prove this a central *topos* in Donne, but to show *how* Donne uses courtship as an effective and readily adaptable means of persuasion.

❧ Courtship as a cultural and rhetorical commonplace

The next, fayre smiling with a pleasing cheeke,
Had power to rauish and inchaunt mens eares,
Hight Rhetorick, whose shadowed vaile showen cleere
With siluer tongues, and ouer it she weares,
A wimpled scarfe, bedewd with hearers teares,
Whose captiue hearts she should detaine long while,
With pleasance of her vnaffected stile.
                    "Rhetoricke" in *Englands Parnassus*[93]

Donne's handling of courtship extends well beyond the particular activities of wooing and political posturing. Various social relations, hierarchically conceived, can evoke similar structures of desire even when courtship opportunities are not readily apparent. In a culture where offenders of all sorts were so clearly stigmatized, one's status before the law held tremendous eulogistic and dyslogistic potential, either to goad one to seek a praiseworthy standing or to avoid a blameworthy one. Many such structures are part of the background of commonplaces from which Donne drew material for both his poetry and his prose. For example, a chart in a legal commentary by Edward Coke illustrates the transference of inheritance as a pyramidal structure where the current legal heir inhabits the apex and is

---

[93] *Englands Parnassus* (1600), 342 [Z3v]. This poem is attributed to Thomas Storer.

therefore displayed as the object of desire (Figure 1).[94] Being biologically determined (according to birth order and sex), these relations are largely fixed, allowing for little or no mobility. Nonetheless, the goad of hierarchy remains in the matter of inheritance, potentially resulting in subversive compensatory action: this is the very situation which motivates Shakespeare's bastards, Edmund and Don John, who struggle against the privileged brother in part out of frustration at their deprived status before the law.

Desire engendered in conditions of estrangement is emblematically present everywhere in Donne's culture, and hence forms part of his original congregations' frame of reference. For example, desire is frequently figured as a city or house on a hill, a commonplace that has its source in biblical imagery (e.g. Matthew 5:14). Northrop Frye, one imagines, would see this topological expression of upwardness as a universal human archetype.[95] Elizabeth Bieman rather sees a transition in the time between Homer and Plato from a metaphoric mode of language where "'Olympus' is simply the place of the gods" to the metonymic where "'Olympus,' for reasons that have recognizably more to do with convention than with the way things 'really' are, signifies a high centre of supernatural (or later, natural) power."[96] Universal or conventional, such a mount as the hill of truth in Donne's third satyre is emblematic of an upward quest toward a desired end. In this case, Donne figures a female object of desire which must be courted through a hierarchical image that, in its context, is charged with both political and transcendent motives. "On a huge hill," says Donne,

> Cragged, and steep, Truth stands, and hee that will
> Reach her, about must, and about must goe;
> And what the'hills suddennes resists, winne so;
> Yet strive so, that before age, deaths twilight,
> Thy Soule rest, for none can worke in that night
> (79–84).

---

[94] Coke, *The First Part of the institutes of the Lawes of England*, vol. 1 (1628), folio 19. Notwithstanding its difficult legal discourse, even at a cursory glance the semiotics of the diagram make clear the basic structure involved, which is our concern here.

[95] Northrop Frye, *Anatomy of Criticism* (Princeton: Princeton University Press, 1957): 99–112.

[96] Elizabeth Bieman, *Plato Baptized* (Toronto: University of Toronto Press, 1988), 26. Bieman takes this shift to indicate a detachment of the signifier from the process of understanding, a function that is fundamental to Plato's sceptical methodology in the dialogues; I am simply using this metonymic association to indicate that this commonplace of the hill as signifier of a desirable end has a long-standing tradition.

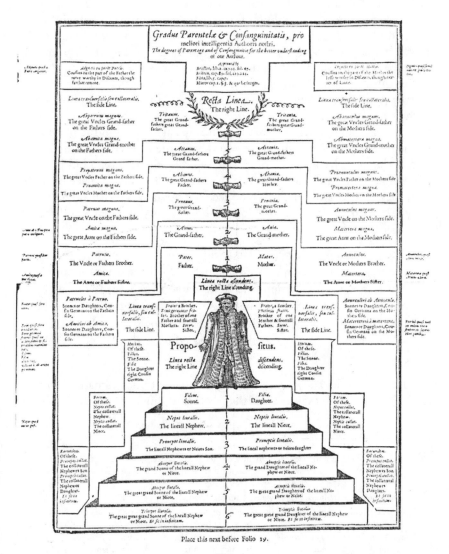

Place this next before Folio 19.

Fig. 1.
"Gradus Parentelæ & Consanguinitatis," *a table in Edward Coke's*
The First Part of the Institutes of the Lawes of England *(1628), vol. 1*

From the *Beinecke Rare Book and Manuscript Library*, Yale University

The hill is at once prohibitive and compelling.[97] To appreciate just how compelling, one must understand the rhetorical function of such scenes. Mounts were a common feature in English Renaissance gardens. Francis Bacon's ideal garden had "in the very middle, a fair mount, with three ascents, and alleys, enough for four to walk abreast," and another at the end of the garden to provide a prospect of the out-lying fields.[98] The prospect was the reward for the climb, affording the subject a commanding view of the area, including the domain of the landlord. Foucault might rather call it a dominating view by which one can, symbolically at least, assert a position of ascendancy.[99] Ben Jonson in "To Penshurst" would make such estates symbols of class structure and, for Jonson, of desire. But Jonson was only adding to a symbol that was already engendered in the placement of the houses themselves in relation to their gardens. As Roy Strong notes, Elizabethan and Jacobean manors were typically situated on a hill in order to see and be seen.[100] To accentuate the sense of ascent to a place of privilege, these houses typically had to be accessed by stairs. One such estate that would have been familiar to Donne, Lord Drury's Hawstead Place, is described by Sir John Cullum:

> The house was on a rise of land with a commanding view of the countryside and bespoke a taste superior to the artificial mount, which in many old gardens was to be clambered up for the sake of prospect. The approach to the house was by a flight of steps, and a strong brick bridge of three arches, through a small jealous wicket, formed in the great well-timbered gate, that rarely grated on its hinges.[101]

The garden in Lady Mary Wroth's title page to her romance, *Urania* (1621), is a good example of the rhetorical function of such scenes

---

[97] John M. Steadman emphasizes the difficulty of the ascent, relating to a desire in the Renaissance for certitude in the middle way between dogmatism and scepticism: *The Hill and the Labyrinth* (Berkeley: University of California Press, 1984), 2–3.

[98] Bacon, *Essays*, intro. Michael J. Hawkins (London: Dent, 1972), 140, 142.

[99] Douglas Chambers notes a shift in the meaning of "survey" in Restoration England from "to look upon" to the modern sense which includes "the panoptic and dominating associations described by Foucault in *Discipline and Punish*" (*The Reinvention of the World* [London: Arnold, 1996], 30). Although the early seventeenth century predates the shift toward the surveillance-oriented model of discipline Foucault describes, the power relations symbolized in the hill resemble quite closely those of the nineteenth-century Panopticon (*Discipline and Punish*, trans. Alan Sheridan [New York: Pantheon, 1977], 195–209).

[100] Roy Strong, *The Renaissance Garden in England* (London: Thames and Hudson, 1979), 12-15, 57.

[101] Sir John Cullum, *The History and Antiquities of Hawstead* (1784), 131.

(Figure 2).[102] The appropriateness of this site for elucidating the courtship *topos* is demonstrated in Gary Waller's description of the "classic romance pattern" (exemplified by *Urania*) as "an often extremely complicated quest, usually that of a young man in search of an ideal, frequently represented by a bride, a lost kingdom, or some personal or communal goal of purity or transformation."[103] Citing Frye, Waller goes on to note that these quests are structured according to an ideology of class hierarchy. This is evident even in heroes and heroines of the lower classes, who either prove themselves by their demonstrated virtue really to be members of a higher class (the common romance *topos* of nobility disguised) or aspire to the values embodied by those in the upper echelons. Throughout the reigns of Elizabeth, James, and Charles I, romance became an increasingly popular metaphor in court circles for inscribing and validating socio-political relations, especially under Henrietta Maria.[104]

Wroth's frontispiece depicts a scene early in the romance where the questing party arrives at a hill crowned with a stately palace, the House of Love. This palace has a sense of mystery about it. It "seem'd as if it hung in the ayre," such that "they imagined it some Magicall work."[105] The gods who are represented in the upper storey add to its sense of transcendence. Clearly the elevated palace represents an achievement in love that is not easily reached. This courtship of love begins at the base of the hill where there is a bridge crossing a river. Three images decorate three towers which comprise the bridge: Cupid with his bow, who is pointing the way to Venus holding a flaming heart, and finally Constancy, who is holding the keys to the palace. These three figures signify the process the courtier must go through: first love is awakened in the Tower of Desire; then it is enflamed in the Tower of Love where the lover is tormented by several attendant affections (jealousy, hope, etc.); finally, one hopes, the lover is admitted entrance. But as the text tells us, the way is opened only to the "few possessed with that vertue." Venus's priest further explains that "heere [in the bridge towers] is the triall of false or faithfull Lovers" — a sort of purification by ordeal. None can proceed to the Tower of Constancy, says the priest, "til the valiantest Knight, with the loyallest Lady come together, and

---

[102] Interestingly, Donne's congregation at St. Dunstan's had ready access to this book, which was sold at a shop in their churchyard and at another in "Paules Ally."

[103] Gary Waller, *The Sidney Family Romance* (Detroit: Wayne State University Press, 1993), 251.

[104] Waller, *Sidney Family Romance*, 252; Carolyn Ruth Swift, "Feminine Identity in Lady Mary Wroth's Romance *Urania*," *Women in the Renaissance*, eds. Kirby Farrell et al (Amherst: University of Massachusetts Press, 1990), 154–84, here 159.

[105] Mary Wroth, *The First Part of The Countess of Montgomery's Urania*, ed. Josephine A. Roberts, MRTS 40 (Binghamton, NY: Medieval & Renaissance Texts & Studies, 1995), 48.

Fig. 2.
Title page to The Countesse of Mountgomeries Urania *(1621)*

This item is reproduced by permission of *The Huntington Library, San Marino, California*

open that gate."[106] In these material details the artist follows the text quite closely, but he adds two very conventional elements to enhance the courtship imagery: a winding path up the side of the hill, and a winding stair along the side of the temple, completing the sense of an ascent-by-degrees.

A similar, fascinating pictorial representation prefaces George Wither's *A Collection of Emblemes* (1635) (Figure 3).[107] Wither's frontispiece clearly illustrates the parallel structure of sacred and profane courtships. On the left extreme of a mountain base, halfway up, is a church with a pastor bidding people to come; on the opposite extreme is a rather more courtly building with Venus also extending an invitation from a doorway, with Cupid before her and a couple (the male in courtier's garb) dallying off to her left. Each building occupies an entrance point at the base, leading upward to a corresponding peak. In the centre are the nine Muses with a chorus in the background who seem to occupy the middle ground, suggesting that verse may serve either amorous or spiritual purposes. Throughout the scene people are at points of decision, their arms extended and pointing in one direction or another.

Structurally, the two ways are identical. In fact, halfway up courtiers on both sides of the mountain are in a similar situation, even though the way of the church is more lush with vegetation and less severe than the way of Venus. Each courtier is climbing the winding route upward: some in danger of falling off the mountain, others with precarious holds on the rocky cliffs, still others in relative security. But in the upper half of Venus's peak, violence erupts between two pairs of rivals; others are found to have been hanged (perhaps suicides of despair). This way, it turns out, leads to death, or at best mutability, at its apex, where a skeleton who holds a counterpart to Cupid's

---

106 Wroth, *First Part of Urania*, 48–49.

107 For another reading of Wither's frontispiece see Michael Bath, *Speaking Pictures: English Emblem Books and Renaissance Culture* (London: Longman, 1994), 111–5. Bath suggests that the iconography of the frontispiece, which was engraved by William Marshall (the engraver of Donne's portrait in the 1635 *Poems*), is based on Renaissance illustrated depictions of a first-century A. D. text attributed to Cebes of Thebes, commonly referred to as *Tabula Cebetis* (Figure 4). This moralizing dialogue is based on the interlocutors' interaction with an allegorical picture of the progress of life, which the elder interlocutor, named Senex, analyzes in detail. The picture includes an ascent up a hill (true education) at the top of which is a citadel (happiness). At the entrance Paideia (Education) purifies and cures the entrants of their vice. Once inside, the pilgrim is led by the Virtues to Happiness who is seated on a throne in the citadel's vestibule: John T. Fitzgerald, *The Tabula of Cebes* (Chico, CA: Scholars Press, 1983), 9–10. Cebes's table was translated into English by Sir Francis Poyntz (d. 1528) and was published c. 1530, going through at least two more editions in the sixteenth century. Several editions were published throughout Europe in the Renaissance. See Stephen Orgel, *Cebes in England* (New York and London: Garland, 1980); *Cebes' Tablet*, intro. Sandra Sider (New York: Renaissance Society of America, 1979); Reinhold Schleier, *Tabula Cebetis* (Berlin: Mann, 1973).

Fig. 3.
Frontispiece to George Wither's A Collection of Emblemes *(1635)*

The Newberry Library, Chicago

Fig. 4.
M. Merian's depiction of Tabula Cebetis

bow also brandishes the sword of death. An eternal end of judgement is also implied in the dark cloud issuing evil spirits to the right of the peak. In contrast, on the left the way of courtship culminates in an apex of life, symbolized by the wings of the eagle (alluding to Isaiah 40:31 [also Exodus 19:4 and Deuteronomy 32:11–12]). This image is typologically as well as topologically charged. On the penultimate peak is the city on a hill, Zion, a biblical commonplace of the Christian's (and before that the Jew's) desired end. On the left, a bright cloud emitting the voices of angels confirms that this is the way to divine favour. Yet these two ways are not entirely divorced after all. The implication of the title at the border of the two peaks suggests that Wither's emblems may do a work of translation in the hearts of the reader, drawing the profane to the sacred. Just above the heavenly muse's head, at least two courtiers appear to be making the translation from one to the other. Wither's muse, it seems, subsumes the pagan Muses to her moral end, to show the way of life and divine love.

Literary uses of similar images abound in this period.[108] I choose visual representations to illustrate this cultural commonplace because, in a society where literacy was still largely limited to a privileged group, pictures were more widely accessible than printed texts.[109] Donne, it should be remembered, preached to a wide cross-section of society. Emblem books were the common person's literature, so much so that Donne could assume that a large portion of his congregation was familiar with the most common emblems.[110] Apart from the very popular emblem books of the period (many of which were written in English, making them accessible to a popular reading audience), emblems frequently turned up in other, non-literary

---

[108] One thinks immediately of the hill of the Muses, and of several mounts in the *Faerie Qveene*, such as Arlo Hill and the Mount of Contemplation. Henry Vaughan, in "Mount of Olives (I)," makes the "sacred hill" the object of a poem on divine love, as so many profane poets apply "Language to love / And idolise some shade, or grove" (1–4). The hill is a recurring feature of the topography along Christian's journey in Bunyan's *Pilgrim's Progress*, where courtship significance abounds. John Steadman lists several such literary sites (*The Hill and the Labyrinth*, 2–3, n. 2).

[109] Notwithstanding John F. Leisher's suggestion that the emblem vogue was largely an upper-class phenomenon, it should be noted that emblem books were being translated into English, presumably to widen the interest to a non-Latinate readership: *Geoffrey Whitney's A Choice of Emblemes and its Relation to the Emblematic Vogue in Tudor England* [Ph.D. diss. Harvard University, 1952] (New York: Garland, 1987): 122. By the early seventeenth century emblem books were targeting a wide reading public: Mario Praz, *Studies in Seventeenth-Century Imagery*, 2nd ed. (Rome: Edizioni di Storia e Letteratura, 1964), 163. See also Mary Cole Sloane, *The Visual in Metaphysical Poetry* (Atlantic Highlands, NJ: Humanities Press, 1981), 24–25.

[110] Joan Webber documents several instances in Donne's sermons where he interprets objects and situations as emblems (*Contrary Music*, esp. 127–33). Clayton G. MacKenzie examines traces of common iconic sources (broadly defined) in Donne's poetry and prose (*Emblem and Icon in John Donne's Poetry and Prose* [New York: Peter Lang, 2001]). See also Joseph Lederer, "John Donne and the Emblematic Practice," *RES* o.s. 22 (1946): 182–200, *passim*.

arts and artifacts, from prints and embroidery to furniture and jewelry.[111] For example, Donne would almost certainly have seen Lady Drury's Oratory at Hawstead Place, seat of his friend and patron Sir Robert Drury, which was richly decorated with emblems from popular emblem books of the period.[112] Emblems literally provide us with the most common imagery patterns available to Donne in inventing matter for a general audience.

Emblems are also culturally significant because they illustrate a manner of picturing or visualizing social structures and relations. The visual impact of these images ensures their memorability and lends a sense of vividness and thoroughness to this field of verbal imagery. As Mary Cole Sloane demonstrates, the emblem books bear many marks of the meditative process, both in the tradition begun in the *Spiritual Exercises* and in the devotional writing of the metaphysical poets.[113] She cites Rosamond Tuve in describing the emblem as a culmination of the medieval mental habit of seeing "the intelligible in the visible," a habit which continued in Donne and Herbert and which was supplemented with their own culture's images.[114] By this means, emblem books served the same deliberative function as sermons in directing their readership toward a proper end. In this vein, Mario Praz describes the Renaissance device (a close relative of the emblem) as "a symbolical representation of a purpose, a wish, a line of conduct (*impresa* is what one intends *imprendere*, i.e. to undertake) by means of a motto and a picture which reciprocally interpret each other."[115] This conceptual structuring of desire and intent is an effective cultural *topos* in part because it is emblematic. Moreover, emblems foster a sense of analogical correspondence between the sensible world and the spiritual that

---

[111] See John Horden's introductory note to Whitney's *A Choice of Emblemes* (1586) (Menston, Eng.: Scholar Press, 1969), and Leisher, *Whitney's A Choice of Emblemes*, esp. chaps. 5 and 6. Leisher also describes the use of emblems in the schools (136–42). On the presence of emblems in various expressions of material culture see also Bath, *Speaking Pictures*, 7–17, and Sloane, *The Visual in Metaphysical Poetry*, 28. Although he excludes emblems from the scope of his study, Anthony Wells-Cole demonstrates how thoroughly ornamental prints from the continent (which nonetheless included emblems) were circulated in England and copied into English decor in portraits, architecture, embroidery, painting, etc. He does, however, note specifically the use of emblems in tapestries (from Whitney and Alciati) and in embroidery (from Paradin): *Art and Decoration in Elizabethan and Jacobean England* (New Haven: Yale University Press, 1997), 232, 240, 256.

[112] Lady Drury's Oratory derived most of its painted decoration from emblem books, including those of Georgette de Montenay, Geffrey Whitney, Claude Paradin, and Peacham (Wells-Cole, *Art and Decoration*, 210–11). Sir John Cullum describes a closet from this oratory and lists forty-one of its emblems (*History and Antiquities of Hawstead*, 134–39). See also R. C. Bald's description in *Donne and the Drurys* (Cambridge: Cambridge University Press, 1959; repr. Westport, CT: Greenwood Press, 1986), 56–57.

[113] Sloane, *The Visual in Metaphysical Poetry*, 24–46.

[114] Sloane, *The Visual in Metaphysical Poetry*, 27–28.

[115] Praz, *Seventeenth-Century Imagery*, 58.

is at work in the relationship between picture and text.[116] On another level, emblem books often symbolize the transference of human love to divine love, a process which is basic both to Christian meditation and to Donne's use of courtship *topoi* in the sermons.[117] Many of the plates Quarles borrowed from *Typus Mundi* and *Pia Desideria* depict Cupid-like figures, Amore (Divine Love) and Anima (Human Soul). Finally, the sermons benefit ethically from this emblematic quality of courtship imagery. The authority engendered in the moral purpose of emblem books ensures that their depictions inscribe clear eulogistic/dyslogistic associations.

The courtship *topos* is well represented in the emblem books of the period. A popular emblem was a spire entwined with ivy accompanied by the epigram "*Te stante, virebo,*" construed as "While thou standest I shall flourish" by P.S., the anonymous English translator of Claude Paradin's *Devises Heroïques* (Lyons, 1557).[118] In addition to this English edition of Paradin, Geoffrey Whitney included the spire and ivy in *A Choice of Emblemes* (1586) (Figure 5). The motto is the same as in Paradin, but the direct source of Whitney's plate is Hadrianus Junius's *Emblemata* (Antwerp, 1565).[119] At a time when emblems were ubiquitous in English culture (coincident with the height of the "Cult of Elizabeth"), this one was particularly common.[120] The spire itself symbolizes hierarchy, a broad base narrowing at the top to a point.[121] This, the opening emblem in Geoffrey Whitney's collection, illustrates not only the visibility of hierarchical paradigms of desire in Elizabethan England, but the readiness with which transcendent, political and, in this case, literary courtships were associated. Whitney's spire reaching to the clouds and entwined with ivy signifies the

---

[116] John Hoskins (writing c. 1599) suggests a close kinship between the emblem and similitude: "an EMBLEM is but the one part of the similitude, the other part (viz., the application) expressed indifferently and jointly in one sentence, with words some proper to the one part, some to the other": *Directions for Speech and Style*, ed. and intro. Hoyt H. Hudson (Princeton: Princeton University Press, 1935), 9–10. Blount echoes Hoskins (*Academy of Eloquence*, 4, [B2v]).

[117] As Sloane notes, "[t]he tendency to associate Divine Love with the secular Cupid was widespread" (*The Visual in Metaphysical Poetry*, 51).

[118] *The Heroicall Devises of M. Claudius Paradin* (1591), 87, F4.

[119] Junius's version of this emblem bears a different motto, with much the same sense, "Principum opes, plebis adminicula": the resources of rulers [are] the prop of the people (*Emblemata* [1565], 20, [B2v]. Translation provided by Leslie MacCoull). Although Junius was born in the Low Countries and lived there most of his life, he spent several years in England.

[120] There were many columns and pyramids of marble in the garden at Nonsuch, home of Lord Lumley, including an obelisk on a platform (Strong, *Renaissance Garden*, 65–66). This obelisk very closely resembles the structure of spires found in Whitney, Junius, P. S. and Paradin, and Bocchi.

[121] P. S.'s description is reminiscent of the triadic platonic scheme outlined by Michael Dixon: "a great foure square pillar, brode beneath, & sharpe on the toppe" (88, [F4v]; cf. Dixon, *The Polliticke Courtier*, 11).

Te stante, virebo.

A MIGHTIE Spyre, whose toppe dothe pierce the skie,
An iuie greene imbraceth rounde about,
And while it standes, the same doth bloome on highe,
But when it shrinkes, the iuie standes in dowt:
The Piller great, our gratious Princes is:
The braunche, the Churche: whoe speakes vnto hir this.

I, that of late with stormes was almoste spent,
And brused sore with Tirants bluddie bloes,
Whome fire, and sworde, with persecution rent,
Am nowe sett free, and ouerlooke my foes,
And whiles thow raignst, oh most renowmed Queene
By thie supporte my blossome shall bee greene.

A

Fig. 5.
Emblem, "Te stante, virebo,"
from Geoffrey Whitney's A Choice of Emblemes *(1586)*

church's dependency on the Queen.[122] But more than dependency, it suggests that the higher motives of the church find their means of fulfilment in a political courtship, signified in the climbing ivy. At the same time, the pillar touching the clouds clearly identifies the sovereign with the upper reaches of a hierarchy which culminates in God, its ultimate fulfilment. In the second stanza, the ivy becomes personalized, so that by the Queen's "supporte my [the poet's] blossome [poesie] shall bee greene" — that is, Whitney's poetry will have borne its fruit if it results in patronage. (Whitney courts the Queen's patronage by *synecdoche*, dedicating his book to a member of the Queen's privy council, and his established patron, Robert Dudley, Earl of Leicester.) Furthermore, the spire (the Queen) touches the clouds, signifying that political structures may lead the subject up to the point of transcendence. The spire could also stand in for the church.[123] Although the great spire of St. Paul's burned down in 1561, many spires remained in London.[124]

Courtship of the Queen is both literally and symbolically a means for the church and/or the moral poet to court God. In fact, the poet gives his whole book a transcendent significance in the inscription on the facing page.

SINCE man is fraile, and all his thoughts are sinne,
And of him selfe he can no good inuent,
Then euerie one, before they oughte beginne,
Should call on GOD, from whome all grace is sent:
So, I beseeche, that he the same will sende,
That, to his praise I maie beginne, and ende.

---

[122] The pillar was a common emblem of Queen Elizabeth in English gardens after 1588, symbolizing her imperial pretensions. One such instance was a crowned pillar embraced by an eglantine tree (Strong, *Renaissance Garden*, 62). Reminiscent of Whitney's emblem, at a reception for Queen Elizabeth in Cecil's garden at Wimbledon, an actor in the character of a gardener likened its plants to "all the Virtues, all the Graces, all the Muses winding and wreathing about [her] majesty, each contending to be chief" (*Renaissance Garden*, 46).

[123] This association between social and religious monuments is expressed in an entertainment by Ben Jonson which welcomed King James I and Queen Anne to Sir William Cornwallis's garden, where Mercury tells the royal couple that Highgate (Cornwallis's house) is upon the Arcadian hill Cyllene: "and from this *Mount*," says Mercury, one may view "these valleyes, yond' lesser hills, those statelier edifices, and towers": "The Entertainment at Highgate," in *Ben Jonson*, eds. C. H. Hereford and Percy and Evelyn Simpson, 11 vols. (Oxford: Clarendon Press, 1941), 7:138. Here, notes Strong, the monuments of the garden are compared with the spires of London (*Renaissance Garden*, 9).

[124] Steeples abounded in Donne's London. St. Dunstan's, where Donne held the vicarage from March 1624, is the most notable example. There is another one block away from St. Paul's at Friday St. and Maiden Lane. See C. J. Visscher, *London Before the Fire: A Grand Panorama* (London: Sidgwick & Jackson, 1973). As Burke would have it, spires are symbolic statements of transcendence over worldly affairs (*RM*, 186).

This short verse anticipates the fragility of the ivy, noting man's frailty owing to sin and his need for divine grace to accomplish anything good. Therefore the poet seeks God's grace to begin, and end. The highest purpose of any human endeavour is God's glory. In each case — political, poetical, spiritual — the pinnacle represents an object of desire, and the narrowing of the spire signifies an increasingly closer approximation to that object. The means of ascent is by winding and clinging, a process of making the appropriate connections — a courtship. Francis Bacon, in his essay "Of Great Place," develops a similar image, observing that "[a]ll rising to great place is by a winding stair."[125]

In Palladin, via his anonymous English translator, the transcendent reaches of the spire are symbolized by a crescent moon at its apex.[126] The spire is a pyramid, reminding us of the close identification of sovereign and deity (in ancient Egypt literally; in Elizabethan England figuratively), while also bespeaking a courtship of transcendence both in the form of lasting fame in this world, and a translation into the next. The pyramid association is expunged from Whitney, but recurs again in Henry Peacham's *Minerva Britanna* (1612) (Figure 6). Here the spire looks much the same, but the ivy is replaced by a personification of Glory. The accompanying verse tells us that this Glory, which supports the monument (the monarch's fame), is found inscribed on money and medals (England's reminder of its sovereign's glory), suggesting that, for the subject, an accumulation of wealth is a means of approaching that political glory.[127] But more importantly, the gems of Glory's crown are described as "glorious proiectes of the mind." These could be policies and projects aimed at improving the commonwealth, or a cultivation of personal and public virtue. In either case, the sovereign is admonished to aim at a higher glory than his/her Memphian counterparts achieved.

Other images of upward progression proliferate in emblem books of the period. In his invocation to the first book of his *Emblemes* (1635), Francis Quarles describes the soul's upward motion which his book aims to induce:

---

[125] Bacon, *Essays*, 33.

[126] In yet another version in Achille Bocchi's *Symbolicarum Quaestionum* (1574), the apex is occupied by a featureless orb, perhaps either a sun or moon (CIIII, [N4v]). The moon was frequently used as a symbol for Queen Elizabeth. The orb can also be taken as any object of desire. In George Peele's *The Araygnement of Paris*, "a ball of golde" is "a faire and worthie prize" over which Venus, Juno, and Pallas argue, each thinking herself fairest and thus worthy to possess it (*The Araygnment of Paris*, ed. R. Mark Benbow in *The Dramatic Works* [New Haven: Yale University Press, 1970], 3:77, line 357); cited by Louis Montrose, "Gifts and Reasons: The Contexts of Peele's *Araygnement of Paris*," *ELH* 47 (1980): 433–61, here 448.

[127] Peacham, *Minerva Britanna* (1612), 21, [E2v].

21   *Gloria Principum.*

To the right truely Noble, and most Honourable Lord
        VVILLIAM, *Earle of Penbrooke.*

In med: Adriani
Imp:

A LADIE faire, who with Maiestique grace,
    Supportes a huge, and stately Pyramis.
(Such as th'old Monarches long agoe did place,
By NILVS bankes, to keepe their memories;)
    Whose brow (with all the orient Pearles beset,)
    Begirte's a rich and pretious Coronet.

Shee Glorie is of Princes, as I find
Describ'd in Moneies, and in Meddailes old;
Those Gemmes are glorious proiectes of the mind,
Adorning more their Roiall heades, then Gold.

* Ingenii prae-   The Pyramis the worldes great wonderment,
clara facinora si-
cut Anima Im-   Is of their fame, some * lasting Moniment.
mortalia sunt.
Salust:
Ovid: ad Liviam.   Facta Ducis vivent operosaque gloria rerum
                        Haec manet haec avidos effugit vna rogos.

                                                    Ragione

Fig. 6.
Emblem, "Gloria Principum," *from Henry Peacham's* Minerva Britanna
(1612)

Rowze thee, my soul; and dreine thee from the dregs
Of vulgar thoughts: Skrue up the heightned pegs
Of thy Sublime Theorboe foure notes higher,
And higher yet ...
         ... Shall we still creepe like Snayles,
That gild their wayes with their owne native slimes?
No, we must flie like Eagles, and our Rhimes
Must mount to heav'n, and reach th'Olympick eare.[128]

Throughout the book this upward movement toward a higher object of
desire is consistently figured as an ascent upward to a destination typically
figured as a hill. In Book 4, emblem 2, the wandering pilgrim seeks his way
through a labyrinth (a symbol of frustrated desire) that prevents him from
a winding path that ascends toward a tower. From the top of the tower the
devout soul, standing beside a fiery beacon, issues its call (Figure 7). In a similar configuration, the "beloved" of Canticles 5:6 meets the devout soul on
the upward way which leads to a tiered tower, again signalled from its apex
by a fiery beacon (Figure 8). In the accompanying text this image of ascent
is made to be emblematic of the ecstasy of divine love in contrast to the
downward-reaching impulse of profane love:

Thy flames O *Cupid* (though the joyfull heart
Feeles neither tang of griefe, nor feares the smart
Of jealous doubts, but drunk with full desires)
Are torments weigh'd with these celestiall fires;
Pleasures that ravish in so high a measure,
That O I languish in excesse of pleasure:
What ravisht heart, that feeles these melting Ioyes,
Would not despise and loathe the trech'rous Toyes
Of dunghill earth![129]

The life-as-journey theme (a favourite in Donne's sermons) is commonly depicted in this manner. In one of Georgette de Montenay's
Emblemes ou Devises Chrestiennes (1571) a "pilgrim by degrees sets out / In
order to arrive at the celestial city," which is figured as a twisting, ascending path leading to a doorway which hovers above the crest of a hill

---

[128] Quarles, *Emblemes*, 1–2, A5–[A5v]. *Emblemes* was published in 1635, but these emblems, originally
published by Hermann Hugo in 1624, circulated widely in Europe before then (Praz, *Seventeenth-
Century Imagery*, 376–78; Sloane, *The Visual in Metaphysical Poetry*, 24–25).
[129] Quarles, *Emblemes*, 262, [S1v].

Fig. 7.
Emblem 2, Book 4, a pilgrim in a labyrinth,
from Francis Quarles's Emblemes *(1635)*

Glasgow University Library, Department of Special Collections, University of Glasgow

Fig. 8.
Emblem 5, Book 5, the devout soul and a tiered tower,
from Quarles's Emblemes

(Figure 9). The pilgrim views this life as a "preamble before a permanent home" and waits to possess a "more elevated place waiting for us" in heaven.[130] An ascent of a different kind is figured by a man ascending a ladder (Figure 10). Waves crash on the rocks below, but the man climbs nonetheless, confident that he will not fall, because God's hand has reached down to pull him up. This is presented as an emblem of the importance of "raising one's steps" (line 3) to God in prayer, with assurance that God will not abandon us if we do not abandon him.[131]

These emblems emerge from notions of hierarchy and human ontology that are fundamental to the intellectual fabric of the period. The Great Chain of Being, the commonplace metaphor for universal order, remained a suitable *topos* for Alexander Pope even in 1733 when he published *An Essay on Man* (see lines 237–44). The upward-reaching aspect of this hierarchy of being which infuses Renaissance thought is evident as early as the work of Ranulf Higden (d.1364), who prefers the metaphor of a "ladder of ascent" where "the top of an inferior class touches the bottom of a superior." Higden continues a few lines later, "[s]o also the noblest entity in the category of bodies, the human body, when its humours are evenly balanced, touches the fringe of the next class above it, namely the human soul, which occupies the lowest rank in the spiritual order."[132] According to the neo-platonic scheme, on which the chain of being is based, a movement from body to spirit is a purification of ascent.

This schema is central to the argument of the Fall in Milton's *Paradise Lost*. The necessity of Adam and Eve's freedom of will is based on their nature as reasonable creatures, just as Satan's rebellion exemplifies a debasement of reason.[133] The proper ambition of all creatures is toward perfection, as described by "the winged Hierarch," Raphael, who tells Adam,

> ...one Almighty is, from whom
> All things proceed, and up to him return,
> If not deprav'd from good, created all
> Such to perfection, one first matter all,

---

[130] Georgette de Montenay, *Emblemes ou Devises Chrestiennes* (1571), 12, E4; my translation from the French. Montenay's book was first published at Lyons and became very popular throughout Europe. It was published in a polyglot version, including English text, at Frankfurt in 1619.

[131] de Montenay, *Emblemes*, 13, F1; cf. Psalms 17:5, 18:36, 37:23, 31, 44:18

[132] Quoted from E. M. W. Tillyard, *The Elizabethan World Picture* (New York: Vintage Books, n. d.), 28–29. Tillyard presents the best summary of this *topos* in relation to Elizabethan England, but a fuller account of its earlier history can be found in A. O. Lovejoy, *The Great Chain of Being* (Cambridge, MA: Harvard University Press, 1957).

[133] *Paradise Lost*, 8.437–444, 9.351–2, 6.29–43. I use *Milton: Complete Poems and Major Prose*, ed. Merrit Y. Hughes (New York: Macmillan, 1957).

Ce pelerin peu à peu s'achemine
Pour arriuer à la cité celeste,
Et n'a regret qui autre que luy domine
Ses champs, chasteaux, & que rien ne luy reste.
Voicy qui fait que rien ne le moleste,
Considerant que maison permanente
N'auons ça bas, mais bien mortelle peste,
A tous qui n'ont plus haut mis leur attente.

Fig. 9.
Emblem of the pilgrim's journey,
from Georgette de Montenay's Emblemes ou Devises Chrestiennes *(1571)*

A QVO TREPIDABO.

Ceſt homme icy preſt à tumber en bas
Et ſe froiſſer, aumoins en apparence,
Monte touſiours, & raſſeure ſon pas,
Sachant que Dieu le ſouſtient d'aſſeurance.
Que tout Chreſtien donc prie en confiance
Dieu, qu'il le tienne, & ne le laiſſe point.
Car s'il nous laiſſe, il n'y a eſperance
D'aucun ſalut iuſqu'à vn petit poinſt.

f   *A ceſt*

Fig. 10.
Emblem of a man ascending a ladder above crashing waves,
from de Montenay's Emblemes ou Devises Chrestiennes

Indu'd with various forms, various degrees
Of substance, and in things that live, of life;
But more refin'd, more spiritous, and pure,
As nearer to him plac't or nearer tending
Each in thir several active Spheres assign'd,
Till body up to spirit work, in bounds
Proportion'd to each kind. So from the root
Springs lighter the green stalk, from thence the leaves
More aery, last the bright consummate flow'r
Spirits odorous breathes: flow'rs and thir fruit
Man's nourishment, by gradual scale sublim'd
To vital spirits aspire, to animal,
To intellectual, give both life and sense,
Fancy and understanding, whence the Soul
Reason receives, and reason is her being,
Discursive, or Intuitive; discourse
Is oftest yours, the latter most is ours,
Differing but in degree, of kind the same (5.469–490).

In exercising right reason in their choices, according to their place in God's
chain of being, Adam and Eve may grow in perfection to be like angels.
Raphael continues, speculating that

                              ... perhaps
Your bodies may at last turn all to spirit
Improv'd by tract of time, and wing'd ascend
Ethereal, as wee, or may at choice
Here or in Heav'nly Paradises dwell;
If ye be found obedient, and retain
Unalterably firm his love entire
Whose progeny you are (5.496–503).

This *topos* of ascent in the hierarchy of being is employed by Thomas
Spencer in his preface to *The Art of Logic* (1628). Spencer very clearly illustrates the courtship potential of Renaissance ontology. Because logic is a
director of reason, and reason defines man's place in the order of being, "the
more logicall a man is, the more is he like a man, and the lesse logicall, the
lesse like a man who is a reasonable Creature."[134] Bound up in this sense of

---

[134] Thomas Spencer, *The Art of Logic* (1628), [A3v]–A4 (n. p.).

order is the Christian humanist project of reversing the effects of the Fall through learning. Spencer insists that logical "precepts are needfull to the promptest witts, for man hath not now so ample vse of reason as *Adam* had at his first Creation, and therefore he needs the helpe of artificiall precepts."[135] The cultivation and use of right reason is a process of identification and ascent to the divine. As Spencer would have it, his audience's very identity (by the very definition of man) is inextricable from this function of reason. Furthermore, there is a scale of purity or perfection within this category of being: to be most logical is to be very much like the celestial beings; conversely, to be least logical is to be least human and most beastlike. No one, of course, wants to be beastly; therefore, everyone will want to be logical (and therefore partake of the benefits of Spencer's book). More specifically, reading and mastering this book provides a sort of ladder, an incremental and therefore temporal process by which one may ascend within the order of humanness, by which one may not only confirm but increase (or purify) one's human dignity. Clearly Spencer's evocation of this commonplace and its appeal to his audience's desire to ascend is, in part, a sales pitch for logic and implicitly for his book. But this is not to say that Spencer is disingenuous.[136] This account of the dignifying effect of logic is persuasive precisely because the hierarchy of being was so basic to the thought of both Spencer and his audience.

This chart of universal order is likewise fundamental to Hooker's appeal to reason in the *Lawes of Ecclesiasticall Politie* and is central to its rhetorical design. From this upward inclination inherent in the Great Chain of Being Hooker extracts an entelechial motive, asserting that "every thing naturally and necessarily doth desire the utmost good and greatest perfection, whereof nature hath made it capable."[137] Hooker plays on this desire as he sets out to present a reason-based defense of ecclesiastical order while at the same time constructing his audience's sense of dignity as God's reasonable creatures. To exercise right reason is to fulfil one's place in the chain of being (reason being a distinguishing characteristic between humans and the lower creatures). Hooker notes that lower creatures sometimes exceed the higher in lesser qualities, as animals often exceed humans

---

[135] Spencer, *The Art of Logic*, [A3v], n. p.

[136] Spencer writes his book largely for an audience that has not had the benefit of a formal education (those who "vnderstäd not Latin") and therefore may not appreciate the importance of the art. In his preface he takes pains to answer the objections of those "Many [who] are of opinion, that *Logicke* is vnprofitable, & of little vse, as serving to exercise the witts of yong Schollers," and therefore neglect it ([A4v], A3).

[137] Richard Hooker, *The Folger Library Edition of the Works of Richard Hooker*, ed. W. Speed Hill, 3 vols. (Cambridge, MA: Belknap Press of Harvard University Press, 1977), 1:82 (1.8.1).

in capacity of sense; however, "[t]he soule of man ... being capable of a more divine perfection, hath (besides the faculties of growing unto sensible knowledge which is common unto us with beasts) a further hability, wherof in them there is no show at all, the abilitie of reaching higher then unto sensible things."[138] This, Hooker makes clear, is the capacity of reason, which can be perfected with education. In striving for the heights of reason attainable to man, Hooker's reader is invited to court identity with those beings perfect in reason, to share in the being of angels and, finally, God. Although each being is ordained to occupy its place in this scale of creatures, each may increase in perfection according to its kind and come closer in proximity and nature to the being above it in the scale. Insofar as Hooker's audience accepts his demonstration of the reasonableness of the Church's policy, they will be compelled to consent as a fulfilment of their identity as reasonable creatures. In this application, appeals to one's sense of dignity can serve as a courtship strategy to bolster one's desire to ascend in the scale of being.

A similar appeal to *dignitas* within hierarchy is evident in Sir Philip Sidney's explanation of the rhetorical function of *exempla*. In his *Defence of Poetry*, Sidney describes the poet's work as a seduction which induces courtship, "For he doth not only show the way, but giveth so sweet a prospect into the way, as will entice any man to enter into it."[139] In the next paragraph, he relates this activity to the use of *exempla* when he asks, "Who readeth Aeneas carrying old Anchises on his back, that wisheth not it were his fortune to perform so excellent an act?"[140] The poet is able to induce this desire because he puts general and abstract principles (heroic benevolence in this case) into particular, vivid "speaking" pictures, such that *exempla* function much like emblems.[141] Later, regarding heroic *exempla*, Sidney says, "the image of each action stirreth and instructeth the mind, so the lofty image of such worthies most inflameth the mind with desire to be worthy, and informs with counsel how to be worthy."[142]

---

[138] Hooker, *Works*, 1:75 (1.6.3).

[139] Sir Philip Sidney, *A Defence of Poetry*, ed. Jan Van Dorsten, corr. ed. (Oxford: Oxford University Press, 1975), 39–40. Later he says the poet's "hand of delight, doth draw the mind" of its audience "more effectually than any other art doth" (*Defence of Poetry*, 42).

[140] *Defence of Poetry*, 41. Sidney's whole treatise, beginning with the anecdote of Pugliano (itself laden with courtship significance), is largely a rhetoric on the use of *exempla*.

[141] See Sidney's famous definition of poetry (*Defence of Poetry*, 25).

[142] *Defence of Poetry*, 47.

⍟ Courtship and the rhetorical and homiletic traditions

The main idea of criticism, as I conceive it, is to use all
that is there to use.

— Kenneth Burke[143]

From these cultural representations of desire through hierarchy emerges a cognitive-affective model of appeal where a reasoned object of desire induces ambition; a similar combination of *logos* and *pathos* can be traced in the rhetorical and homiletic traditions that Donne inherited as a preacher in early seventeenth-century England. Burke's courtship model of human motivation is, of course, not entirely new. A desire to mount within a hierarchy is implicit in Aristotle's deliberative topic of "the good." Aristotle says, "There is pretty much an objective at which everybody aims, both each in private and all together, both in pursuit and in avoidance": that objective is happiness or well-being.[144] Included as species of this common end are several implicitly hierarchical "goods" such as reputation, status, wealth, friends and associates. Furthermore, all goods are not equal. One seeks a greater good over a lesser good, and a lesser evil over a greater. Yet all things must remain in proportion to their place in a given order: "What is not excessive is good and what is greater than it should be bad."[145] Aristotle continues under the rubric of "relative expedience" to suggest that the nobler is to be preferred over the less noble and the longer-lasting over the shorter-lived.[146] Cicero, in *De Inventione*, draws a sharper distinction than does Aristotle between the good of advantage and the good of honour. First and foremost among things to be sought are those of "intrinsic merit" and "natural goodness": these are things honourable.[147] The ultimate term, then, is the greatest good to which everyone aspires within a given hierarchy, relative to which all other goods find their proper place or value. To move upward through a hierarchy (i.e. to court) is therefore to undergo a purification of sorts.

---

[143] *PLF*, 23.
[144] Aristotle, *Art of Rhetoric*, trans. H. C. Lawson-Tancred (New York: Penguin, 1991), 87 (3.1.5 = 1360b 4–6).
[145] Aristotle, *Art of Rhetoric*, 93 (1363a 2–3).
[146] Aristotle, *Art of Rhetoric*, 99 (1364b 26–28, 30–31).
[147] Cicero, *De Inventione; De Optimo Genere Oratorum; Topica*, trans. H. M. Hubbell, Loeb Classical Library (Cambridge, MA: Harvard University Press, 1960), 325 (=*De Inventione* 2.52.157).

Central to the appeal of the greater good is the human faculty of the passions or affections. In her standard work on the subject, Susan James summarizes early modern understanding of the passions (which include desire) as "thoughts or states of the soul which represent things as good or evil for us, and are therefore seen as objects of inclination or aversion."[148] Technical distinctions among the various passions and their relevant objects of good or evil vary from writer to writer in the period, but consistent among them is the general notion that the passions both "incite us to avoid danger" and "create our attachments and aspirations."[149] Basic to early modern psychology, then, is a close relationship between the passions and actions of either attraction or avoidance. The affections are thus both means for distinguishing good or bad objects and the impulses that define one's response (action) to these objects.

The challenge facing the rhetor is to bring his audience to desire the greater good over the lesser; this problem is aggravated for the Christian preacher who begins with the premise of his audience's depravity. A preacher manages this situation by appealing to and purifying his audience's native desires. In his *Art of Rhetoric* (1560), written in part for the aid of preachers, Thomas Wilson rather optimistically characterizes the objects of human desire as those things "that appear in our judgment to be godly" and the object of human loathing as "those things that seem naught, ungodly," adding almost as an afterthought, "or harmful unto us."[150] In a less optimistic moment Wilson says, under the topic of things that are profitable, "[t]ake away the hope of lucre, and you shall see few take any pains, no, not in the vineyard of the Lord."[151] In both cases, spiritual motives seem to be bolstered by less lofty, more immediate desires, either to avoid what is harmful to us or to gain what is materially profitable. According to Alexander Richardson, the manipulation of basic human desire is commonly considered the proper function of rhetoric: it is the "art of affection as it sweeteneth the speech, for the affection of love is so greedy of it, that it will not let the understanding take it, therefore Rhetorick is said to be the art of affection."[152] Notwithstanding the ambiguity of his second "it,"

---

[148] Susan James, *Passion and Action: The Emotions in Seventeenth-Century Philosophy* (Oxford: Clarendon Press, 1997), 4.

[149] James, *Passion and Action*, 10.

[150] Thomas Wilson, *The Art of Rhetoric*, ed. Peter E. Medine (University Park, PA: Pennsylvania State University Press, 1994), 160.

[151] Wilson, *Art of Rhetoric*, ed. Medine, 77 (alluding to Matthew 20:1–16, 21:28–40).

[152] "Rhetorical Notes" (32, [C8v]) in *The Logicians School-Master* (1657). In the interest of *technometria*, however, Richardson refutes this rigid distinction between the function of rhetoric (to move the affections) and that of grammar (to be understood).

Richardson clearly identifies a traditional association between rhetoric and the goad of desire, which is implicitly hierarchical in that it is always greedy for more.

So, then, central to the rhetorical operations of hierarchy and courtship, and rhetoric in general, is the generation and manipulation of desire. There is good authority for such a view of the Christian sermon. In *Sacred Rhetoric* Debora Shuger demonstrates that affective appeal was central to the Renaissance ideal of sermonic eloquence. The passionate grand style, as Shuger describes it, addressed a basic psychological dilemma facing Renaissance preachers: the most excellent objects of desire are the least apprehensible; indeed, by their very nature they transcend human understanding. These most excellent objects must therefore be presented vividly to the imagination in order to incite desire, specifically love. This is achieved in the union of *magnitudo*, a sense of the magnitude of the object achieved through amplification, and *praesentia*, a present apprehension of the object, a sense of immediacy, by means of *hypotyposis*, or vivid depictions. What I aim to show in the following pages is *how* this appeal is conceived to work.[153]

"To delight" and "to move" an audience had long been recognized as the double objective of rhetoric. Furthermore, it is clear to rhetorical thinkers, when addressing issues of motivation, that the former is necessary to achieve the latter. Roger Ascham's *Scholemaster* provides a convenient example of how this motivational model works. Ascham describes his method for motivating grammar school students to do their translation exercises: the schoolmaster must, in a "streight, plaine, & easie" manner, set out the exercise "Which, bicause he [the pupil] shall do always in order, he shall do it always with pleasure: And pleasure allureth loue: loue hath lust to labor: labor always obteineth his purpose."[154] Ascham's use of *anadiplosis* accentuates a logical process through steps or degrees which models a sort of courtship of advancement. The master's clearly presented assignment conduces to the student's orderly execution of it, which gives the student pleasure, causing him to love the activity, thereby producing a "lusty" work ethic which culminates in his successful completion of the assignment. A delight in the task thereby moves the student to achieve the master's objective.

---

153 See chap. 5 in Debora Shuger, *Sacred Rhetoric: The Christian Grand Style in the English Renaissance* (Princeton: Princeton University Press, 1988), on this ancient dilemma and the relationship between Renaissance psychology and strategies of affective appeal.

154 Roger Ascham, *English Works*, ed. William Aldis Wright (Cambridge: Cambridge University Press, 1904), 239–40.

St. Augustine, Donne's favourite authority on all matters religious, similarly observes that, in order to move an audience, one must draw on the resources of the grand style to affect them with delight. Augustine describes, in essence, a courtship of identification where the preacher seeks common ground with his audience in order to begin bending them to his chart of values. He says:

> A hearer must be delighted, so that he can be gripped and made to listen, and moved so that he can be impelled to action. Your hearer is delighted if you speak agreeably, and moved if he values what you promise, fears what you threaten, hates what you condemn, embraces what you commend, and rues the thing which you insist that he must regret; and if he rejoices at what you set forth in your preaching as something joyful, pities those whom by your words you present to his mind's eye as miserable, and shuns those whom with terrifying language you urge him to avoid.[155]

The preacher's message and the congregant's order of values must be brought into accord. This is managed by evoking a conducive affective response. The first approach to a congregation involves meeting them on their emotive ground. Therefore, the preacher, no less than the schoolmaster, must understand human desire. To move or impel a congregation one must work within their motivational-affective framework. In *The Country Parson*, George Herbert describes the parson's study of human passions: "having studied, and mastered all his lusts and affections within, and the whole Army of Temptations without, [he] hath ever so many sermons ready penn'd, as he hath victories."[156] Here Herbert has in mind the "sermon" of the parson's exemplary life, but for preachers like Donne (and probably Herbert too) the study of human passions is a great source of matter for spoken sermons as well.

Thomas Wright, an English Roman Catholic priest, offered his treatise on *the Passions of the Minde in Generall* (1604) with such preachers in mind. He declares in the opening pages that "passions are meanes to help vs, and impediments to withdraw vs from our end: the Diuine therefore, who specially entreateth of our last end, and of the meanes to atchiue it, and difficulties to obtaine it, must of necessitie extend the sphere of his knowledge

---

155 Augustine, *De Doctrina*, IV.74.

156 George Herbert, *Works of George Herbert*, ed. F. E. Hutchinson, cor. ed (Oxford: Clarendon Press, 1959), 278 (recalling Gregory the Great, *Pastoral Care*, 2.2, 3, 5, 7). All quotations from Herbert are from this edition.

to this subiect of our Passions." A right directing of emotions counters the effects of the Fall by pruning "the inordinate motions of Passions" which, in preventing reason, "are thorny bryars sprung from the infected root of originall sinne."[157] The preacher undoes the effects of the Fall by purifying (pruning) the congregants' desires by cultivating right reason (*right* reason because reason might also "inuen[t] tenne thousand sorts of new delights, which the passions neuer could haue imagined") but especially by bolstering their wills.[158] Later, in the fourth chapter, Wright says, "if the motions of our wils be vertuous, directed with the square of Gods law, and prudence, if the inferiour appetite or passions obey and concur with the will, then with much more ease, pleasure, and delight, vertuous actions are accomplished and performed."[159] Note that Wright conceives of the preacher's task as an entelechial courtship bringing the congregation's wills to their proper end, i.e. true identification. Furthermore, the lower desires, when properly oriented, can be used to draw an audience toward their proper end.

Also in the fourth chapter, Wright draws on classical authority to demonstrate that the passions may thus be directed to serve as instruments of virtue rather than vice. Cicero, he says, describes the passions as "sparks of fire apt to kindle virtue"; or, in Lactantius's analogy, as horses draw a coach, "so the passions draw the soule to the fruition of her vertuous obiects."[160] "By this Discourse," says Wright, "may be gathered, that Passions, are not only, not wholy to be extinguished (as the Stoicks seemed to affirme) but sometimes to be moued, & stirred vp for the seruice of vertue, as learnedly *Plutarch* teacheth."[161] Similarly, the Bible teaches that passions can function as "spurres to stirre vp sluggish and idle soules, from sloathfulnesse to diligence, from carelesnesse to consideration."[162] The human subject, then, is set in motion by the passions, which the preacher draws toward their proper object. The good pastor ought not therefore deny human desires, but rather extend them higher.

In a sub-section entitled *"How to moue Passions by reason,"* Wright turns to the means of *inventio* for producing pathetic proof, noting the importance of exercising the judgement exemplified by physicians who adjust their cure to meet the capacity of their patient. The preacher must

---

[157] Thomas Wright, *the Passions of the Minde in Generall* (1604), 2, [B1v].

[158] Wright, *Passions of the Minde*, 10, [B5v].

[159] Wright, *Passions of the Minde*, 16, [B8v].

[160] Wright, *Passions of the Minde*, 16, [B8v]. Lactantius, *Lucii Caecilii Firmiani Lactantii Divinarum Institutionum*, 6.17 (PL 6.695A–695B): Wright cites 6:7, which appears to be a mistake for 6:17.

[161] Wright, *Passions of the Minde*, 17, C1.

[162] Wright, *Passions of the Minde*, 18, [C1v].

similarly know his audience in order to determine what reasons will be emotionally "vrgent and potent."163 He gives an example of how God induced a desire in the Hebrews for the promised land by describing it as "a countrie flowing with milke and honie."164 Wright teaches that urgent reasons proceed from amplification of the rhetorical commonplaces (one thinks of Aristotle's general topic, or commonplace, of "the good"). He develops in fuller detail the usefulness of the circumstances and predicables in presenting a vivid portrayal (*hypotyposis*) of the proper object of desire. In a section on amplification, he also lists, as means of inventing "pithy short descriptions," "similitudes or dissimilitudes, examples, contrarieties, effects, repugnant" as useful for instructing, delighting and moving an auditory.165

Even such adherents of the plain style as the Puritan William Ames acknowledge that appeal to the affections is necessary to induce devotion.166 In a section on preaching in *Medulla S. S. theologiæ* (1629),167 Ames expands on the latter half of the Puritan doctrine-use method of sermon composition, giving special attention to pathetic appeal. "To apply a doctrine to its use," says Ames, "is to sharpen and make specially relevant some general truth with such effect that it may pierce the minds of those present with the stirring up of godly affections." Ames is alluding here to the two-edged sword of Hebrews 4.12, which he describes as "piercing to the inward thoughts and affections and going through to the joining of bones and marrow."168 One would expect pathetic proof to have a place in sermons, even to someone as cautious toward the humane art as is Ames. But what is significant in all this is the notion that desire can be used as a goad to "pierce" and to "stir" the congregant to action. It is for this very same reason that George Herbert, another proponent of the plain style (ostensibly at least), urges that preachers choose "moving and ravishing texts."169 In describing the activity of a sermon, Herbert similarly uses such verbs as "kindle" and "inflame."170 Ames, however, carefully qualifies the limits of rhetoric: "The doing of all these things must have in it no show of human

---

163 Again as in Gregory the Great, *Pastoral Care*, 3.1.

164 Wright, *Passions of the Minde*, 184, [N4v]. (Exodus 3:8 and many other places).

165 Wright, *Passions of the Minde*, 192–93, [N8v]–O.

166 Peter Auksi finds that conformists and non-conformists alike were able to promote a plain style along with pathetical appeal for stimulating an audience in devotion (*Christian Plain Style*, 266–303 and *passim*). Oddly, Auksi does not include Ames in his study.

167 Although *Medulla theologiæ* first appeared in England in 1629, two editions were previously published in Amsterdam.

168 Ames, *The Marrow of Theology*, trans. John D. Eusden, 193–94.

169 Herbert, *Country Parson* 7 (233).

170 Herbert, *Country Parson* 7, 21 (233, 257).

wisdom or mixture of carnal affections; it should manifest itself throughout as the demonstration of the Spirit."[171] Ever sceptical toward any human additions in the communication of Scripture, Ames is much more reluctant than is Wright (or Donne, as we will see) to draw on basic human motives for devout purposes. Nonetheless, in *Conscience with the Power and Cases Thereof* (1639), Ames's definition of devotion draws on an order of motivation that is recognizably similar to the social courtship of ambition. In answer to his question "*In what things doth Devotion consist?*" Ames answers first with "patience and constancie," then with a sort of holy ambition: "It is required that men rest not themselves contented in any degree of godlinesse, through luke warmenesse, sloth, and dulnesse, but that they aspire to the highest perfection. In this respect Devotion is the zeale of Religion."[172] By this means, the devout direct and concentrate their "thoughts and affections" toward their proper end.[173]

The goad of desire is effectively described by Richard Bernard in his devotional allegory *The Isle of Man* (1626). Bernard describes Desire, one of Heart's eleven daughters, as being "neuer content, but would haue sometimes this, and then that, now here, now there, neuer resting, neuer satisfied with either riches or honours, or varietie of pleasures."[174] Francis Bacon expresses a similar understanding of ambition. He says, "AMBITION is like a choler; which is an humour that maketh men active, earnest, full of alacrity, and stirring, if it not be stopped."[175] In a manner typical of the essays, Bacon goes on to qualify his opening statement by saying that ambition should rather be directed than stopped, for "ambitious men, if they find the way open for their rising, and still get forward, they are rather busy than dangerous; but if they be checked in their desires, they become secretly discontent, and look upon men and matters with an evil eye."[176] Conversely, ambition is a necessary "spur" if a soldier uses it to achieve the goal of victory in a war.[177]

---

[171] Ames, *Marrow*, 194.

[172] William Ames, *Conscience with the Power and Cases Thereof* (1639), Book 4, 93, 2M3 (each Book has separate pagination).

[173] Ames, *Conscience*, Book 4, 94, [2M3v].

[174] Richard Bernard, *The Isle of Man*, 4th ed. (1627), 65, D10.

[175] Bacon, *Essays*, 113. Robert Burton's characterization of desire and ambition is similar to those of Bernard and Bacon (although Burton's interest is in the humourous *effect* of ambition, melancholy). In a subsection devoted to ambition, Burton notes, "A true saying it is, 'Desire hath no rest,' is infinite in itself, endless, and, as one calls it, a perpetual rack, or horse-mill, according to Austin, still going round as in a ring": *The Anatomy of Melancholy*, vol. 1 (London: Dent, 1932), 280.

[176] Bacon, *Essays*, 113.

[177] Of corollary interest is Bacon's description of the object of ambition, honour, and its three aspects: "the vantage ground to do good; the approach to kings and principal persons; and the raising of a

Desire, or ambition, keeps the subject always in motion; once evoked, the preacher needs only to give desire its proper direction. Such is the advice Bishop Jeremy Taylor gives to his ministers:

> He that observes any of his people to be zealous, let him be careful to conduct that zeal into such channels where there is least danger of inconveniency; let him employ it in something that is good; let it be pressed to fight against sin. For zeal is like a cancer in the breast; feed it with good flesh, or it will devour the heart.[178]

Similarly, Richard Bernard in his preaching handbook cautions preachers that "affection is heady without wisdom: this moderates as the other pricks forward: they must be linked inseparably."[179] Desire will set the congregant to motion, but the preacher must be sure to direct this motion in its proper application. For Bernard, the role of the affections is to move the congregant in the direction set out in the doctrine of the text. Expounding on the second part of his doctrine-use-application method, Bernard says, "vse must bee made to gaine the affection."[180] Similarly, in exhorting the congregation to act upon the use, the preacher "must consider of the *motiues* to perswade and draw them to the practise, and to continue therein."[181] Among the resources Bernard lists for instilling these motives are examples drawn from economics and politics. For evoking motives he also recommends similitudes,

> which may bee taken from persons, things and actions to explaine the necessity, the equity and easinesse of the practise vrged, & also they serue to win the hearers by such euident demonstrations. These will draw an assent to the Parable being propounded ..., and will cause them to giue sentence at vnawares vpon theselues, which being then wisely applyed, will greatly strike the heart.[182]

---

man's own fortunes." "He that hath the best of these intentions," continues Bacon, "when he aspireth, is an honest man" (*Essays*, 114).

[178] Jeremy Taylor, *Rules and Advices to the Clergy of the Diocese of Down and Connor* in *The Whole Works*, ed. Reginald Heber, rev. ed. Charles Page Eden, 10 vols. (London: Longman, 1847–1854; repr. Hildesheim: Georg Olms Verlag, 1969), 1:106.

[179] Bernard, *The Faithfvll Shepherd*, A6 (n. p.).

[180] *Faithfvll Shepherd*, 272, [N5v].

[181] *Faithfvll Shepherd*, 294, [O5v].

[182] *Faithfvll Shepherd*, 297–98, O7–[O7v].

Again, Bernard comes back to the emotive impulse of desire as he continues, "in pressing this duty a Minister must consider how to moue and gaine
the affections."[183] Affective patterns drawn from socio-political situations
may be used to "demonstrate" similar spiritual motives.

At the same time that the affections are stimulated, they are governed
by a cognitive framework (relating to the will and reason) which channels
them in a proper direction, according to a determined set of values based
on the doctrine of Scripture. These values are determined by the prescribed
"end" of courtship. The cognitive aspect of this appeal is emphasized by
Andreas Hyperius, as translated by John Ludham. Hyperius asserts that
"The Preacher shall not employ his least care in mouinge of affections,
forsomuch as all the learned sorte doe confesse, that he stãdeth of no one
thing more in neede, then he doth of this one onely faculty."[184]
Interestingly, the purpose of this appeal to the affections is almost exclusively expressed in terms of mental stimulation: "to excite the myndes of
their hearers"; to "styrre vpp the myndes of menne vnto virtue"; to "induce
the myndes of the hearers to bountifulnesse"; "to prouoke the mindes of
men."[185] Ludham repeatedly chooses, with apparent consciousness, to talk
about the effect of the affective appeal as a mental activity (only once does
he mention the hearts of the hearers). He goes on to note that the rhetorical figures commonly serve this purpose, but adds that the preacher should
emulate these same affections, both in his delivery and in his lifestyle, so
that "hee by his oration and (as it were) by his owne example may incense
others to enterprise the lyke."[186] The preacher's example provides an affective structure for his congregation to emulate. An *exemplum*, almost by definition, is a greater good which, by virtue of its transcendent place, is
worthy of one's ambition. The congregation is therefore "incensed" not
merely by an inner impulse, but by an observable and extrinsic pattern of
what   is   good   and   therefore   desirable.   As   Sidney   says,   the
exemplum both stirs and instructs the mind, inflaming the mind with desire
to be worthy even as it defines what is worthy. The *exemplum* is an epitome
of hierarchy, such that the subject will be moved only if he approves of the
chart of values that the *exemplum* assumes.

The cognitive-affective function of hierarchy is implicit in Thomas
Traherne's treatment of desire under the title of "Approbation" in his

---

183 *Faithfull Shepherd*, 299, O8.

184 Andreas Hyperius, *The practise of preaching*, trans. John Ludham (1577), 41a, C1.

185 Hyperius, *The practise of preaching*, trans. Ludham, 41a–46b, C1–[C6v].

186 Hyperius, *The practise of preaching*, trans. Ludham, 43a, C3.

Commentaries of Heaven.[187] Here Traherne implies a courtship model wherein desire brings the subject to approve of an object based on a recognition of its relative goodness, leading him or her to desire that object all the more in its perfection. Traherne defines his term, approbation, as

> an Affection of the Soul allowing and consenting to the Truth of that Goodness, which is in any Object. It is a cool and moderate Affection: and if it pass noe further, the Soul is still an Alien and a Stranger to the thing it Approves: Approbation ther fore is of value, only as it is the Way to Esteem, Desire, Joy, Love etc. Desire glues the Soul to an Object, Esteem obliges it, Honor crowns it, love embraceth it, Zeal ravisheth it Joy possesseth it Praise and Glory Beautifie and make it excellent.[188]

One approves of an object according to its state of perfection (and by implication according to its place within a hierarchy of degrees). It is from this approval, this agreement with a given chart of advantage, that desire derives. Traherne continues,

> The Particular Excellencies in each ... [thing], by how much the greater they are by so much the more Approbation and Esteem, and Love and Joy they occasion. ... Perfection in all which is so necessary a propertie causing an Approbation, that if any of these we perceiv the least Defect, we cannot approve the same.[189]

Even though he classifies approbation as an affection, it is an affection which derives from cognitive distinction and recognition of value. Developing the cognitive-affective relation further, Traherne implies a dialectical relation whereby approbation, a moderate affection, brings recognition of what is honourable and beautiful (i.e. perfect or upward in a valuative series); this recognition of a thing's perfection in turn amplifies one's approval of the same.

I conclude by returning to Richard Hooker, who gives occasion for an apt summary of these ideas in relation to Burke's notion of courtship. In the *Lawes of Ecclesiasticall Politie*, Hooker, conservative voice of the

---

[187] Although he is not writing about preaching *per se*, Traherne was a minister and is writing here in a devotional mode that shares many of the rhetorical concerns of preaching.

[188] Thomas Traherne, *Commentaries of Heaven*, ed. D. D. C. Chambers (Salzburg: Institüt für Anglistik und Amerikanistik, 1989), 72.

[189] Traherne, *Commentaries*, 73.

Elizabethan church, says that "sermons [are] as keyes to the kingdom of heaven, as winges to the soule, as spurres to the good affections of man."[190] He too envisions the sermon's activity as a manipulation of desire to induce in the congregant a holy ambition. Although not directly related to preaching, much of Hooker's earlier discussion of the faculties of reason, will, and affections expresses principles that are fundamental to Burke's courtship principle and can be easily related to the preacher's consideration of audience. In regard to "how man attaineth unto the knowledge of such things unsensible," Hooker says, "Seeing then that nothing can move unlesse there be some ende, the desire whereof provoketh unto motion; how should that divine power of the soule ... ever stir it selfe unto action, unlesse it have also the like spurre?"[191] There are "two principall fountaines ... of humaine action," continues Hooker, "*Knowledge* and *Will.*" Expanding on the latter, he adds that will is the greater desire in relation to appetite. But the will is often recalcitrant, while the appetite is readily moved but easily strays. Therefore, "appetite is the wills sollicitor, and the will is appetites controller."[192] And again, he says that the will works on an "object by desire, which is as it were a motion towards the end as yet unobtained."[193] Appetite is a spur which may be used to draw the subject to transcendent motives.

This drawing upward of desire works according to the analogy of the good: "Whereas wee now love the thing that is good, but good especially in respect of benefit unto us, we shall then love the thing that is good, only or principally for the goodnes of beautie in it self."[194] That is, temporal desire, if extended, is a step toward a refined, spiritual desire. Moreover, the topic of a desirable "good" relates very closely to notions of identity mentioned earlier regarding Hooker's use of the entelechial motive inherent in the Great Chain of Being. Hooker says that "there is in all things an appetite or desire, whereby they inclyne to something which they may be: and when they are it, they shall be perfecter then nowe they are. All which perfections are conteyned under the generall name of *Goodnesse.*"[195] To ascend in this hierarchy, to seek the greatest good, is to undergo a purification.[196] Furthermore, to seek any good is to be in the process of seeking identification with God. For, says Hooker,

---

[190] Hooker, *Works*, 2:87 (5.22.1).

[191] Hooker, *Works*, 1:77 (1.7.1).

[192] Hooker, *Works*, 1:78 (1.7.2–3).

[193] Hooker, *Works*, 1:113 (1.11.3).

[194] Hooker, *Works*, 1:113 (1.11.3).

[195] Hooker, *Works*, 1:73 (1.5.1).

[196] Hooker's description of the effect of sermons as an ascent of the soul carries connotations of purification, functioning also as "phisicke unto diseased mindes" (*Works*, 2:87 [1.22.1]).

there can bee no goodnesse desired which proceedeth not from God himselfe, as from the supreme cause of all things; and every effect doth after a sort conteine, at least wise resemble the cause from which it proceedeth: all things in the worlde are saide in some sort to seeke the highest, and to covet more or lesse the participation of God himselfe.[197]

To evoke good affections in a congregation is to set them on a courtship of God, for God, being infinitely good, is "the highest of all thinges that are desired," and "desire tendeth unto union with that it desireth."[198]

Natural affections, extended by reason to their proper object, result in the will and ability to overcome the estrangement of human limitations and to ascend to God. Of this courtship of God, the highest object of our faith, hope, and love, Hooker says,

> concerning these vertues, the first of which beginning here with a weake apprehension of things not sene, endeth with the intuitive vision of God in the world to come; the second beginning here with a trembling expectation of thinges far removed and as yet but onely heard of, endeth with reall and actual fruition of that which no tongue can expresse; the third beginning here with a weake inclynation of heart towardes him unto whome wee are not able to aproch, endeth with endlesse union, the misterie wherof is higher then the reach of the thoughts of men.[199]

The courtship *topos* aptly describes the preacher's task of leading his congregation from a condition of estrangement from God to one of endless union, a process which begins with weak inclinations to virtue which need to be goaded and extended toward fulfilment in God.

All notions of progress are modes of courtship of a "good" — a desired end that is better or more complete or more pure than the present condition in the process. The entelechial end of every paradigm of progress is an ultimate term functioning as an ordering principle, arranging every step, every action, in proximate relation to itself. Many such models of progress function as courtships even where hierarchy is ancillary and sometimes only vaguely evident. As Burke notes, capitalist accumulation may become a

---

[197] Hooker, *Works*, 1:73 (1.5.2).
[198] Hooker, *Works*, 1:112 (1.11.2).
[199] Hooker, *Works*, 1:119 (1.11.6) (commenting on 1 Corinthians 2:9).

courtship, with money as its ultimate term.[200] Any arrangement which promotes a system of values presents a hierarchy of desire (however truncated) which urges the subject to abandon the lesser in pursuit of the former. My aim in the following chapter is to extend this field to include various orders of desire, or courtships, employed by Donne in his sermons.

---

[200] Speaking of an author of a book promoting laissez-faire capitalism, Burke notes, "In the stress he places upon the price system, or monetary motivation, as a device for rationalizing the structure and trends of the free market, we probably come upon the crucial moment in his concept of substance. Money would be, in the technical sense, his 'God term.' For a God term designates the ultimate motivation, or substance, of a Constitutional frame" (*GM*, 355).

CHAPTER TWO

"Like an Angel from a cloud": Donne and Courtship as a Topic of Inventio

matter stately and high ... require a stile to be lift vp and aduaunced by choyse of wordes, phrases, sentences, and fig-ures, high, loftie, eloquent, and magnifik in proportion ... mounting vpwardes, with the wings of the stately subiects and stile.

— George Puttenham[201]

IN THE RENAISSANCE, DISCUSSIONS OF ELOQUENCE invariably led to imagery of ascent, and hence of courtship. Donne's seventeenth-century biographer, Izaak Walton, describes Donne as preaching

> like an Angel from a cloud, but in none; carrying some, as St. *Paul* was, to Heaven in holy raptures, and inticing others by a sacred Art and Courtship to amend their lives; here picturing a vice so as to make it ugly to those that practised it; and a vertue so, as to make it be beloved even by those that lov'd it not.[202]

---

[201] George Puttenham, *The Arte of English Poesie*, ed. Edward Arber, intro. Baxter Hathaway (London: A. Constable, 1906; repr. Kent, OH: Kent State University Press, 1970), 164.

[202] Walton, *Lives*, 49.

Walton anticipates some of the strategy I will discuss under the rubric of Donne's rhetoric of courtship in the sermons. Donne indeed had his feet firmly on the ground. We might even go so far as to call him a worldly preacher in that he understood mundane concerns and tailored his sermons to reach an audience that was "in the world." Even when he brings his audience to a beatific vision, it is not with the aim of obfuscating their workaday world but rather of bringing a bit of heaven back down to baptize their earth-bound perspective. As Horton Davies puts it, "Like all the metaphysicals his imagination soared to heaven, whose cartographer he was, but his message was meant for the evasive earthbound man in the pew, lost in the labyrinthine mazes of his own heart or the ambush of his excuses."[203] One of Donne's frequently visited strategies is precisely as Walton describes: to purify his audience's worldliness by repelling them from the worst and by enticing them to pursue what is best. God's courtier enlarges his congregation's desire in a "holy rapture" for the finer things not of this world, but of heaven. But whereas Walton credits this effect to Donne's passionate and powerful *pronuntiatio*, I will argue that it results from a fundamental and common principle of *inventio* in Donne's sermons.[204]

The notion of courtship I have outlined in the first chapter could be used in various applications to Donne. One could, for example, look for ways in which Donne's courtship of the divine functions rather as a "stylization of motives belonging to the social hierarchy." This is what Burke does with Shakespeare's *Venus and Adonis*, where he observes that "vocabularies of social and sexual courtship are so readily interchangeable, not because one is a mere 'substitute' for the other, but because sexual courtship is intrinsically fused with the motives of social hierarchy."[205] Although Burke notes that any one order of motives may stand in for another, his tendency is to place the social in a privileged position. Donne would rather agree with Hooker that mundane desires are a stylization of a spiritual desire for God. A current species of Burke's socio-political bias often comes under the guise of unmasking power relations. Bryan Crockett contends that "[d]espite the enormous appeal of this kind of analysis ... it ascribes to early

---

[203] Horton Davies, *Like Angels From a Cloud* (San Marino, CA: Huntington Library, 1986), 5.

[204] Walton views Donne's eloquence in terms of a common seventeenth-century notion of the grand style which is characterized by vehement delivery and a personal investment in and internalization of the matter at hand. On this definition of the grand style see Shuger, *Sacred Rhetoric*, 53–55, 67–68. Walton describes Donne as "preaching the Word so, as shewed his own heart was possest with those very thoughts and joys that he laboured to distill into others: A Preacher in earnest; weeping sometimes for his Auditory, sometimes with them" (*Lives*, 49).

[205] *RM*, 217.

modern thought an anachronistic innocence of the mask's potential. ... If ever a culture understood what a mask can and can not disguise, it is that one."[206] Similarly, if any culture understood how closely profane motives impinge upon the sacred, it was Donne's. In fact, this fine line is one that Donne regularly exploits for devotional purposes. In his theory of motives, Burke allows for a measure of self-awareness. Concluding his criticism of psychoanalysis, he objects to the Freudian emphasis on sexual motives to the exclusion of other motives. (He cites contemporary treatments of St. Augustine as an example.) Burke says, "I am merely attempting to suggest that a terminology of motives is not evasive or self-deceptive, but is moulded to fit our general orientation as to purposes, instrumentalities, the 'good life,' etc."[207] Nowhere is this more true than in Donne's employment of the courtship *topos*.

Donne himself is aware that the pulpit is frequently a means for courting social position and promoting policy. Moreover, he readily acknowledges the pulpit's potential for achieving political ends and is well aware that ambiguities invariably arise between these analogous courtships. In a sermon preached before the Countess of Montgomery Donne nonetheless warns an audience consisting of the ruling class not to "bring a misbelief, a mis-conceipt, that all this religion is but a part of civill government and order" (2:8.343–345). At Whitehall he refutes those who "thinke scornefully that *preaching* is indeed but the *foolishnesse of preaching*, and that as the Church is within the State, so preaching is a part of State government, flexible to the present occasions of time, appliable to the present dispositions of men" (2:18.8–12). In another sermon, about rendering each man his due, Donne scrutinizes himself in the first person as an *exemplum* of those who praise princes. Even though princes and the favour they bestow are "Images of God ... in a proportion," God is not satisfied with us praising the creature in substitution for the Creator (4:12.194–6). Using himself as an *exemplum*, Donne criticizes such gestures in preaching:

---

[206] Bryan Crockett, *The Play of Paradox: Stage and Sermon in Renaissance England* (Philadelphia: University of Pennsylvania Press, 1995), ix. As Debora Shuger notes, "The almost total neglect of society's religious aspects in favor of political ones — a reaction against the theological bias of earlier Renaissance criticism — has produced in recent literary scholarship a curiously distorted picture of the period": *Habits of Thought in the English Renaissance* (Berkeley: University of California Press, 1990; repr. Toronto: University of Toronto Press, 1997), 5. Although my focus is on rhetoric, not theology, I choose to emphasize its religious function rather than its political function, and perhaps to redress some of the imbalance Shuger has identified.

[207] *PC*, 29. On the treatment of St. Augustine, Burke says, "The error is exposed in its fullest parochialism when the contemporary epigones [undistinguished imitators] of psycho-analysis set about to interpret for us the hidden sexual motives at the roots of such intense and brilliant theologians as Saint Augustine. The entire motivation by which Augustine lived and wrote is categorically discarded in favor of a few sexual impulses which can, at best, be shown to have been an ingredient in his motivation" (*PC*, 27).

though I spend my nights, and dayes, and thoughts, and spirits, and words, and preaching, and writing, upon Princes, and Judges, and Magistrates, and persons of estimation, and their praise, yet my intention determines in that use which I have of their favour, and respects not the glory of God in them (4:12.199–203).

All respect for earthly honour and authority must conduce to God's glory, not to the subject's personal advancement nor the prince's gratification. In short, the right end of preaching, says Donne elsewhere, is "edification, and advancing the kingdom of God" (8:6.83–4).

I am not interested in arguing with Donne's publicly stated purpose as a preacher, nor will I attempt to show how Donne uses transcendent discourse to court social ends in the sermons.[208] Donne did spend a great deal of his life seeking social advancement. Even after taking orders, he was suspected by some of calculating his preferment in the church.[209] Yet Donne's chief purpose as preacher, the one to which he again and again applied his rhetorical energies, is to induce his congregation to court the divine. Donne's rhetorical situation as I define it is precisely that of a preacher who aims to persuade his congregation to increasing devotion, to turn their eyes from perceived material urgencies to less appreciable spiritual necessities. To this end, Donne freely borrows resources from the social realm to bring his audience into spiritual identifications similar to those they would readily recognize in their workaday world.

First, then, this paradigm of courtship functions as a language of accommodation whereby Donne can bring spiritual issues into contact with his audience's own world of concerns.[210] But more importantly, it enlarges

---

[208] George Parfitt stresses Donne's use of his status as preacher as a means of self-aggrandizement (104–10). In their lives of Donne, R. C. Bald and John Carey also pursue the characterization of Donne as an ambitionist throughout his tenure at St. Paul's. Bald describes Donne "as one who had mastered at last the arts of the courtier, and it is clear, even when he finally turned to the Church, that he did not intend to abandon those arts, but to rise by them": *John Donne* (Oxford: Clarendon Press, 1970), 301. More recently, Arthur Marotti has continued this course in his article, "Donne as Social Exile and Jacobean Courtier," 77–102). A common (and wrong-headed) assumption in these critics is that a man with such mixed motives cannot be genuinely devout. I am not going to enter into this argument here, but a case can be made for Donne's embracing of courtship modes as a *deliberate* means of addressing and ultimately purifying his own motives, of drawing them into his religious experience. As I will demonstrate, this is precisely what he does for his congregation in the sermons.

[209] Bald, *John Donne*, 309.

[210] Donne understands this accommodation both in the sense of accommodating spiritual ideas to the understanding of a worldly audience and, as Shuger points out, in the sense of interpreting a passage of Scripture so as to meet the present needs of his audience (*Habits of Thought*, 206). In this latter application of accommodation Donne is following in the tradition of Augustinian exegesis as described above in my "Introduction."

these worldly concerns, extending them to a higher end and thereby purifying and transforming worldly motives into spiritual ones. The second
function of the courtship *topos*, which this chapter will develop in some
detail, is to use these mundane motives to induce a parallel desire for God.
In Walton's picture of Donne in the pulpit we once again see the preacher
depicted as one who stirs and then directs his congregation's affections.
Indeed, Donne's manipulation of desire, seen within a Burkeian framework, accounts for a great deal of Donne's *inventio* in the sermons. He uses
courtship structures to define the good (that which is desirable) and to
chart the appropriate channels for his audience's awakened desires. Or, to
borrow Hooker's words, Donne "spurres ... the good affections of man"[211]
using courtship through hierarchy to define, stimulate, and direct his audience's motives in their proper direction.

This is not simply achieved in the manner Walton suggests, in holy
raptures in the sense of emotional *pronuntiatio* (although passionate delivery must at times have been *part* of Donne's appeal); nor is Donne's
method of inducing desire and of "mounting" his congregation "vpwardes"
based on grand and lofty *elocutio* such as Puttenham describes in this chapter's header. Rather, Donne evokes desire in his audience at the most basic
level of *inventio*, in the cognitive and affective structures he finds both in
his text and in the circumstances of his congregation "in the world." That
is, he uses courtship structures as both pathetic and logical proof to reorient his audience and to instill in them a new habit of thought and feeling
about their lives in relation to the divine. Before turning directly to these
issues of audience and proof, I will briefly survey the field of courtship
imagery in Donne's sermons and some of the *topoi* Donne visits in developing the courtship principle.

❧ *The courtship* topos *in Donne's sermons*

Donne's sermons are replete with images of courtship. Typically, these are
figured archetypally in various hierarchical configurations of upwardness
and downwardness, often in relation to man's place in the created order:

> God hath given Man that forme in nature, much more in grace,
> that he should be upright, and looke up, and contemplate Heaven,
> and God there. And therefore to bend downwards upon the earth,
> to fix our breast, our heart to the earth, to lick the dust of the earth
> with the Serpent, to inhere upon the profits and pleasures of the

---

[211] cf. above, chap. 1, n. 190.

earth, and to make that which God intended for our way, and our rise to heaven, (the blessings of this world) the way to hell; this is a manifest Declination from this Uprightnesse, from this Rectitude (7:9.239–247).

Donne frequently expresses temporal-spiritual correspondences in this manner, where the latter is a "higher" manifestation of the former. After treating the social virtue of liberality, Donne brings his audience to "a higher exaltation" of its spiritual counterpart (8:10.315). These directional references carry eulogistic/dyslogistic connotations: upwardness signifying release and purification; downwardness suggesting imprisonment and pollution.[212] There is great motivational potential in this imagery, as when Donne says of the ministry of the Gospel in each believer, "If thou finde it not ascending, it descends" (10:1.419–420). A steep slope will not allow complacency. Donne, in a favourite formulation, describes conversion as "a *Resurrection*, and an *ascension*" of the soul from "that darke, and durty prison" of the flesh; it is a rising "from the durt and Mud of this world," symbolized in his text as the washing of one's feet (5:8.74–78).[213] Throughout the sermons the red mud of the earth, out of which we rise, symbolizes our identification with Adam (Adam, Donne notes, literally means "red earth"); in this case, mud appropriately signifies the pollution of original sin. Alluding to his text, Donne then asks, "how is it possible that I should descend, to so low a disposition, as to foule them [those feet] againe?" (85–86). The purification image derives from the text; the directional associations are Donne's addition.

Although this upward/downward imagery is often found in a biblical text, Donne typically amplifies it along socio-political lines. In Job 5:7, "*Man is borne unto travaile,*[214] *as the sparks fly upward,*" Donne finds an image of upwardness, but he develops it in relation to vocation (8:8.226–7). The association of this passage with issues of career appears to have been commonplace, even though it is not obvious in the text. Joseph Hall, for example, makes the same connection in his occasional meditation

---

[212] Instances of ascent/descent imagery can be found throughout Donne's sermons, as in 5:8.71–88 cited below. Some others are 1:9.494–502; 5:9.37–50 and *passim*; 9:14.52–66; 10:1.396–439 and *passim*.

[213] Canticles 5:3. The text reads: "I have washed my feet, how shall I defile them?" In chap. 6, I discuss in greater detail a similar configuration of descent and ascent in *Deaths Duell*.

[214] Donne uses the Geneva Bible translation, "travaile," which is more fitting for his rhetorical purposes than is the "trouble" of the King James Version.

on this passage.[215] Special to Donne, however, is the specifically hierarchical cast he gives to this notion of vocation. Whereas Hall develops the image to signify the irregularity of youth, which in adulthood finally settles upon a vocation, Donne takes it as an emblem of properly or improperly motivated ambition. Dutiful labour in a lawful calling is "a flying upward," while the labour of the wicked is "a depressing downward" (227–233). Subsequently, these directions of professional conduct are symbolically associated with hell, the lowest point of descent, and heaven, the final reward of just labour (234–238).

Donne's amplification of biblical matter along socio-political lines is again evident in a sermon on the twin vices of lust and pride (a perverse ascent), where he warns in his *exordium* against descending into the debasement of sin. The Fall of course typifies the paradox of humankind's upward (pride) and downward (judgement) inclinations, but Donne amplifies this point according to current social values. The original sin was "an ascending, a climing too high," a "clambring" after place which resulted in a descent in sin such that "Ever since this fall, man is so far from affecting higher places, then his nature is capable of, that he is still groveling upon the ground, and participates, and imitates, and expresses more of the nature of the Beast then of his owne" (9:17.39–53). The whole sermon is structured on this opposition of descent and ascent in relation to God. Here the doctrine of the Fall is invested with contemporary social prejudice against social upstarts. Whether preached at Lincoln's Inn or at St. Paul's (as seems likely), Donne's urban-London congregation would have been aware of the careers of such social climbers as Sir Walter Ralegh.[216] Ralegh typifies his political reputation in "My first borne love vnhappily conceived," a penitential poem to Queen Elizabeth. In what seems to have been an attempt at damage control after a falling-out with the Queen, Ralegh chides his first-born love for "too hie flieng" in its approach to her, the apparent cause of his current troubles.[217] At court, as in Eden, over-reaching is a sure way to fall.

---

[215] *Occasional Meditations*, no. LXVII in Frank Livingstone Huntley, *Bishop Joseph Hall and Protestant Meditation in Seventeenth-Century England*, MRTS 1 (Binghamton, NY: Medieval & Renaissance Texts & Studies, 1981), 157.

[216] See Potter and Simpson for the dating and placing of this series on Psalm 32 (*Sermons*, 9:34–37).

[217] This poem probably belongs to the period around 1590 when Ralegh was seeking to consolidate his return to favour after having been opposed by Essex (Queen Elizabeth's new favourite) for his socio-political pretensions (Oakeshott, *The Queen and the Poet*, 37–38). Oakeshott notes in both Ralegh and Spenser (in Book III of *The Faerie Qveene*, first published in 1590) a subsequent emphasis on Ralegh's humility and an acknowledgement that he had "flown too high" (39). As Stephen May describes, the upstart Ralegh infuriated his fellow courtiers all the more because he "wore his newly acquired wealth and status with a haughty swagger": *Sir Walter Ralegh* (Boston: Twayne, 1989), 9. See also Oakeshott, *The Queen and the Poet*, 27–29, 31. Ralegh's troubles continued into the reign of King James until his execution in 1618.

In Donne's sermon, the political reference to social climbing combines with a notion of order and human dignity grounded in the great chain of being, another overtly hierarchical image, to instill a properly motivated ascent. This is a common strategy in Donne, who often defines his audience as occupying a particular place in this order (often lower than they would like) and then asserting their potential to slide either upward or downward in the scale of being. Within their proper stratum of the hierarchy (but not beyond) each being may move either upward, toward identification with higher beings, or downward, toward identification with lower beings.[218] Here Donne asserts that all creatures know and adhere to their place in the chain, except humans, who remove themselves from their place of dignity and so disrupt God's order (9:17.76–94).[219] Donne proceeds to characterize his audience as inclined to move downward in being rather than upward, such that "we all follow our Mother, we grovell upon the earth [inclined toward our mineral selves], whose children we are, and being made like our Father, in his Image [our spiritual selves], we neglect him" (96–98). So, says Donne, "we have forfeited this Jurisdiction, this Dominion, and more, our owne Essence; we are not onely inferior to the Beasts ... but we are our selves become Beasts" (106–109).

Donne then turns this "increpation" into an exhortation. To remedy their debasement of themselves within the created order, he calls his congregation to attend to that very trait which distinguishes their proper place within that order: "Consider the dignitie of thy soule, which onely, of all other Creatures is capable, susceptible of Grace" (109–110). To attend to one's soul makes one less beastly and more godly. A proper ascent, then, is spiritually, not politically motivated. The capacity of humankind (this unique ability to receive God's grace) argues the necessity of fulfilling that capacity, so that one is compelled to achieve the highest dignity possible. Motives of political courtship have thus been transplanted into the spiritual order. Moreover, Donne aggravates this situation of lapsed courtship (a process which would involve seeking identity with God, the apex of the grand hierarchy, in whose image man is made) by drawing out a principle from the upper reaches of the spirit world. Among angels in heaven there is no allowance for falling even one or two levels in status; rather, "those of that place that fell, fell into the bottomlesse pit" (119–120). And so Donne

---

[218] With reference to Ralegh, Steven May goes on to note that this attitude toward social upstarts was based on "[c]enturies of religious and philosophical teaching [which] held that such drastic elevations in status disrupted the order of things" (*Sir Walter Ralegh*, 9). May quotes an anonymous contemporary: "A Lewder wretche ther lyves not under skye, / Then clown that climes from base estate to hie."

[219] Another well-developed instance of Donne's use of the hierarchy of being is 2:5.38–89; some others are 5:13.310–330; 5:18.379–388; 4:12.478–488; 8:1.818–831; 8:7.95–98.

(somewhat uncharacteristically) draws his audience to confront the possibility of complete damnation, a total descent.

Emblematic of these hierarchical structures of thought are the concrete images Donne frequently uses to symbolize ascent. These images were commonly inscribed in emblematic representations of this period, as described in the previous chapter. Common to Donne's configuring of upwardness and downwardness is the sense of a progression through a graded series. In one sermon the injunctions of a biblical text are described as "steps" and "degrees" by which one can approach God (6:14.150).[220] Similarly, in his prayer for Sodom, Abraham approached God by steps as on "a winding staire" (5:17.334).[221] Reminiscent of the Wither and Wroth frontispieces is Donne's justification of this "winding" approach "which our Saviour recommends unto us, in such a Serpentine line, (as the Artists call it) to get up to God, and get into God by such degrees" (336–338).[222] This is the route of Satyre III where the pursuer of Truth "about must, and about must goe" in ascending her hill.

The hill or mount of ascent is perhaps the most explicit symbol of courtship in Donne's sermons. Donne draws out the eulogistic potential of the hill image in a sermon on the Book of Lamentations (4:20) which is likened to a "pit" that becomes a "hill," a book of psalms and thanksgiving (4:9.850–859). Hilltops consistently symbolize a position of desire which is achieved through process. In a sermon where he applies John the Baptist's commission[223] to his congregation, urging them to communicate God's

---

[220] Donne also conflates Jacob's ladder with the straight and narrow path of Matthew 7:14 to describe the Christian lifestyle as set down throughout Christian history (7:9.261–267). Also, Satan's (and after him, Adam's) inordinate ambition is a "clambring" up a ladder (9:17.44–45). Donne quite possibly could have know and adapted ideas in John Climacus's *The Ladder of Divine Ascent* (perhaps in the Latin translation by Ambrogio Traversari), which is based on Jacob's ladder. On the availability of Climacus's text in Donne's time see Robert Boenig, "George Herbert and John Climacus: A Note on 'Prayer (1)'," *N&Q* n.s. 37 (1990): 209–211.

[221] For stair imagery see also 10:1.423. Elsewhere Donne develops an image of justification as a chain consisting of four links which lead the subject step by step upward to God. To begin his congregation in the right way, he urges them to "take hold of that linke that is next us, A good life, and keepe a fast and inseparable hold upon that" (7:8.498–499). I discuss this passage more fully in the next chapter.

[222] The most relevant reference I could find is Matthew 10:16, where Jesus advises his disciples as they set out on an itinerant ministry to be wise as serpents and gentle as doves, that is, to combine a godly demeanour with worldly cunning — a combination that is appropriate to the method I am describing in Donne's sermons (I am indebted to Jay Gurnett for this reference). Earlier in this sermon, Donne notes that Bernard derives from 1 Timothy 2:1 "certaine gradations, and steps, and ascensions of the soule in prayer" (5:17.101–102), a commonplace of mystical writing.

[223] John 1:8 — "*He was not that light, but was sent to beare witnesse of that light*" — is Donne's primary text, but the secondary text which he develops here in the second partition of the sermon is Isaiah

light to the world, Donne notes that mountains in the Bible express an advanced point of progress in one's purpose or end: Moses's sight of the promised land and Christ's transfiguration, crucifixion, and ascension all occurred on mountain tops (4:8.598–606).[224] In a sermon at Lincoln's Inn on the Reformation, Donne again begins with the image of a hill of ascent, this time drawn from Psalm 24:3: "*Who shall ascend into the hill of the Lord?*" (4:4.2–3). Donne takes the hill to represent a perfect completion of one's calling, in this case the completion of the Reformation. Moses's destruction of the places of idol worship in Donne's principal text (Deuteronomy 12) is presented as the first "step," the "inchoation of this ascension" to a completion of God's work — the complete abolition of idolatry (1–15). This passage is packed with images of ascent. Donne even describes the language of the biblical text as "a vehement gradation and heightening of the commandment [given to Moses]" (14–15). "Gradation" calls to mind the rhetorical figure *gradatio*, or *climax*, a figure which enacts an ascent. As with the Hebrews, suggests Donne, the current Reformers need to be diligent: "so far we are ascended, and so the Inhibition lies upon us, that we slide not back again" (33–34).

These images are significant to my argument because they demonstrate the vivid appeal of this aspect of the courtship *topos* so common in the emblems of the period (again see figs. 1–10 in chap. 1). Images of ascent inscribe in compact form a recognizable structure of cultural experience, to which I now turn.

♣ Socio-political sources of courtship

Donne's courtship imagery draws extensively from recognizable socio-political relations. Sexual courtship does not figure as prominently in the sermons as readers of Donne's poetry might expect. Decorum would not allow the preacher to handle sexual themes as freely as could the poet, not even the divine poet. Donne of course makes the usual associations between marriage and the union of the Church (and sometimes of the individual soul) with Christ, but only once does he make extensive use of the

---

40:3 — "*To prepare the way of the Lord, to make streight his paths, that therefore every valley should be exalted, every mountaine made low*" (4:8.517–519).

[224] On the mount as an emblem of ascent see 4:9.150ff: Christ chose to ascend from a mount because it served as an emblematic picture of the act of ascent itself, in the same way that, of all types of government, monarchy best serves to aid Donne's contemplation of heaven. In 8:8.293–298 true holy tears carry us higher than any other hill, signifying either power, oppression, pride, or ambition. Other instances are 1:3.535–575; 5:13.215; and 9:14.569–574.

analogy between a love for a woman and a love for God.[225] In a sermon specially commissioned to be preached before Queen Anne at Denmark House, Donne turns to carnal love in developing the theme of seeking God.[226] In the first partition of the sermon, where he talks about Christ's love, Donne notes that whereas in most places in the Bible the writers use a non-erotic version of the word "love" so as not to confuse divine and profane love, in Proverbs, whence Donne has taken his text, Christ's love is expressed as Amor (1:5.155–173). Furthermore, Donne points out the structural similarity between sexual and divine courtship in Solomon,

> whose disposition was amorous, and excessive in the love of women, when he turn'd to God, he departed not utterly from his old phrase and language, but having put a new, and a spiritual tincture, and form and habit into all his thoughts, and words, he conveys all his loving approaches and applications to God, and all Gods gracious answers to his amorous soul, into songs, and Epithalamions (42–48).

Solomon's ultimate term was replaced, but the language and manner of approach remained much the same. I will have more to say on this sermon later (in chap. 3), but for now it is important simply to note that Donne recognizes courtship not simply as a field of imagery for ornamentation, but as *inventio*, providing a source of analogous structures of experience that are readily transferable to religious experience.

Similarly, in a sermon preached at Whitehall, Donne notes that profane and divine courtships are so similar, that the worldly-minded may easily confuse the latter with the former. Taking the example of St. Stephen and St. Paul (then Saul), fellow pupils under Gamaliel until the former became a disciple of Jesus, Donne exhorts his congregation,

> Though then thy kinsmen in the flesh, and thy fellow pupils under *Gamaliel*, men whom thou hast accompanied heretofore in other waies, think thy present fear of God, but a childishness and pusilanimity, and thy present zeal to his service but an infatuation and a melancholy, and thy present application of thy self to God in

---

[225] One notable exception is in 7:1.267–271, where private prayer is likened to decorum in sexual courtships, but here the association is very briefly and delicately handled. When Donne uses the analogy of marriage, it is usually in the sense of a contract which is a type of God's covenant or "contract" with humankind (9:18.286–303).

[226] Bald, *John Donne*, 329.

prayer, but an argument of thy Court-dispaire, and of thy falling
from former hopes there; yet ... come apace to Christ Jesus: how
learned soever thou art, thou art yet to learn thy first letters, if thou
know not that Christ Jesus is *Alpha* and *Omega* (8:7.305–315).

Although worldly ambitions seem indistinguishable from devout zeal, they
are but a simple reflection of a higher achievement. Yet as Donne notes here
and in his sermon to Queen Anne, these courtships are functionally similar.

References to socio-political structures provide the lion's share of
Donne's courtship analogues. Donne frequently draws on courtship situations — obeisance, patronage, diplomacy — as recognizable patterns of
experience. Rather than simply cataloguing these, I want to focus on the
way courtship modes inform Donne's presentation of such religious activities as prayer. His conflating in the Holy Sonnets of prayer with "flattering
speaches" that "court God" is carried over into the sermons.[227] Preaching
before Charles I, Donne relates a well-known axiom of patronage in application to God: "there cannot be a more effectuall prayer for the future, then
a thankfull acknowledgement of former benefits" (9:9.184–185). In a similar way, Donne tells his congregation at St. Paul's that "Prayer and Praise
is the same thing" (5:14.79). "Our Prayers besiege God," says Donne, "but
our praises prescribe in God, we urge him, and presse him with his ancient
mercies, his mercies of old; By Prayer we incline him, we bend him, but by
praise we bind him" (5:14.147–151). These posturings toward God are
variants of recognizable modes of political persuasion, such as those
employed by Roman orators who used panegyric "to make those *Emperours*
see, what they were bound to doe" (4:10.582–584).[228]

These culturally defined approaches to God also inscribe a hierarchically defined desire that Donne can use to "stir up" a like desire for Divine
favour. In one of the sermons in his series on Psalm 32, Donne makes
explicit the analogy between social courtship and prayer, suggesting that "If

---

[227] In "Oh, to vex me, contraryes meete in one." Here too Donne notes an analogy of experience
between profane and divine courtships: the latter is marked by contradictory impulses that are typified in the fickleness and inconstancy of profane love.

[228] In a Letter to Sir Henry Goodyer, again in the context of prayer, Donne states the maxim "nothing doth so innocently provoke new graces, as gratitude" (*Letters*, 96). This strategy of gratitude is
ubiquitous in Donne's letters to "persons of honour." Angel Day describes the strategic use of gratitude for writing petitionary letters (*The English Secretary* [1599], 91–92, B2–[B2v]). See also
Michael C. Schoenfeldt, *Prayer and Power* (Chicago: University of Chicago Press, 1991), 184–87
on the coercive power of gratitude in relation to George Herbert's poetry. The related tactic of *lau-
dando praecipere*, to teach by praising, is described throughout Book 4 of Castiglione's *Book of the
Courtier* and by Bacon in his essay "Of Praise" where he notes, "by telling men what they are, [we]
represent to them what they should be" (*Essays*, 156).

any man have tasted at Court, what it is to be ever welcome to the King himselfe, and what it is to speake to another to speake for him, he will blesse that happinesse, of having an immediate accesse to God himselfe in his prayers" (9:14.198–201). Courtship structures can also be used to evoke negative emotions that are equally motivational. In this passage, Donne's congregation is made to feel repulsion at the Roman Catholic practice of invoking the saints, an implicit analogue of political courtship through intermediaries. This Papist/Protestant *agon* is implicit in another passage where Donne again draws on courtly protocol, this time to explain his congregation's position of grace before God:

> In benefits that pass from men of higher ranck, to persons of lower condition, it is not the way to get them, to ground the request upon our own merit; Merit implies an obligation, that we have laid upon them; and that implies a debt. And a Petition for a due debt is an affront; it is not so much a Petition delivered as a writ served upon him, to call him to answer his injust deteining of a just debt (1:7.86–91).[229]

Such boldness, Donne goes on to say, is bad enough in a social context where relative merit *may* exist (Donne's congregation is made to feel the shame of committing such an affront), but it is absolutely inexcusable to approach God with such pretension. Here Donne effectively blends doctrinal issues of grace vs. works with socially defined notions of grace.

Although many of Donne's explicit references to political courtship are directed at courtly audiences, this is not always the case. In sermons outside of court as well Donne draws on courtship practice to describe his congregants' relationship with God. In a 1622 Whitsunday sermon, probably preached at St. Paul's, he warns not to importune or flatter God and cautions that "though God be our businesse, we may be too busie with God" (5:2.1–20). At Lincoln's Inn[230] Donne expands on a statement by St.

---

[229] In a similar passage, George Puttenham describes the manner in which one ought to petition a prince: "they are not to be chalenged for right or iustice, for that is a maner of accusation: nor to be charged with their promises, for that is a kinde of condemnation: and at their request we ought not to be hardly entreated but easily, for that is a signe of deffidence and mistrust in their bountie and gratitude: nor to recite the good seruices which they haue receiued at our hands, for that is but a kind of exprobation, but in crauing their bountie or largesse to remember vnto them all their former beneficences, making no mention of our owne merites, and so it is thankfull, and in praysing them to their faces to do it very modestly" (*Arte of English Poesie*, ed. Arber, 299–300).

[230] Potter and Simpson argue that this undated sermon was part of a series preached during the Trinity Term at Lincoln's Inn (*Sermons*, 3:26–27).

Bernard, evoking a familiar instance of political courtship as he describes
God's comfort as a benefice (a gift or grant of patronage) which comes

> *Non subtus*, not from below thee, from the reverence and acclama-
> tion of thy inferiours; *Non circa*, not from about thee, when all
> places, all preferments are within thy reach, so that thou maist lay
> thy hand, and set thy foote where thou wilt; *Non intus*, not from
> within thee, though thou have an inward testimony of a morall
> constancy, in all afflictions that can fall, yet not from below thee,
> not from above thee, not from within thee, but from above must
> come thy comfort, or it is mistaken (3:12.550–557).[231]

Donne's use of *anaphora* and *parison* emphasizes the hierarchical structure
he uses to direct (along socio–political lines) his congregation's response to
God's benefits. This is a good illustration of how *elocutio* functions as more
than mere ornament; it derives directly from (and hence serves) the *inventio* of the sermon.

Donne develops the same similitude more fully in another sermon
preached at St. Paul's (10:5). Here he uses it as ornament, as the sugar
which entices the reader to receive the bitter pill; but he also uses it as a crucial proof in his argument to win his audience's assent to the idea he promotes. He begins this sermon about reconciliation with God (a direct
reference to a condition of estrangement) with a discussion of the patronage
system. It is a well-executed *exordium* that appeals to a set of circumstances
that would certainly win the sympathy of his audience, as an *exordium* ought
to do. He describes some conditions in which benefactors "vitiate and
deprave the nature of the benefit" they aim to bestow, as when they give
with the intention of receiving something in return, or when the benefice
is too small to do any good (10:5.1–11). Donne then amplifies the point:

> And then there are circumstances, that doe absolutely *annihilate* a
> benefit, amongst which, one is, if the giver take so expresse, so
> direct, so publique knowledge of the wants of the receiver, as that
> he shall be more ashamed by it, then refreshed with it; for in many
> courses of life, it does more deject a man, in his own heart, and in

---

231 In the context, Donne is speaking about the "benefits" (largely interchangeable with "benefice")
God has given (559–560). In usage contemporary to Donne, a "benefit" invariably carries connotations of class advantage and patronage: "2a. A kind deed, a kindness; a favour, gift" and "2c. Law.
the advantage of belonging to a privileged order which was exempted from the jurisdiction or sentence of ordinary courts of law" (*OED*).

the opinion of others too, and more retard him in any preferment, to be *known* to be *poore*, then to *be* so indeed; And he that gives so, does not onely make him that receives, his *Debtor*, but his *Prisoner*, for he takes away his liberty of applying himselfe to others, who might be more beneficiall to him, then *he* that captivated, and ensnared him, with that small benefit (11–21).

Donne puts his finger on a very sensitive situation of social embarrassment (an inevitable condition of cross-class communication, Burke would say) that is aggravated by a lack of due courtesy on the part of the benefactor. By way of contrast, Jacob, who considered Esau's reception of his gift an act of grace, is presented in the ensuing lines as a model of courtesy.[232] Donne evokes these courtship motives to prepare his congregation for the reconciliation offered by God in his text (2 Corinthians 5:20). Happily, Christ, our benefactor and negotiator of this reconciliation, approaches us with courtesy:

he delivers that benefit of all those accidents, or circumstances, that might vitiate it; and amongst those, of this, that we should not be confounded with the notice taken of our poverty, and indigence; for he proceeds with man, as though man might be of some use to him, and with whom it were fit for him to hold good correspondence (27–32).

Donne continues throughout the sermon to describe the benefice of spiritual reconciliation in similar terms.

These few instances are enough to establish a prominent pattern of courtship imagery in Donne's sermons. But as I will demonstrate, political courtship is only the most obvious social structure of desire. Donne finds many others which speak to the desires and ambitions of his mixed congregation at St. Paul's and, to a lesser degree, at the other churches where he preached. It now remains to describe the place of these images in the rhetorical strategies of Donne's sermons.

๛ Courtship as language of accommodation

Donne's strategy of courtship is directed at the needs and condition of his audience who, being human and fallen, are inclined more to the ways of the flesh than to the ways of the spirit. In a sermon on heaven preached at

---

[232] Donne also finds biblical examples of courtesy in Abraham, David, and Abigail (3:5.71–118).

Whitehall, Donne characterizes his congregation's hearts as nullified, divided, and wandering. Consequently, their hearts need to be brought to attention and given a new orientation. Donne expresses this condition and its effects in one of his typically masterful deployments of *isocolon*:

> Except the Lord of heaven create new hearts in us, of our selves, we have *Cor nullum*, no heart; all vanishes into Incogitancy. Except the Lord of heaven con-centre our affections, of our selves, we have *Cor & Cor*, a cloven, a divided heart, a heart of Irresolution. Except the Lord of heaven fix our Resolutions, of our selves, we have *Cor vagum*, a various, a wandering heart; all smoaks into Inconstancie. And all these three are Enemies to that firmness, and fixation of the heart, which God loves, and we seek after (9:7.290–297).[233]

Like Richard Bernard's allegorical Heart, theirs is "a heart that should not know where to settle, nor what to wish," yet one which by nature seeks constancy (9:7.195–96). Donne's sermon takes as its text Matthew 6:21, "*For, where your treasure is, there will your heart be also,*" the biblical *locus classicus* on the alignment of mundane and spiritual motives. To amplify this passage somewhat in Burkeian terms, the ultimate term of any given motivational hierarchy goads and therefore determines the direction of the heart's desire. The condition to which Donne continually preaches is one of misdirected or inconstant devotion, so that the heart's errant desire must be directed and fixed to its proper object.

Richard Hooker describes the preacher's consideration of audience when he says, "[i]t is true that the weakenes of our wittes and the dulnes of our affections doe make us for the most parte ... hard and slowe to beleve what is written." For this reason even such a reluctant advocate of the preaching ministry as Hooker admits that sermons are necessary helps for the congregation's recalcitrance.[234] Yet Hooker argues elsewhere that while nature is deficient, Scripture is entirely efficient in communicating divine truth and does not need the help of sermons.[235] Scripture is not deficient

---

[233] On this characterization of the human heart see also Donne's *Devotions*, expostulation 9. See also Rosemary Boston, "The Variable Heart in Donne's Sermons," *CSR* 1 (1971): 36–41.

[234] Hooker, *Works*, 2:104 (5.22.17). Hooker's coolness toward sermons can be explained in part by the fact that in the *Lawes of Ecclesiasticall Politie* he is reacting to the exclusive emphasis Puritans placed on preaching over other forms of public worship. Cf. Donne, *Sermons*, 9:7.98–100.

[235] According to Hooker, the public reading of Scripture is enough to impart the mysteries and articles of faith (*Works*, 2:91–2 [5.22.4–6]).

in Donne's mind either, but his congregants, with their inconstant hearts, are. Donne includes himself among them as an *exemplum* of one who lacks the spiritual attention even to pray. He admits that he is easily engaged "in musique, in feasting, in Comedies, in wantonnesse"; but though "some beam of [God's] grace shines out upon me," says Donne, he cannot attend to his prayers but easily becomes distracted (10:1.542, 545).[236] Donne is not quite so bald as Hooker in describing his congregation's condition, but he does recognize that they are bound up in present and pressing concerns. As to "the in corrigible stiffenesse of mans disobedience," Donne explains that "he is not afraid of future judgements, because they are remote" (8:13.617–620). The preacher must therefore make the remote, eternal concern present. It is Donne's understanding too that Scripture is effectual, but he also understands, as a rhetorician, that that other book of revelation, the "book of creatures," is a profound analogy for giving divine truth passage into his audience's affections and thought.

Nor is the problem of inattention to spiritual matters attributable only to an audience's indolence. The matters that a preacher deals with are by nature transcendent and difficult or even impossible to apprehend — a circumstance which causes George Herbert to ask, "Lord, how can man preach thy eternall word?" (1).[237] Similarly in Donne, "There is nothing so little in heaven, as that we can express it" (7:15.711–712). Donne tells his congregation that the humane arts (arithmetic, rhetoric, poetry) are unable to bring them to an apprehension of eternity (4:2.899ff). The benefit of divine forgiveness, for example, is "so inexpressible a comfort, to that soule that hath wrastled with the indignation of God, and is now refreshed and released, as whosoever should goe about to describe it, should diminish it; He hath it not that thinks he can utter it" (9:14.370–374). The best Donne can do is to liken those who prefer earthly blessing (which is easy to apprehend) over the blessing of forgiveness (which is difficult to apprehend) to one who goes to market and buys only unwholesome herbs, or to an apothecary's shop to ask for poison (362–368). His answer is to accommodate his congregation's understood needs and desires by speaking the language of the marketplace and court.[238] In speaking their language, Donne, the preacher of the Word, emulates the methods of the divine author of the

---

[236] cf. Donne's famous passage on the distractions that prevent prayer, in his funeral sermon for Sir William Cokayne (7:10.271–286).

[237] "The Windows" (*Works*, ed. F. E. Hutchinson, 67).

[238] To meet this need Donne of course uses strategies other than the one I am developing here. Patricia M. Howison describes some of Donne's other means of leading his audience to an apprehension of elusive matters of spirit ("Donne's Sermons and the Rhetoric of Prophecy," *ESC* 15 [1989]: 134–48).

Word. This is the pattern set down by God who "provide[s] man meanes proportionable to man" in order "to expresse his unexpressible mercy" (5:13.343–345; cf. 9:5.392–396).

Donne uses mundane concerns to speak not only to the understanding, but to the appetite as well. He takes his oft-cited image of "Manna [which] tasted to every man like that that he liked best" as an emblem of Scripture's applicability to man's needs, interests, affections, and capacity (7:1.1–15, also 2:13.265–292). Understanding that his congregant is inclined rather more to motives of the social order than to those of the spiritual, Donne relates transcendent matters to the things that motivate humans. Leonard Wright, in *A Svmmons for Sleepers* (1596), describes the rhetorical situation Donne faces. As the title suggests, Wright's concern is to awaken his audience out of spiritual lethargy and ignorance, and he conceives of the solution in terms of a mounting achieved through similitude:

> The ioies of heauen are pleasant ioies, our eies cannot see them, our eares cannot heare them, our hearts cannot vnderstand them, nor our tongues expresse them, as if a man should promise his horses a good banquet, they could imagine no other but prouender and water to bee their best cheere, because they know no daintier dishes, euen so the naturall man accustomed to the puddle of fleshlie pleasure, his mind can mount no higher, to perceiue, discern, or vnderstand the things that bee of God, so as the ioifull pleasures of heauen, are hidden from his sences.[239]

Wright then introduces a series of similitudes of comparison to aid the reader's understanding of heaven's joys, which are like in kind but greater in degree than temporal pleasures. For example: "seeing wee receiue so manie comfortable blessings in the day of sorrow and mourning [on earth], much greater shall our pleasures bee in the ioifull day of mariage [in heaven]."[240] Note that this use of similitude accommodates both the affections and the intellect.

From Wright we can derive a twofold process of similitude by which the heart and mind "mount higher": first, the similitude establishes an understanding of the likeness between temporal and eternal; then it brings a recognition of the transcendence of the latter. Donne's strategy in using the courtship similitude is similar to that of the Holy Ghost who "brings

---

[239] Wright, *A Svmmons for Sleepers* (1596), [G1v].
[240] Wright, *A Svmmons for Sleepers*, [G1v].

us here to the consideration of some lesser pieces, things which are always within distance and apprehension, always in our eye" (9:17.135–136). The effectiveness of similitude, as Bartholemew Keckermann points out, derives from its accommodation to what is known and familiar to the audience. In *Rhetorica Ecclesiastica* (1606), Keckermann thus advises, "[l]et similitudes be drawn from things pertaining to the senses ... and placed in the midst of common life."[241]

In drawing out likenesses to spiritual motives, Donne routinely turns to common experience: buying and selling, making a will, sexual desire, professional advancement, political advantage. Herbert H. Umbach, in arguing that Donne's preaching was moderately metaphysical by the standards of his time, notes that the imagery of metaphysical preachers was characteristically strange and unfamiliar and that while they found in Jesus's parables a precedent for their use of similitude, "[t]he most important point seems to have been overlooked, namely that Jesus's parables recall the more familiar occupations or circumstances in life."[242] Although Umbach implies that Donne escaped this excess, when he goes on to discuss Donne's similitudes he admits to omitting "[a] large percentage [which] is ordinary *and hence not quoteworthy here."*[243] Rather, I am arguing that this wide and frequently visited field of courtship imagery in Donne's sermons is powerful (and hence noteworthy, if not quoteworthy) precisely because these images "recall the more familiar occupations or circumstances in life."

♣ Desire and the affective structure of social courtships

For the rest of this chapter I want to focus on the function of courtship structures as rhetorical proof. Most obviously, Donne uses courtship analogies to evoke a whole range of desires that he can use for motivating his congregation. Donne, like many of his contemporaries, also describes the activity of a sermon as a spurring and directing of the affections. In contrast to a lecture, "a Sermon," says Donne, "intends *Exhortation* principally and *Edification,* and a holy stirring of religious affections" (8:3.10–12). Like the eagle who stirs up her nest (Deuteronomy 32:11), "The Preacher stirres and moves, and agitates the holy affections of the Congregation, that they slumber not in a senselesnesse of that which is said" (8:1.239–241). But he goes on to indicate that the preacher directs these emotions into a fear of

---

[241] Auksi's translation (*Christian Plain Style,* 273).

[242] Herbert H. Umbach, "The Merit of Metaphysical Style in Donne's Easter Sermons," *ELH* 12 (1945): 108–29, here 113.

[243] Umbach, "Merit of Metaphysical Style," 113–14, emphasis mine.

God that draws their attention upward, and then the preacher-as-mother-eagle "armes them with her wings, so as that no other terror, no other fluttering but that which comes from her, can come upon them" (250–252). The preacher incites but also manages his congregation's emotions.

The courtier-turned-preacher understood very well the workings of desire within hierarchy. Donne sees his audience as continually goaded with a desire for more — "rotten with perfection" as Burke puts it.[244] Preaching at St. Paul's on the satisfaction that comes only from God, Donne notes that there may be fullness without satisfaction. There will be a fullness upon arriving in heaven, says Donne, but not complete satisfaction, "because we shall desire, and expect a fuller satisfaction in the reunion of body and soule" (5:14.234–235). How much less can we expect satisfaction here on earth? Donne turns to social referents to amplify his point about the elusiveness of satisfaction: "Pleasure and sensuality, and the giving to our selves all that we desire, cannot give this; ... Labor for profit, or for preferment, cannot doe it; ... If these things could fill us, yet they could not satisfie us, because they cannot stay with us" (239–250). Over forty-three lines of text (226–268), Donne both evokes and frustrates his congregation's expectations for fullness in their earthly courtships, only to offer them instead a more promising courtship in the spiritual order. But though there is fullness in the ways of the Spirit, there is still no complete satisfaction for the human spirit on earth: "The desire of spirituall graces begets a satiety, if I would be, I am full of them, And then this satiety begets a farther desire, still we have a new appetite to those spirituall graces: This is a holy ambition, a sacred covetousnesse, and a wholsome Dropsie" (277–281). Here Donne depicts the psychological structure of courtship: a never-ending cycle where appetite begets satiety, and satiety begets a new appetite. As Donne says in another sermon, "nothing supplies, nor fills, nor satisfies the desire of man, on this side of God; Every man hath something to love, and desire, till he determine it in God; because God only hath ... an inexhaustible goodnesse" (6:11.338–342).[245] Yet because God's goodness is inexhaustible, the courtship of God never ends.

---

[244] *LASA*, 16. Adapting Aristotle's notion of *entelechy*, Burke notes that "there is a principle of perfection implicit in the nature of symbol systems; and in keeping with his nature as a symbol-using animal, man is moved by this principle." For example, in *RR* Burke refers to "the linguistic drive towards the Title of Titles, a logic of entitlement that is completed by thus rising to ever and ever higher orders of generalization" (25). The socio-political counterpart to this drive is courtship, and implicit in all of Burke's models of purification is a basic structure of hierarchy.

[245] Donne cites [Pseudo] Dionysius the Areopagite as his source for the phrase "inexhaustible goodnesse." Dionysius's *Celestial Hierarchies* is an excellent example of how a hierarchical order of being lends itself to notions of purification.

The goad of desire in this life is for Donne a temporal manifestation of a greater, more profound desire for a spiritual end. It is for him a proof of eternity.[246] In his commemorative sermon on Lady Danvers's death, Donne says,

> As God hath provided us an *Endlesnesse*, in the world to come, so, to give us an Inchoation, a Representation of the next world, in this, *God* hath instituted an *endlesnesse* in this world too; *God* hath imprinted in every *naturall man*, and doth exalt in the *super-naturall*, and *regenerate* man, an endlesse, and Undeterminable desire of more, then this life can minister unto him (8:2.450–455).

This word "inchoation" is a favourite of Donne's when talking about this life in relation to the next, a point which will be explored more fully in the next chapter. What is significant for my present purposes is the idea that the unsatisfied desire of the natural man in worldly affairs points to a desire which is even more acutely felt by those of a regenerate nature (who are higher in Donne's scale of being), because their desires are enlarged to include spiritual objectives. There is a clear and continuous scale of progression away from the worldly-minded, leading to their ultimate object (whether they realize it or not) of the fullness of heaven. Furthermore, this desire is enlarged in an upward movement in the scale until only the eternal can satisfy. In this light, the famous and disquieting (and to many, puzzling) image of Lady Danvers's remarkably active corpse crawling with worms below the feet of the congregation is fittingly emblematic of the incessant goad of desire in the flesh that is never satisfied.[247]

Donne's objective in this sermon is not simply to bring consolation in the assurance that Lady Danvers is in a better place, but to goad his audi-

---

[246] This mode of proof is the product of what Debora Shuger calls a "participatory consciousness," one of the "habits of thought" she identifies in the Renaissance, and one which is typified by the following line of reasoning: "The fact that all men desire infinite happiness, a happiness not given in this world, itself guarantees the existence of something 'above the capacity of reason,' something 'divine and heavenly' capable of satisfying that desire" (*Habits of Thought*, 44). In other words, "the desires of the mind assure the reality of the desired object" (45).

[247] John Carey sees this image as an example of Donne's athletic view of death, a typically self-gratifying image, but "not ... an aspect of the affair her relatives would much wish to contemplate" (*John Donne*, 201). To Carey, Donne's consideration of audience and occasion does not extend beyond the preacher's personal preoccupations. Yet decorum must be located in the sermon's broader purpose not simply to pacify an audience but to spur them on to greater devotion. On the popular iconography of the "Transi Tomb" depicting the body's putrefaction see Kathleen Cohen, *Metamorphosis of a Death Symbol: The Transi Tomb in the Late Middle Ages and the Renaissance* (Berkeley: University of California Press, 1973).

ence to desire the same for themselves. As his chosen text of 2 Peter 3:13 attests, he aims to enlarge their desire for the "*new heavens, and new earth.*" Donne goes on to demonstrate that an extension of mundane desires is a common feature of biblical rhetoric. He notes that elsewhere, "the *holy Ghost* applies himselfe, to the naturall affections of men. To those that are affected with *riches*, he saies, that *that new City shall be all of gold*, and in the *foundations, all manner of precious stones*" (720–723). In the same way, he notes, the lovers' discourse in Canticles 1:15–16 bespeaks the union between Christ and his church in heaven; and to "those, whose thoughts are exerciz'd upon *Honour*, and *Titles, Civill*, or *Ecclesiasticall*," God promises a royal priesthood (730–731). Yet in this verse an even greater desire is extended and satisfied in heaven, one which has no comparable satisfaction here on earth: the desire here and now for justice or righteousness. It is significant that here Donne mingles an explicit instance of courtship motives with other desire structures. Whether they be basic motives such as riches and title, or higher motives of justice, the Holy Spirit's procedure (and Donne's by imitation) is the same: to take existing structures and enlarge and extend them toward heaven, their true *telos*.

Socio-political relations afforded Donne an effective structure for directing his congregation's desires. In his second extant sermon at Whitehall, on the passage "*Because they have no changes, therefore they fear not God*" (Psalm 55:19), Donne begins by applying the general principle of the text to the particular context of his courtly audience. Whereas a prison or a galley is a place "where any change that could come, would put them [the inmates] in a better state, then they were before," court seems a relatively desirable place

> where every man having set his foot, or plac'd his hopes upon the present happy state, and blessed Government, every man is rather to be presum'd to love God, because there are no changes, then to take occasion of murmuring at the constancie of Gods goodness toward us (1:4.3–9).

Donne promptly warns, however, that Lucifer and his followers were discontent with their place in heaven, and that as good as the current political environment seems, it is a "copy" of heaven, and an imperfect one at that. Donne implies that there may be some subjects present who are wrongly discontent with their present level of favour not only with God, but with the king: many (if not all) in the upper reaches of hierarchy (both in the king's and God's blessing) desire more. Donne is no doubt addressing a political problem of murmuring about the king and his regime (a frequent point of exhortation in the sermons).[248] But he further identifies the political context of his listeners with what should be their spiritual concerns. Throughout the sermon he warns of the slipperiness of sin, which his congregation cannot but associate with the slipperiness of positions at court, even though Donne delicately avoids direct reference to this political analogue.[249] Francis Bacon, in his essay "Of Great Place," describes the political ascent as "slippery"; conversely, "the regress is either a downfall, or at least an eclipse."[250] Donne's sermon may serve a political purpose of quieting discontent at court, but equally (indeed more importantly to the preacher) the political purposes of the sermon's context serve to advance the pastor's spiritual agenda, enabling him to draw on political anxieties at court to instill an anxiety about the courtier's position before God, and thereby correct the condition described in the text.

Throughout this sermon, Donne maintains a close identification between notions of temporal and spiritual hierarchy, but as he moves toward his conclusion he uses this analogy to instruct the king as well as the subject. Donne again directs his fellow subjects' devotion to God with respect to their allegiance toward the king: "so the love of man towards God, and those who represent him, is not permanently setled, if there be not a reverential fear, a due consideration of greatness, a distance, a distinction, a respect of Rank, and Order, and Majestie" (414–417). But he concludes by noting that in the text it is *Deus* who is to be feared, not *Jehovah* or *Adonai*, names which connote God's absolute Lordship, so that "God calls not upon us, to be consider'd as God in himself, but as God towards us; not as he is in heaven, but as he works upon earth" (427–429). Emphasized in the text is the relationship between God and his subject. The application of this is that God chooses not to proceed with us according to his absolute will, but "according to that Contract which he hath made with us, and that Law which he hath given to us" (436–438). The model Donne presents here is

---

[248] In 9:12 Donne commends reverential silence of private men regarding those in positions of authority (224–326). In 7:5.377–378 he warns against "privy whisperings and calumnies" and in 9:9.84–86 against "calumny" and "misinterpretation" of church and political leaders.

[249] In the months just prior to Donne's delivery of this sermon (2 November 1617), Francis Bacon, newly appointed Lord Chancellor, drew the ire of King James and his new favourite, the Earl of Buckingham, over his resistance to a proposed match between Buckingham's brother and the disgraced Sir Edward Coke's daughter (or rather, Bacon opposed the manner in which it was being executed). Upon explaining himself to the king, Bacon was returned to favour. See Mary Sturt, *Francis Bacon* (London: Kegan Paul, 1932), 177–85. A more notorious example of the slippery slope of political courtship was Sir Walter Ralegh, who was finally sentenced to death by Bacon in 1618.

[250] Bacon, *Essays*, 31.

one of mutual obligation. Insofar as Donne's socio-spiritual similitude serves the political order, it must do so both upward and downward in the hierarchy. Potter and Simpson, in their introduction to this sermon, suggest that Donne was "still working toward a *rapport* with his audiences that would make them receptive to the doctrine he was expounding" but that he still hadn't quite learned how to touch the hearts of his listeners.[251] Yet clearly in his handling of motives familiar to his audience, even at this early stage in his preaching career, Donne was well on his way.

Donne finds a wide range of other social relational structures, besides the sexual and political, that are able to induce desire and thus operate as models of courtship. Another instance of hierarchically defined desire can be found in a sermon preached at St. Dunstan's on the believer's filial relation to God. As he begins the first partition, Donne explains that the word signifying "children" in his chosen text (Psalm 34:11) is the Hebrew *Banim*, which has three acceptable connotations. These he casts into a hierarchy. He tells his congregation, "you are not onely *Filii familiares*, children because *servants*, nor onely *Filii mammillares*, children because *noursed* by him, but you are also *Filii viscerales*, children of his bowells" (6:4.130–133). Here Donne uses *climax*, a figure of grammatical arrangement, to configure a series of increasingly desirable positions with respect to the patriarch (God) — those of a servant, an adopted child, and a natural child — which point the congregation toward what should be the object of their desire, the one with whom they ought, as true sons, to identify. As Donne makes clear, the ascendant position of sonship connotes freedom and intimacy with God, while the lower status of the servant connotes bondage and servitude. He uses this sense of familial hierarchy to repel his congregation from identifying with the Roman religion. He tells his congregation that in contrast to the law and order of "old *Rome*," where one could not be adopted by a citizen lower in the social hierarchy, "the new *Rome*" (i.e. the church of Rome) would like to adopt them out of their position of freedom in the Reformed religion into one of slavery to the human traditions of Papistry (106–129). To adhere to the Roman church would be to descend in socio-familial (not to mention spiritual) status.

For non-courtly audiences, Donne frequently uses the economic motives of the marketplace as a courtship structure. In the emerging capitalist society of seventeenth-century England, economic enterprise became an increasingly dominant means of courting social status. Donne tells his St. Dunstan's congregation that as loath as they would be to cast the

---

[251] Potter and Simpson, *Sermons*, 1:132–33.

"Fraight, the Cargason, the Merchandise" out of their ship, so they should be loath to cast off religious zeal; discretion (the ship's ballast) keeps them secure, but zeal (their merchandise, and by extension their whole enterprise) brings profit (6:18.453–458). Donne completes his allegory by charging that they have taken more care to please men with their discretion, than God with their zeal. They "thought it sufficient," he declares, "to sail on smoothly, and steadily, and calmly, and discreetly in the world, and with the time, though not so directly to the right Haven" (462–464). The profitability of the destination ought to energize his congregation to steer a direct (rectified) course.

In a sermon in his series on the Penitential Psalms, Donne likens remembering and confessing one's sins to "an Audit, a casting up of our accounts" wherein we recount "our prodigality, our unthriftinesse, our ill bargaine" (5:15.36, 27). Donne frequently evokes this *topos* of improvident bargaining in urging his audience toward spiritual prudence. Here, with reference to our own account of sin, we are made to feel the shame of one who is "loath to see a list of their debts," while at the same time feeling the legal-economic necessity of doing so (38–39). Conversely, at St. Paul's Donne directs his congregation's attitude toward spiritual richness with an allusion to the economic motive of accumulation. He refers to Redemption as a purchase and Christ's blood as the currency. Every blessing (Christ's blood chief among them) is currency if it bears his image and name in its inscription. These blessings are distinguished according to economic values: "the temporall is my silver, and the spirituall is my Gold" (6:13.506–507). But these are "illusory shadows" (he might have said counterfeits) if not made current by Christ: "except I have it, in, and for, and by Christ Jesus" — that is, unless this accumulation of blessing has its proper source and end (509–510).[252]

Nor is imagery of the marketplace excluded from Donne's sermons at court. In a sermon preached before King Charles, Donne likens his courtly congregation to an art collector (a market limited to the privileged few, one would expect) who has masterpieces at home, yet goes out to country fairs

---

[252] The *OED* lists a figurative usage of "shadow" in application to a portrait as contrasted with its subject (Shakespeare's *TGV*, IV.iii.126–127 and *MND*, V.i.209). Shakespeare's use of "shadow" in sonnet 43 to signify an image — "Then thou, whose shadow shadows doth make bright" — is augmented by his use of "mirroring" schemes: *antistasis, epizeuxis, diacope, polyptoton,* and others (see Stephen Booth's notes in his edition, *Shakespeare's Sonnets* [New Haven: Yale University Press, 1977], 203). A sense of "shadow" as an imitation or copy is first cited in 1693. In the context of this sermon, it may be that Donne is already stretching the sense to signify something like a counterfeit copy. The advantage of choosing "shadow" over "counterfeit" is that "shadow" evokes a sense of transitoriness common in its usage at the time, which is appropriate to the temporal-spiritual distinction Donne makes here.

to buy cheap copies (9:2.455–458).[253] Similarly, God's image, the genuine "master-peece," is at home in our souls; it is a debasement of ambition to seek counterfeits abroad (458–459). Donne draws in other instances of perverse courtships as he drives his point home:

> we indure the oppositions, and scornes, and triumphs of a rivall, and competitor, that seeks with us, and shares with us: we indure the guiltinesse, and reproach of having deceived the trust, which a confident friend reposes in us, and solicit his wife, or daughter: we endure the decay of fortune, of body, of soule, of honour, to possesse lower Pictures; pictures that are not originalls, not made by that hand of God, nature; but Artificiall beauties. And for that body, we give a soule, and for that drugge, which might have been bought, where they bought it, for a shilling, we give an estate. The Image of God is more worth then all substances; and we give it, for colours, for dreames, for shadowes (462–472).[254]

Donne adapts his mercantile field of reference to the pretensions of a courtly audience, configuring their spiritual interests as a matter of refined or unrefined taste (quality art vs. kitsch) and of business sense (paying too much for inferior merchandise).

Another common field of imagery in Donne's sermons is found in legal discourse, which he also uses as a recognizable frame of reference for codifying his congregation's motives. These juridical references are not limited to Donne's Lincoln's Inn sermons. A good example is a sermon preached at a christening, presumably at St. Paul's. In this sermon addressing the difficulty of apprehending Jesus's incarnation, Donne notes in the first part of his *divisio* that "God descends to meanes proportionable to Man; he affords him witnesse" (5:6.88–89). Specifically, Donne derives three witnesses from his text of 1 John 5:7–8: spirit, water, and blood. In his amplification of this first point, he notes that in the Old Testament Jesus is figured in ablutions of water and sacrifices of blood, and in the New Testament in the sacraments of his visible church, including the one which was the occasion of this sermon. Donne makes the water and blood (conceptual means of

---

253 Donne evidently had some personal experience with paintings. According to Oliver Millar, Donne owned a Titian described as "our Lady and Christ and St John half figures": *The Queen's Pictures* (London: Weidenfeld & Nicolson, 1977), 35.

254 Other instances of Donne's use of economic imagery in engendering desire for spiritual matters are 2:11.369–383 (at Lincoln's Inn); 4:5.165–206 (at Lincoln's Inn); 4:11.171–201 (at St. Paul's); 4:12.1–59 and *passim*; 9:11.611–617; 9:14.1–12 (these last two were probably preached at St. Paul's).

grace) concrete in application to Christ, relating them to his physical tears and his sweat which poured out as blood in Gethsemane, and which finally issued from his side on the cross.

Furthermore, these "witnesses" carry extra force because of a similitude Donne develops in his *exordium* between an instance of English law and the sentence of God's spiritual law on fallen humanity. Donne begins the sermon by relating his audience's spiritual condition to an undesirable status under common law:

> IN GREAT and enormous offences, we find that the law, in a well governed State, expressed the punishment upon such a delinquent, in that form, in that curse, *Igni & aqua interdicitur,* let him have no use of *fire,* and *water,* that is, no use of any thing, necessary for the sustentation of life (1–5).[255]

Similarly, under the curse of the Fall,

> we have nothing to doe, naturally, with the spirituall *water of life,* with the fiery *beames* of the holy *Ghost,* till he that hath wrought our restitution from this banishment, restore us to this *water,* by powring out his owne *bloud,* and to this lively *fire,* by laying himselfe a cold, and bloudlesse carcasse in the bowels of the Earth (7–12).

Donne's reference to law in the *exordium* is designed to enlarge his audience's desire for the restitution Jesus offers.

Donne continues this pathetic appeal with reference to "another Malediction, upon such offenders, appliable also to us, *Intestabiles sunto,* let them be Intestable" (18–19). Such an offender is intestable in four ways: 1) "he was able to make no *Testament* [i.e. a will] of his owne"; 2) "he could receive no profit by any testament of any other Man"; 3) "he could not testifie, he should not be beleeved in the behalfe of another"; 4) "the testimony of another could doe him no good, no Man could be admitted to

---

[255] Donne is referring to an aspect of English law inherited from the Romans. Thomas Blount provides this gloss from Livy: "Interdicted of Water and Fire, Were in old time those, who, for some crime were banished; which Judgment, though it was not by express sentence pronounced, yet, by giving order, That no man should receive them into his house, but deny them Fire and Water, (the two necessary elements of life) they were condemned, as it were to a Civil death; and this was called *legitimum exilium*" (*Νομο-λεζικον: a Law-Dictionary* [1670], 2P). Donne picks up on the banishment aspect in the application which follows, though he does not draw direct attention to this aspect of the law itself.

speake for him" (22–29).[256] Then Donne presses an application to spiritual matters. Because humankind is under the Malediction of Maledictions (the curse of the Fall), "we cannot thinke to scape any lesse malediction of any law," including *Intestabiles sunto* (36–37). Therefore, corresponding to the four aspects of civil intestability, before God: 1) "we can make no *testament* of our owne; we have no good thing in us to dispose"; 2) "we can make no use of *anothers* testament," neither the Old Testament (lacking faith, we cannot apprehend its promises of the Messiah) nor the New Testament (the Messiah is communicable in baptism, but we cannot baptize ourselves); 3) "we can profit no body else by our testimony," because we are not able to live exemplary lives; 4) "Neither doth the testimony of others doe us any good," because we do not heed their godly example which is their "testimony" (40–51). "As long, as we are considered under the penalty of that law," says Donne, "this is our case ... that we are *intestable*" (64–66). This condition of "being under the law" has its theological parallel in being "under the Law" of the Old Testament which, St. Paul says, has the function of making us aware of sin (Romans 6:14–7:7). The social analogue helps to bring a sense of immediacy to its spiritual counterpart. While Donne's audience may be insensible to the judgement of their sin, they cannot be unmoved by this reference to the censure of civil law.

In the same way that Donne's delineation of the implications of intestability descends by degrees to the status of least advantage, so the reversal proceeds as an ascent by degrees: in Christ's redemption, "this great reedification of mankind, he beginnes at the lowest step" (76–77). The reversal of this sentence (speaking juristically) begins with a readmission of the testimony of others on our behalf (77–78) — a restoration of the fourth point of testability. By analogy, one who wants pardon from this undesirable status before the Law must attend to the message of this sermon: he must receive the testimony of these witnesses (spirit, water, and blood) that Jesus is come to earth and come to each individual soul. Because "Christ Jesus makes us all our owne *Iury*," these witnesses speak both *to us*

---

[256] The first two applications of this law pertain to making a testament or will, the second two to giving testimony in court. Theodosian law rendered Donatists and heretics intestable and prevented them from entering into contracts of any kind (*Codex Theodosianus* 16.5.54). As to the ability to make a will, W. S. Holdsworth cites William Lynwood, a fifteenth-century authority on canon law, on the disqualification of "'ratione pœnalitatis,' as those condemned of crimes which rendered them intestabilis" (*A History of English Law*, vol. 3, 7th ed. [London: Methuen, 1956], 424). According to Sir William Blackstone, the crimes which rendered one "intestabilis" were those which by their very nature caused the malefactors to forfeit their lands and goods: treason and felony (*Commentaries on the Laws of England*, vol. 3 [Oxford and London: printed for W. Strahan and T. Cadell, and D. Prince, 1783; repr. New York: Garland, 1978], 499).

regarding Christ and *to Christ* on behalf of us (84). In this way, the sermon initiates the congregant on the first step of an upward ascent toward a right standing before God.

By this strategy of borrowing a similitude from law, Donne too descends to make the ways of God proportional to his audience; he translates their social desires (regarding their status before the law) into a higher concern over their status before God. And he does so to facilitate his audience's ascent in spiritual capacity, so that in receiving testimony of these three witnesses in the text, they will begin a process which will finally release them to be able and inclined to dispose of their own affairs before God, that is, to respond to the incarnation. Interestingly, Donne later on uses another courtship conceit to give the general doctrine of the incarnation a personal application. He tells his congregation that Jesus is a "mighty prince" and that "[t]hough the whole world be his *Court*, thy soule is his *bedchamber*" (259, 261–262).

Much of Donne's other imagery in the sermons can be related to the function of courtship. His goading of his audience with restlessness (and therefore, in a sense, courtship) is always at work in his imagery of life-as-journey. Donne typically presents this image by juxtaposing the present state of wandering and anticipation with the desired end of rest at the destination. In a typical treatment of this theme, Donne remarks, "the world is a Sea, but especially it is a Sea in this respect, that the Sea is no place of habitation, but a passage to our habitations" (2:14.724–726). Donne goes on to amplify the restlessness of this condition, and the transience of rest in this life, in contrast to the final and true rest which comes beyond the grave. He then develops the navigational imagery in a unique direction. He describes the necessity of having the bottom of the ship immersed in the sea of worldly concerns, but notes that it is the upper part of the ship, which is above water and directed at eternity, that sails the vessel. Again, mundane concerns are accepted but reoriented.

Winfried Schleiner does a good job of cataloguing this journey imagery in Donne's sermons, but stops short of suggesting reasons why "the field in which life was seen as a pilgrimage seemed to exert something like compelling influence."[257] Schleiner himself cites some possible reasons, without appearing to recognize (at least not stating in so many words) their rhetorical significance, namely the *ethos* of its source in Scripture and Christian tradition and the *pathos* of the difficulties and dangers associated with travel in early modern times and the resulting relief of arriving at the

---

[257] Schleiner, *Imagery*, 91–92.

destination.[258] But the suasive force of this *topos* makes most sense when viewed as a species of courtship, where each step brings the subject into closer relation with his object of desire. This is a configuration made common by many emblem books of the period, where the devout pilgrim is represented on a winding path leading upward toward a destination on a hill.[259] Part of the tradition Schleiner cites is the idea of *status viatoris*, of "being on the way."[260] This is an element that is common to courtship motives, of being in the process of identification with the object of desire. Furthermore, the life-as-journey image both evokes desire (for completion and rest) and gives it a proper end and orientation (home) which combines motives of identity (one's proper place), fulfilment, and ultimately purification.[261]

Courtship strategies are not limited to instances of Donne's use of sociopolitical similitudes and related imagery. This strategy is also at work in Donne's use of *exempla*. Upwardness and downwardness are given an explicitly hierarchical cast in a sermon preached at Whitehall where Donne stresses that diligently performing the duties of one's place can serve as a goad to others within the hierarchy. He says,

> as a perfume intended only for that room, where the entertainment is to be made, breaths upward and downward, and round about it; so the doing of the duties of the place, by men that move in middle Sphears, breath upwards and downwards, and about too, that is, cast a little shame upon inferiors if they doe not so, and a little remembrance upon Superiors that they should doe so (8:7.165–170).

The *exemplum* is effective because of the class-consciousness (the goad of hierarchy) at work in both those below and above him.

---

[258] Spenser's Despaire in Book I of *The Faerie Qveene* assumes the desire-evoking ability of the journey motif, and other, analogous structures of desire, when he suggests to Redcrosse Knight, "Sleepe after toyle, port after stormie seas, / Ease after warre, death after life does greatly please" (1.9.40.8–9). Despaire's great sleight of hand, of course, is to invert the eulogistic/dyslogistic correspondence between "death" and "life" and the other pairings in the sequence. This *topos* is also evoked in Hamlet's famous "To be, or not to be" speech where life is a sea of troubles and death a "consummation / Devoutly to be wished" (3:1.63–64).

[259] Refer to figs. 7–10.

[260] Schleiner, *Imagery*, 86.

[261] Dante begins *The Divine Comedy* with "NEL MEZZO del cammin di nostra vita"; "MIDWAY in the journey of our life." The purification significance of this journey-quest is obvious (trans. Charles S. Singleton, vol. 1 [Princeton: Princeton University Press, 1970], 3).

Elsewhere Donne makes clear that the eulogistic/dyslogistic associations implicit in the *exemplum*'s place in the hierarchy of being are central to its motivational power:

> First, to raise us to the best height, God makes himselfe our example, *Sicut Pater, Be holy as your Father in heaven is holy.* Then, because we cannot reach to that, he makes men like our selves (at least, such as we should be) our example, *Sicut Elias, Elias was a man subject to like passions as wee are, and hee prayed that it might not raine, and it rained not, and that it might, and it did.* If wee be not able to conforme our selves to the singularity of one particular and transcendent man, hee sends us to the whole body of good men, his servants, *Sicut Prophetæ, Take, my brethren, the Prophets, for an example of long patience.* And because he knowes our inclination, to be a declination, and that we cast those lookes, which hee made upward towards him, downward towards the creature, he sends us to creatures of an ignobler nature, *Vade ad formicam, Goe to the Ant,* doe as shee doth, be as industrious in thy businesse, as she is in hers. And then, as in inclining us to good, so also for avoiding of sinfull courses, he leades us by example too, *Non sicut quidam eorum, Bee not idolaters as some of them, nor fornicators, nor tempters of Christ, nor murmurers, as some of them* (9:14.53–70).

Donne's arrangement from highest to lowest in the order of being emphasizes the hierarchical cast implicit in the operation of *exempla*. It also draws attention to the accommodating function of *exempla*, moving from the lower, apprehensible world to the higher, transcendent world of being.

Jeanne Shami finds that Donne's *exempla* are typically men and women of a "middle nature" (neither saint nor sinner) who demonstrate a careful deliberation in cases of conscience.[262] These models achieve a commerce between God and Donne's auditory, drawing them into the pattern of human experience and spiritual progress which they model. Donne's *exempla* are near enough to his struggling congregants that they are not out of

---

[262] Jeanne Shami, "Donne's Protestant Casuistry: Cases of Conscience in the *Sermons*," *SP* 80 (1983): 53–66. Shami argues that the continual emphasis on Donne's ideal *exempla* (i.e. Elizabeth Drury in the *Anniversaries*) "wrenches from Donne a dichotomy between matter and spirit that is not borne out by Donne's practice." Rather, "Donne's focus is much more sharply on *this* world and on the application of the examples of struggling men and women to the difficult lives of seventeenth-century Christians" ("Protestant Casuistry," 55).

reach, yet ascendant enough to draw observers of them higher in the way that leads to the prime *exemplum*, Jesus Christ. Donne takes David as a key *exemplum*, not because he is perfect, but because he represents the full scope of the human condition. He "includes all states, betweene a shepherd and a King, and his sinne includes all sinne" (5:15.118–120). Furthermore, David symbolizes the nexus of mundane and spiritual motives which Donne seeks to reconcile. He embodies "affections of a middle nature, that participate of nature, and of grace too, and in which the Spirit of God moves, and naturall affections move too" (5:16.387–389). Again, there is persuasive potential here because David appeals to motives and desires of the natural man, and because the Holy Spirit works in conjunction with, not in opposition to, these natural affections.

❧ Logical and pathetic proof: courtship as analogical induction

> *Make not then your owne mischance,*
> *Wake your selfe from Passions-traunce,*
> *And let Reason guide affection,*
> *From despaire to new election.*
> — Fulke Greville, *Cælica*, no. 75[263]

Donne's manipulation of desire through hierarchy operates on both the passions and reason. The process I describe here, which I call analogical induction, is one where the affections are both stirred and guided discursively towards a proper orientation.[264] Burke describes the basic function of rhetoric (another of his many formulations of it) as "the use of words by human agents to form attitudes or to induce actions in other human agents."[265] I wish to expand on this function of induction by saying that one mode of courtship can be used to induce attitudes and actions within another, analogous order of courtship. That is, sexual and socio-political motives may be used to stimulate and direct spiritual motives or *vice versa*. To draw a metaphor from physics, in laying two orders of motives side by side in an analogical relation, one may induce a current of desire in the same way that an electrically charged coil can induce an electrical current

---

[263] Fulke Greville, *Certaine Learned and Elegant Workes* (1633), 220, [2H3v].

[264] All rhetorical proof is in a sense analogical, in that it deals with open systems, in contradistinction to logic. What I describe here is a special case of argument by analogy.

[265] *RM*, 41.

in the same direction within another, parallel coil.[266] This process of induction both stimulates and directs the electrical flow.

Burke describes a similar rhetorical situation in terms of the priority of the "idea" where analogically "the principles of one order are transferred to another order."[267] This "idea" provides a transferable mode of thought that allows a similar organization of material. For example:

> Given an economic situation, there are ways of thinking that arise in response to it. But these ways of living and thinking, in complex relationship with both specific and generic motives, can go deep, to the level of *principles*. For a way of living and thinking is reducible to terms of an 'idea'—and that 'idea' will be 'creative' in the sense that anyone who grasps it will embody it or represent it in any mode of action he may choose. The idea, or underlying principle, must be approached by him through the sensory images of his cultural scene. But until he intuitively grasps the principle of such an imaginal clutter, he cannot be profoundly creative, so far as the genius of that 'idea' is concerned.[268]

Indeed, Donne's profound creativity derives from his ability to extract the idea of hierarchical motives from his cultural clutter that includes economic, sexual, legal, and political insignia and apply it to religious motives. He derives imagery from these and related fields to map out his audience's spiritual condition in terms they will readily apprehend and accept. More importantly, he extracts from these common cultural experiences a mode of thought that is appealing to his congregation and then, sometimes tacitly, sometimes directly, invites them to transfer it to their spiritual condition. He thus uses things of apparent advantage (politically, economically, juridically defined) to generate an analogous sense of value in the less palpable mat-

---

[266] This process is called electromotive or electromagnetic induction. The flow of electrical current is induced in the secondary coil when the current of the primary coil is interrupted. It is as if the secondary coil extends the initial current beyond the limitations externally imposed on the primary coil (Lenz's law states that the direction of the induced current opposes the change of flux which generated it). The analogy, if taken too far, breaks down. The current induced in the secondary coil is temporary, whereas Donne's aim is to induce a courtship of God (in the "secondary coil") which continues well beyond the limitations of earthly courtships (the "primary coil"). I owe the lectures of my late High School shop teacher, Mr. Thalheimer, for this reference. I have confirmed my memory with reference to J. T. Davies, et al., *Electricity and Electrons* (Harmondsworth, Eng.: Penguin, 1973), 72–73.

[267] *RM*, 133.

[268] *RM*, 137.

ters of the spirit. Quotidian necessities of temporal life and death, for example, serve as analogies to induce a similar sense of *necessitas* (a common topic of deliberation) in spiritual life and death.

In this way, Donne's sermons function by and large as deliberative discourse, seeking to motivate his audience to seek out a particular end, to make them amorous and ambitious for God. Thomas Wilson's description of the purpose of the deliberative mode is much like that of a sermon: to "persuade or dissuade, entreat or rebuke, exhort or dehort, commend or comfort any man"; and "to advise our neighbor to that thing which we think most needful for him, or else to call him back from that folly which hindereth much his estimation."[269] As Aristotle's modern editor notes,

> The business of deliberation and advice is to present the advocated course of action as likely to promote some desired end, so that it is by investigating the ends of conduct, those things which men actually tend to seek out, that we will discover the sources of deliberative persuasiveness.[270]

Much of Donne's use of forensic imagery (and there is a great deal of it) in fact serves this deliberative function of defining his audience's desired end — that which is deemed advantageous — rather than the proper function of forensic rhetoric, which is to determine the nature of past events.[271] Cicero discusses the topics of honour and advantage in his section on forensic rhetoric, but here too they serve a deliberative function of defining the proper end and use of the law, not of arguing the matter of law.[272] In his sermon on the three witnesses discussed above (5:6), Donne borrows from the law pertaining to testability to impel and direct his audience's desire for spiritual testability, a spiritual status juridically defined. Similarly, in his first extant sermon, which will be the focus of chapter 4 below, Donne uses the strong social censure of prodigality in post-Elizabethan England (a status of disadvantage) to induce a similar repulsion toward spiritual prodigality.

---

[269] Wilson, *Art of Rhetoric*, 70. It should be remembered that Wilson had preachers in mind when he wrote his treatise.

[270] Aristotle, *Art of Rhetoric*, trans. Lawson-Tancred, 86 (an editorial comment).

[271] The topic of advantage was a mainstay of deliberative discourse. See for example Wilson, *Art of Rhetoric*, 70–72. Geoffrey Bullough provides a survey of Donne's use of juridical imagery in the sermons in "Donne the Man of Law," in *Just So Much Honor*, ed. Peter Amadeus Fiore (University Park: Pennsylvania State University Press, 1972), 73–93. Although an excellent survey, Bullough's article does little to account for the rhetorical impact of these juridical references.

[272] Cicero, *De Inventione*, trans. Hubbell, 309 (2.48.141).

Yet Donne's use of the courtship principle works discursively, as well as affectively, in a manner similar to Cicero's argument by legal analogy, where a case is argued according to its similarity to a previously decided case. This is "to proceed by inference from what is written to what is not written."[273] This procedure, of course, is the process of induction (here as defined within the field of dialectic) whereby general principles are derived or confirmed from a multitude of similar cases.[274] Induction, says Aristotle, is commonly used with a popular audience because it argues from premises based on perception and things that are most familiar.[275] Donne similarly proceeds by inference from what is immediately apprehensible (advantage in the order of social courtships) to what is not (advantage in courting God). What I want to emphasize here is that induction involves a transfer of discursive structure, an analogous mode of thinking. Donne borrows from the similitude of worldly affairs an accepted chart of advantage defined according to social hierarchies as a means of structuring his audience's motives in religious devotion.[276]

On this discursive function, Donovan J. Ochs's article on Cicero's *Topica* is useful. Ochs argues that Cicero's topics are "categories, types, or kinds of thinking processes," or discursive structures, rather than simply premises from which arguments may be drawn (as in Aristotle).[277] He demonstrates the element of process implicit in Cicero's notion of the topics with reference to the "relational pattern" of similitude, which he formulates as "if *A* is *like B*, then *C* is *like x*."[278] In this case a relational pattern, a way of thinking about a set of objects, is transferred from one set to another. Moreover, Cicero notes that similitude can have a cumulative effect: "proofs from similarity ... result in credibility by means of many comparisons." Cicero calls this process induction, in contradistinction to other types of similitude, "as when one item is compared to one item, or an equal is compared to an equal."[279] Donne's use of the similitude of

---

[273] Cicero, *De Inventione*, trans. Hubbell, 321 (2.50.152).

[274] See Aristotle's *Topics* 1.8 (108a–108b 33) on the usefulness of similitude in inductive argumentation (*Topics: Books I and VIII*, trans. Robin Smith [Oxford: Clarendon Press, 1997], 18–19).

[275] Aristotle, *Topics* 8.1 (155b 1 – 156a 22), trans. Smith, 20–21.

[276] Bernard Dupriez describes similitude as "a type of parallel which may be used in a process of reasoning" and which is based on qualities held in common: *A Dictionary of Literary Devices*, trans. and adapted by Albert W. Halsall (Toronto: University of Toronto Press, 1991), 418. Under the heading of "Reasoning" Dupriez includes similitude as a device of inductive reasoning (*Dictionary of Literary Devices*, 378–79).

[277] Donovan J. Ochs, "Cicero's *Topica*: A Process View of Invention," in *Explorations in Rhetoric*, ed. Ray E. McKerrow (Glenview, IL: Scott, Foresman & Co., 1982), 107–18, here 109.

[278] Ochs, "Cicero's *Topica*," 111.

[279] cf. Cicero, *Topica* 10.41–43.

courtship functions in this manner: the various species in the field of courtship from which Donne draws all conduce to the same pattern of thought. Ochs goes on to say that Cicero's topics "are suited for oratorical amplification because his notion of relational patterns does not restrict an orator to deal only with premises."[280] In the same way, Donne's similitude of courtship provides a discursive structure that affords many possible variants that can be extended and multiplied throughout the whole *inventio* and *dispositio* of a sermon. The principle of courtship, then, involves two discursive modes: one is the pattern itself, advantage hierarchically defined; the other is similitude, the means of cognitively transferring a principle-pattern from one order of experience to another.

Similitude is generally assumed to belong to *elocutio*; but in Burke's theory, and in Donne's practice, its most important function is on the level of *inventio*. In *The Faithfull Shepherd*, Richard Bernard's first criteria for the use of similitude are brevity and infrequency.[281] William Perkins also requires that allegories ("arguments taken from things that are like") be "quickly dispatcht."[282] One of the distinctive features of Donne's sermons is in direct violation of this principle. Donne's similitudes are striking in that they often pervade an entire sermon, or large portions of it, and form an essential part of its argument and arrangement, unlike the practice of Lancelot Andrewes, for example, whose similes are typically brief and illustrative. Sidney also assumes similitude to be a function of *elocutio*, for the purpose of clarification. In *A Defence of Poetry*, similitude is prescribed "not ... to prove anything to a contrary disputer, but only to explain to a willing hearer, [and] when that is done, the rest is a most tedious prattling, rather over-swaying the memory from the purpose whereto they were applied."[283] Donne is not interested in disputing either, nor even in convincing his audience of truth, but rather in moving them to act upon what they already know or should know to be true. In this Donne is in agreement with William Perkins, who sees the value of similitude in instructing on how to live, rather than in proving points of doctrine.[284] But because Donne in his sermons typically uses similitude to win assent to a prescribed course of action rather than as a means of illustrating and clarifying a point, he extends it further than either Sidney or even Perkins allows.

---

[280] Ochs, "Cicero's *Topica*," 112.

[281] Bernard, *Faithfull Shepherd*, 246, [M5v]. Specifically, Bernard is talking about allegorizing, where "an argument [is] drawn from a similitude, when the words are expounded mystically" (*Faithfull Shepherd*, 244, [M4v]).

[282] Perkins, *Arte of Prophecying*, 97, G6.

[283] Sidney, *Defence of Poetry*, 71.

[284] Perkins, *Arte of Prophecying*, 97, G6. Bernard echoes Perkins in *The Faithfull Shepherd*, 246, [M5v].

Robert Cawdrey ambiguously suggests that similitude can offer pathetic and logical proof. In his preface to *A Treasury or Store-house of Similies* (1600), Cawdrey states his hope that his collection of similes will cause the reader to become "mightily inflamed with an earnest liking, and a loue vnto [virtue]."[285] He further notes that his similes (drawn chiefly from Scripture) carry an ethical appeal to the affections, causing one both to recognize vice and virtue and to detest the former while approving the latter. They also serve *logos*, benefiting the understanding by their "plaine opening of many grounds and principles of Christian Religion."[286] Cawdrey equivocates, however, on the exact place of similes in the invention of proof. He refers to the biblical passages listed under each head as "*proofe*" of that commonplace.[287] He further implies an inductive mode of proof in his assertion that similitude "reasoneth from things confessed," drawing analogies from common experience to enable apprehension of the ineffable mysteries of heaven.[288] Yet he maintains that "*Similitudes are neuer set out to confirme or confute, but to adorne, and to make a matter more plaine.*" His reason seems to be that a simile needs to bear a likeness in only one aspect and therefore can serve only as an approximation, being "*euermore inferiour to the matter at hand.*"[289]

Notwithstanding Cawdrey's equivocation, it is clear that similitude was allowed a place in the office of *inventio*. Similarly, Donne's socio-political similitudes serve not as mere ornament, but as proof by analogy of experience, both pathetic *and* logical. Terry Sherwood resists a trend in modern criticism, as he sees it, "to regard Donne's figurative language as a retreat from reason, as another example of his appeal to emotion."[290] He quotes Donne's own description of the Holy Spirit, in his role as divine author of Scripture, as a "Metaphoricall, and Figurative expresser of himselfe, *to the reason, and understanding of man*" (9:14.560–561, emphasis mine). Sherwood applies this passage to Donne's similitudes, which function ana-

---

[285] Cawdrey, *Treasury*, [A2v], n. p.

[286] Cawdrey, *Treasury*, [A2v], n. p. A "ground" was commonly considered a basis for argument derived by means of the dialectical topics. "Logicke," says Sir John Doddridge, "teacheth a man to collect the Axiomes, principles, grounds and rules observed in that Art which he studieth, and being so collected to dispose the same, which yeeldeth diversity of matter, and ready furniture for disputation" (*The English Lawyer* [1631], 62, [I3v]). Richard Bernard says that in composing sermons the preacher should also show the "ground" of the doctrine by expounding the circumstances of the text and then, "by the Logicall affection of Arguments," demonstrate how the doctrine "may bee seene to arise necessarily" from the text (*Faithfull Shepherd*, 216, [L2v]).

[287] Cawdrey, *Treasury*, [A5v].

[288] Cawdrey, *Treasury*, [A4v].

[289] Cawdrey, *Treasury*, A6.

[290] Terry Sherwood, *Fulfilling the Circle* (Toronto: University of Toronto Press, 1984), 42.

logically, referring to mundane things in order to enable apprehension of their spiritual analogues.[291] Similarly, what I am talking about here is not so much figurative language as figurative thought. Yet *pathos* and *logos* rarely, if ever, work in isolation, and this is especially true in Donne's sermons. The cooperation between these two means of proof is aptly illustrated from very different perspectives by two sources contemporary and familiar to Donne: Francis Bacon, and writing on the art of Christian meditation.

❧ Courtship, similitude, and the relationship between *logos* and *pathos*

Francis Bacon provides a seventeenth-century perspective on the relation between *logos* and *pathos* by way of the human faculties. For Bacon, as for Burke and Donne, the goal of rhetoric is to induce action.[292] As to its function,

> the duty and office of Rhetoric, if it be deeply looked into is no other than to apply and recommend the dictates of reason to imagination, in order to excite the appetite and will .... The end of rhetoric is to fill the imagination with manifestations and likenesses that bring aid to the reason, not oppress it.[293]

Rhetoric excites the appetite and will and brings aid to reason. It is reason (*logos*), *via* the imagination, that excites desire (*pathos*), while at the same time reason (*logos*) is bolstered by means of familiar similitudes produced by the imagination. (For Bacon, imagination is the faculty that composes images from known experience, and did not carry the sense of fantasy that it now does.) Somewhat paradoxically, reason is both cause (applied to) and effect (aided by) in relation to imagination. Notwithstanding Bacon's logical conundrum, the discursive structure of these images of similitude, these "manifestations and likenesses," seems to be basic to Bacon's formula of rhetoric. Imagination provides mental representations (images) of the physical evidence of sense, or the concrete ends of appetite and desire.[294] These images, says Bacon, bear "the print of truth."[295]

---

[291] Sherwood, *Fulfilling the Circle*, 42–43.

[292] See Marc Cogan, "Rhetoric and Action in Francis Bacon," *PR* 14 (1981): 212–33. I am indebted to Cogan for much of my distillation of Bacon's rhetoric.

[293] Quoted from Cogan, "Rhetoric and Action," 214, who emends Spedding's translation of *De Augmentis* somewhat. Cf. Bacon, *Works*, 4:455.

[294] Cogan, "Rhetoric and Action," 215.

[295] Cogan, "Rhetoric and Action," 216.

Bacon observes that rhetoric is necessary because human desire is fired by short-sighted thinking rather than prudent reason:

The affections themselves carry ever an appetite to apparent good, and have this in common with reason; but the difference is that affection beholds principally the good which is present; reason looks beyond and beholds likewise the future and sum of all. And therefore since what manifests itself as present fills the imagination more strongly, reason is commonly vanquished and overcome.[296]

This is where rhetoric comes into play. Rhetoric functions as a bridge between what we *would* (fired by the affections) and what we *should* (guided by the dictates of reason). Bacon continues, "After eloquence and force of persuasion have made things future and remote appear as present, then upon the revolt of imagination to reason, reason prevails." According to Bacon, the images of sense and desire have an immediately perceptible, empirical (and therefore compelling) presence, but images shaped by reason and judgement, being abstract rather than concrete, lack such presence. In a similar way, Donne describes rhetoric's ability to "make absent and remote things present to your understanding" (4:2.900–901).[297] Because it deals with things "absent and remote," the faculty of reason is unable to appeal to the will to incite desire and action. To compensate, says Bacon, the imagination, through the seductive power of rhetoric, appeals to and motivates the will to action. The imagination shapes reasoned images "in such a way that they appear as good to the will, desirable or worth of choice."[298] In the manner that Bacon describes, Donne's images of secular life, similitudes of spiritual relations, are shaped by reason (the apparently reasonable order of the ways of the world) but also aid reason, imputing the same sense of order to spiritual matters; these same reasoned images excite desire in the subject, first regarding objects in the socio-political realm (the world of images), but also in the spiritual world to which these similitudes apply.

More simply stated, the process I describe here is one where the affections are evoked and then guided through a discursive structure from com-

---

[296] Cogan, "Rhetoric and Action," 218. Cf. Bacon, *Works*, 4:457 (Cf. Aristotle, *De Anima* 3.10 [433a 10 – 433b 30]).

[297] Here Donne says that rhetoric is unable to bring an apprehension of eternity, so that he must use the strategy of relating eternity symbolically to their present lives (St. Gregory calls the present life "an eternity"). But this identification of the temporal and spiritual, as I have outlined it here, is precisely a rhetorical strategy.

[298] Cogan, "Rhetoric and Action," 217.

mon experience (hierarchy) toward a proper orientation (God). As in other species of deliberative discourse, this close association between passions and the operations of the mind is fundamental to meditative practices common in the seventeenth century, where the devotional writer sought to instill in the devotee a method of thought that would channel his desire to an appropriate end.[299] Barbara Lewalski describes the "near-identification of sermon and meditation in terms of methods and purposes" in English Protestantism.[300] To better understand the co-operation of *pathos* and *logos* in Donne's sermons, then, we may consider briefly the theory of seventeenth-century meditation.

Augustine Baker illustrates the close relationship between courtship and meditative structures when he describes the process of "internal prayer" (a species of meditation) wherein "*the soule* in a Holy ambition doth *aspire*, to rayse & eleuate her selfe out of inferiour Nature, & to mount to the *Apicem spiritus*, which is Gods throne."[301] Anthony Low takes Donne as an example of the meditative mode which, taking his cue from Baker, he describes as a function of the intellect and imagination. Low quotes from Baker:

Meditation is such an Internall Prayer, in which a Deuout Soule doth in the first place take in hand the consideration of some particular *Mystery of Faith*, to the end that by a serious and exact search into the seuerall points and circumstances in it with the Vnderstanding or Imagination, she may extract Motiues of good Affections to God, and consequently produce suitable Affections in vertue of the said Motiues, as long as such vertue will last.[302]

Although Low, again following Baker, distinguishes meditation from "sensible affection," another devotional mode, it is clear from Baker's definition

---

[299] I speak of meditative practices, plural, based on the rich variety of influences that contributed to Christian meditation in early modern England as outlined collectively by Louis L. Martz, *The Poetry of Meditation* (New Haven: Yale University Press; London: Oxford University Press, 1954); Anthony Low, *Love's Architecture* (New York: New York University Press, 1978); and Barbara Lewalski, *Protestant Poetics* (Princeton: Princeton University Press, 1979). There is no reason to exclude any meditative influence from the resources available to Donne.

[300] As described by Lewalski in chap. 3 of *Donne's Anniversaries and the Poetry of Praise* (Princeton: Princeton University Press, 1973), especially 83–92. Walter R. Davis argues that meditative practice provides a recurring structure in Donne's sermons ("Meditation, Typology, and the Structure of John Donne's Sermons," *The Eagle and the Dove*, eds. Claude J. Summers and Ted-Larry Pebworth [Columbia: University of Missouri Press, 1986], 172–88).

[301] Augustine Baker, *Sancta Sophia* (1657), 250–1; [2H1v]–2H2.

[302] Baker, *Sancta Sophia*, 100–1, [N2v]–N3; quoted by Low, *Love's Architecture*, 36–37.

above that both intellect and affections are central to the process of meditation.[303] The model of analogical induction I have been developing has
many of the same elements described by Baker, except that Donne draws
his audience into a consideration of their circumstances *vis à vis* worldly
courtships (sometimes instead of, but usually in addition to mysteries of
faith) to extract motives of ambition which he then *redirects*, through a similar courtship mode of thought, toward a new object of courtship, thus translating these motives into "good Affections to God."

In this way, Donne's sermons closely adhere to the method and aim of
meditation as described by Robert Southwell in his preface to *Marie
Magdalens Funeral Teares* (1591).[304] Both Donne and Southwell aim to
draw worldly passions heavenward. Referring to contemporary social conditions, Southwell notes that

> as passion, and especially this of loue, is in these daies the chiefe
> commaunder of moste mens actions … so is there nothing nowe
> more needefull to bee intreated, then how to direct these humors
> vnto their due courses, and to draw this floud of affections into the
> righte chanel. Passions I allow, and loues I approue, onely I would
> wishe that men would alter their obiect and better their intent.[305]

In his ensuing meditation on Mary Magdalene, an illustration of this redirection of desire, Southwell sets out to win patrons of love poetry over to a
divine passion for Christ. To Southwell, this is simply a matter of taking
the existing passion and aligning it in the proper direction.

To Joseph Hall, this redirection of the subject's affections from mundane to spiritual matters is part of the discursive function of meditation.
The matter of meditation, says Hall, is either of knowledge or "of affection
for the enkindling of our love of God," but Hall agrees with an undisclosed
authority that "God's school is more of affection than understanding." This
is not to say that there is no intellectual function in meditation. On the contrary, meditation is a process of "bending … the mind upon some spiritual

---

[303] Baker names four main categories of mental prayer, which Low adapts as his four devotional
modes: vocal prayer, meditation, sensible affection, and immediate acts (Low, *Love's Architecture*,
6).

[304] Although Southwell does not explicitly call his discourse a meditation, Vincent Leitch, who introduces the facsimile text, classifies it as an Ignatian meditation: *Marie Magdalens Funeral Teares*
(1591), intro. Vincent B. Leitch (Delmar, NY: Scholars' Facsimiles & Reprints, 1975), n. p.

[305] Southwell, *Funeral Teares*, [A3v].

object, through divers forms of discourse, until our thoughts come to an issue."[306] As his own *Occasional Meditations* make clear, by "spiritual object" Hall means any object or experience which, by similitude, can evoke a spiritual application. This discursive function is evident in Hall's outline of the process of deliberate meditation (as distinguished from extemporal or occasional meditation) which draws its steps from the dialectical topics of *inventio*, and bears some similarity to the *dispositio* of sermons.[307]

The discursive mode of Hall's *Occasional Meditations*, however, more closely parallels Donne's use of the courtship *topos*. In his meditation V, "Upon a Fair Prospect," for example, Hall describes the pleasure afforded by the view: "What a pleasing variety is here of towns, rivers, hills, dales, woods, meadows, each of them striving to set forth other and all of them to delight the eye!"[308] But he immediately goes on to note that of God's earthly creatures, only man (a *reasonable* creature) is capable of apprehending this beauty. From the outset of the meditative process, a discursive faculty is required. Hall proceeds, of course, to recognize that he should then turn his eyes to praise the Creator. This reorientation transforms the very scene, so that Hall concludes, "It is the intermixture and change of these objects [the prospect and the Creator together] that yields this contentment both to the sense and mind."[309] Hall goes on to make a further association, telling his soul that there is "a truer and fuller delight" above in the heavens and that "[a]ll thy other prospects end in this." The heavens, this greater prospect, is a "glorious circumference" which enlightens all that the subject sees on earth (literally and figuratively) and draws the mind upward. Yet Hall's mind reaches higher yet: this firmament is but the bottom of the curtain of the tabernacle which houses God's "incomprehensible light." By metonymic progression, Hall ascends from earth to the heavens to the upper heavens, from an initial earthly delight to an approxi-

---

[306] Huntley, *Bishop Joseph Hall*, 72.

[307] Huntley, *Bishop Joseph Hall*, 88–100. Hall illustrates his method with a meditation on death which proceeds in this order: the entrance [*exordium*]; description [*propositio*]; *divisio*; causes; effects; subjects; adjunct; contrary; comparisons [similitude]; names; testimonies; followed by six non-dialectical steps and concluding with thanksgiving [conclusion] (Huntley, *Bishop Joseph Hall*, 109–118). Conversely, John Brinsley, in his educator's handbook *Ludus Literarius* (1612), says that "The arte of meditation [is] most profitable for inuention." In particular, for supply of matter he recommends, as a supplement to Reusner's *Symbola*, Erasmus's adages, Aphthonius and Lycosthenes, and "that little booke called the Arte of Meditation" (*Ludus Literarius*, 182, 2A4). On the close relation between *inventio* and the meditative process see chap. 4 in Ceri Sullivan, *Dismembered Rhetoric* (Madison: Fairleigh Dickinson University Press, 1995).

[308] Huntley, *Bishop Joseph Hall*, 126.

[309] Huntley, *Bishop Joseph Hall*, 126.

mation of the ineffable delight in God himself. Concomitantly, the meditator sets out a dialectic between Creator and creature, heaven and earth, which infuses mundane occasions with spiritual significance.

♣ The sermon as equipment for living

In both his deliberate meditations, and especially in the occasional meditations, Hall sets out a mode of thought which the devotee can transfer and apply to almost any occasion. Similarly, meditative practice informs the sermons in the same manner as attributed by Helen Gardner to the Holy Sonnets: as a way of thinking.[310] What is important for rhetorical purposes is the way in which meditative modes can be used to structure an audience's thinking about their lives and their world. Donne aims not to win a momentary conviction of truth in the mind of his readers, but rather to infuse patterns of thought, to teach new ways to see the world and themselves in relation to God. Mindful of the memory's importance in perpetuating devout motives, Donne thoroughly relates these patterns of thought to recognizable patterns of experience in their workaday world. Like the meditator who aims to "bend" his thinking to attend to spiritual matters, Donne seeks to incline his audience always to see a correspondence between mundane and spiritual motives. The effect is like that in Sir Thomas Browne who, once he recognizes a pattern of quincunxes in the world, cannot but see them everywhere about him.

As Donne says in one of his sermons, "the best arguments we can prove our Sermons by, is our owne life. The whole weekes conversation, is a good paraphrase upon the Sundayes Sermon" (5:13.677–679). Donne is specifically talking about the preacher's life as an *exemplum*, but the same principle applies to his congregation. His intention is that the whole week be an extension of the pattern set down in the Sunday sermon, that his and his congregation's weekly lives be proof of Sunday's *propositio*. The preparative function of the sermon's rhetoric is perhaps best expressed by Augustine, as adapted by Burke. For Donne, as for Augustine, the task of the rhetor is to induce action — *ad agendum* in Augustine's phrase.[311] With the purpose of broadening the province of rhetoric to include poetry, Burke notes the shift from Aristotle's *movere* (to move) to Augustine's *flectere* (to bend) as a change in emphasis from action to attitude. Rhetoric, like meditation, now works

---

310 Donne, *The Divine Poems*, ed. Helen Gardner (Oxford: Oxford University Press, 1952), liv.

311 *RM*, 50 (taken from Augustine, *De Doctrina Christiana* 4.12.27).

upon the mind and affection as a preparative to action, "attitude being an incipient act, a leaning or inclination."[312] This is consonant with Donne's continual reminding of his congregation that the sermon is a preparation, a bending of their attitudes toward the act of the communion sacrament. It is also a preparation for their re-emergence into the world beyond the church doors — "equipment for living," as Burke would put it.[313] Donne, probably better than any other preacher of his time, knew the difficulty of escaping the motives that operate from Monday to Saturday. Nor does he ask his congregation to do so. Rather, he equips them with a mode of thinking and feeling that will sanctify and reorient their worldly involvements, and will draw them from the immediate concerns of the world around them upward to the realm of ultimate concerns. It is to this purifying effect that I turn in the next chapter.

❧ An after-word on *ethos* and identification

So far I have emphasized the operations of *pathos* and *logos* in Donne's rhetoric of courtship, but *ethos* is also at work to a significant degree. Although Donne as a divine and scholar was no Lancelot Andrewes, his handling of patristic and contemporary authorities, and especially of Scripture, is admirable. But Donne commands a unique authority in his adeptness at dealing with the secular world of his congregation's everyday lives. His handling of economics is a case in point. Coburn Freer convincingly demonstrates that Donne's poetry evinces an understanding of contemporary economic theory that is uncommon among poets.[314] Oddly, Freer suggests that economic metaphors seldom appear in Donne's later poetry and the sermons. On the contrary, economic metaphors abound in the sermons, and Donne's facility in manipulating economic motives for spiritual ends is, as we have seen, impressive. His facility with the law is equally evident. And to those who knew his reputation as a poet, he would have carried some authority on matters of sexual courtship as well. But Donne commands respect not only for his understanding of the marketplace and court,

---

[312] *RM*, 50.

[313] *PLF*, 293–304. Under this rubric Burke talks about literature as strategies for sizing up and responding to situations in life.

[314] Freer specifically cites Donne's sophisticated references to various theories regarding the debasement of currency (and its causes) during the Tudor and Stuart periods: "John Donne and Elizabethan Economic Theory," *Criticism* 38 (1996): 497–520, here 498–501, as well as to credit, debt and borrowing (501–505).

but especially for his ability (the ability of a good casuist) to accommodate this world to the greater demands of the spirit.[315] In this study of Donne as preacher, my concern is with the way Donne induces his audience to court God, rather than in his strategies for courting identity with his audience. But as Burke points out, identification with the audience one wishes to persuade is an essential part of any rhetorical appeal. Donne meets his congregation on common ground, and he identifies with those motives so that they might meet with God on hallowed ground.

---

[315] Donne's ability as casuist is demonstrated in his own work in *Biathanatos* and on the Oath of Supremacy in *Pseudo-Martyr*. John Donne, *Pseudo-Martyr*, ed. Anthony Raspa (Montreal and Kingston: McGill-Queen's University Press, 1993), xi–lxxxix (esp. xiii–liv). See also Camille Wells Slights's chap. 4 in *The Casuistical Tradition* (Princeton: Princeton University Press, 1981) on casuistry in both the prose and the poems.

CHAPTER THREE

Courtship and the Dispositio of Form

*For every thing is made, and governed to an end, and Art is
the rule of the making and governing of things to their end.*
— Alexander Richardson[316]

COURTSHIP PROVIDES DONNE WITH A RICH STRUCTURE for both
inventio and *dispositio*. We have seen that Donne frequently visits courtship
structures for finding and developing the matter of his sermon. Courtship
is also frequently an informing principle in his arrangement of his matter,
either in the actual disposing of the elements of his sermon, or in his ordering of his audience's values and thoughts regarding the issue at hand.[317]
With respect to matters of courtship, these two offices of rhetoric are not
easily distinguished, since courtship is itself a *topos* that is characterized by
a particular principle of arrangement: hierarchy. Furthermore, this *topos*
achieves its effect largely at the level of *dispositio* — not only in Donne's
arrangement of his sermon's material, but also in his *elocutio* and in the discursive and emotive patterns his material evokes. Donne uses these same
structures to arrange his sermonic matter, both conceptually and materially,
so as to lead his congregation to a right orientation toward their proper
object of desire.

---

[316] Richardson, *The Logicians School-Master*. 2nd. ed. (London, 1657), 25, C5.

[317] In his article on the dynamic function of Cicero's topics, Donovan Ochs argues that "since the relationship is the key component, Cicero's *loci* are capable of providing the architectural structure for
the entire *confirmatio* or *refutatio* as parts of an oration" ("Cicero's *Topica*," 112). The relational
nature of the courtship *topos* makes it equally important to both the larger and smaller units of a
sermon's structure.

The more common contemporary term for *dispositio* is form. M. H. Abrams's definition of form illustrates the close relationship between *inventio*, the central generating principle, and *dispositio*, the arrangement of material according to that idea: "The 'form' of a work, in [the] central sense, is its essential organizing principle."[318] In this sense, form belongs to both *inventio* and *dispositio*. This aspect of form, which I will distinguish as "conceptual arrangement," is similarly described by Holman and Harmon as "the organization or structure of thought in the work."[319] More in keeping with traditional notions of *dispositio* is their first definition of form: "the organization of the elementary parts of a work of art in relation to its total effect." This I will distinguish as "material arrangement," which is concerned with what-follows-what in a given sermon (in our case), and to what end.

I will begin by relating some of the material I have discussed in connection with Donne's *inventio* to this first aspect of "conceptual arrangement." I will then discuss material arrangement with respect to the formal operation of courtship in Donne's sermons, with reference to Burke's relevant ideas on form. Finally, I will conclude by drawing in another Burkeian notion, "temporizing of essence," which, I will argue, is essential to the suasive function of courtship and, therefore, of Donne's sermons as well.

❧ Purification and cure: the conceptual end of Donne's sermons

It is perhaps appropriate to begin this discussion of *dispositio* with reference to the sermon's desired end, the place to which Donne ostensibly wishes to bring his audience. As one critic paraphrases Burke, "[i]f you find the end toward which a work moves, you should then know the logic of its progression."[320] Donne frequently expresses his objective for his congregation in terms of purification and cure. Donne's *peroratio* typically brings the congregation into consideration of Christ or his sacraments. Sixteen of his sermons, for example, end with reference to "the inestimable price of his incorruptible blood." Significant of Christ's work of redemption and of Donne's conception of the sacraments are images of purification and heal-

---

[318] M. H. Abrams, *A Glossary of Literary Terms*, 3rd ed. (New York: Holt, Rinehart and Winston, 1971), 64–65.

[319] William Harmon and C. Hugh Holman, *A Handbook to Literature*, 8th ed. (Upper Saddle River, NJ: Prentice Hall, 2000), 221.

[320] George Knox, *Critical Moments* (Seattle: University of Washington Press, 1957), 46. Knox is generalizing Burke's comments made in relation to a poem by Marianne Moore (*GM*, 490).

ing. Christ's blood is the "physick" or "soveraigne balme of our soules" (6:17.475–476), and a "tide" which washes away our sin in baptism (8:15.459–464).[321]

Donne frequently conceives of sermonic activity as medicine. In the Renaissance there was both a metaphorical and a literal connection between rhetoric and medical practice. The medicinal quality of eloquence was commonplace: Apollo, whose symbols were the lyre and the bow, is god both of poetry and of healing.[322] In one of his *Amorum Emblemata* (1608), Otto van Veen includes a picture of a Cupid-like cherub presenting a caduceus to a love-wounded man.[323] The picture is accompanied by a verse entitled "Loue is the author of eloquence," which reads:

> Loue doth the louers toung to eloquence dispose,
> With sweet conceats of loue his ladies eares to please,
> And thereby moue her harte his restlesse care to ease,
> For loues inuentions oft great science do disclose.[324]

Relief of a love-agitated heart is conceived of as a science of cure. Renaissance love poets commonly employed physical affliction as a metaphor for estrangement from the beloved, for which sexual union was posited as a cure. Paradoxically, in love poetry, affliction from the beloved was a means of asserting union (however perverse) with the beloved; similarly, in Christian thinking of the period, and saliently in Donne's sermons, to feel God's affliction was to be assured of his care and concern.[325]

---

[321] Christ's blood, by metonymic relation to the "stripes" received before his crucifixion, is attributed healing properties in Isaiah 53:5, a passage which has traditionally been taken to be a prefiguring of Christ's crucifixion. The cleansing power of Christ's blood is expressed in 1 John 1:7. See also Ephesians 5:26 on the cleansing power of the Word. On the blood of Christ as medicine see Augustine, *Sermo* 284.6.

[322] Raymond A. Anselment traces the historic development of this association in *The Realms of Apollo* (Newark, DE: University of Delaware Press, 1995), 23–24, 42–48.

[323] The caduceus is the symbol for medicine used by various health organizations. It consists of a pole (the term is derived from a staff carried by Mercury) with entwined serpents upon it. In Numbers 21:8–9 Moses, following God's instructions, lifts a bronze serpent upon a pole above his people to heal them from a plague of snake-bites; the Gospel of John makes a typological comparison between this event and Christ being lifted up on the cross (John 3:14–15).

[324] Otto van Veen, *Amorum Emblemata* (Antwerp: 1608), 80, [K4v].

[325] See *Astrophil and Stella*, nos. 6, 20, 34, 48 for examples from love poetry. A similar strategy is at work in Donne's Holy Sonnet, "Batter my heart." In the realm of religion, John Downame refers to temporal affliction as "rather signes of Gods loue than of his hatred; and markes rather of our election and adoption, than of reprobation and eternall damnation." Among the biblical passages he cites for support is Hebrews 12:6: "whom the Lord loueth he chasteneth: and scourgeth euery son that he receiueth" (*The Christian Warfare* [1604], 157, L7). Donne also frequently expresses this sense of physical affliction as spiritual benefits and "Medicinall assistances" (9:13.635–639)

Illustrative of the close relationship between rhetoric and medicine is the title page of Gabriel Harvey's *Ciceronianus* (1577), which depicts the serpent held up by Moses in the wilderness, implying a divinely ordained power of healing inherent in rhetoric rightly applied. Furthermore, in an age that was still dominated by humour theory, rhetoric, which had as its purpose the stimulation and proper direction of the passions, could literally determine the physical health of an audience.[326] Thomas Wright, in *The Passions of the Minde*, states that "[a]s this Treatise affordeth great riches to the Physitian of the soule, so it importeth much the Physitian of the body, for that there is no Passion very vehement, but that it alters extreamly some of the foure humors of the body."[327] Health of the body quite literally required health of the soul. It is appropriate, then, that Richard Hooker, who describes sermons as "spurres to the good affections of man," should also characterize them as "phisicke unto diseased mindes."[328] The goal of preaching, and the end of a sermon's *dispositio*, were the health of the whole person, body and soul.

Donne expresses a similar view of the preacher's curative end. In a sermon preached at St. Paul's, he bases this characterization of the preacher's activity on various Hebrew and Latin equivalents for *Obsecramus*, the Latin equivalent of the Greek word δεόμεθα (which he does not supply) which is translated "we pray you" in 2 Corinthians 5:20, his text for this sermon: "We pray yee in Christs stead, be ye reconciled to God." From one Hebrew equivalent, *Napal* (or *Naphal*), Donne derives two Latin translations, *Ruere* and *Postrare* (a mistake for *Prosternere*), meaning "to throw down, to deject our selves, to admit any undervalue, any exinanition, any evacuation of our selves, so we may advance this great work" (10:5.149–151). The connection Donne then makes to medicine seems somewhat tenuous, notwithstanding his pun on "evacuation." He continues, "as Physicians must consider excrements, so we must consider sin, the leprosie, the pestilence,

---

and as occasions for "physick," which signify God's love and concern (7:1.710–714). On sickness as an occasion for grace see Troy Dale Reeves, *"Sana Me Domine*: Bodily Sickness as a Means of Grace in Donne's Sermons and Devotions," *ABR* 33 (1982): 270–75.

[326] Robert Burton cites Plato — "all the mischiefs of the body proceed from the soul" (*Charmides*, 156E–157B) — and other authorities on this idea (*Anatomy of Melancholy*, 1.250–53). Raymond Anselment, in discussing images of Apollo in seventeenth-century literature, notes the close relationship attributed between spiritual causes, physical ailments, and their cure, in both poetry and pastoral ministry (*Realms of Apollo*, 27–30, 42–48).

[327] Wright, *Passions of the Minde*, 4, [B2v]; see also 16–7, [B8v]–C1.

[328] cf. above, chap. 1, n. 190 and n. 196. Anselment also describes the close connection between pastoral ministry and medical practice (*Realms of Apollo*, 27–30). This imagery pattern is established in Luke 4:18 and throughout Jesus's ministry where his healing of bodies was routinely associated with his healing of the soul.

the ordure of the soule" (160–161). Donne's change of emphasis from the dejection of the preacher to the effect on the congregant is made complete as Donne adds an economic metaphor to describe the sermon's effect of "mak[ing] you see your poverty and indigence" (162–163).

Donne's second Hebrew equivalent, *Calah* (or *Chalah*), further signifies both "*Dolere*, to grieve within our selves, for the affliction of another" and "*vulnerare*, to wound, and afflict another" (166–168). And so, says Donne, "we [preachers] wound your consciences, with a sense of your sins" (171). This paradoxical activity is further expressed by two more Latin equivalents: "*Cruciare*, to vex, and ... *Placare* too, to appease, to restore to rest and quiet" (174–175). This single Greek-Latin term is thus made to imply a process that includes both affliction and cure. Donne then makes a direct application to the activity of the sermon:

> And therefore, if from our words proceed any vexation to your consciences, you must not say, *Transeat calix, let that Cup passe* [Matthew 26:39], no more of that matter, for it is the *physick* that must first *stirre* the humour, before it can *purge* it; And if our words apply to your consciences, the soverain balm of the merits of your Saviour, and that thereupon your troubled consciences finde some rest, be not too soon secure, but proceed in your good beginnings (178–185).

This passage is particularly significant here, first because it illustrates a method of *inventio* (discussed in the introduction), that of Donne's polyglot amplification of a biblical text.[329] Second, this double activity of afflicting and healing is an instance of a common pattern in Donne's sermons (to which I will turn shortly) and one which Donne often "finds" in Scripture. But here I want to emphasize that for Donne, a sermon is a ritual of cure which both pollutes the subjects by reminding them of their corruption in sin (hence their estrangement from God) and purifies them by confirming their identification (union) with Christ.

More important perhaps than the medical imagery Donne uses to characterize his sermon's activity is the great deliberative potential he finds in the promise of health. His use of medicinal and curative references should be seen as elemental to the broader *topos* of courtship. At the most

---

[329] Donne amplifies the Greek word with various Hebrew and Latin connotations that, in the Holy Spirit's wisdom, were foreseen in this single Greek word: "Scarce any where hath the Holy Ghost taken a word of larger signification, then here" (10:5.140–141).

basic level, health is a good to which all people aspire.[330] But more specifically, like all "courtships" (in the broadest sense, as I have been using it), it envisions a desired end which is achieved through a process of improvement.

With respect to transcendent courtship, a ritual of cure is necessary for establishing a means of connecting with the divine. Donne of course makes the traditional association between sin and sickness, but he also finds in the quest for health a process that has a compelling object of desire.[331] He warns his congregation at Lincoln's Inn not to cover their desire for forgiveness under a spirit of dejection so that they fail to see that their sins "ly upon Christs shoulders," nor to obfuscate true contrition by rushing into facile confession of sin (2:6.540). "We must hide neither," says Donne, "but anatomize our soule in both, and find every sinnewe, and fiber, every lineament and ligament of this body of sinne, and then every breath of that newe spirit, every drop of that newe blood that must restore and repayre us" (548–52). Sickness requires a diligent searching out of the cause in order to find the diseased element and effect a cure. This new form of desire-quest would have been familiar to much of Donne's audience at the Inns of Court. As a finishing school for young gentlemen, Lincoln's Inn would have included a number of students who had visited anatomy theatres on the continent during their Grand Tour.[332] That anatomy was conceived of as a quest is evident in its common association during this period with geographical exploration.[333]

---

[330] Physical well-being is an element in Aristotle's notion of happiness and the good things that attend it; one could easily conceive of purity in this list as well (*Art of Rhetoric*, trans. Lawson-Tancred, 87, 89–90 [1.5, 1360b 14 – 24, 1361b 3–34]).

[331] For a survey of this field of imagery see Schleiner, *Imagery*, 68–85. Schleiner notes that Donne is working within a long-standing tradition of representing sin as sickness that extends at least as far back as St. Augustine. By the time Donne inherited it, this field of imagery had become very well developed. Further, Schleiner insists that Donne's use of medical imagery does not necessarily indicate a particular intellectual interest, but rather (and here I am extending his argument somewhat) a rhetorical interest (*Imagery*, 81).

[332] This would especially be true of Donne's audience at court. On the audiences (including English travellers) who attended anatomy theatres and on the fashion for anatomy in this period see Jonathan Sawday's *The Body Emblazoned* (London: Routledge, 1995), 42–43. Prest describes the class-composition of the Inns in *The Inns of Court*, 21–32.

[333] See Donne's treatment of the human body as microcosm in *Devotions*, meditation 4, and as a site of geographical exploration in "Love's Progress." Donne is also the chief figure in Sawday's discussion of the association between geographical and anatomical exploration, which also includes anatomist Andreas Vesalius, scientist Joseph Glanvill, and poet Abraham Cowley (*The Body Emblazoned*, 25–8). See also Michael Neill, *Issues of Death: Mortality and Identity in English Renaissance Tragedy* (Oxford: Clarendon Press, 1997), 125–30.

❧ The conceptual arrangement of courtship: dialectical inclusion

The preacher's purpose in "stirring up humours" is to transform mundane affections and motives into heavenly ones, as is frequently expressed by Donne's grammatical sanctification of dubious nouns by modifying them with the adjective "holy". Thus he leads his congregation to a "holy ambition" (5:14.280), a "holy amorousnesse" (7:10.368–369), a "holy industry" (7:17.325). Elsewhere Donne stimulates the "Amorous soule, ambitious soule, covetous soule, voluptuous soule" in its " holy amorousnesse," "holy covetousnesse" and "holy ambition" for the eternal (7:15.723–727).[334] And he tells his congregation at court that he wants to imprint on them a "holy noblenesse" and a "religious ambition" (9:2.823). He assures another that

> If thou have truly given thy selfe to him in the Sacrament, God
> hath given thee thy selfe back, so much mended, as that thou hast
> received thy self and him too; Thy selfe, in a holy liberty, to walk
> in the world in a calling, and himself, in giving a blessing upon all
> the works of thy calling, and imprinting in thee a holy desire to do
> all those works to his glory (7:11.147–152).

This sanctifying of "liberty" and "desire" comes from a reorientation effected by a thoughtful participation in the sacraments, such that one's worldly calling is given new direction and purpose in bringing glory to God. Worldly ambition is, in a similar way, transformed into holy ambition.

Thus one of Donne's simplest methods of transforming carnal desire is to use "perspective by incongruity" (Burke's term) to transform social terms so that they signify within a higher moral order: hence a purification strategy which Burke calls "terministic purification." One can, for example, provide a "moral revaluation or perspective by putting the wrong words together." In rhetorical terms, we might rather call this perspective by indecorum. Burke cites as an example Nietzsche who continually undermined common notions, "carefully qualifying his nouns by the juxtaposition of modifying matter that had the 'wrong' moral inclination." An example from Donne is "holy ambition" (and the numerous similar noun phrases noted above) where "holy" is literally an indecorous modifier for

---

[334] In other instances, Donne speaks of an ambition for more and more grace (7:9.116), "a spiritual covetousness" (I.5.15), "a holy ambition, a sacred covetousnesse, and a wholsome Dropsie" (5:14.280–1).

"ambition."[335] This juxtaposition of terms transforms our notions of both holiness and ambition: ambition is purified in its reorientation to an higher order (holiness) where God is the ultimate term; holiness, at the same time, is given an athletic, dynamic quality that draws on the energy of mundane motives. In this way, Donne's discordant conjunction becomes a bridging term, extending the divine down to the human and drawing the human toward the divine. It is not difficult to see, then, how notions of courtship and hierarchy can function as the rhetorical basis of even a simple noun phrase. I might add that this is just as Walton describes Donne: as one who deployed a "*sacred* Art and Courtship" to persuade his audience (emphasis mine).[336]

The purpose of these apparently indecorous modifications, then, is to impose a new principle of decorum, a new orientation to the terms. To recapitulate somewhat, this rhetorical reorientation is conceived, by both Donne and Burke, as a purification (cure) through hierarchy. Conditions of estrangement invariably carry connotations of pollution, so that to mount within a hierarchy is to engage in a process of purification in relation to the object of desire. Donne brings purification and health to his congregation by conceptually reordering their motives as he draws them into a courtship of God. The objective of courtship, then, is an ever-increasing state of perfection within a given order. In *The Book of the Courtier*, for example, Burke finds "a series of formal operations for the dialectical purifying of a rhetorical motive." He notes that "[b]y its gradations, it builds a ladder of courtship dialectically, into a grand design that, in its ultimate stage, would transcend the social mystery, ending Platonically on a mystic, mythic vision of celestial mystery."[337] Sociopolitical courtships are thereby subsumed by a courtship of the divine. The important feature of this dialectic for our purposes is that it works at inclusion of the profane within the holy.

In a similar manner, Donne is able to purify social ambitions by giving them an anagogic significance. Rather than excluding various elements of human experience, Donne purifies them by including them within a hierarchy that has its end in God. Far from the self-persuasion of "positive

---

[335] *PC*, 91. Notwithstanding Anthony Esler's contention that ambition lost much of its moral disapprobation among the younger generation of Elizabethan courtiers in the 1570s and 1580s, Donne, in the early seventeenth century, still assumed that ambition carried dyslogistic connotations that needed purification: *The Aspiring Mind of the Elizabethan Younger Generation* (Durham, NC: Duke University Press, 1966), 51–86. Louis Montrose suggests that Esler overstates the case: "Gifts and Reasons," 460, n.10.

[336] Walton, *Life*, 49.

[337] *RM*, 221.

thinking," Donne would see his audience fundamentally changed by the sermon's symbolic act of conceptualizing this re-orientation.[338] The degree to which this identification between worldly and spiritual motives is either truly suasive (i.e. life-changing) or merely sophistic (self-justifying) is determined by the degree to which the congregant internalizes or "digests" it, to borrow a seventeenth-century metaphor. Donne frequently uses this metaphor to emphasize his congregant's need to incorporate and assimilate mundane motives into a higher order, characterizing the reception of spiritual benefit as either good digestion or its implicit effect, a good bowel movement (a sign of good health).[339] As George Herbert suggests, this model of dialectical inclusion (as I am calling the process outlined above) leads to good health. Donne also makes an explicit connection between desire and physical well-being, characterizing impure motives as indigestion. Proper prayer requires "rumination, a chawing of the cud," by which Donne means a second examination of one's motives (6:1.474–475). Conversely, improperly motivated prayer (prayer which is not aimed at our good *and* God's glory) derives from "indigested apprehensions" (476–477).

In a sermon at Whitehall based on Proverbs 25:16 — *"Hast thou found honey? Eat so much as is sufficient for thee, lest thou be filled therewith, and vomit it"* — Donne takes honey to signify temporal ambition. He notes that the limits and capacities of the body's internal organs are known,

> But this infinite Hive of honey, this insatiable whirlpoole of the covetous mind, no Anatomy, no dissection hath discovered to us. When I looke into the larders, and cellars, and vaults, into the vessels of our body for drink, for blood, for urine, they are pottles, and gallons; when I looke into the furnaces of our spirits, the ventricles of the

---

338 Dale A. Bertelsen describes Burke's view of reality as a dialectic between biological and cultural determinants. This dialectic gives rise to rhetorical opportunities for transforming reality by instilling new orientations which bring new perceptions of reality: "Transformation, then, is the process Burke relies on to explain the ineffable movement between subjective perception and social context, from biological to symbolic and *vice versa*: the redefinition or recontextualization of individuated perception in a socially recognizable form, or the influence of that form on human perception: "Kenneth Burke's Conception of Reality: The Process of Transformation and Its Implications for Rhetorical Criticism," in *Extensions of the Burkeian System*, ed. James W. Chesebro (Tuscaloosa, AL: University of Alabama Press, 1993): 230–247, here 235.

339 The preacher's aim, says Donne, is "that you may always suck pure milk from us, and then not cast it up, but digest it, to your spirituall growth" (6:3.391–392). Donne characterizes good rhetoric as digestive medicine. He notes that *exempla* are useful when "a Rule would be of hard digestion to weake understandings" (9:12.3–4). The *exemplum* is as a laxative which "concocts it [the rule], and makes it easie" (4). He goes on to elaborate: "Example in matter of Doctrine, is an Assimilation in matter of Nourishment; The Example makes that that is proposed for our learning and farther instruction, like something which we knew before, as Assimilation makes that meat, which we have received, and digested, like those parts, which are in our bodies before" (5–9).

heart and of the braine, they are not thimbles; for spirituall things, the things of the next world, we have no roome; for temporall things, the things of this world, we have no bounds (3:10.391–399).

Donne goes on to say that this anatomy is characteristic of men who prefer Old Testament religion, which offers immediate, temporal blessing, over New Testament religion, which involves a labour in this world for payment that is reserved for the next (418–419). The vomiting man, the man of excessive temporal ambition, is characterized as one who "could see nothing but worldly things, things nearest to him." Formerly this man at least "saw some glimmering, some colour of comfort" in temporal blessings; now, having lost all benefit of these attainments (having vomited them without digesting them to receive their spiritual benefit), he now "sees no comfort at all" (467–470). Donne handles this theme extensively and brilliantly, concluding with an exhortation to "make this Honey (Christs true Religion) thy meate; digest that, assimilate that, incorporate that" so that his congregation might extend worldly courtships to a higher one: "desire better gifts; and ever think it a title of dignity which the Angel gave *Daniel*, to be *Vir desideriorum*; To have still some farther object of thy desires" (518–520, 536–539, referring to Daniel 9:23, 10:11, 19 [Vulgate]).

In taking his congregation into the digestive tracts of their motives, Donne repels them from the pollution of worldliness with the repulsiveness of indigestion. In Jonathan Sawday's Bakhtinian reading of this sermon, the interior of the body which Donne so laboriously describes is the "grotesque" body associated with the lower, marginal class, as distinct from the "classical," outer body, which is associated with high official culture.[340] Sawday concludes that for Donne, "writing on the brink of scientific transformation of the body," "[i]t is as if the encounter with the body's interior has suddenly revealed a vista of an alternative (and dangerous) mode of existence in which the marginal, the low, the anti-rationalistic, reigns supreme."[341] But Sawday attributes to Donne no sense of audience. More significant than Donne's vague position *vis à vis* scientific change is the formal operation of purification he produces in this sermon. In insinuating his courtly congregation's guilt in association with the hierarchically low, he engenders in them a desire to reclaim their proper status within the body

---

[340] Sawday observes: "In Donne's anatomical journey, we do not encounter staterooms, halls, or a privileged public space. Instead, we wander through service chambers, and gaze into barely understood industrial processes" (*The Body Emblazoned*, 19).

[341] Sawday, *The Body Emblazoned*, 19–20.

politic. This status is characterized as health. A good digestion (as opposed to vomiting) involves expelling these polluting elements from the body's interior (here configured as the excess of worldly motives) and incorporating the beneficial nutrients (worldly pursuits brought into the higher, spiritual order oriented toward a higher object of desire).

In a very long *exordium* to a similar sermon, again preached at Whitehall (the first in a two-part series), Donne introduces Solomon's warning in Ecclesiastes 5:13–14 against the dangers of riches. He characterizes the problem identified by Solomon as a "sickness" and Solomon's method as "anatomy" and then "cure". Donne begins by framing these themes in terms of the relationship between temporal and eternal desires:

> But because there is no third object for mans love, this world, and
> the next, are all that he can consider, as he hath but two eyes, so
> he hath but two objects, and then *Primus actus voluntatis est Amor*,
> Mans love is never idle, it is ever directed upon somthing, if our
> love might be drawn from this world, *Solomon* thought it a direct
> way to convay it upon the next (3:1.29–34).

From this he expounds Solomon's method of dealing with this world: "he dissects it, and cuts it up before thee, that so thou mayest the better see, how poor a thing, that particular is" (42–43). The problem revealed by this anatomy is that of an improper relationship, not between the humours, but between temporal and eternal desire.

The *exordium* of this sermon is the closest Donne comes to *contemptus mundi*; he could hardly avoid it given Solomon's famous *vanitas vantitatum*, which Donne discusses here at length to conclude that "[m]an therefore can have no deeper discouragement, from enclining to the things of this world, then to be taught that they are nothing" (115–117). Yet from "*Solomons* Anatomy," Donne proceeds in the *divisio* and *confirmatio* of the sermon to address the cure of this worldly malaise of misdirected motives (155–156). In the *divisio* he introduces an important qualification: that "though Riches be not *in themselves* ill, yet we are to be abstinent from an over-studious heaping of them, because naturally they are mingled with that danger, that they may be for the owners evil" (161–164, emphasis mine). This mingling of unwholesomeness, this "sickness" as Donne describes it, is a problem that he addresses with assimilative imagery (165). In his first partition, Donne prescribes a reorientation of humility and reverent fear toward God: a subordination of "riches" to spiritual objectives. And then he adds, "If we were able to digest, and concoct these temporal things into good nourishment, Gods natural way is, and would be, to convay to us the testimony of his spiritual graces in outward and temporal benefits" (189–192). What was mingled with danger becomes assimilated into nourishment when motives are brought into proper alignment.[342]

As Donne turns toward application of the sermon, he concludes that the healthiness of riches is determined in their use: "But God holds that ladder there, whose foot stands upon the earth here, and all those good works, which are put upon the lowest step of that Ladder here, that is, that are done in contemplation of him, they ascend to him, and descend again to us (421–425)."[343] Brought to proper use, riches are a means of ascent to God. Implicit in Donne's metaphor is a patronage system to which his congregation could easily relate, where service properly directed may result in benefits bestowed from above. In the moral application of this image, all ambitions of accumulation are set right when brought into a proper courtship.

๙ Dialectical inclusion as equipment for living

One strategic advantage of extending heavenly aims downward to include the mundane is that while mundane motives receive the benefit of purification by their inclusion in a higher order of motives, the transcendent borrows from the mundane an immediate sense of *necessitas*. In his version of the debate between the active life and the contemplative life, Donne sees the active life as potentially polluting, yet necessary.[344] In his verse epistle to Henry Wotton, "Sir, more than kisses, letters mingle Soules," Donne writes,

> Life is a voyage, and in our lifes wayes
> Countries, Courts, Towns are Rockes, or Remoraes;
> They breake or stop all ships, yet our state's such,
> That though then pitch they staine worse, wee must touch
> (7–10).

---

[342] Later, Donne explores a possible literal interpretation of his text, that this inordinate love of riches actually results in "a disordering, a discomposing, a distemper of the mind" (294–295). In this case physical sickness, if rightly considered, can become a blessing: if it motivates us to bring our desires back into proper order, the soul might thereby become physician to the body (302–303).

[343] See chap. 2, n. 220.

[344] In Donne's *Satyres*, for example, the speaker begins in a state of being dead to the world in the seclusion of his study, while the public figures in this and the other satyres are characterized with reference to pollution and filth, as is the speaker's own lapse in attending court ("Satyre IV"). The *Satyres* end with the speaker (identifiable as Donne) taking up a public position as secretary to Lord Keeper Sir Thomas Egerton, whose responsibilities included purifying the legal system of corruption. On this commonplace of the active vs. contemplative and on Donne's deployment of deliberative strategies in addressing the issue, see Allen Barry Cameron, "Donne's Deliberative Verse Epistles," *ELR* 6 (1976): 373–381.

Even though these places of worldly business stain worse than pitch, one must be involved in them. Both in his verse epistle to Wotton and in his *Satyres*, Donne expresses his uneasiness at the imperative of public service, which must be pursued in often-corrupt circles of power and influence. But neither is the indolence of country life a real option, so Donne offers this prescription:

> Onely'in this one thing, be no Galenist. To make
> Courts hot ambitions wholesome, do not take
> A dramme of Countries dulnesse; do not adde
> Correctives, but as chymiques, purge the bad (59–62).

That is, Donne's prescribed course is the Paracelsian practice of purging the bad humour rather than the Galenic method of applying correctives to balance the humours.[345] Donne concludes by declaring that in offering this counsel he is only putting into principle the example of Wotton himself, who, having returned from his travels in Europe, has been able to extract the best of the faith of the German, French, and Italian churches, "Having from these suck'd all they had of worth, / And brought home that faith, which you carried forth" (67–68). The issue of earthly ambition is recast in terms of religious faith. It seems the solution is to filter (purge) one's experience in the world through a process of dialectically engaging one's faith with experience in the public arena. The courtier can survive the ambitions of court as long as, like the snail, he carries his home (faith) with him with perseverance (49–50).[346] This poem, probably written before 1600, foreshadows the sort of religious *consolatio* Donne would more fully develop as a preacher.[347] Donne understands that his congregation must exit the church doors to re-enter the world of business and that in doing so they need equipment for engaging that world.

In his sermon preached before Queen Anne, Donne finds that in the book of Proverbs Christ is identified with Wisdom who (similar to Mistress Truth who stands on a hill in Donne's third Satyre) "offers himselfe to be found in the tops of high places, and in the gates of Cities" (1:5.401–402).

---

[345] Again, Donne uses these two medical schools of thought for rhetorical purposes; this should not be taken as a statement of Donne's intellectual adherence to one or the other.

[346] This is similar to the compasses imagery in "A Valediction forbidding mourning" where the fixed foot keeps the wandering foot in proper orientation.

[347] On the date of this poem see Bald, *John Donne*, 100, n. 1.

This indicates to Donne that Christ is to be found in all professions: not only in the cloister, but in such high places of worldly activity as the courts of princes and of judges (403–410). One's profession, then, becomes a courtship not only of power, but of Christ, for "when all our actions in our severall courses are directed principally upon his glory, Christ is eminent, and may easily be found," even in these places of power (399–400). The catch, of course, is that the courtier must act wisely — that is, must court wisdom.

Brought into an order which is presided over by God, man's worldly passions and pursuits are justified in the theological sense. This strategy is illustrated in a sermon preached at Lincoln's Inn where Donne revisits his *dignitas topos*. Preaching from Psalm 38:4 on the heavy burden of sin, Donne begins his first partition with St. Augustine's definition of sin as "a withdrawing of man to the creature,"[348] which Donne amplifies:

> And every such turning to the creature, let it be upon his side, to *her* whom he loves, let it be upwards, to *honour* that he affects, yet it is still down-ward, in respect of him, whom he was made by, and should direct himselfe to. Every inordinate love of the Creature is a descent from the dignity of our Creation (2:5.41–46).

Three orders of courtship are represented here: the sexual ("to her whom he loves"); the political ("to *honour* that he affects," honour being an appropriate response to one's superior); and of course, the transcendent (the one whom he "should direct himself to"). The first two orders, it seems, are in conflict with the latter. But Donne also raised here the issue of what constitutes "inordinate love." He continues,

> There are good things in the world, which it is a sin for man to love, *Quia infra illum ordinantur*, because though they *be good*, they are not *so good* as man; And man may not decline, and every thing, except God himself, is inferiour to man, and so, it is a *declination*, a *stooping* in man, to apply himselfe to any Creature (48–53).

Any love of any creature is inordinate, but Donne makes an important qualification. Love of the creature is inordinate

> *till* [emphasis mine] he meet that Creature in God; for there, it is above him; And so, as *Beauty* and *Riches*, and *Honour* are beames

---

[348] Augustine, *Ad Simplicianum* 1.2.18 (PL 40.122) (altered).

that issue from God, and glasses that represent God to us, and ideas that return us into him, in our glorifying of him, by these helpes, so we may apply our selves to them; for, in this considera-tion, as they assist us in our way to God, they are above us, other-wise, to love them for themselves, is a *declination*, a *stooping* under a *burden* (53–59).

Purification from sin in effect becomes a matter of hierarchy, of reordering the inordinate into proper relation with the ultimate term of desire.

At least one contemporary recognized this function in Donne's ser-mons. In an *apostrophe* to the deceased Dean on behalf of those who grieve his passing, fellow poet Sidney Godolphin, in his "Elegie on D. D.," brings consolation that

> Passions excesse for thee wee need not feare,
> Since first by thee our passions hallowed were;
> Thou mad'st our sorrowes, which before had bin
> Onely for the Successe, sorrowes for sinne,
> We owe thee all those teares, now thou art dead,
> Which we shed not, which for our selves we shed.
> Nor didst thou onely consecrate our teares,
> Give a religious tincture to our feares;
> But even our joyes had learn'd an innocence,
> Thou didst from gladnesse separate offence (11–20).[349]

Donne's mourning congregation need not fear because of their excessive passions, a reference to their present grief, but implicitly any and all human passion previous to this as well when they used to hear Donne preach. They need not fear because in his preaching Donne "consecrated" and "hal-lowed" these same passions by drawing them to a new object.

The principle behind Donne's conceptual arrangement in these exam-ples is Platonic rather than Pauline. In her study of Platonic Christian thought, Elizabeth Bieman observes that "in the attitudes he conveys towards the world of 'the flesh' Paul departs both from earlier Jewish norms and from Platonic insights upon the axis that conjoins the physical to the spiritual in the experience of sexual love" — and, I would add, of other "worldly" desires as well.[350] In this respect Donne differs markedly from his

---

[349] *Poems*, ed. Grierson, 1:392–93, here 393.
[350] Bieman, *Plato Baptized*, 83.

favourite biblical author. This dialectical inclusion of all goods within the larger order of the Good, which marks Donne's conceptual arrangement of motives, is basic to courtship structures. Courtesy handbooks of the period were infused with Platonic thought. In Stefano Guazzo's *Civile Conversation* (1586), the character of Anniball qualifies what he means by a courtier who is classifiable as good with respect to his conversation:

> when I name the good, I meane not onley that excellencie of good-nesse, which is not any way imperfect, and which is in a manner as rare on earth as the Phœnix: but I include in that number, all those which are well reported and reputed of in the world, and which approach so neare as they can to that excellencie before spoken of.[351]

This model of relative perfection is exemplified by the man who is healthy, despite his humours being not quite perfectly balanced (no one, says Anniball, is ever perfectly balanced).[352] In Guazzo, as in Castiglione, courtly virtues are seen as "in the way" to higher, spiritual attainments, a paradigm that is set out in Socrates's allegory of the horses and chariot in Plato's *Phaedrus*.[353] Significantly, in *The Courtiers Academie* (1598), Annibale Romei begins his dialogue on the topic "of Honour" (both a courtly and a rhetorical topic) by alluding to Plato's famous allegory.[354]

This allegory is richly resonant with the courtship *topoi* we have been discussing and is a *locus classicus* for so much that Burke finds useful in Castiglione's dialectic. Elizabeth Bieman succinctly summarizes the basic import of this allegory of the soul, which consists of a charioteer (the rational soul) driving a winged chariot pulled by a mixed team consisting of a spirited white horse (the animal soul) and an unruly black horse (the appetitive soul). Bieman elaborates: "The turbulence of bodily passion, always dangerous, is intimately involved in the higher erotic energies that motivate the lover of wisdom, the philosopher, in his ascent."[355] The team represents a dialectic of compulsion and control, impulse and refinement, which must be brought into proper relation to the higher, "real" objects of desire (Love, Beauty, Justice, etc.). Bieman summarizes:

---

[351] Stefano Guazzo, *The Civile Conversation* (1586), trans. George Pettie and Barth Young, vol. 1 (London: Constable, 1925), 58.

[352] Guazzo, *Civile Conversation*, trans. Pettie and Young, 1:57.

[353] Plato, *Phaedrus*, 248A–E, 253C–256E

[354] Annibale Romei, *The Courtiers Academie* (London, 1598), 78, [L3v].

[355] Bieman, *Plato Baptized*, 50. Again, it should be remembered that this dialogue is also contingent upon rhetorical purposes: Socrates delivers it to Phaedrus as a rhetorical demonstration.

If the charioteer is strongly 'winged' in the righteousness derived through philosophic recollection [of his origin or *telos*, hence true identity], he will succeed in directing his team upwards through the strait of mixed opportunity and threat. He may, impelled by love rightly directed, even reach the heaven of bliss in which strong united souls are 'carried round with the gods' in the contemplation of eternal truth.[356]

In his later reiteration of his allegory, Socrates makes it clear that given a proper orientation by the rational soul, lower loves may draw the soul through a process of refinement into higher love.[357]

Similarly, Donne's purification of his congregation's motives does not involve denying the concerns of this life, but rather extending these concerns to make them continuous with the *next* life. Donne denies both the Sadducee, "our great and worldly man" who sees humanity as "all body" and his counterpart, the Pharisee, who "is so super-spirituall, as that he beleeves, that is, considers no body; He imagines such a Purification, such an Angelification, such a Deification in this life, as though the heavenly Jerusalem were descended already" (9:6.479–482).[358] Donne's persistent emphasis on body and soul together is in a sense an insistence on a bridging of this life and the next, of worldly and spiritual motives. Donne repeatedly expresses the idea that this world is an "inchoation" of the next, and that this world and the next are but two rooms of the same house. In a sermon on the relationship between terrestrial and heavenly blessings, he says,

> The pure in heart are blessed already, not onely comparatively, that they are in a better way of Blessednesse, then others are, but actually in a present possession of it: for this world and the next world, are not, to the pure in heart, two houses, but two roomes, a Gallery to passe thorough, and a Lodging to rest in, in the same House, which are both under one roofe, Christ Jesus (7:13.559–565).[359]

---

[356] Bieman, *Plato Baptized*, 50.

[357] *Phaedrus* in *Complete Works*, ed. John M. Cooper (Indianapolis: Hackett, 1997), 253D–256E.

[358] The allusion is to Revelation 21:2.

[359] For similar instances of this image of the two rooms see 4:2.10–14; 7:6.221–222. On this life as an "inchoation" of the next see 7:5.612–614; 8:2.450–456; 9:4.632–633; 9:11.215–219.

Donne differs from many of his contemporaries in his resistance to dichotomizing social and spiritual courtships.[360] To Donne preaching at St. Paul's Cross, amid London's centre of business, it is a scandal to think that Christ "induced a Religion incapable of the honours, or the pleasures, or profits of this world" (9:4.96–97). Just as he tells his congregation in St. Paul's that

> we bid you not to raise your selves in this world, to such a *spiritu-all heighth*, as to have no regard to this world, to your *bodies*, to your *fortunes*, to your *families*. Man is not all soule, but a body too; and, as God hath married them together in thee, so hath he com-manded them mutuall duties towards one another (4:8.588–592).

Donne more typically urges identification between mundane and spiritual courtships. He seeks rather to translate desire: not to eliminate passions but to redirect them. Commenting on John the Baptist's commission that "*every valley should be exalted, every mountaine ... made low*" (518–519), Donne says that to emulate the Baptist,

> is not to bring our mountainous, and swelling affections, and pas-sions, to that flatnesse, as that we become stupid, and insensible. Mortification is not to kill nature, but to kill sinne. Bring there-fore your *Ambition* to that bent, to covet a place in the kingdome of heaven, bring your *anger*, to flow into *zeale*, bring your *love* to enamour you of that face, which is *fairer then the children of men*, that face, on which the Angels desire to look, Christ Jesus, and you have brought your mountains to that lownesse, which is intended, and required here (665–673).

Donne deals with worldly desires by subsuming them within his courtship of heaven, causing them to "flow" into a transcendent order of motives which has God as its apex. Reminiscent of Guazzo's characterization of the good man's conversation, Donne says earlier in this sermon,

> we do not require, that you should absolutely rectifie all the defor-mities and crookednesses, which that *Tortuositas Serpentis*, the winding of the old Serpent hath brought you to; for, now the

---

[360] Similarly, Tracy Ware notes that Donne differs from Augustine's "tendency to oppose the temporal to the eternal, a tendency which is conspicuously absent in Donne": "Donne and Augustine: A Qualification," *N&Q* 228 (1983): 425–27, here 426.

streame of our corrupt nature, is accustomed to that crooked chan-
nell, and we cannot divert that, we cannot come to an absolute
directnesse, and streightnesse, and profession in this life (553–558).

He goes on to describe rather a process of courtship, adding that "the holy
Ghost speaks but of a *way*, a path; not of *our rest* in the end, but of our
labour in the way" (559–560).

For Donne, secular and sacred modes of courtship are not only analogous but con-substantial. What Dennis Quinn says of Donne's development of similitude in a single passage from the sermons holds true to his
courtship similitude writ large: "The exhaustiveness of Donne's parallels
suggests not comparability but identity in the two terms of the
metaphor."361 This identity in *elocutio* engenders a corresponding identity
in thought. And so in another sermon he encourages his congregation to
"Employ then this noblest sense [sight] upon the noblest object, see God;
see God in every thing, and then thou needst not take off thine eye from
Beauty, from Riches, from Honour, from any thing" (8:9.69–72). With
God, the ultimate term, in clear view, every other desire is duly incorporated within the compass of the holy. Furthermore, there is, says Donne, an
inchoation of virtue even in the perversely ambitious, in that ambition at
least sets men in the right direction of desiring something better. Donne
amplifies this point with his congregation at St. Paul's:

> Whosoever labours to supplant another, that he may succeed, will
> in some measure endeavour to be fit for that succession. So that,
> though it be but a *squint-eye*, and not a direct look, yet some eye,
> some aspect, the envious man hath upon *vertue* (8:12.349–352).

Worldly ambition and holy ambition are substantially the same: the
former is lower in the scale of perfection, but a starting point on that
scale nonetheless.

More typically, Donne's fellow clergymen saw a strong disjunction
between carnal and spiritual motives. Unlike Donne, Richard Baxter
employs the more common rhetorical strategy of antithesis. Baxter, too,
evokes social motives in order to induce spiritual motivation, but he does
so by emphasizing a disjunction between the two rather than a continuity,
as he interrogates his reader:

---

361 Quinn, "Donne's Christian Eloquence," 364. Quinn says this metaphoric amplification is not a
"mere rhetorical device" but a hallmark of exegesis in the Augustinian tradition. But as we have
seen, Augustinian exegesis is deliberately rhetorical in its orientation. There is nothing "mere" in its
"rhetoricalness."

Quest. 1. If you could grow rich by religion, or get lands and lord-
ships by being diligent in godliness; or if you could get honour or
preferment by it in the world; or could be recovered from sickness
by it, or could live for ever in prosperity on earth; what kind of
lives would you then lead, and what pains would you take in the
service of God? And is not the rest of the saints a more excellent
happiness than all this?

Quest. 2. If the law of the land did punish every breach of the sab-
bath, or every omission of family duties, or secret duties, or every
cold and heartless prayer, with death: if it were felony or treason to
be ungodly and negligent in worship, and loose in your lives, what
manner of persons would you then be, and what lives would you
lead! And is not eternal death more terrible than temporal?[362]

Baxter bases his appeal on mere similitude in form, whereas Donne typically asserts a consubstantiality of form.[363] The difference is that Baxter
evokes the association between the worldly and the heavenly heuristically,
whereas Donne seeks permanently to fuse the two orders of motives in the
minds and hearts of his auditory. Baxter is much more heavenly-minded
than Donne, always leading his reader to a future consideration.[364] Donne
frequently leads his congregation to consider heaven as well, but always
with respect to living this present life.

---

[362] Richard Baxter, *The Saint's Everlasting Rest*, in *The Practical Works*, ed. William Orme, 23 vols.
(London: James Duncan Downame, 1830), 22:26–540, here 474.

[363] Thomas Becon (1512–1567) expresses an even more forceful sense of division between the human
and the divine: "God's word is most highly worthy to be wished and desired," while "Man's invention is most worthy to be despised and cast away, forasmuch as it is nothing else than the lewd imagination of filthy flesh, and by that means hated of God and of all good men": *The Diversity Between
God's Word and Man's Invention*, in *Prayers and Other Pieces of Thomas Becon*, ed. John Ayre
(Cambridge: Cambridge University Press, 1844; repr. New York: Johnson Reprint, 1968),
484–497, here 496. This whole tract consists of a series of similar juxtapositions amplifying this
theme.

[364] Lewalski notes that *The Saint's Everlasting Rest* "was a central document in systematizing and
disseminating" a method she calls "Heavenly Meditation" (*Protestant Poetics*, 165–66).

❧ Conceptual arrangement in a sermon preached before Queen Anne

As a transition to issues of material arrangement, I would like to look at one sermon which draws together several of the strategies I have discussed in relation to courtship as a principle of conceptual arrangement. As Peter E. McCullough points out, Donne used his sermon preached before Queen Anne at Denmark House boldly to urge the Queen to return completely from her Roman Catholic leanings to the Church of her birth, but Donne's chief concern transcends such political distinctions, aiming primarily at urging the Queen and her court to bring all desire within the purview of a pursuit of godliness.[365] Donne begins by saying that as the biblical writers retained some of the character of their profession in their writing style,

> so that soul, that hath been transported upon any particular worldly pleasure, when it is intirely turn'd upon God, and the contemplation of his all-sufficiency and abundance, doth find in God fit subject, and just occasion to exercise the same affection piously, and religiously, which had before so sinfully transported, and possest it (1:5.8–13).

He continues to amplify the point in economic terms, speaking of a "spiritual covetousness" and using such words as "gain," "wages," "possession," and "purchase" (14–28). Similarly, the voluptuous man and the angry man will find completion of their passions in God. Carnal appetites have not only their counterparts, but their fulfilment in the spiritual order of motives:

> So will a voluptuous man, who is turned to God, find plenty and deliciousnes enough in him, to feed his soul, as with marrow, and with fatness, as *David* expresses it; and so an angry and passionate man, will find zeal enough in the house of God to eat him up (29–32).

Donne then extends these desires (and the courtships they imply) so that they become perpetual and without end: these

> affections which are common to all men, and those too, which in particular, particular men have been addicted unto, shall not only

---

[365] McCullough, *Sermons at Court*, 169–82.

be justly employed upon God, but also securely employed [unlike tenuous, earthly courtships], because we cannot exceed, nor go too far in imploying them upon him (33–36).

Unlike the socio-political arena, God's kingdom imposes no ceiling on one's advancement. Here Donne introduces as his *exemplum* Solomon (in a passage cited in the previous chapter), whose excessive amorousness was transferred to and satisfied by God.

Donne charts his congregation's emotive experience by dividing love into two constituent parts: desire and enjoyment (53). From this definition he derives the affective structure of his sermon: "for to desire without fruition, is a rage, and to enjoy [i.e. to have] without desire is stupidity" (53–54). He evokes the frustration of false loves in order to direct his congregation to true love and fulfilment in a relationship with Christ. In other words, those who pursue worldly passions will be ever goaded, never satisfied, and never at rest. But one who extends these passions higher to seek God is promised enjoyment and satisfaction. This configuration is aimed at infecting his congregation with the same dissatisfaction Solomon experienced, with the goal of effecting in them a similar translation of desire.

Throughout the first half of the sermon, the congregation's definition of love (or at least their thinking about love) undergoes a terministic purification. To begin with, sensual love is "nothing but to be scourg'd with burning iron rods, rods of jealousie, of suspition, and of quarrels"366 (68–69): this love is all desire and no satisfaction. But Donne concludes the first partition with the love of God which "is the consummation, that is, the marriage, and union of thy soul, and thy Saviour" (281–282). In this way he awakens his audience's desire for God and leaves them in hope of satisfaction. At the same time, Donne enlarges the love of the Saviour, describing it within a hierarchy of species culminating in "true" love, as he has defined it — as "a desire, that they whom we love should be happy" (177):

> *He loves us* as his ancient inheritance, as the first amongst his creatures in the creation of the world, which he created for us: *He loves us* more as his purchase, whom he hath bought with his blood; for even man takes most pleasure in things of his own getting; *But he loves us most* for our improvement, when by his ploughing up of our hearts, and the dew of his grace, and the seed of his word, we come to give a greater rent, in the fruites of sanctification than before (181–188, emphasis mine).

---

366 Donne's source here is Augustine, *Confessions* 3.1.1 [altered].

Donne has already depicted Christ as the perfect lover, an amalgam of the best qualities of male and female love: in his masculinity, Christ's love is constant and durable; in his feminine figuration as Wisdom in Proverbs, his love is vehement and earnest (107–108). Now we are made to feel, in Donne's arrangement of *auxesis*, the largeness of his love.

Having enlarged the desirability of Christ's love, Donne goads his congregation into seeking the same by depicting the condition which should be avoided at all costs:

> That stupid inconsideration, which passes on drowsilie, and negligently upon Gods creatures, that sullen indifferency in ones disposition, to love one thing no more than another, not to value, not to chuse, not to prefer, that stoniness, that inhumanity, not to be affected, not to be entendred, toward those things which God hath made objects and subjects of affections (206–211).

To desire something, anything, is to be moving in the right direction, for "St. *Paul* places in the bottome, and lees, and dregs of all the sins of the Jews, to be without natural affections" (212–213, cf. Romans 1:31). Not only does Donne heighten the desirability of Christ by elevating his love (distance induces desire), but he characterizes indifference in this matter as a shameful condition which can be remedied only by an awakening and a cultivation of desire for Christ.

This reorientation and enlargement of his congregation's love of God is essential to a purification of their mundane passions. Otherwise, says Donne, based on his earlier definition of love ("a desire, that they whom we love should be happy") there can be no love on earth. He asks,

> doth any ambitious man love honor or office therefore, because he thinks that title, or that place should receive a dignity by his having it, or an excellency by his executing it? doth any covetous man love a house or horse therefore, because he thinks that house or horse should be happy in such a Master or such a Rider? doth any licentious man covet or solicite a woman therefore, because he thinks it a happiness to her, to have such a servant? (246–253).

Quite the contrary, says Donne. Such a man is content that these should serve his own "imaginary happiness" (256). But all this changes if the love of creatures raises us up to the love of the Creator. "[F]or if it do so," says Donne, "we may love our selves, as we are the Images of God; and so we may love other men, as they are the Images of us, and our nature; yea, as they are all the members of the same body" (261–263).

♣ Material arrangement: the formal operation of courtship

> *Therfore they that wyll not go to farre in playing, let them folowe this coūsell of the Poete.*
> Stoppe the begynninges.
> — Roger Ascham[367]

When Donne thus stylistically infects his congregation with a sense of sin in order to incite them to accept the cure he will finally offer, he is employing a rhetoric of form. And when he makes his congregation to feel their pollution, and thus feel their distance from "the Good" (however defined), and thereby establishes the conditions of estrangement that will give rise to courtship motives and a desire to ascend in the proper direction he lays before them, Donne is capitalizing on the formal qualities inherent in courtship. This is where the conceptual arrangement of courtship bears significantly upon material arrangement.

Form is a function of *dispositio*.[368] Furthermore, desire is the central agent in Kenneth Burke's notion of literary form and, I suggest, in the *dispositio* of a Donne sermon. Simply stated, form is the arousal and fulfilment of desire. "A work has form," says Burke, "in so far as one part of it *leads* a reader to anticipate another part, to be gratified by the *sequence*" (emphasis mine).[369] As to its rhetorical effect, Burke says that "[f]orm, having to do with the creation and gratification of needs, is 'correct' [decorous] in so far as it gratifies the needs which it creates. The appeal of the form in this sense is obvious: form *is* the appeal."[370] The gratification of sequence is at the heart of courtship, a process which leads to the fulfilment of a desired end. Courtship, then, is inextricable from the formal operations of desire.

The appeal of the courtship *topos* is attributable in part to the suasiveness of process itself. There is a narrative momentum, a logic of sequence, that is augmented by a desired end that is engendered in the arrangement of the elements of a work. Describing what he calls the "kinetic" decorum of narrative sequence, Michael Dixon says, "Dispositional sequence in nar-

---

[367] Ascham, *Toxophilus*, in *Works*, ed. Wright, 29.
[368] In *RM*, Burke identifies form with the traditional term *dispositio* (69).
[369] *CS*, 124.
[370] *CS*, 138.

rative thus implies consequence: placement in time and space for an event asserts both causal and logical significance"[371] A sequence, once begun, thus acquires a force of momentum. One common instance of this is Donne's argument by precedent, where an established pattern of behaviour argues, by force of logic, a continuation of that pattern: "The Memory is as the conclusion of a Syllogisme, which being inferred upon true propositions, cannot be denied: He that remembers Gods former blessings, concludes infallibly upon his future" (8:11.321–324). Donne repeatedly asserts that God works according to precedent.[372] In a discussion of prevenient grace, he suggests that God's manner of proceeding with others in the past is an argument that he will proceed in the same manner with each of his St. Paul's congregants in the future; conversely, to seek comfort in drink, music, comedies, and conversation implies, by *logos* of sequence, the continuation of seeking comfort in these areas (4:8.538–551).

Donne employs this *logos* of precedent in his second prebend sermon, where he finds in the inexorable process of time — past, present, and future — a basis for future expectation. David serves as an *exemplum* of one who seeks assurance in God's past providence in order to find confidence for a continuation into the future. At the beginning of the second partition, Donne outlines the logic implicit in the pattern he describes, taking David's words (Psalm 63:7) — "Because it hath beene thus heretofore, sayes *David*, I will resolve upon this course for the future" — as his own pattern: "Because God hath already gone this way, this way I will awaite his going still" (7:1.320–330).[373] The formal quality here is one where repetition engenders an expectation of continued performance. This pattern has recognizable analogues in juridical practice as well as in the political patronage system.[374] Donne goes so far as to say that precedent binds God to continue his benefits, asserting that "[t]here is no State, no Church, no Man, that hath not this tie upon God, that hath not God in these bands,

---

[371] Dixon, *The Polliticke Courtier*, 32.

[372] Among the many instances are 5:18.1–49, 7:1.394–413, and 8:14.301–302.

[373] As Judith H. Anderson observes, this idea of God proceeding according to preset patterns is a recurring theme in Donne's sermons and descriptive of Donne's method in this sermon. Her argument would benefit from a clearer conception of form and Donne's strategies of arrangement: "Patterns Proposed Beforehand: Donne's Second Prebend Sermon," *PS* 11 (1988): 37–48, esp. 42–43.

[374] Although argument by precedent did not yet hold the central place it does in the present legal system, in the sixteenth and seventeenth centuries precedents increasingly gained importance: see A. K. R. Kiralfy, *Potter's Historical Introduction to English Law and its Institutions*, 4th ed. (London: Sweet & Maxwell, 1958), 274–78; and Max Radin, *Handbook of Anglo-American Legal History* (St. Paul: West, 1936), 343–53. See 6:18.35–74 for another instance of God's binding principle of precedence expressed in political and juridical terms.

That God by having done much for them already, hath bound himselfe to doe more" (411–413).

There is also a formal aspect to Donne's use of courtship as a language of accommodation, where he arranges elements of a discourse in such a manner as will lead the subject in an easy way to truth. A graded series of steps is in itself compelling, where gratification is derived from both the manageability and progressiveness of the process. Richard Hooker quotes Walafrid Strabo, Abbot of Reichenau (A.D. 807–849), on the arrangement of public Scripture readings for the greater benefit of the congregation, so "*[t]hat from smaller things the minde of the hearers may goe forwarde to the knowledge of greater, and by degrees clime up from the lowest to the highest things.*"[375] Later Hooker makes use of this hierarchical model, asserting that his objective in discussing the controversy over the public administration of the Word is "to lead on the mindes of the simpler sorte by plaine and easie degrees, till the verie nature of the thinge itselfe doe make manifest what is truth."[376] The process itself seems to carry a suasive force, where one small step leads easily to another.

But more fundamentally, the formal operation of Donne's sermons is based on the very foundation of Christian theology. For Donne, the generating idea of Christian courtship is the estrangement between God and man resulting from the Fall. Naturally, then, Donne's sermons often take a two-part structure of Fall and Redemption, or in courtship terms, estrangement and reunion (what Northrop Frye describes as the U-shaped pattern of biblical narrative).[377] Part of the effect of this two-part structure is that the first part sets the conditions which evoke a desire for the second. Burke describes the formal operation of this structure:

> if an author managed over a certain number of his pages to produce a feeling of sultriness, or oppression, in the reader, this would unconsciously awaken in the reader the desire for a cold, fresh northwind — and thus some aspect of a northwind would be effective if called forth by some aspect of stuffiness.[378]

---

[375] Hooker, *Works*, 2:77 (5.20.6).

[376] Hooker, *Works*, 2:84 (5.21.2).

[377] Northrop Frye, *The Great Code* (New York: Harcourt, Brace, Jovanovich, 1982), 169. Frye compiles an impressive catalogue of biblical instances of this "U-shaped pattern," which he considers a narrative archetype of Western culture (169–98).

[378] *CS*, 39.

In stylistically engendering an atmosphere of fallenness in his congregation (configured as illness, socio-political estrangement, or general downwardness, etc.) he creates an expectation for a corresponding redemption.

Donne's paradigm of salvation in the sermons is typically Protestant and theologically orthodox in this respect; furthermore, it bears a common cultural pattern.[379] Richard Bernard finds in Scripture a common two-part structure, where "[t]he Law [is] to the stubborne, to breake their hearts; and the Gospell to the repentant, to comfort their spirits."[380] As might be expected, this bipartite structure held particular appeal for such Ramists as John Stoughton. The title of two Stoughton sermons typifies the form of fall and redemption in connection with overt healing imagery. *Baruch's Sore Gently Opened: God's Salve Skilfvlly Applied* (1640), as Stoughton collectively names these two sermons, sets out a series of binary equivalents to the two parts of Jeremiah's message to Baruch in Jeremiah 45. Jeremiah operates:

1. As a Chirurgion [who "gently opened" the wound]
2. As a Physitian [who "skilfvlly applied" the salve][381]

He applies:

1. A Corrosive Plaister ["to cut the tough humour"], which is
2. Incarnative ["which assures him, and makes it good"][382]

Jeremiah provides:

1. The Prognosticke of *Baruchs* Maladie
2. The Practicke of Gods Remedy

And Jeremiah proceeds:

1. First, by way of spirituall and grave instruction ...
2. By way of sweet Consolation[383]

A similar twofold pattern is evident in other aspects of culture as well, including courtship. George Wither takes the gamesters' bouncing balls, which enact this falling and rising motion, as emblems of the courtier's sit-

---

[379] Lewalski provides a convenient summary of Donne's Protestant soteriology in *Protestant Poetics*, 13–27.

[380] Bernard, *The Shepherds Practise* in *The Faithfvll Shepherd*, 369, R7.

[381] John Stoughton, *Baruch's Sore Gently Opened: God's Salve Skilfvlly Applied* (1640), 4, [B2v].

[382] Stoughton, *Baruch's Sore*, 5, B3.

[383] Stoughton, *Baruch's Sore*, 8, [B8v].

uation, heading his emblem with the couplet, "*When to* suppresse *us, Men intend, / They make us higher to* ascend."384 Suppression, or descent, induces a desire to rebound. Augustine Baker infuses the upward-downward pattern of religious meditation with a similar sense of courtship when he describes the fulfilment of "Holy ambition" in the state of internal prayer. In this state, "*the soule* being inflamed with Diuine Loue, doth *breath* forth her ardent affections to God ... that they may draw in fresher aire." Baker goes on to describe the form of this dialectical purification as one "of emptying & filling, of rising & falling. For after euery *Aspiration* there is a short descent; & then a mounting higher then before."385 The continual reiteration of this natural dialectic of breathing argues that every descent is matched and, Baker adds, exceeded by a corresponding ascent.

Nowhere is this pattern more evident than in Donne. Writing on the seventeenth-century devotional poets, William H. Halewood introduces to the Ignatian model of meditation, as described by Louis Martz, the Protestant emphasis on prevenient grace — "the grace which is required to make men *want* to be saved by softening the stony in their hearts."386 This emphasis leads Halewood to find in Donne's Holy Sonnets a form much like that I describe here, of a descent into desolation which sets the conditions that cause a desire for an ascent to consolation; Halewood alternately describes this form as a movement from a state of unrest to one of rest, a formal operation that is at the heart of *Deaths Duell*, as I will demonstrate in chapter 6.387

Donne often infuses his ostensible three-part sermon structure with this pattern. Preaching on Paul's commission, Donne divides his sermon into three sections. First is the "who" of the text, Paul, and then his two-part activity (the "what"): "his humiliation, his exinanition of himselfe, his devesting, putting off of himselfe, *He fell to the earth*; and lastly, his investing of Christ, his putting on of Christ, his rising againe by the power of a new inanimation" (6:10.26–30). In another instance, Donne's *divisio* begins with "The generall impotency of man, in spirituall duties" and then, after a middle section describing those duties, answers in the third partition with "the meanes of repairing this naturall impotency" (6:5.35–39). In another, he adds to the bipartite structure to draw out the process, moving from "*Commination*" (threat) to "*Commonition*" (instruction) to "*Consolation*" ("the rising at the generall Judgement") (5:9.9–13).

---

384 George Wither, *A Collection of Emblemes* (1635), 16, [C4v].

385 Baker, *Sancta Sophia*, 250–1, [2H1v]–2H2.

386 William H. Halewood, *The Poetry of Grace* (New Haven: Yale University Press, 1970), 74.

387 Halewood, *The Poetry of Grace*, 75–83.

Donne often uses images of downwardness (a well) and upwardness (a steeple) to define his audience's sermonic experience (4:6.285–288). "The naturall ways is *upward*," says Donne, yet sometimes we see better by being brought low. He goes on to elucidate:

> Gods meaning was, that by the sun-shine of prosperity, and by the beames of honour, and temporall blessings, a man should see farre into him; but I know not how he is come to need *spectacles*; scarce any man sees much in this matter, till affliction shew it him (308–312).

Donne's *dispositio* is thus frequently designed to bring his congregation low in order to raise them up again with a new vision. In this sermon Donne exploits the dyslogistic associations of downwardness (a well) and their eulogistic counterparts (associated with a spire) to structure his audience's desire. It is much more desirable, in this case, to appreciate one's prosperity, and to see God at the end of it, than to need humiliation through affliction in order to have one's vision retrained on God.

While the formal operation of the sermons typically stages the congregation's fall so that they might feel the force of their redemption, Donne realizes he must at the same time prepare them to live in a fallen world. While he often raises them toward union with the divine object of desire, he knows he must release them into a life of mundane passions. Armin Paul Frank describes in Burke "the Plotinistic-mystical strategy of supplementing the 'Upward Way' toward the divine vantage point ('god-term') by a corresponding 'Downward Way' back to the minutiae of life."[388] For rhetorical purposes it does not matter whether Donne was either a Platonist or a mystic. What does matter is that Donne takes full advantage of these recognizable cultural forms in arranging the matter of his sermons. Once the subject recognizes the conventions of the form, either consciously or unconsciously, he or she will anticipate the remaining elements that are necessary for its completion, and is thus led to participate in the process of its completion.[389] Insofar as Donne's congregation recognizes and goes along with this standard Christian form, it too functions as a conventional form.

---

[388] Armin Paul Frank, *Kenneth Burke* (New York: Twayne, 1969), 132. This is the formal principle of Donne's poem "The Extasie" as described by George Williamson: "As sphere to intelligence, or as air to heaven, the body is the agent or medium of the soul. As blood ascends to spirits to unite body and soul, so even pure lovers' souls must descend to affections and faculties which sense may reach, or else the living soul is locked in a bodily prison, except in ecstasy": "The Convention of *The Extasie*," in *Seventeenth-Century English Poetry*, ed. William R. Keast (Oxford: Oxford University Press, 1962), 132–43, here 141.

[389] *CS*, 126–27.

❧ The grammar of courtship: *elocutio* and sequence

When Burke first turns to issues of formal appeal in *A Rhetoric of Motives*, it is with reference to *elocutio*, noting that, even among the sophists, the most ostentatious use of rhetorical figures "arose out of great functional urgency."[390] "In its simplest manifestation," says Burke, "style is ingratiation."[391] Virginia Holland expands on this statement, adding that "[t]his makes style a part of form because the speaker *must* say the right thing (style) if he adequately satisfies the appetites which he has aroused in the audience (form)."[392] Elsewhere Burke notes that even a fragmentary utterance, if it creates anticipation or expectation, functions as form. He observes that if someone states only a subject — "The man" — a desire for the verb is immediately awakened in his auditor.[393] A periodic sentence is a perfect example of form at the sentence-level, where the deferred closure of the sense drives the reader-auditor toward the end. Donne's use of longer sentences with parallel clauses and repetitive forms has this effect. Moreover, such figures of grammatical arrangement as *climax* function formally in that they create an atmosphere of anticipation and expectancy. Alexander Richardson makes clear the implicit courtship-form at work in some of Donne's favourite grammatical figures, such as *auxesis* (words arranged in ascending order of importance), and especially *climax*. "*Climax*," says Richardson, "signifieth a *gradatio*, or a climbing up the ladder of stairs, or the like: it is a manifold *anadiplosis*."[394] The form of courtship reflected in *climax* is one of awakened expectation that each step in this process leads toward an implied end.

Furthermore, grammatical form implies sequence and hence functions as a form of logic. Walter J. Ong, in his introduction to Milton's *Art of Logic*, says that logic pertains to "utterances in which if something is posited something else follows."[395] The formal operation of *climax* carries a sense of logic in this sense. Taking an example from World War II — "Who controls Berlin, controls Germany; who controls Germany controls Europe; who controls Europe controls the world" — Burke notes that

---

[390] *RM*, 66. Here Burke makes no connection to form as he defines it elsewhere in *RM* and in *CS*, but instead limits himself to traditional categories of rhetoric.

[391] *PC*, 50.

[392] Virginia Holland, *Counterpoint* (New York: Philosophical Library, 1959): 70.

[393] *CS*, 140.

[394] Richardson, "Rhetorical Notes" (84–5, [G2v]–G3) in *The Logicians School-Master*.

[395] Walter J. Ong, "Introduction" to *A Fuller Course in the Art of Logic* in *Complete Prose Works of John Milton*, vol. 8 (New Haven: Yale University Press, 1953), 153.

regardless of ... doubts about it as a proposition, by the time you arrive at the second of its three stages, you feel how it is destined to develop — and on the level of purely formal assent you would collaborate to round out its symmetry by spontaneously willing its completion and perfection as an utterance.[396]

In a similar manner, Donne uses *climax* in his commemorative sermon on Lady Danvers to instill in the minds of his congregation at Chelsea a discursive pattern which leads from lesser to greater, from this earth to the new earth in eternity, in order to enlarge their desire for the new heaven and new earth of his text (2 Peter 3:13). In the new earth, says Donne,

> all their *waters* are *milke*, and all their *milke, honey*, where all their *grasse* is *corne*, and all their *corne, Manna*; where all their *glebe*, all their *clods* of earth are *gold*, and all their *gold* of innumberable *carats*; Where all their *minutes* are *ages*, and all their *ages, Eternity* (8:2.700–704).

He goes on to make clear that this line of thinking bears a purification significance (implicit in *climax*) as it moves toward fulfilment, "Where every thing, is every minute, in the highest exaltation, as good as it can be, and yet super-exalted, and infinitely multiplied, by every minutes addition; every minute, *infinitely* better, then ever it was before" (704–707). Donne's Dionysian language[397] of "super-exaltedness" extends the logic of his grammatical arrangement and emphasizes the transcendent movement of mundane desires toward complete fulfilment.

At St. Dunstan's church, Donne employs elocutionary form to complement dispositional form in a sermon on the suffering of affliction, which he divides into a series of binaries:

> these are our two parts; first the *Burden*, and then the *Ease*, first the *waight*, and then the *Alleviation*, first the *Discomfort*, and then the *Refreshing*, the sea of afflictions that overflow, and surround us all, and then our emergency and lifting up our head above that sea (10:9.75–79).

In the first partition, where he aims to sink his congregation into a sense of their affliction in their fallenness, Donne uses *climax* to say, "We make all

---

[396] *RM*, 58–9.
[397] Pseudo-Dionysius, *De Divinis Nominibus*, 1.1, 5.1, 7.1.

our worms snakes, all our snakes vipers, all our vipers dragons, by our murmuring" (231–232). In contrast to this despairing image of human agency,
he goes on later in the second partition to round out the sermon's form by
concluding on the comfort that comes in knowing that God's grace is oper-
ative in all our suffering. He sets his sub-points out as "three gradations in
our text, three circumstances, which, as they aggravated the discomfort in
the former, so they exalt the comfort in this part, That they are *His*, *The
Lords*, That they are *from his rod*, That they are *from the rod of his wrath*"
(597–601). Here form derives from a grammatical sequence that moves
toward syntactic completion. In the same way, Donne's grammar of affliction brings meaning to personal suffering as he concludes the sermon with
a favourable semantic analysis of these parts of this phrase, so that God's
affliction is finally seen to signify his mercy (688–732).

Grammatical form operates somewhat differently in a sermon on
Jesus's healing of a man sick with palsy (Matthew 9:2), where Donne very
carefully cultivates an association between the desire for physical well-being
and the desire for spiritual well-being, to which he adds a hierarchical
arrangement of priority. Here he uses the figures of *auxesis* and *anaphora* to
establish the logical priority of sin (the cause) over physical illness (the
effect). "What ease were it," he asks,

> to be delivered of a palsie, of slack and dissolv'd sinews, and
> remaine under the tyranny of a lustfull heart, of licentious eyes, of
> slacke and dissolute speech and conversation? What ease to be
> delivered of the putrefaction of a wound in my body, and meet a
> murder in my conscience, done, or intended, or desired upon my
> neighbour? To be delivered of a fever in my spirits, and to have my
> spirit troubled with the guiltinesse of an adultery? To be delivered
> of Cramps, and Coliques, and Convulsions in my joynts and
> sinewes, and suffer in my soule all these, from my oppressions, and
> extortions, by which I have ground the face of the poore
> (10:2.545–555).

Donne's amplification of the rhetorical topic "of ease" argues a process that
his congregation wants to avoid, that of attending to physical effects and
failing to recognize the more troubling spiritual causes. His series of "to be
..." statements, an arrangement of *anaphora*, sets out a pattern of contrast
between physical ailments and more serious spiritual afflictions. This
anaphora, together with *auxesis*, establishes a pattern of deteriorating health:
from an infected wound in the first; to a fever in the second; to a sub-series

in the third (heightened by the use of consonance) culminating in convulsions. This same pattern in relation to spiritual health is established at the outset in a series which moves from private, passive sin ("a lustfull heart") to increasingly public and active sin ("licentious eyes" followed by "dissolute speech"). The logic of this sequence is all the more forceful owing to the congregation's common experience of physical disease which all too commonly led the patient relentlessly toward death.

Donne counters this downward movement by citing the good medical practice of treating causes rather than symptoms as a warning to his audience against a regression in the disease of sin:

> It is but lost labour, and cost, to give a man a precious cordiall, when he hath a thorne in his foote, or an arrow in his flesh; for, as long as the sinne, which is the cause of the sicknesse, remaines, *Deterius sequetur*, A worse thing will follow; we may be rid of a Fever, and the Pestilence will follow, rid of the Cramp, and a Gout will follow, rid of sicknesse, and Death, eternall death will follow (555–560).

Donne aggravates his congregation's anxiety by arranging his material in a manner that leads them in a direction (from bad to worse) that is opposite to the one they desire, building their sense of estrangement from their goal of well-being and thus goading their desire to ascend the scale of spiritual health. In this way, he evokes desires associated with physical health in order to deflect his congregation's desire to a more important kind of well-being, and hence to take the Saviour's "prescription": "sinne no more sins" (562).

Sir Philip Sidney's first sonnet in *Astrophil and Stella* aptly illustrates the courtship potential of such grammatical arrangements as I have described. Neither Sidney nor Astrophil is courting in earnest, in the way Donne would have his congregation court God (Astrophil seems as interested in his own process of writing as he is in the lady to whom he writes). But despite this difference in tone, this poem is ideal for my purposes precisely because of its self-conscious rhetoricity. In this sonnet, Astrophil first addresses his condition of estrangement from Stella with a symbolic assertion of identification with her. Astrophil sets out a series of increments by which he may cover the distance to his beloved. Emblematic of the condition of estrangement in courtship are Sidney's persona signifying a stargazer and his object of desire, a transcendent star. Astrophil's means for overcoming this estrangement is the symbolic activity of language — more specifically, the rhetorical figure of *climax*. In the opening lines, this figure builds, in a series of steps, a linguistic bridge between the estranged parties, both literally in the syntax of the sentence and potentially in the relational process it describes:

> LOVING in truth, and faine in verse my love to show,
> That the deare She might take some pleasure of my paine:
> Pleasure might cause her reade, reading might make her know,
> Knowledge might pitie winne, and pitie grace obtaine
> (1–4).[398]

Beginning the process of writing already identifies Astrophil in a process which logically implies his identification with his beloved. His writing is a cause which, through a series of intermediate effects/causes (pleasure, reading, knowledge, pity), will lead to an ultimate effect of grace. This implicit identification is strengthened by the organic effect of a figure which links each step together by making each effect the cause of the next effect.

The progression of the *climax* also enacts a purification of Astrophil's position *vis à vis* Stella, transforming his position of pain into a state of grace, which implies that his initial condition is one of sin and pollution, a symptom of estrangement from the divine. This progression is really just an extension of a more compact cultural logic of courtship which is both socially and religiously defined. Grace is possible only in a situation of estrangement, so that in a sense the condition itself *produces* the desire. Yet at the same time the superior position of the object of desire implies, culturally, a responsibility to come to the aid of the needy subject.[399] A common strategy of patronage is to cast oneself as a dependent in order to induce a sense of obligation in the potential patron. But perhaps more significantly, this is a model that derives from divine example. This cultural logic is strengthened by the religious overtones in Sidney's diction, implying the precedent of God who binds himself to give grace to all who ask for it.

But to return to our primary concern here, Sidney's grammatical arrangement illustrates the logical operation of sequence itself. In relation to the subject, this expression has the effect of putting Astrophil (symbolically at least) in a process that culminates in his object of desire who is oth-

---

[398] *The Poems of Sir Philip Sidney*, ed. William A. Ringler Jr. (Oxford: Clarendon Press, 1962), 165.

[399] William Ames in his casuistical book, *Conscience with the Power and Cases Thereof*, describes the "*mutuall obligation betwixt those that are superiour onely in age, and gifts, and their inferiours.*" In answer to "*What is the duty of such Superiours?*" he says, "Hee which excels in some gift, ought readily to impart it to the benefit of others" because the privileged are "only dispensers" of the blessings they have received from God (Book IV, 153, V2). This is in the context of the fifth book, "of the Dvties of Man Towards his Neighbour" (91, 2N2).

erwise beyond his reach. With respect to the object of desire, Stella, this sequence implies the reasonableness of accepting Astrophil's advance based on the logical momentum it initiates and enacts.

℞ Temporizing of essence as a courtship strategy

This portion of Sidney's sonnet aptly illustrates Burke's principle of "temporizing of essence," a principle which, I will contend, is elemental to the suasive power of courtship with respect to its *dispositio*, yet one which Burke, to my knowledge, never explicitly connected to courtship. Burke first defines his term in *A Grammar of Motives* where he states,

> Because of the pun whereby the logically prior can be expressed in terms of the temporally prior, and *v.v.*, the ways of transcendence, in aiming at the discovery of *essential* motives, may often take the historicist form of symbolic *regression*. That is, if one is seeking for the 'essence' of motives, one can only express such a search in the temporal terms of imaginative literature as a process of 'going back.'

Or conversely, in the "remembrance of things past" one may lay claim to an essential origin and thereby assert one's identity.[400] This pun of priority allows one to "translate back and forth between logical and temporal vocabularies."[401] But more importantly for Donne's salvatory purposes, it affords easy convertibility between essentialist and temporalist thought. For example, "original sin" is a historicist way of talking about "essential sin." Here temporizing functions as *causa*, "a form of apologia accounting for present conditions through a narrative, historical or mythic, of their provenance."[402] Conversely, Donne frequently uses historicist vocabulary (both biblically and culturally derived) to define his congregation's essence, or identity.

"Temporizing of essence" should be seen as a function of courtship, one to which Donne returns over and over again. In this application temporizing of essence operates as a reversed *metalepsis*, a trope "in which a remote cause is signified by a series of metaphoric steps to a present effect."[403]

---

[400] *GM*, 430.

[401] *GM*, 430.

[402] Dixon, *The Polliticke Courtier*, 208.

[403] Dixon, *The Polliticke Courtier*, 208. Peacham's example of *metalepsis* from Virgil illustrates the implicit logic in such figures of process: "Virgil by eares of Corn, he signifyeth haruestes, by haruestes, sommers, and by sommers, yeares": *The Garden of Eloquence* (1577), [C4v].

Here narrative and logical forms merge, where any point in a sequence implies its end. Consequently, one's end (and therefore, by the pun of logic, one's essence) can be represented by *synecdoche* as any one of the steps in the process toward that end, so that to be in process is to identify with the end of the process. As we noted in relation to *Astrophil and Stella*, to court is to declare one's essence (either aspired-to or actual) in temporal or narrative terms. A person can symbolically change his essence, then, by putting himself "in the way" (as Donne might put it).[404]

Before falling into the fault of anachronism, I should make a distinction between Burke's modern sense of "temporizing" and usage contemporary to Donne. This distinction, in fact, engenders a certain irony in my argument regarding Donne's managing of this principle. In the context of a discussion of Christian devotion, Richard Baxter provides a standard seventeenth-century sense of temporizing as "*[t]he prevalence of worldly, fleshly interests too much against the interest and work of Christ,*" and specifically, "Our too much minding worldly things, and shrinking from duties that will hinder our commodity."[405] Ironically, Donne uses temporal (i.e. "worldly, fleshly") interests to generate an analogous interest in Christian duty. Fundamentally, Baxter and Donne agree: the process of spiritual improvement involves bringing worldly motives into proper relations. It is in their methods that they differ.

Donne typically responds to the difficulty of rendering the ineffable by translating the essential into temporal terms. In this application, it will be helpful to take another approach via Burke's *logological* thesis, which states that "since the theological use of language is thorough, the close study of theology and its forms will provide us with good insight into the nature of language itself as a motive."[406] I am rather interested in this process in reverse, to see how the linguistic analogy serves Donne rhetorically as a means of configuring a courtship of the divine. Burke's fifth logological analogy states, "'Time' is to 'eternity' as the particulars in the unfolding of a sentence are to the sentence's unitary meaning."[407] Donne makes a similar correlation in his *Devotions*, where he says, "*Eternity* is not an everlast-

---

[404] cf. my earlier discussion of 8:12.560.

[405] Baxter, *Gildas Salvianus* in *The Practical Works*, ed. Orme, 14:198. There is also the sense of temporizing where one might object *now* to something one opposes *categorically* to avoid having to say so (*GM*, 439). This is closer to the third sense cited in the *OED*: "to act, negotiate, parley, treat, deal (with a person, etc.), so as to gain time."

[406] *RR*, vi. In *RR*, Burke develops six analogies between theology (words about God) and "logology" (words about words).

[407] *RR*, 33.

ing flux of *Tyme*; but *Tyme* is as a short *parenthesis* in a longe *period*."[408] St. Augustine sets out the theological relation that gives rise to Burke's logological analogy, and provides Donne with a framework for relating this life in time to the next in eternity. Addressing God in prayer, Augustine says,

> Your 'years' neither go nor come. Ours come and go so that all may come in succession. All your 'years' subsist in simultaneity, because they do not change; those going away are not thrust out by those coming in. But the years which are ours will not all be until all years have ceased to be. Your 'years' are 'one day' ... and your 'day' is not any and every day but Today, because your Today does not yield to a tomorrow, nor did it follow on a yesterday. Your Today is eternity.[409]

This mode of thought is evident in Donne's statement that

> Christ does not call us to an immediate possession of glory, without doing any thing between. Our Glorification was in his intention, as soon as our Election: in God who sees all things at once, both entred at once; but in the Execution of his Decrees here, God carries us by steps; he calls us to Repentance (7:5.764–768).

Like Burke, Donne is interested in the implications of this temporal-eternal relationship for human action.

This paradox of time and eternity is the basis of Donne's repeated assertion that this temporal life is a participation in eternal life. The humane arts, says Donne, are impotent to bring us an understanding of eternity: "The best help that I can assigne you, is, to use well *Æternum vestrum*, your owne Eternity; as S. *Gregory* calls our whole course of this life, *Æternum nostrum*, our Eternity" (4:2.904–907). In this sermon about the final resurrection, and in others as well, Donne's point is to emphasise that what his congregation does today is consubstantial with eternity, that it is in many ways a participation in eternity. This sermon is largely an amplification of his proposition that "our blessed Saviour thus mingles his

---

[408] Donne, *Devotions Upon Emergent Occasions*, meditation 14, ed. Anthony Raspa (Montreal and London: McGill-Queen's UP, 1975), 71.

[409] St. Augustine, *Confessions*, trans. Henry Chadwick (Oxford: Oxford University Press, 1991), 230 (11.13.16). Burke takes as his text a more grammar-oriented passage (4.10.15), but the basic mode of thought is the same (RR, 27). See also John M. Quinn, "Eternity" and "Time" in *Augustine Through the Ages*, 318–20, 832–8 and Simo Knuuttila, "Time and Eternity in Augustine," in *The Cambridge Companion to Augustine*, ed. E. Stump and N. Kretzmann (Cambridge: Cambridge University Press, 2001), 103–15.

Kingdomes, that he makes the Kingdome of Grace, and the Kingdome of Glory, all one" (371–373). This statement comes in the middle of a long *confirmatio* where Donne depicts the final resurrection as typologically present in various "resurrections" in this life (a common strategy in Donne's sermons). It is in this temporal paradox that Donne finds a solution to the rhetorical problem posed by Calvinist soteriology.[410]

❧ Temporizing of election

Donne's strategy of temporizing essence is part of a larger preoccupation with time in the sermons. Eiléan Ní Chuilleanáin notes, as an aspect of this persistent concern, Donne's frequent reference to the circumstances of the sermonic occasion. She describes "the energy of his 'now,' often repeated and emphasised as the true time of salvation."[411] This, however, is much more true of Andrewes than of Donne. Andrewes frequently refers to the "*hodie*" of the sermon. Ní Chuilleanáin also mentions the Puritan emphasis on methods for determining one's status among the elect in conjunction with "autobiographical narratives in which conversion was located in time," but she goes on to suggest that Donne rejects these means of addressing the doctrine of election.[412] This is not entirely the case. Donne persistently translates the essential status of the elect into terms of temporal experience, and in doing so he frequently uses himself, as well as others, as an *exemplum*.

It may be unthinkable to some to associate Donne with Puritan theology, but we should not let theological prejudice set limits on Donne's rhetorical options. Critics have frequently used Donne's prose as a site for excavating his theological positions, and have typically done so without adequate recognition that Donne's doctrine comes to us by means of highly rhetorical discourses.[413] For Donne, in the sermons at least, doctrine is often contingent upon rhetorical-devotional need. Dewey D. Wallace notes

[410] I specify Calvinist doctrine because this was, by and large, the dominant theological culture into which Donne preached. The Roman Catholic and Arminian paradigms produced a different set of rhetorical-devotional problems.

[411] Eiléan Ní Chuilleanáin, "Time, Place and the Congregation in Donne's Sermons," in *Literature and Learning in Medieval and Renaissance England*, ed. John Scattergood (Dublin: Irish Academic Press, 1984), 197–216, here 198.

[412] Ní Chuilleanáin, "Time, Place and the Congregation," 205.

[413] Jeanne Shami similarly criticises those who pick selectively through Donne's sermons to argue his theological affiliation: Horton Davies that Donne was an Arminian; Barbara Lewalski and Paul R. Sellin that Donne was a Calvinist: "Introduction: Reading Donne's Sermons," *JDJ* 11 (1992): 1–20, here 6. More recently, Daniel Doerksen has argued, by way of the sermons, Donne's sympa-

that in post-Reformation England, doctrines grew out of religious experience and that "different theologies [of grace] were not mainly different
solutions to intellectual puzzles, carried on by dint of the ineluctable
curiosity of the human mind, but were formulations that expressed,
enshrined, and stimulated particular pieties."[414] In the same way, Donne's
doctrine can be seen to reflect the devotional needs (the "pieties") of his congregants, as he perceives them. This is especially true of his formulation of
election, which, I will argue, grows out of the religious experience of an audience that has difficulty living with the ambiguities of the nominal status of
the elect. Donne's persistent emphasis on human agency has less to do with
any quarrel between faith and works, Calvinism and Arminianism, than with
the needs of a congregation who seek assurance in this life of their status in
the next. The doctrine of election, then, is inherently rhetorical in that it
involves notions of belonging and hence identification: "we are clearly in the
region of rhetoric," says Burke, "when considering the identifications
whereby a specialized activity makes one a participant in some social or economic [or spiritual, we should add] class."[415] Therefore we are also in the
realm of courtship, where one desires to belong to a desirable class.

Burke's "grammar of motives" is helpful in understanding Donne's
handling of the doctrine of salvation. As explained in Burke's book by the
same name, five terms (called the pentad) must be included in a "rounded
statement about motives": act, scene, agent, agency, and purpose. The
philosophical inclination or "terminology" of one's accounting of motives
is revealed by which term is featured: the featuring of "scene" corresponds
to materialism; "agent" to idealism; "agency" to pragmatism; "purpose" to
mysticism; "act" to realism.[416] In meeting the devotional needs of his congregation, Donne typically emphasizes process rather than essence, moving
from an orientation of idealism, which emphasizes the agent, to realism or
pragmatism, which emphasize act and agency respectively. The first agent-
act ratio involves God who elects the elect. Donne is interested in the

---

thies with moderate Calvinist Puritans: *Conforming to the Word* (Lewisburg: Bucknell University
Press, 1997), *passim*. Obversely, Achsah Guibbory uses the sermons to demonstrate Donne's softening of the rigours of Calvinist doctrine as he moves toward an Arminian position in the latter
part of his career: "Donne's Religion: Montagu, Arminianism and Donne's Sermons, 1624–1630,"
ELR 31 (2001): 412–39. Shami's objection is chiefly over methodology of proof-texting; my com-
plaint is against an often attendant insensitivity to the rhetorical quality of the text, which includes
the place of a given passage in the overall *dispositio*.

[414] Dewey D. Wallace, *Puritans and Predestination* (Chapel Hill: University of North Carolina Press,
1982), ix.

[415] *RM*, 27–28.

[416] *GM*, xv, 128.

divine act of election in eternity, but he is even more interested in the act of the second agent-act ratio: the elect (who is a patient with respect to the first agent, but still an agent in his own right) and his activity as one of the elect. Donne's interest in the act of the secondary agent derives from the inscrutability of both the mind of the Elector and his act, and therefore of the essential identity of the second agent (the potentially-elect) as well. Donne frequently uses the circumstances (which would include the terms of Burke's pentad) in analyzing his text, and he typically emphasizes the activity of the agent — the "what" and "how." When using the circumstances to divide his text, Donne typically moves from agent to act and/or agency. In his sermon preached to Queen Anne, for example, Donne began with the persons ("who are the lovers in this text") before moving on to their act of love ("the affection it self" characterized as "enjoying" and "seeking") and its agency, the how ("early seeking") (1:5.75, 80–87). In a sermon on the penitential Psalms Donne, in typical fashion, takes two parts: the agent, David, and the act, his prayer (5:16.47–79).

This emphasis on the activity of the agent is an instance of temporized essence functioning as a courtship strategy. It is a strategy that is also found in Donne's frequent use of *exempla*, especially biblical *exempla*, figures who incarnate in historical time the eternal principles of Scripture. Again, this strategy is illuminated when seen as a grammar (this time not in Burke's specialized sense) of courtship, as Donne tells his congregation,

> His [Simeon's] example, and the characters that are upon him, are our Alphabet. I shall onely have time to name the rest of those characters; you must spell them, and put them into their syllables; you must forme them, and put them into their words; you must compose them, and put them into their Syntaxis, and sentences; that is, you must pursue the imitation, that when I have told you what he was, you may present your selves to God, such as he was (7:11.370–376).

This method of instilling Christian identity is overtly rhetorical. Here Donne plays the role of Roger Ascham's schoolmaster, who teaches eloquence in Latin by leading his pupils in examining first the grammar and later the rhetoric of the best models, with the aim of teaching them to imitate the style of the most eloquent authors.[417] But the passage also resonates with the

---

[417] Perhaps even more precisely, Donne's method here resembles that of Edmund Coote in *The English Schoole-Maister* (1596), who sets out a series of tables of letters and syllables to assist novice grammarians in English to begin putting words together. Coote's book,

Augustinian-Burkeian idea that this grammatical process of imitation in time (a courtly as well as a rhetorical gesture) is constitutive of an essential identity, a meaning, that is manifest at one's final presentation before God in eternity. Similarly, in the sermons, one's election (an essential status) is found in the grammar of a rightly ordered life in present historical time.

This proof of daily experience is very different from the rhetorical approach of the Calvinists. Alister McGrath notes that later Calvinists in the sixteenth century systematized Calvin's Institutes into "a logically coherent and rationally defensible system, derived from syllogistic deductions based upon known axioms."[418] Concomitantly, predestination became a "controlling principle" for establishing general principles from which to deduce consequences.[419] McGrath summarizes Theodore Beza's "*ordo rerum decretarum,*" a chart depicting the divine decree of election, in which "[e]verything in the history of salvation is shown to be the logical execution in time of the 'eternal and immutable purpose of God'."[420] This scholastic-Calvinist influence (as McGrath characterizes it) is clearly evident in William Ames's syllogistic approach to the man who wants to know if he has eternal life. Ames sets out his syllogism, based on John 11:26 and Psalm 118:17, thus:

> *Whosoever beleeues in Christ, shall not dye but liue.*
> *I beleeue in Christ:*
> Therefore, *I shall not dye but liue.*[421]

Donne, in contrast, seeks more concrete, palpable proof, addressing the problem of assurance *vis à vis* the minor term or "witness," as Ames calls it.

For Donne, his audience's problem is not one of doctrinal belief, but of personal assurance, not of understanding (*logos*), but of feeling (*pathos*). Donne's approach to *consolatio* is to help his audience find assurance of their election in a rightly ordered and interpreted life. He states this prob-

---

which was aimed at a popular audience, was sold in St. Paul's Churchyard and was in print throughout Donne's tenure at St. Paul's (see my introduction to the *RET* electronic edition at http://www.library.utoronto.ca/www/utel/ret/coote/ret2.html). Robert Whalen interprets this passage as an instance of Donne's sacramental poetics of immanence whereby one's election is seen to be infused in current devotional experience (*Poetry of Immanence*, 100–9).

[418] Alister McGrath, *A Life of John Calvin* (Oxford: Basil Blackwell, 1990), 212.

[419] McGrath, *A Life of John Calvin*, 213.

[420] McGrath, *A Life of John Calvin*, 214.

[421] Ames, *Conscience*, Book I, p.3, B2. Dykstra Eusden describes Ames's adaptation of the traditional syllogism into terms appropriate to religious "proof," where the major term becomes the "light" of Scripture, the minor term the "witness," and the conclusion (also scriptural) the "judgment": "Introduction," in *The Marrow of Theology*, 44.

lem in application to the early preachers of the Gospel. "It cost the Apostles, and their Successors," says Donne,

> more paines and more labour, *ut persuaderent hominibus, dona Dei iis indulta*, To perswade men that this mercy of God, and these merits of Christ Jesus were intended to them, and directed upon them, in particular, then to perswade them that such things were done: they can beleeve the promise, and the performance in generall, but they cannot finde the application thereof in particular; the voice that is neerest us we least heare, not because God speaks not loud enough, but because we stop our eares; nor that neyther; for wee doe hear, but because we do not hearken then, nor consider; no nor that neyther, but because we doe not answere, nor cooperate, nor assist God, in doing that which he hath made us able to doe by his grace, towards our own Salvation (1:8.250–262).

While grace (the cause of election) is eternal in God, it takes the form of an unbroken sequence in our experience, a sequence which argues continuance. Donne's characterization of God's grace as "precedent and subsequent, and concommitant," this emphasis on continuity through time, is a temporal approximation of the eternal quality of grace (281–282). Thus grace is concurrent with works, for "without such Grace and such succession of Grace, our Will is so far unable to pre-dispose it selfe to any good" (282–283). In other words, to do good is to find evidence of one's participation in God's eternal grace. Donne adds to this narrative logic an organic metaphor in combination with a Christological precedent to bolster its *pathetic* effect:

> since Grace is our Father, that Parent that begets all goodness in us, *In similitudine ejus*, sayes *Origen*, conformable to the Pattern Christ himself, *Qui non nascitur & desinit*, who hath a continuall generation ... in all the acts of our understanding, and in a ready concurrence of our Will, let us every day, every minute *feele* [emphasis mine] this new generation of spirituall children (312–318).

Confirmatio comes through personal action (agency) which has its final source in the Divine agent and its effect in affective assurance.

In the same manner, sickness serves Donne as an "objective correlative" for structuring his congregation's thinking and feeling about God's salvatory means of grace. Troy Dale Reeves argues that notwithstanding any possible underlying psychosis in Donne, his keen interest in sickness and

death is best understood as "an existential means of approaching and com-
prehending the single most significant mystery of Christian experience:
grace."[422] That is, medicine is used by Donne in the *Devotions* and *Sermons*
as an analogue of "God's *real* cure."[423] This analogue, in Reeves's representation of it, enables Donne to focus (rhetorically, I would add) on the
human and visible means of a cure which only God can administer. Thus
Donne's curative imagery is commonly associated with the sacraments,
God's visible means of grace in the church.

Justification is another difficult theological idea which Donne brings
into closer temporal proximity to his congregation. Donne uses the topic
"of the cause" to amplify his doctrinal point. He describes justification as a
chain with four causal links: God, Christ, faith, and works. The logical
relation is augmented by Donne's inverted *climax* of descent from the ineffable final cause, God, to his effect on earth upon the elect. Again, the
emphasis is upon agency:

> As the efficient justification, the gracious purpose of God had
> done us no good, without the materiall satisfaction, the death of
> Christ had followed; And as that materiall satisfaction, the death
> of Christ would do me no good, without the instrumentall justifi-
> cation, the apprehension by faith; so neither would this profit
> without the declaratory justification, by which all is pleaded and
> established. God enters not into our materiall justification, that is
> onely Christs; Christ enters not into our instrumentall justifica-
> tion, that is onely faiths; Faith enters not into our declaratory jus-
> tification, (for faith is secret) and declaration belongs to workes
> (7:8.480–489).[424]

This conceptual chain acquires distinct upward and downward connotations as it is recast in historicist vocabulary:

> Consider we then our selves, as men fallen downe into a darke and
> deepe pit; and justification as a chaine, consisting of these foure
> links, to be let downe to us, and let us take hold of that linke that
> is next us, A good life, and keepe a fast and inseparable hold upon
> that .... God comes downeward to us; but we must go upward to

---

[422] Reeves, "*Sana Me Domine*," 270.

[423] Reeves, "*Sana Me Domine*," 273.

[424] The traditional causes in Aristotelian logic are material, formal, efficient, and final. I am unaware
of any precedent for Donne's "declaratory" cause.

God; not to get above him in his unrevealed Decrees, but to go up towards him, in laying hold upon that lowest linke; that as the holy Ghost shall reprove, that is, convince the world, that there is no other righteousnesse but that of Christ, so he may enable you to passe a judgement upon your selves, and to testifie to the world that you have apprehended that righteousness (496–509).

This is Donne's way of reconciling God's unrevealed decrees, such as election and justification, to the individual's need for assurance. What Donne offers here is proof of the eternal by means of temporal experience, in essence a proof by courtship. In putting the congregants on the way, upon the first link in the chain, Donne enables them to apprehend their essential position at the topmost link of the chain. This first link (consubstantial with the final cause by means of this causal chain) is one of declaration, a laying claim to an essential identity through deeds done in time. Achsah Guibbory uses this passage to prove an Arminian turn in Donne's soteriology, but to take this as a bald statement of theology is to distort the import of the text. This is not a theological statement *per se*, but rather a rhetorical appeal designed to meet the devotional needs of a congregation, and it is informed as much by a culture of courtship as it is by dogma and ecclesiastical polity.[425]

There are good cultural reasons for viewing Donne's temporizing of election as a courtship strategy. The term *election* itself carried political overtones in usage contemporary to Donne: Sir Thomas Elyot uses it in application to the art of courtesy and patronage promotion.[426] Moreover, Donne's emphasis on actualizing or authenticating one's status among the elect by one's manner of life shares kinship with a fundamental principle of courtship begun as early as Castiglione and carried throughout the courtesy literature of the period. Frank Whigham describes the semiotics of Elizabethan courtship: "[e]lite status no longer rested upon the absolute, given base of birth, the received ontology of social being; instead it had increasingly become a matter of doing, and so of *showing*."[427] Castiglione's *sprezzatura* thus reflected a nonchalance that bespoke a native ability; a

---

[425] Guibbory, "Donne's Religion," 430–31. For a nuanced study of Donne's strategic handling of soteriology in the interest of his congregation's needs, see Robert Whalen, *The Poetry of Immanence*, ch. 3.

[426] Sir Thomas Elyot, *The Book named The Governor*, ed. S. E. Lehmberg (London: Dent, 1962), 154–58.

[427] Whigham, *Ambition and Privilege*, 32–33.

courtier confirmed his *telos* by his manner of conduct. Whigham further points out the ambiguity that arises where these outward signs can be declared as a natural outworking of one's position by birth or of inner quality.[428] This temporal-essential ambiguity is at work in John Ferne's *The Blazon of the Gentrie* (1586), where he notes that historically, nobility was originally achieved on the basis of one's reputation of character and deeds. Extending this narrative of origins forward, Ferne adds that presently, "A Gentleman or a Nobleman is he ... which is knowne, and through the heroycall vertues of his life, talked of in euery mans mouth."[429]

In the same way, this enactment of one's essence among the elect is a mode of courtship, a conventional way of declaring and proving one's nature where it may seem to be in question. To adapt Whigham to our purposes, this courtship strategy of temporizing essence "works through the inferential movement from stylistic action to ontological conclusion."[430] Or as Burke puts it, a thing's *essence* or *quiddity* becomes identical with its principle of action, as when Hamlet says that "use almost can change the stamp of nature" (*Hamlet*, 3.4.169).[431] In an image resonant with courtship significance, Donne tells his congregation at Lincoln's Inn that "[a]lways from that mount of *sanctification* arises our prospect to *election*" (3:7.264–265).[432] Conversely, temptation or "scandal" may cause one to "fall ... into dangerous and ruinous action," to descend the hill and to lose sight of one's election (268–269). Here Donne plays with notions of narrative and essential order in adapting the common notion that sanctification is a mark of the elect. Logically, election precedes sanctification, but experientially, narratively, sanctification leads to an apprehension of election. Theologically, sanctification, one's present ascent in purity of action, has no causal bearing on election; but experientially, it does.

Donne uses the hill image again in a sermon that addresses the abuses of the doctrine of election. In opposition to the Pharisees (stand-ins for English nonconformists) who believe they have God communicated to themselves all

---

[428] Whigham, *Ambition and Privilege*, 33.

[429] John Ferne, *The Blazon of the Gentrie* (1586), 4, [B2v]. In his prefatory letter to Sir Walter Ralegh in the *Faerie Queene*, Spenser states the purpose of his book: "to fashion a gentleman or noble person in vertuous and gentle discipline" (ed. A. C. Hamilton [London: Longman, 1977]: 737). Similarly, the anonymous author of *The Institucion of a Gentleman* (1555) remarks that though a gentleman is born, he must work to become worthy of his birth (K3).

[430] Whigham, *Ambition and Privilege*, 35.

[431] *GM*, 249.

[432] Donne frames his subject of "scandals" with respect to courtship motives. He warns that, "[t]o hinder the feet of another, that would goe farther, or climbe higher in the ways of godlinesse, but for me; to say to any man, What need you be so pure, so devout, so godly, so zealous, will this make you rich, will this bring you to preferment? this is an active scandall in me" (3:7.52–56).

at once "intirely and irrevocably," Donne poses a courtship model where one approaches God "by participation of his successive Grace, more and more, as he receives more and more grace" (9:6.520–522). In contrast to the courtship image of ascent up a hill, these "Pharisees" see this life "but as an easie walk downe a hill" (526): the goal already attained, the subject has nothing to do but enjoy a perfunctory descent. In promoting his progressive model of spiritual purification, Donne does not deny the doctrine of grace and unconditional election, but rather the extreme versions of it (535–545). But more importantly, in doing so Donne provides his congregation with equipment for living, a sacramental vision of this life infused with the essence of grace.

So then, in emphasizing the signs or activity of the elect, Donne suggests that action will bring the inner life into line and experientially determine one's essence as one of the elect. Donald Friedman describe's Donne's approach to his vocation in similar terms. Lacking any intuitive or communal sense of God's calling to ministry, Donne found his calling confirmed in his enactment of it — in his activity as a priest. Friedman says,

> Donne's apprehension of the failure of agency in the absence of an identity confirmed by community [i.e. failure to find a suitable career] ... is resolved when he finds his calling in the offices of the church, when he finally 'hears' the voice that summons him to the priesthood in day-to-day acts that constitute its work in the world. Characteristically, he defines himself by what he sees and does, rather than by any conviction of being moved by providential will. The moment of ultimate vision, the confrontation with the face of God, is indefinitely postponed; but never does he contemplate hearing the voice of God directly.[433]

This is fundamentally a rhetorical gesture. To act called is to have a calling: or, to act elected is to be elected. That is, essence is confirmed temporally by one's enacting of it. Consequently, Donne's way of calling his congregation to an assurance of their election is to call them to action.

---

[433] Donald M. Friedman, "Donne, Herbert, and Vocation," *GHJ* 18 (1994): 135–58, here 144. Whether Donne felt that a priestly calling was a matter of personal choice (as Friedman says he did) or not, remains unclear (139). What is clear is that in the absence of any direct apprehension of the mind of God, Donne looks for confirmation in experience.

❧ A brief conclusion on *dispositio* and the eloquence of Donne's sermons

The basic *dispositio* of a Donne sermon is (to borrow another Burkeian formulation) "an individuation of formal principles" which are drawn from "experience outside of art."[434] Donne's sermons enable the audience, in the course of the canonical hour, to engage symbolically in the basic Christian forms of Fall and Redemption. Burke goes so far as to relate this individuation of form to Platonic idealism, where the form is a way of experiencing the ideal; in this way it has much the same rhetorical effect as temporizing of essence, where the temporized process enables an immediate experience of the essential and ineffable. Each sermon, then, is an individualization of Christian forms, or, in Donne's register, a sacrament. The effective power of symbolism, says Burke, depends on shared experience between the artist (and his work) and the audience.[435] The rhetorical power of Donne's sermons as symbolic action thus derives from his rigorous engagement of biblical forms with the conventional forms of his congregation's experience in the world. In the chapters that follow, I will explore this quality in Donne's rhetoric with close readings of three sermons which infuse experiences common to his congregation with spiritual significance.

---

[434] *CS*, 143.
[435] *CS*, 153.

CHAPTER FOUR

Courtship and the Discourse of Prodigality in Donne's Sermon on Isaiah 52:3

Isaiah 52:3
YE HAVE SOLD YOUR SELVES FOR NOUGHT, AND
YE SHALL BE REDEEMED WITHOUT MONEY.

DONNE'S *INVENTIO* IN THE SERMONS FOLLOWS the rhetorical tradition of "finding" matter in the circumstances of his oration;[436] but as Donne himself suggests in his first extant sermon, preached "at Greenwich" on 30 April 1615 (the third Sunday after Easter), invention involves not only finding the material available, but also amplifying that material. Indeed, for Donne, finding and amplifying are all one. Donne's perspective on invention begins with his understanding of the Bible. His job as a preacher is to "find" his matter and argument in his text. His *inventio*, the overall argument of the text from "the miserable condition of man" to "the abundant mercy of our Redeemer," is a "model" or "designe" to which "those words

---

[436] Walter J. Ong describes the "rhapsodic" method of invention (borrowed from oral-formulaic composition) whereby the rhetor "stitches" together a discourse from the common storehouse of material: *Rhetoric, Romance, and Technology* (Ithaca: Cornell University Press, 1971), 34–38; preaching manuals of Donne's time added the element of finding matter in Scripture (of course) but also in the circumstances of the sermon (the time, place, audience, and the particulars of the occasion).

which the Holy Ghost hath chosen in this text, hath invited and led us" (1:1.124–127). In amplifying this matter, Donne does not conceive of something new, but merely opens up the text to its fullness. In other words, *inventio* is, from the human perspective, a discovery of the abundance the Holy Spirit has placed in the text. At the same time, to amplify the matter of the text is to find the order inherent in the matter. For Donne, then, both amplification and arrangement are integral aspects of invention.

Donne's deployment of the courtship *topos* in this sermon provides a prime example of the centrality of arrangement in his *inventio* and amplification of his argument. Peter E. McCullough argues convincingly that this sermon preached "at Greenwich" was not delivered in the parish church as Potter and Simpson suggest, but rather at court, possibly with King James in attendance. Although Donne drew on these same fields of reference in addressing diverse audiences (as I demonstrate above), the degree of Donne's concentration on juridical and socio-economic matters, in addition to the linguistic complexities of his hermeneutic, support McCollough's attribution of audience.[437] From the text of the sermon, "Ye have sold your selves for nought, and ye shall be redeemed without money" (Isaiah 52:3), Donne derives a basic two-part structure of fall and redemption consisting of "the miserable condition of man, wherin he enwraped himself, and of the aboundant mercy of Christ Jesus in withdrawing him from that universal calamity"; and he will derive this structure, he says, "by considering onely the sense, and largeness, and extention of those words, in which the holy Ghost hath been pleased to express both these in this Text" (39–43). Donne begins to open up the riches of the text by amplifying the definition of two Hebrew terms he finds there: *machar* ("sold your selves") and *kinnan* ("for nought"). In each case, he extrapolates his definition into a progressive series or hierarchy, moving from the term's mildest to its most dyslogistic synonym. This process is then cast into a narrative in the first person plural by which Donne insinuates his and his audience's fall into spiritual destitution.

But Donne also finds in these words and in his audience's common experience an analogy between the socio-political and the spiritual, which he will use to give a particular emotional colouring to his sermon's argument. Drawing on legal and popular discourse, Donne develops a simili-

---

[437] For McCullough's full argument see "Donne as Preacher at Court: Precarious 'Inthronization'," ed. David Colclough, *John Donne's Professional Lives* (Cambridge: D. S. Brewer, 2003): 180–2. Potter and Simpson find Donne's references to commerce and prodigals apt material for "a congregation of practical men in trade or business" such as would attend the parish church (I:117). One ought to be careful not to infer too much from Donne's fields of reference. As I think my analysis will demonstrate, Donne's handling of these cultural *topoi* could appeal to a diverse audience.

tude between social and spiritual prodigality to evoke in his audience a sense of repulsion and shame associated with the low status of the prodigal in early modern England. His vivid depiction of prodigality, as I will demonstrate, bears a close similarity to the diction of Tudor poor-laws and to various other cultural representations of the prodigal. In evoking this similitude, Donne borrows from the social order of motives to induce a reordering of his congregation's spiritual values and a reorientation within the hierarchy of the text. That is, he uses this judicial procedure for a deliberative end: to define his audience, to name them prodigals, so that he might motivate them to court a new identity.

These two means of *inventio*, definition and similitude, become rich resources for amplifying the *topos* of courtship as I have described it in the previous chapters. First, in arranging his material hierarchically, in accordance with the principle of courtship, Donne establishes in his audience a mode of thought, urging them to think of their present state as a point leading either in an upward aspiration or a downward slide. Yet closely related, indeed inseparable from this discursive pattern, is an affective impulse which inheres in all such formal structures. Donne's use of a socially-derived notion of prodigality as a similitude of his audience's spiritual malaise (as he constructs it) establishes a pattern of affection, where an appeal to an emotionally charged instance of social hierarchy goads and affectively re-enforces the upward-striving thoughts of his audience. This cognitive-affective pattern, combining modes of *logos* and *pathos*, aids the two-part structure of his *divisio* — "*Exprobrationem*, and *Consolationem*" — by engendering a dissatisfaction with the "miserable condition of man" and an attendant desire for "the abundant mercy of our Redeemer" (125–132). Finally, by this means, Donne quite literally moves his audience through the text toward a re-identification with their Saviour and purification from their implication in spiritual prodigality. All this Donne "finds" in Isaiah 52:3.

~· II ·~

Donne's *inventio* largely consists of amplifying the order of the matter in the text, from which he derives the *dispositio* or movement of his argument. Thomas Wilson in *The Art of Rhetoric* (1560), defines amplification as "a figure in rhetoric which consisteth most in augmenting and diminishing of any matter, and that divers ways."[438] Later in the same section he adds that

---

438 Wilson, *Art of Rhetoric*, 152.

"[w]e increase our cause by heaping of words and sentences together, couching many reasons into one corner which before were scattered abroad, to the intent that our talk might appear more vehement."[439] This is similar to Kenneth Burke's description of amplification as "the saying of something in various ways until it increases in persuasiveness by sheer accumulation."[440] Donne goes one step further. He augments this sense of accumulation in the way he arranges his material. He uses definition to derive from the text a hierarchy of near-synonyms through which he moves his audience in a replication of an archetypal Edenic fall. For Burke, hierarchy always implies motives of courtship, a desire to move up or down a scale. Burke might paraphrase Donne's *propositio* to say that humanity is goaded by the impetus of sin in a downward courtship of the Devil. Donne uses his series of terms to implicate his audience in such a movement, in a downward slide into spiritual prodigality.

To define the word translated in the text as "ye have sold," Donne uses a collection of Latin equivalents which he arranges in a graded connotative series. He then "invents" his matter here according to "many places of Scripture" where these synonyms are found. The Hebrew *Machar* signifies

> *dare pro re alia*, a permutation, an exchange of one thing for another; and in other places it signifies *Dedere*, upon any little attempt to forsake and abandon our defences, and to suffer the enemy easily to prevail upon us; so also it signifies *Tradere*, not onely to forsake our selves, but to concur actually to the delivering up of our selves; and lastly, it signifies *Repellere*, to joyn with our enemies in beating back any that should come to our relief, and rescue (45–52).

By so paraphrasing his terms, Donne already begins addressing these definitions to his audience's situation. He then personalizes his semantic progression, implicating his audience in this falling action and repeating the phrase "worse than that" to emphasize the descent. He continues,

> we have so sold our selves, for the substance of the Act, as is expressed in that word *Machar*, we have exchanged our selves at an undervalue, and worse than that, we have yeelded up our selves upon easie tentations, and worse than that, we have offered our

---

[439] Wilson, *Art of Rhetoric*, 158–59.
[440] *RM*, 69.

selves, exposed our selves, invited the devil, and tempted temptations, and worse than that, we have Rejected the succours and the
supplies which have been offered us in the means and conduits,
and seals of his Graces (52–59).

With each "worse than that" Donne successively introduces an application
of each of the three definitions he used to amplify the meaning of *Machar*,
thereby augmenting the progressive wretchedness of the prodigal act, while
insinuating his audience's involvement in the process. In this way, the word
of the text signifies not just an action, but a progressive series of actions.
The word itself becomes a symbol of his audience's movement in the first
half of the sermon. Donne's use of amplification here is much as Wilson
describes it, bringing together synonyms which before were "scattered
about" throughout the Vulgate, although his words are not exactly
"heaped," as in Wilson's definition; in fact, they are, as we have noted,
ordered in a deliberate way. Wilson seems to have *congeries* in mind
(whereby we "lay on such load and so go to it by heapes," in Puttenham's
words),[441] whereas Donne's words are arranged by *auxesis*, in a climactic
order. But the effect is no less vehement. Indeed, it is augmented by his use
of repetition.

Wilson goes on to discuss the pathetic function of amplification: "the
beauty of amplifying standeth most in apt moving of affections."[442] Wilson
defines affections, or passions, as "none other thing but a stirring or forcing of the mind either to desire or else to detest and loathe anything more
vehemently than by nature we are commonly wont to do." Significantly, it
is "out of the substance in things" as well as out "of words" that "affections
are derived": it is in matter, or *inventio*, not merely *elocutio*, that an argument achieves *pathos*.[443] To move the affections, says Wilson, "the weight
of the matter must be so set forth as though they saw it plain before their
eyes; the report must be such and the offense made so heinous, that the like
hath not been seen heretofore, and all the circumstances must thus be heaped
together."[444] Whereas Wilson speaks in the context of a juridical mode,
where the *narratio* sets out the full details of a legal case in a vivid description (the who, what, where, when, and how), Donne's amplification is

---

[441] Under its alternate name, *sinathrismus* (Puttenham, *Arte of English Poesie*, 243).
[442] Wilson, *Art of Rhetoric*, 160.
[443] Wilson, *Art of Rhetoric*, 152.
[444] Wilson, *Art of Rhetoric*, 161.

exegetical. Yet there is a sense in which Donne too is making a case against his audience. His heap consists of only one circumstance, the action (the "what"), but the action also implies the character of the agent (the "who") whom Donne identifies as his audience. Despite the limited range of circumstances, this personalized and graded presentation of the act sets the matter out plainly and pathetically, as Wilson prescribes.

Donne adds another form of amplification. This form is described by Wilson as occurring "when things increased and things diminished are both set together, that one may the rather beautify the other. As if when God's goodness towards us were largely amplified, we did straight extenuate our unthankfulness towards him again."[445] Juxtaposition, a principle of arrangement, is seen as an amplifying device where one's given matter is viewed in the broader relations where comparison helps determine the order of things. This is the very relation Donne uses, though not so much to render God's mercy beautiful as to build on his definition of prodigality to emphasize human wretchedness in contrast with God's munificence and therefore the distance between man and God on the scale of prudence. He defines another word from his text according to the "places of Scripture", this time to describe the manner of man's repudiation of God. He continues,

> how we have done this ... is expressed in that other word, *kinnan*, which signifies *fecit*, as it is here, *Gratis*, for nought. And in another place, *Frustra*, to no purpose; for it is a void bargain, because we had no title, no interest in our selves, when we sold our selves; and it signifies, *temere*, rashly, without consideration of our own value, upon whom God had stamped his Image; And then again it signifies, *Immerito*, undeservedly, before God, in whose jurisdiction we were by many titles, had forsaken us, or done any thing to make us forsake him (60–68).

Again he expands his word into an implicit progression of Latin synonyms from the word of the English text "for nought" (*Gratis*) to a statement of man's purposelessness and rashness, culminating in human undeservedness in *Immerito*.

Once more Donne uses *narratio* to personalize his definition and implicate his audience in this imprudent bargaining. He augments the travesty of this act by comparing the munificence of the rejected with the profligacy of the rejecter,

---

[445] Wilson, *Art of Rhetoric*, 159.

[s]o that our action in selling our selves for nothing, hath this latitude, That man whom God hath dignified so much, as that in the
Creation he imprinted his Image in him, and in the Redemption
he assumed not the Image, but the very nature of man, That man
whom God still preserved as the Aple of his Eye, and (as he
expresses himself often in the Prophets) is content to reason, and
to dispute with man, and to submit himself to any tryal whither
he have not been a gracious God unto him: That this man should
thus abandon this God, and exchange his soul for any thing in this
world, when as it can profit nothing, to gain the whole world and
loose our own soul, and not exchange it, but give it away, thrust it
off, and be a devil to the devil, to tempt the tempter himself to
take it (68–79).

The periodic structure of the first half of this long sentence heightens the
audience's apprehension regarding the matter of "selling our selves." Two
long dependent clauses beginning with "that man whom God" amplify or
"heap up" the blessedness of "this man" who "should thus abandon this
God," the source of blessing. But the audience is not allowed to rest through
the loose structure of the rest of the sentence, as Donne compounds the van-
ity and willfulness of the action in a series of parallel statements. He further
appeals to the emotion of his audience by placing them in the midst of an
agon between God at the beginning of the sentence and at the end the Devil,
to whom they are grammatically if not morally inclined.

   As in his definition of *Machar*, Donne's amplification gives *kinnan* a
dynamic role in his argument. To use Donne's own words, "the word [*kinnan*] aggravates our condemnation" and "multiplies our fault" — as does
his explication of *Machar* (79–80, 82). That is, the words themselves,
which are found in the text, aggravate the congregation. In expanding and
personalizing the definition of these words, Donne insinuates a whole story
which is already implied, in which his audience are agents of their own
descent into sin, repeating the universal fall from the dignity of creation
and identity with God to alliance and ultimate identification with the Devil.
Donne effectively identifies his audience with the Devil to shock them out of
their current state — in Wilson's words, to move or to stir their minds to
detest this condition, and to desire a reversal of this downward movement.
This dramatic realignment is designed to repel/impel his audience to a re-
identification with God through a reformation of their prodigal ways.

   So far I have emphasized Donne's appeal to *pathos* in his aggravation of
his congregation's guilt through his arrangement of the material of his text.

Yet even Wilson surreptitiously acknowledges that amplification can likewise provoke thought, along with emotion. In fact, when he speaks of moving the affections, it is in reference to the "mind." "He that loveth to enlarge by this kind," says Wilson, "must mark well the circumstances of things, and heaping them altogether he shall with ease espy how one thing riseth above another."[446] In other words, the arrangement or form of the matter is to be found in the inherent order or logic of the matter at hand, "how one riseth above another." Presumably, then, the rhetor's task is to lead his audience to discover and understand the inherent order of his matter, in this case the text. The logic Donne finds in his amplification of the first half of Isaiah 52:3 is one of each stage leading to the next in a downward slide, from the precipitous act of compromising oneself to the final end of debauchery. In reiterating this pattern, Donne establishes in his audience a pattern of thought as well as of feeling.

Burke helps clarify this relation between *logos* and *pathos* in his notion of form, or (because form involves sequence) *dispositio*. As described in chapter 3, the central agent in literary form, according to Burke, is desire (or its reverse, loathing). Form in art is simply the arousal and fulfilment of desire. But as he goes on to explain, desire derives from established patterns of thought: "A work has form in so far as one part of it leads a reader to anticipate another part, to be gratified by the sequence."[447] This anticipation derives from cognitive expectations akin to cause and effect, which in turn evoke a concomitant emotive impulse.

In the same section, Burke offers five principal types of form, three of which are at work here in Donne's sermon. These will serve to illustrate the close working between *pathos* and *logos* in the sermon's *dispositio*. First, Donne's definitions take a progressive form, where each in a series of elements seems a logical outcome of what has gone before.[448] Under the impetus of sin (the logic of the Fall), the prodigal act leads further and further away from the felicity of association with God. Second, Donne's definition and narration bear a repetitive form which, for rhetorical purposes, is best defined in *A Rhetoric of Motives*. Here Burke writes, "we know that many purely formal patterns can readily awaken an attitude of collaborative expectancy in us." He cites as an example a passage built about a set of oppositions (*We do this*, but *they look down*, etc.) where "[f]ormally, you will find yourself swinging along with the succession of antitheses, even

---

446 Wilson, *Art of Rhetoric*, 153.
447 *CS*, 124.
448 *CS*, 124.

though you may not agree with the proposition that is being presented in this form."[449] Similarly, in his repetitive and hierarchical arrangement of his matter, Donne invites his audience's cognitive participation in a paradigmatic fall.

This operation of *logos*, the engendering of cognitive expectation, provides occasion for an affective appeal. Earlier in *Counter-Statement*, Burke defines form in terms of the psychology of audience, where

> form is the creation of an appetite in the mind of the auditor, and the adequate satisfying of that appetite. This satisfaction—so complicated is the human mechanism—at times involves a temporary set of frustrations, but in the end these frustrations prove to be simply a more involved kind of satisfaction, and furthermore serve to make the satisfaction of fulfilment more intense.[450]

Frustration is very much Donne's strategy as he incessantly asserts his audience's downward motion throughout the *exordium* and early part of the *confirmatio*, only to defer the way out until the second half of the sermon. Formally, this arrangement functions to induce despair and an accompanying desire for relief, and then to provide the opportunity to gain that relief. At the same time that the formal operation of his progression entices his audience to assent, Donne's definition of that process urges that this is not the direction they want to go. Yet even as Donne's audience recognizes their desire to resist the slide into prodigality, the text incessantly pushes their thoughts in this very direction. In this state of tension, his audience is made ready to respond to his offer of a release from the process and to follow a reversal of the discursive pattern in an ascent toward God — once the opportunity is finally offered.

Finally, in its broadest operation, Donne's sermon brings its audience through the recognizable form of fall-redemption, which Donne finds in the rudiments of Christian doctrine implicit in the words of the text; this is the third type of form, which Burke calls "conventional form."[451] In the same way as a Shakespearean comedy evokes in the audience anterior expectations of marriage and restored social order, so in the Christian story (the argument of every sermon) the Fall holds promise of redemption. In

---

[449] *RM*, 58.
[450] *CS*, 31.
[451] *CS*, 126.

leading his audience in an enactment of a fall, Donne thus awakens their desire for deliverance, a desire that is predicated on recognition of a conventional form.

In this sermon the felt necessity of redemption follows closely on the heels of a recognition of need in the prodigal state. Donne meets this expectation of redemption as he rounds out his definition of his text, giving his *incrementum* of *kinnan*-connotations a twist. With the intervention of Christ, the word signifies quite differently.

> But then, as the word aggravates our condemnation, so it implies a consolation too; for it is *frustra*, That is unprovidently, unthriftily, inconsiderately, vainly, and that multiplies our fault, but then it is invalidly, and uneffectually too; that is, it is a void bargain; and when our powerful Redeemer, is pleased to come, and claim his right, and set on foot his title, all this improvident bargain of ours is voided, and reversed (79–85).

Whereas Donne's previous amplification of *kinnan* has directed the reader in a downward process, now this movement is turned back with the conjunction "but." This logical turn presents a loophole in Donne's semantic progression and foreshadows the completion of the sermon's emotive pattern in the redemption offered in Christ.

Gratification for his audience, however, is delayed. Throughout the first partition of the sermon, Donne focuses on the negative side of motives with his naming and defining of prodigality as he continues to identify his audience with the downward movement of the text.

⌣· III ·⌣

In the middle third of the sermon, Donne builds on his discursive framework with a social similitude that is laden with hierarchical motives. This second invention-amplification strategy also begins in the *exordium*. In his development of the word *kinnan*, Donne introduces a legal-commercial analogy which forms the basis of his argument throughout his *confirmatio*. Like his use of definition, Donne's extension of the analogy throughout the greater portion of the sermon is a variant of amplification which "increases in persuasiveness by the sheer accumulation" of the analogy.[452] To begin with, "selling" is seen primarily in its spiritual application of selling out to the Devil. But the social analogy quickly takes over as Donne structures his

---

[452] *RM*, 69.

audience's thinking and feeling about spiritual matters with reference to the more accessible ways of the world. In evoking a temporal order of motives which his audience readily accepts, he aims at inducing a similar assent to a spiritual order of motives.

By the time Donne introduces his socio-economic analogy, his audience is primed for the process it evokes by the semantic (and discursive) fall rehearsed in the *exordium*, and by his first reference to the text where he establishes a model of temporal-spiritual correspondence. Again Donne finds his temporal-spiritual analogy in the text, which he amplifies to derive his argument. He begins the sermon by setting out three sets of circumstances. After establishing the "what" — deliverance from calamity — he considers who was delivered, by whom, and from what. One possible exposition (allegorically considered) has the Jews delivered by Cyrus from Babylon, another poses the primitive church delivered by Constantine from years of Roman persecution, and the last sees the whole world delivered from the "bondage of death by sin" by the Redeemer Christ Jesus (1–12).

From the outset a hierarchy is evident as Donne moves from the most temporal (the most limited in place and time) to the most spiritual (the least tied to place and time). In each the temporal and spiritual cohere, but in varying relations. He rejects the first interpretation because even the Jews see more than a "temporal deliverance" in the text; even they recognize in it a type of the Messiah. He eliminates the second because the primitive church did not "sell themselves"; we might, however, note that typologically this interpretation represents an advance over the previous on the temporal-spiritual scale. Finally, Donne prefers the last option simply because it features spiritual deliverance in the Passion of Christ. But he cites as support the close correspondence between the temporal events described by Isaiah and those of the Gospel of Christ such that, as St. Jerome says,[453] "this Prophet *Esay*, is rather an Evangelist, than a Prophet" (31–32). In semiotic terms, the Babylonian captivity is but another temporal signifier of a more profound, spiritual redemption, while the persecution of the early church fails to signify altogether because it lacks correspondence to the text; but his own audience's need for deliverance from sin corresponds perfectly to the pattern of the text as fulfilled in the Passion of Christ. For Donne, meaning is in some respect contingent upon the need of his audience.[454] That is, the rhetorical situation plays a determining role in his interpretation of Scripture.

---

453 Jerome, *In Isa.* Prologue 3–4 (PL 24.18A).

454 Gale Carrithers, in a rather oblique way, makes a similar point under the rubric of Donne's existential thought. For Carrithers, Donne's sense of religious truth is experiential in so far as he always

Donne's similitude, then, is found through the typology inherent in the text and in relation to his audience's circumstances. The important point, for the moment, is the discursive pattern Donne establishes in his exegesis which reflects the hierarchical arrangement of his definitions, moving from the temporal signifier of the text to the spiritual meaning to which it corresponds: or as Donne expresses it, from the literal to a "secondary sense of accommodation" (35). Rhetorically, he urges his audience to make the same transition from the temporal signifiers of their quotidian experience to the corresponding meaning in their religious experience.

As an intermediate step in this process, Donne relates the events of the Old Testament to the experience of his audience. Still in the *exordium*, Donne derives his definition of redemption (amplifying the word "redeemed" from Isaiah) from three socio-political customs of the Old Testament, noting that "Christ Jesus ... is our Redeemer in all these acceptations of the word" (102–104). In explicating his term for his audience, he does two things at once. First, he gives the social function of the Old Testament a spiritual application to Christ and the church (corresponding to the last two steps of Donne's typological series). The provision of cities of refuge (Numbers 35:12), where murderers could escape the vengeance of their victim's kin, is a type of Christ who "is our sanctuary and refuge; when we have commited spiritual murder upon our own Souls, he preserves us, and delivers us to the redemption ordained for us" (104–106). And as provision was made for a man to redeem his neighbour's forfeited possessions (Leviticus 25:25), so "when we have sold our possessions, our natural faculties, He supplies us with grace, and feeds us with his Word, and cloaths us with his Sacraments, and warms us with his Absolutions, against all diffidence, which had formerly frozen us up" (106–109). And then, like the kinsman redeemer whose duty it was to propagate his family's line through his kin's widow (Ruth 3:13), so "in our barrenness, he raises up seed unto our dead souls, thoughts, and works, worthy of repentance" (110–112).

Second, even while spiritualizing these social customs in application to Christ, Donne relays them to his audience in terms immediately applicable to their own circumstances, again urging their identification in these spiritual applications by expressing the action in the first person plural. He begins with the most basic of needs, preservation from death ("murder"), proceeding to the body's need for food, clothes, and warmth, and finally to

---

aims at making his Christian teaching present to his audience's experience within and without the walls of the church: *Donne at Sermons*, 69–90, esp. 82.

the highest of basic human needs, generation (104–111). As before, Donne's formal use of parallelism and hierarchy encourages his audience's assent (and in this case ascent) to the similitude he continues to explore in his *confirmatio* (to which I will turn shortly).

This recourse to the similitude of socio-economic experience addresses a perceived problem in his audience's faculties of understanding and will. Donne raises this problem in relation to another definition, this time of the noun *Casaph*, which "signifies not onely money, but, *Omne appetibile*, any thing that we can place our desires, or cast our thoughts, upon" (113–115). He takes the opportunity to point out the limiting scope (to both the understanding and the will) of human desire:

> This Redemption of ours, is wrought by such means, as the desire
> of man could never have fortuned upon; The Incarnation of God,
> and then the death and Crucifying of that God, so Incarnate,
> could never have fallen within the desire, nor wish of any man
> (115–118).

Emblematic of this truant desire are the Sacraments, "poor and naked things of themselves, (for all that the wit of man could imagine in them, or allow to them)," which are both physical and spiritual food and drink (120–121). The objective, then, in this socio-economic similitude is to turn the audience's desire from money to the higher matter of the soul in the same way that the food of the Eucharist signifies a spiritual desire and satiety.

Donne uses his similitude, then, as a language of accommodation, employing a lower order of motives as "poor emblems" to help his audience apprehend a greater good which is much more difficult to conceive. He later observes that while his audience can readily discern how their material goods come and go, and even how their physical life proceeds, their souls are not so readily apprehended. Consequently, "because we know not, how they came into us, we care not how they go out" (238–239). This is fundamentally a rhetorical problem, as Wilson recognizes in *The Art of Rhetoric* where he notes,

> because we are all so weak of wit in our tender years that we cannot
> weigh with ourselves what is best, and our body so nesh that it
> looketh ever to be cherished, we take that which is most gainful for
> us, and forsake that altogether which we ought most to follow.[455]

---

[455] Wilson, *Art of Rhetoric*, 77.

Donne responds to this problem with a strategy that permeates his sermons: rendering spiritual motives in terms of the workaday world. We have already seen how the social world reinforces the discursive pattern of hierarchy established in Donne's definitions. This use of analogy also carries an emotive force in the vividness with which it renders spiritual relations. As in Donne's use of definition, the economic similitude (to recall the effects of amplification as described by Wilson) "set[s] forth" the issues "as though they saw it plain before their eyes." His analogue introduces a set of circumstances which are more palpable for their commonness in the lives of his audience. From a preacher's perspective, because the socio-economic motive is more easily realized, it can serve to bolster the less tractable spiritual motives of man.

∽· IV ·∾

Donne has already confronted his audience with the social analogue of this model in "the miserable conditions of man" who is destitute of basic human needs. He continues along these lines in the first part of his *confirmatio*, where he introduces a new focus to his similitude with reference to a readily recognizable, commonplace social condition in Tudor England: prodigality.[456] In evoking this correspondence between the temporal and spiritual, Donne aims at inducing desire by aligning his audience's spiritual position of courting the Devil (as he defines it in the hierarchy of the text) with decidedly detrimental social possibilities. Like his amplification by definition in the *exordium*, Donne's use of prodigality functions as a "repugning argument." Roland MacIlmaine, in his translation of Ramus's *Logike* (1574), describes this device as "contrarie affirmatiues, which amonge them selues do repugne continually."[457] As an example, he offers, "*There is no healthe in warre, therfore we aske the peace.*" Similarly, Donne's argument might run, "there is no happiness in prodigality, therefore I urge you to be prudent." Or more accurately the reverse, "there is great shame in prodigality, so don't be prodigal!" Either way, Donne relies on his audience's repugnance at prodigality and destitution in general to compel them similarly to

---

[456] cf. Aristotle, *Nicomachean Ethics*, 4.1 (1119b 25 – 1120a 4, 1121a 8 – 1122a 17).

[457] Roland MacIlmaine, trans., *The Logike of The Moste Excellent Philosopher P. Ramus Martyr* (1574), ed. Catherine M. Dunn (Northridge, CA: San Fernando Valley State College, 1969), 23. Burke describes how a rhetor can use an audience's ideology to advantage: "[i]f they despise treachery, for instance, he can awaken their detestation by the portrait of a traitor" (*CS*, 161).

choose one spiritual lifestyle over a contrary one that he has identified with prodigality. As vigorously as his audience would resist fiscal prodigality before the law, Donne urges them to eschew spiritual prodigality before God. Conversely, social ambition for both personal and public good should have its counterpart in the spiritual order of motives.

Donne depicts his prodigal in such a way as to evoke a whole set of related contemporary motives. He begins by giving a name, "prodigality," to the downward part of his process as outlined in his *exordium* and *divisio*. And in having identified his audience in that process, he effectively names them prodigals. Donne makes passing reference to a famous Old Testament prodigal, Esau, and the Prodigal Son of the New Testament must certainly come to mind, though he is not mentioned until late in the sermon. He defines his term as sin, however, with reference not to the Bible, nor even to ecclesiastical tradition, but to contemporary law. The cause of its sinfulness is twofold. First, it ironically "destroys even the means of liberality." That is, it is a false liberality that prevents true liberality: "If a man wast so, as that he becomes unable to releive others, by this wast, this is a sinful prodigality; but much more, if he wast so, as that he is not able to subsist, and maintain himself; and this is our case, who have even annihilated our selves, by our profuseness" (139–142).[458] The relief of others and the ability to maintain oneself are social ideals reflected in the Elizabethan Poor Laws, especially in the significantly revised statutes of 1572. Like the previous statutes of Henry VIII, these came in response to the perceived social burden of those unable or unwilling to support themselves. Consequently, rogues, vagabonds and beggars are described as "outragious Enemyes to the Cōmon Weale."[459] These subjects, who posed a burden to public resources "to the highe displeasure of Almightye God, & to the greate annoye of the Cōmon Weale," were marked out as offenders against both social and spiritual authority.[460] In fact, these offenders were visibly stigmatized. The act stipulates that the subject be imprisoned, "grevouslye whipped, and burnte through the gristle of the right Eare with

---

[458] For legal commentary on this law see Michael Dalton, *The Countrey Iustice* (1618), 96ff, [J8v]; for moral commentary on the social problem of prodigality, see John Carr, *The Ruinous fal of Prodigalitie: with the notable examples of the best aprooued aucthours* (1573), *passim*.

[459] *The Statutes of the Realm*, vol. 4 (London: Dawsons of Pall Mall, 1963), 14E Eliz. c. 5 (1572): ¶.II. On the Poor Laws and attitudes toward the "undeserving poor" see Linda Woodbridge, *Vagrancy, Homelessness, and English Renaissance Literature* (Urbana, IL: University of Illinois Press, 2001), 1–37. For a brief history of the Poor Laws see Paul Slack, *Poverty and Policy in Tudor and Stuart England* (London: Longman, 1988), esp. 124–31.

[460] *Statutes of the Realm*, 4: 14E Eliz. c. 5, ¶.I.

a hot Yron of the compasse of an Ynche about, manifestinge his or her rogyshe kynde of Lyef, and his or her Punyshment receaved for the same."[461] This physical stigma was removed in the statute of 1598 but was replaced by the first Jacobean parliament in 1604 with a branded "R" on the left shoulder.[462]

It is precisely the inability "to subsist, and maintain himself" that Donne identifies as the result of the prodigal's wastefulness (141). He also names as a concomitant cause for blame the inability to "releive others," which is likewise relevant to the Elizabethan Poor Laws. The statute of 1572 makes the provision that "yf any p[er]son or p[er]sons beinge able to further this charitable Worcke will obstinatly refuse to geve towardes the Helpe and Relief of the said poore people," they shall be called to account to the authority of the shire.[463] Management of personal wealth is a public issue. To refuse to use (or to waste) one's ability to help the legitimate poor is seen as a violation of law and, by the same token, is sinful prodigality.

A court audience familiar with this law, in theory and perhaps in its actual application, would also be reminded to anticipate the second part of Donne's sermon concerning the Redeemer. The law provides one exception to the said punishment, that

> Except some honest p[er]son, valued at the last Subsidie next before that tyme to Five Pounde[s] in Goode[s] or Twentye Shillinge[s] in Lande[s], or els some suche honeste Householder as by the Justice[s] of Peace of the same Countie or two of them shalbe allowed, wyll of his Charitye be contented p[re]sentlye to take suche Offendour before the same Justice[s] into his Service for one whole yere next followinge.[464]

The whole of Donne's structural paradigm, then — the fall into prodigality followed by redemption — has a close and recognizable analogue in contemporary law.

Although this statute does not name prodigality specifically, William Vaughan makes the connection for us. The statute defines rogues as any "ydel p[er]sones goinge aboute in any Countrey of the said Realme." It fur-

---

[461] *Statutes of the Realm*, 4: 14E Eliz. c. 5, ¶.III.

[462] *Statutes of the Realm*, 4: 1E Ja. c. 7. Cf. George Nicholls, *A History of the English Poor Law*, rev. ed. (London: P. S. King & Sons, 1898; repr. New York: Augustus M. Kelley, 1967), 2:211.

[463] *Statutes of the Realm*, 4: 14E Eliz. c. 5, ¶.XXI.

[464] *Statutes of the Realm*, 4: 14E Eliz. c. 5, ¶.II.

ther specifies certain types of people — students, mountebanks, soldiers — who are especially given to roguishly "wander abroade" in the realm. And special provision is made for soldiers who have license to move about when on leave.[465] William Vaughan speaks of soldiers in similar terms in *The Golden-groue* (1600), a book of virtues and vices pertaining to personal and public governance. In his chapter *"Of Prodigalitie,"* he notes that "[i]nto the listes of this vice many of our English Caualeers & souldiers do enter, who bestow al that they haue on gorgeous raiments & in visiting of queanes [i.e. prostitutes]."[466] Vaughan, too, faults them for their wandering. He adds that "[i]t becommeth them not to follow crowes abroad through thicke & thinne; but to respect, whither they go."[467]

Even members of Donne's auditory who did not known the Poor Laws *per se* would have been fully aware of their implications expressed in other cultural discourses of the time.[468] In the late morality play, *The Contention Between Liberality and Prodigality*, both Soldier and Courtier are presented as potential candidates for Prodigality's influence.[469] But the Soldier proves worthy of Liberality, while the Courtier does not. This anonymous play was performed in 1601, a year in which new revisions to the Poor Laws were passed.[470] In it Prodigality and Tenacity court Fortune to gain her son, Money. Prodigality claims for himself that

> *The Princely heart, that freely spends,*
> *Relieues full many a thousand more,*
> *He getteth praise, he gaineth friends,*
> *And peoples loue procures therefore* (437–440).[471]

None of these claimed effects, however, proves true. Having won Fortune's decision in his favour, Prodigality promptly proceeds to waste Money.

---

[465] *Statutes of the Realm*, 4: 14E Eliz. c. 5, ¶.IX. Cf, Woodbridge, *Vagrancy*.

[466] William Vaughan, *The Golden-groue* (1600), [H5v].

[467] Vaughan, *The Golden-groue*, [H5v].

[468] Christopher Hill describes some popular manifestations of the attitude expressed in these laws in *Liberty Against the Law* (New York: Penguin, 1996), *passim*, esp. chap. 3.

[469] On the ubiquity of the Prodigal Son in English Renaissance drama see Erwin Beck, "Terence Improved: The Paradigm of the Prodigal Son in English Renaissance Comedy," *RD*, n. s. 6 (1973): 107–22; and for the visual arts, Darryl Tippens, "Shakespeare and the Prodigal Son Tradition," *ERC* 14 (1988): 57–77.

[470] Interestingly, John Carr's *The Ruinous fal of Prodigalitie* was published a year after the first introduction of the Poor Law in 1572, apparently for the purpose of adding moral support to Elizabeth's legislation. The revival of this outmoded morality play may have served a similar purpose.

[471] *The Contention Between Liberality and Prodigality* (1602), ed. W. W. Greg (Oxford: Oxford University Press, 1913), [C2v].

Subsequently, Fortune grants Money to Tenacity, whom Prodigality robs and kills in desperation. At Prodigality's murder trial (the climax of the play), Money testifies that both Prodigality and Tenacity are culpable for their ill-use of him without regard for the common good:

> He [Tenacity] would neuer let me abroad to goe,
> But lockt me vp in coffers, or in bags bound me fast,
> That like a Bore in a stie, he fed me at last.
> Thus Tenacitie did spoile me, for want of exercise:
> But Prodigalitie, cleane contrarywise,
> Did tosse me, and fleece me, so bare and so thinne,
> That he left nothing on me, but very bone and skinne
> (1182–1188).

Money is therefore entrusted to Liberality, who will "keepe [Money] from these extremities," and Prodigality is hanged (1190). In Donne's words, Prodigality "destroy[ed] all means of liberality" to the point of being "not able to subsist, and maintain himself" much less "releive others."

This same association of prodigality with the frustration of the greater public good is expressed by Samuel Daniel in *The Civil Wars* (1609). Daniel laments England's misfortune in the Wars of the Roses, describing it as a prodigal act of waste.

> What furie, ô what madnes held thee so,
> Deare *England* (too too prodigall of blood)
> To waste so much, and warre without a foe,
> Whilst *Fraunce*, to see thy spoyles, at pleasure stood![472]

This lapse in England's history resulted in the waste of all that Edward III had achieved. Nature, too, is partly responsible for being spendthrift with her resources, loading Edward and his son and heir with an exceeding amount of virtue and shortchanging their successors. Daniel exclaims,

> O more then men! (two thunderbolts of warre)
> Why did not Time your ioyned worth diuorce,
> T'haue made your seueral glories greater farre?
> Too prodigall was Nature, thus to doe;
> To spend in one Age, what should serue for two (I.20).

---

[472] Samuel Daniel, *The Civil Wars*, ed. Laurence Michel (New Haven: Yale University Press, 1958), I.2.

In William Dunbar's (born c. 1460) "The Tabill of Confessioun," religious sentiment predates the social concerns of both the historiographer and the legislator. Here the penitent speaker confesses he has sinned, among other ways, "In prodigall spending but reuth of pure folkis neding" (124).[473] Dunbar's editor glosses "but" as the preposition "without,"[474] which gives us the same formula expressed in law and in Donne decades later: prodigality is a guilty neglect of social duty.

Indeed, the vice of prodigality was an ethical commonplace of the period. Thomas Gainsford, in a published commonplace book, includes under the head of "Pouertie" this statement: "Pouertie that comes by prodigalitie, is rather to be derided with scorn, then relieued by pitie: and meriteth so much the more reproch, by how much the more intemperately the prodigall liued in his former iollitie."[475] Gainsford distinguishes this prodigality from poverty which comes by no vice, which is deserving of pity rather than censure. Donne thus delivers his censure in a culture well familiar with the identification of prodigality with the default of social responsibility to the needy and to the greater good. The social stigma of the prodigal that Donne evokes goes beyond a mark on the ear.

Having evoked this socio-political censure of prodigality, Donne turns to another application of contemporary law where he derives a spiritual parallel much as he did with the Old Testament provisions for redemption. In particular, Donne is concerned with the law's function in defining the legal subject. Here he states his similitude directly:

> as in civil Prodigalities, in a wastfulness of our temporal estate, the
> Law inflicts three kinds of punishment, three incommodities upon
> him that is a Prodigal, so have the same punishments a proportion,
> and some things that answer them, in this spiritual prodigality of
> the soul by sin (147–151).

Rhetorically, Donne uses his legal analogy to evoke motives related to his audience's sense of identity and selfhood; he engenders in them a dissatisfaction with social place, while at the same time providing a valuative series through which his audience may ascend to a more desirable status. In the first case, a prodigal cannot dispose of his own estate. Such a person has no

---

[473] William Dunbar, *The Poems of William Dunbar*, ed. James Kinsley (Oxford: Oxford University Press, 1979), 15–21, here 19.

[474] *The Poems of William Dunbar*, ed. Kinsley, 393.

[475] Thomas Gainsford, *The Rich Cabinet* (1616), 113–14, Q1–[Q1v].

more legal right than that of a "mad-man, or of an Infant" (153).[476] Donne
adds that "such is the condition of a man in sin; He hath no interest in his
own natural faculties; He cannot think, he cannot wish, he cannot do any
thing of himself" (154–156). In his inability to act, the prodigal is all but
stripped of his personhood.

A similar loss of agency marks the second case, the prodigal's disqualification from making a will.[477] In amplifying this example, Donne follows
an arrangement like that of his opening typological interpretation of his
text, moving from the temporal, to the ecclesiastical, to the spiritual.

> I give my Soul to God, my Body to such a Church, my Goods to
> such, and such persons: But if those Goods be liable to other debts,
> the Legataries shall have no profit; If the person be under excommu-
> nication, he shall not lye in that Church; If his soul be under the
> weight of unrepented sins, God will do the devil no wrong, he will
> not take a soul, that is sold to him before (162–167).

A prodigal, social or spiritual, forfeits his ability to bequeath an inheritance.
Conversely, as a prodigal is assumed to be disinherited unless specifically
named in a father's will, says Donne, so it may be feared that a spiritual
prodigal is disinherited if signs of repentance are lacking at death. As the
social prodigal loses certain rights relating to his status before the law, so
the spiritual prodigal in selling himself to the Devil loses the right to his
soul. As advantageous as it is to avoid such a legal predicament, it is much
more so in spiritual matters, according to Donne's typological series.
Moreover, Donne appeals to motives of hierarchy as he first suggests his
audience's identity with a low state of being before the law (that of a mad-
man, infant, prodigal) and then invites them instead to aspire to a higher
state of identity as an heir of God. In urging this upward turn in motives,
Donne employs one more instance of law to emphasize the spiritual prodigal's loss of status in compromising his selfhood. He evokes his audience's
abhorrence of "those Laws barbarous and inhumane, which permit the sale

---

476 The three exceptions Donne names here are set down by Justinian, *Institutes*, 2.12. Incidentally,
   William Vaughan, in describing the carelessness of the prodigal, uses madness as a similitude: "It
   becōmeth thē I say, not to imitate Bedlems, who iourney still that way, where the staffe falleth. God
   hath appointed euery man to be of some calling or other" (*The Golden-groue*, [H5v]).

477 W. S. Holdsworth cites this particular disqualification from the right to make a will as "propter
   defectum mentis" which he interprets: "as the impubes, the madman, or the prodigal": *A History
   of English Law*, 7th ed., vol. 3 (London: Methuen, 1956), 424. Cf. Justinian, Institutes, 2.12.

of men in debt, for the satisfaction of Creditors" (219–220). But what is worse, adds Donne, is that "we *sell our selves,* and grow the farther in debt, by being sold; we are sold, and to even rate our debts, and *to aggravate our condemnation*" (220–222, emphasis mine).

This last phrase signals a central strategy in this sermon. One aspect of Donne's genius in the sermons is his ability to make the rhetorical activity of the sermon seem identical with his audience's actual behaviour. Here he conflates his text's rhetorical aggravation of his audience's guilt — "the word aggravates our condemnation" (79–80) — with their actual aggravation of guilt in their actions, or at least the actions he imputes to them in lines 220–222 above. In this way, the text becomes a symbol in action. This barbarous selling of ourselves is an actualization of the downward slide with which Donne characterizes his definition of *Machar.* His use of amplification in definition, examples, narration, comparison, and the rest, thus serves as an identification strategy whereby he marks out the text of his sermon as a site for his audience's rehearsal of their guilt. The text becomes their daily life experience in microcosm. But then it also becomes a means of changing or purifying that life.

Donne reinforces the connection between the text's rhetorical and his audience's actual "aggravation" as he again insinuates his audience's guilt in a narration of the first person plural. He draws from popular history an even worse case of enslavement in the reportedly common practice among "*Muscovits*" of drinking themselves and their progeny into insupportable debt and ultimately slavery. This time Donne uses comparison, adding, "But we sell our selves, not for drink, but for thirst: we are sory when our appetite too soon decaies, and we would fain sin more than we do" (226–228). To emphasize the point, he adds a contrast of extremes between the blessed martyrs who "got heaven for their bodies, and we [who] give bodies, and souls for hell" (231–232). His "worse yet" strategy of comparison marks another increment in his audience's debasement of themselves in exchange for the most ephemeral of pleasures.

Continuing his appeal to his audience's sense of self and identity, Donne turns to another, economic aspect of his juridical analogy. His appeal to the legal status of the self has its counterpart in a right economy of the self. Here Donne's prudential argument is expressed in the most explicit hierarchical arrangement of the sermon:

> In a right inventary, every man that ascends to a true value of himself, considers it thus; First, His Soul, then His life; after his fame and good name: And lastly, his goods and estate; for thus their own

nature hath ranked them, and thus they are (as in nature) so ordi-
narily in legal consideration preferred before one another
(233–237).

Donne derives authority for his arrangement from the course of nature —
"for thus their own nature hath ranked them" — and from law — "so ordi-
narily in legal consideration." The causal relation implied in the "as ... so"
structure of the final clause suggests that law also derives its ethical appeal
from a pre-established condition in nature.

Donne's *ethos* as rhetor also gains by the suggestion that the hierarchical structure of his argument is not an arbitrary invention, but one that is
"found" in nature. As well, William Vaughan helps to uncover the culturally derived sense of *ethos* at work here *vis à vis* Donne's audience. Vaughan
notes that liberality is a means for a gentleman to "vphold his reputatiõ"
(corresponding to Donne's "good name" — a high-reaching motive),
whereas those who are prodigal should "cõsider with thẽselues, *what they
are ... of what vocation they are.*"[478] The agonistic scale between liberality
and prodigality functions as a social index of character. To employ one's
material wealth properly is to earn a good reputation, and thus to ascend
in Donne's inventory of values. Donne's argument from natural and social
order leads in the ensuing lines to an assertion of his audience's unnatural-
ness in their careless dealing with their souls. Once more Donne appeals to
the first-person experience of his audience as he laments, "But for our
souls, because we know not, how they came into us, we care not how they
go out" (237–239).

This negligence of the soul derives from a failure to understand its
coming and going. Such a problem, however, can only be addressed indi-
rectly through analogy. Donne approaches this problem not in the heady
manner of the philosopher, who cannot tell "whither my soul came in," nor
of the theologian, who "can no more tell me" where the soul goes out, but
in the earthly vocabulary of the economist where the coming and going of
goods can be readily accounted for, again with the purpose of making spiritual matters more apprehensible (399–42). In this way, Donne deflects
attention from the unclear causes of the soul's issue to the present and relat-
able experience of the manner of spending. In his "inventary" Donne por-
trays an increase in his audience's concern as he descends his scale from
soul, to life, to reputation, to natural goods where "our covetousness
appears most, in the love of them, in that lowest thing of all" (256–257).

---

[478] Vaughan, *The Golden-groue*, [H3v], [H5v].

This, says Donne, "is a most perverse undervaluing of himself, and a damnable humility" (259–260).

Donne adds yet one more condition that is even worse yet: there are those who are willing to part even with their goods to maintain their sin. These are both spiritual and social prodigals who misspend their social estate for their spiritual perversity, and thus travesty the natural order: "that which is the most precious, our souls, we undervalue most; and that which we do esteem most, (though naturally it should be lowest) our estate, we are content to wast, and dissipate for our sins" (263–265). Donne uses the instance of material goods to show that the source of a given possession is of no consequence when sin is the governing principle of one's desire. At the same time, the progressive debasement in nature that Donne depicts rebukes this desire. To shame his congregation further, Donne adds, by way of contrast, that "the Heathens needed laws to restrain them, from an expensive, and wastful worship of their Gods," whereas his audience (good Christian people) become prodigal in a courtship of the Devil (266–267).

A right inventory also rectifies a lapsing memory. Even the Devil knows that under usual conditions "*all that a man hath, will he give for his life*" (245). But intemperate devotion to physical gratification (the sin principle) causes one's life to slip away unnoticed:

> we do not easily give away our lives expresly, and at once; but we
> do very easily suffer our selves to be cousened of our lives: we pour
> in death in drink, and we call that health, we know our life to be
> but a span, and yet we can wash away one inche in ryot, we can
> burn away one inch in lust, we can bleed away one inch in quar-
> rels, we have not an inch for every sin; and if we do not pour out
> our lives, yet we drop them away (246–252).

One who does not value the soul will not attend to it and thus will part too easily with it; while he who pursues sin will do so at any cost without giving thought to the soul. Throughout the sermon Donne diligently exposes this incremental dissipation in stark, concrete terms to cause his audience to take notice, to awaken their memory to the value of their souls.

In addition to understanding and memory, the audience's problem, as Donne sees it, is one of will, or, more specifically, of motives. Having shown how readily soul and life will be forfeited for sin, Donne approaches the third item in his inventory of values, a good name, with a rhetorical question which is at first puzzling. He ironically asks, "For the third peece of our self, our fame and reputation, who had not rather be thought an usurer, then a beggar? who had not rather be the object of envy, by being great, than of scorn and contempt, by being poor, upon any condition?"

(252–255). What is being forfeited here, and where does sin enter the picture? Although neither label is socially desirable, Donne expects his audience to prefer enduring envy as a usurer rather than contempt as a beggar. Their concern is not for a good name (a higher value) but rather for the mere economic advantage (a lower motive) that comes with usury, regardless of the dyslogistic appellative. Yet it is the usurer who is culpable *ipso facto*, while the beggar is censured, as we have seen, primarily for being prodigal. Here Donne questions the purity of his audience's motives. His audience, he insinuates, would not want to be poor "upon any condition," even upon the condition of moral innocence. Usury is a sin; begging is not.[479] And whereas the beggar may be poor for no fault of his own, the motives which lead the usurer to riches are inevitably dubious.[480] Economic motives must be subject to the higher, ethical concerns.

What is interesting about Donne's inventory is that he does not deny desire for wealth, these lower motives, but rather seeks to establish the proper conditions for this desire, and to take the desire higher. There is, for Donne, a discernible continuity between the two parts of his similitude, between the material and the spiritual. His similitude derives from a conviction of the wholeness of life. The *divisio* states his intention to "look better upon some pieces of it [the text], that we may take such a sight of this Redeemer here, as that we may know Him, when we meet Him at home, at our house, in our private meditations, at His house, in the last judgement" (127–130). In enabling his audience to see Christ at home (and in the marketplace) as well as at church, Donne aims not to supplant the socio-economic urge but to give it a proper orientation and extension. Although he begins by placing two orders of motives side by side, referring his spiritual motivation to the socio-economic, he includes both in his "right inventory." Donne teaches his audience to value their goods (to eschew prodigality) and to value more so their good name, in order to avoid social censure reserved for the prodigal. But in extending his hierarchy into spiritual matters, Donne hopes the impetus of desire will continue

---

[479] Usury was debated on moral grounds into the early seventeenth-century. See R. H. Tawney, "Introduction," in Thomas Wilson, *A Discourse Upon Usury ... [1572]* (London: G. Bell and Sons, 1925), pp. 106–121; and Norman Jones, *God and the Moneylenders: Usury and Law in Early Modern England* (London: Basil Blackwell, 1989), 24–46, 145–74.

[480] cf. Gainsford, *The Rich Cabinet*, 113–14, Q1–[Q1v] (quoted above). Attitudes varied, but Christopher Hill notes in the anti-enclosure sentiment of the period a sympathy for those who were reduced to begging owing to the economic conditions resulting from this political policy: *Liberty Against the Law*, chap. 3. Arthur Kinney (ed.) describes these economic conditions with respect to the underworld of Elizabethan vagabonds: *Rogues, Vagabonds, & Sturdy Beggars*, 2nd ed. (Amherst, MA: University of Massachusetts Press, 1990), 11–58. See also Woodbridge, *Vagrancy*.

to goad his audience higher yet to a proper valuation of their souls, and consequently of all of their "possessions."

Rather than denying the basic motives of his congregation's quotidian life, Donne urges that even the highest of these ambitions be brought into proper relation to what should be their highest concern: "Let no man present his Dotals, his Court-rolls, his Baculs, his good Debts, his titles of honour, his Maces, or his Staves, or his Ensignes of power and Office, and say, call you all this nothing? Compare all these with thy soul, and they are nothing" (361–364). In this way, the soul functions as Burke's ultimate term, the principle by which all other possessions are valued and ordered. At death, continues Donne,

> What hast thou of all that thou hast received? Is not all that come to nothing? and then thou that thoughtest thy self strong enough in purse, in power, in favour, to compass any thing, and to embrace many things, shalt not finde thy self able to attain to a door-keepers place in the kingdome of heaven (368–372).

Those who value their soul will, of course, seek its preservation in eternity. In this light, all other property is put in its proper place.

This revaluation is the solution to the prodigal's predicament and forms the basis for the *consolatio* of redemption whereby "God pursues the devil, in all those steps, by which he had made his profit, of a prodigality" (418–419). Only in acknowledging the immense value of the soul can one see the legal loophole found in the "for naught" of the text. Again Donne uses a social analogue to amplify the principle behind the word: "the laws presume fraud in the conveyance, if at least half the value of the thing be not given: now if the whole world be not worth one soul, who can say, that he hath half his value?" (294–296). In the second part of his *confirmatio*, Donne pushes this point where he interprets the "therefore" of the text according to the law of equity, the secondary cause of this void bargain:

> this reason, relates to the price, not to the worke of the Redemption, Because it was for nothing, that we were sold, it is without money, that we are Redeemed: for, for that, there is reason in Equity: but for the Redemption itself, there is no therfore, no reason at all to be assigned, but onely the Eternall goodness of God himself, and the Eternall purpose of his will (409–414).

Donne points out the confusing logic of the "therefore" of the text, asserting that the "therefore" applies, as a secondary cause of redemption, to the price of the arrangement. The implication is that because the value of the soul so far outstrips the value received in exchange, the bargain is void, and we are therefore redeemed without money.[481] But the ultimate cause of redemption in the first place is beyond economics, accountable only by God's grace. Again, spiritual causes transcend the social. While the secondary cause has its analogue in civil law, the primary cause of redemption, God's grace, is inscrutable and transcends the laws of economics, even as the soul transcends other possessions in value.

◡· V ·◡

This transcendence of the spiritual over the temporal is signalled in one of Donne's favourite images, the coin, which marks a turn between the first and second partitions from an economic order of motives to the purgative. Yet it is not a turn exactly, because as Burke suggests, upward movement through any hierarchy carries connotations of purification. Indeed, the coin here shares both purgative and economic fields of imagery, and again it is a socio-economic model that clarifies this cleansing process. Donne's identification of his audience with the coin image implies his congregation's circulation, their involvement in the world, yet also their consecration, being marked or set apart with a particular value and purpose. The coin is, in a sense, an emblem of how worldly motives can be transformed when given a heavenly orientation — and *vice versa*. Donne uses this imagery once more to talk about man's fall from native dignity in association with God, but this time in terms of pollution:

> whensoever we commit any sin, upon discourse, upon consideration, upon purpose, and plot, the image of God which is engraved and imprinted in us, and lodged in our understanding, and in that reason which we employ in that sin, is mingled with that sin; we draw the image of God into all our incontinencies, into all our oppressions, into all our extortions, and supplantations: we carry his image, into all foul places, which we haunt upon earth; yea we carry his image down with us, to eternal condemnation ... in Hell (336–344).

---

[481] The principle of equity (line 412) allows for a given law to be excepted on the basis of another law which speaks to the case. In this case, the contract is void because of the unequal value of the price paid and the goods received. See Doddridge's *The English Lawyer* (1631), for the provision of equity as an exception to law (209–215, Ee–[Ee4]).

The process of pollution, parallelling the process of prodigality, is similarly naturalized into a narrative sequence from "discourse" to "plot." The proximity of the coin image to Donne's assertion fifteen lines later of the ephemerality of "Ensignes of power and office" at court in contrast to the endurance of the soul could not have been missed by Donne's audience, for it is the king's image which impresses the coin, while it is God's which marks the soul. In the same way that the king is the ultimate term (the ordering principle) in socio-economic courtships, so God brings a proper and ultimate order (and value) to these and to the higher pursuits of the soul. Moreover, certain socio-economic activities associable with public life — "oppressions," "extortions," and "supplantations" — pollute the right inventory Donne promotes. These debase God's image by "mingling" it with sins of "plot and purpose," which carry it into "foul places, which we haunt upon earth."

Earlier in the sermon Donne briefly looks beyond his socio-economic field of reference for a simile of pollution to augment his audience's feelings toward this compromise of selfhood. Like a viper which "eats out his own womb," so "The Prodigal consumes that that should maintain his Prodigality." Donne uses this image to reiterate the theme of "spiritual murder" from line 105, calling prodigality "a sin that murders it self" (145–146). Here Donne introduces another strategic appeal to motives, likening prodigality, which feeds on and ultimately destroys the prodigal, to poison: "the venem and the malignity of his sin goes through all his actions, and he cannot purge it" (156–157). This image of pollution is another instance of Donne's repulsion/attraction strategy. He introduces a related image in a parallel comparing "disease," which is a privation of health, with poverty (a privation of wealth), and "unsensibleness" ("a privation of tenderness of Conscience") (284–285). In the order of things to be desired, a clean conscience is included along with health and wealth. Donne brings three orders of motives together, implying that prodigality and hardness of conscience are diseases or pollutants which, like venom, need to be purged. Donne draws on Augustine's notion of sin as privation[482] to develop the "for naught" of the text, but venom and disease also strongly connote a positive presence of pollution. His audience's sinful prodigality is not just a privation of good, but a pollution with evil. This coining, venom, and disease imagery thus develops a close connection between the audience's socio-anagogic prodigality and their need for purification.

---

[482] As in *Confessions* 3.7.12 and *Enchiridion* 11 [PL 40.236].

The aim of the sermon, then, is to purify the audience's motives through its extended hierarchy. This formal function becomes explicit in the second partition, the sermon's *consolatio*. Donne draws out the purification significance of Isaiah's text by finally turning to the parable of the Prodigal Son as a model for his audience's repentance and restoration to their native *dignitas*, and he gives the story a characteristic emphasis on process, a process that recalls the collect of the day.[483] The son did not come to "some sudden thoughts of Repentance, but he put himself actually in the way" (430–431). Donne's model of repentance, for rhetorical purposes at least, is not one of Calvinistic crisis, but of continuing courtship. The robe (here Donne follows St. Augustine) signifies not just the son's restoration to "integrity", but "an ability to preserve himself in that integrity," to remain in process (435–437).

In the same way, says Donne, one's incorporation into the church by baptism is a double "cure" (444). As in law, which reverses all contracts by which the prodigal is bound and then assigns guardians to prevent them from making new contracts, so

> this blessed [Holy] Spirit of consolation, by his sanctification, seals to our consciences a *Quietus est*,[484] a discharge of all former spiritual debts, he cancells all them, he nails them to the cross of Christ, and then he strengthens us against relapses into the same sins again (451–455).

Donne continues in language which reminds us of his earlier semantic hierarchies and which gives this pattern a purifying significance: "He proceeds farther than this; beyond restoring us, beyond preserving us; for he betters us, he improves us, to a better condition, than we were in, at first. And this he does, first by purging and purifying us, and then by changing, and transmuting us" (456–459). Purification, he continues, may come by the "sunshine" of temporal blessing. Here again Donne draws a close identity between material prosperity and spiritual prosperity. He who has enjoyed "prosperous fortune, should have received the best concoction, the best digestion of the testimonies of his [God's] love, and consequently be the

---

[483] The collect reads, "ALMIGHTY God, who shewest to them that be in error the light of thy truth, to the intent that they may return into the way of righteousness; Grant unto all them that are admitted into the fellowship of Christ's Religion, that they may eschew those things that are contrary to their profession, and follow all such things as are agreeable to the same; through our Lord Jesus Christ."

[484] The legal formula of discharge.

purer, and the more refined mettall" [using alchemical terminology] (463–466). Should, that is, if that person has acknowledged the correspondence between this and the higher blessing of God. If not, purification by the fire of affliction may come to melt away the "dross" of the prodigal's life (470). It matters very much how one *thinks* about these blessings.[485] If such tribulations come, says Donne, we should "think" of them as needed correctives from a caring God (469). Indeed, the discursive structure of the sermon has been working to establish this pattern of correspondence between temporal and spiritual experience.

In moving "from this purifying" to "our transmutation," Donne reverses the agonistic relation established in the *exordium*. By this purging "we are changed" and brought into identity with God, so that "this grace makes us as properly the seed of God, as sin makes us the seed of the Devill" (475, 480–482). Donne goes on to reject false notions of consubstantiality with God (those of the Manicheans and of Origen) before giving the true relation:

> But this transmutation is a glorious restoring of Gods image in us, and it is our conformity to him; and when either his temporal blessings, or his afflictions, his sun, or his fire, hath tried us up to that height, to a conformity to him, then come we to that transmutation, which admits no re-transmutation, which is a modest, but infalible assurance of a final perseverance, so to be joyned to the Lord, as to be one spirit with him; for as a spirit cannot be divided, so they who are thus changed into him, are so much His, so much He, as that nothing can separate them from him; and this is the ladder, by which we may try, how far we are in the way to heaven (494–503).

Process is expressed in an explicitly hierarchical image. "Height" is rendered as "conformity" with God, either in temporal blessing or tribulation. And this "transmutation" through experience is "the ladder" indexing the status of one's spiritual ascent.

Donne ends by reminding us of the transcendent value of the blood which purchased redemption: "therefore we were not redeemed with corruptable things, as silver and gold, but with the precious blood of Christ"

---

[485] Donne's congregation would have been prepared for this idea by the collect of the day, which exhorts them to "eschew those things that are contrary to their profession, and follow all such things as are agreeable to the same."

(557–559). Donne's aim has been to dilate his audience's desire, to evoke that which desire could comprehend in order to extend it beyond to what it cannot yet fully appreciate. "The blood of Christ by which we are redeemed," he reminds us, "was not this *Casaph*, it was no *Res appetibilis*, a thing that a sinner might, or could desire to be shed for him, though being shed, he must desire, that it may be applied to him" (578–583). So that even as he concludes his sermon, Donne situates salvation within the full range of human desire. He first quotes and then paraphrases, into the language of the marketplace, the call of Isaiah 55:1:

> But you must come; and you must come to the market; to the Magazine of his graces, his Church; And you must buy, though you have no money: he paid obedience, and he asks obedience to himself, and his Church, at your hands. And then, as *Joseph* did to his brethren, he will give you your corn, and your money again; he will give you grace, and temporal blessings too: he will refresh and re-establish your natural faculties, and give you supernatural (593–599).

⌣· VI ·⌣

R. C. Bald says of this sermon that Donne "keeps strictly to his primary concern, that of interpreting Scripture, and offers little in the way of advice or exhortation to his congregation. He was evidently too unsure of himself as yet to attempt much in this line."[486] If exhortation must be presented explicitly and directly as such, then Bald is correct. But as I have demonstrated, Donne uses his interpretation of Scripture precisely for this purpose of edifying, and he does it not on the level of *elocutio*, by speaking words of exhortation, but in his *inventio* and *dispositio*, by amplifying and arranging his matter in a manner which leads his congregation to pursue godly behaviour.

   Donne's *inventio* in his first extant sermon is well rounded, employing complementary modes of *pathos* and *logos*. His use of definition and similitude under the *topos* of courtship creates a mode of thought whereby he invites his audience to induce desire from a socio-economic order into their spiritual values. We have also seen how Donne's ethical appeal to notions of selfhood, as constituted by social relations, also urges a revaluation of his

---

[486] Bald, *John Donne*, 312.

audience's personal values. Furthermore, the dialectical nature of the similitude creates an *ethos*-building cycle whereby the immediacy of the social order borrows authority from the transcendence of the spiritual, and *vice versa*. In one sense, Donne's argument for a right valuation of the soul gains authority by its analogy to the worldly wisdom of economic prudence. In another sense, notions of social prodigality, framed in the transcendent language of God's censure, both in the Poor Laws and in the biblical text of Donne's sermon, borrow from divine authority.

It remains to say something about Donne's *ethos* as rhetor. Donne commands a certain authority not only as a man of God in his handling of the Word, but as a man of the world as well in his demonstrated knowledge of legal and social practice. In appealing to common social sense, Donne evinces Aristotle's first species of *ethos*, practical wisdom (*phronēsis*), or as Edward Corbett paraphrases it, "sound sense."[487] Donne's performance in dealing with the economic motives of his audience demonstrates that he is a priest who understands worldly needs and concerns. In this way, his adept handling of the socio-economic analogue functions as an identification strategy. He achieves identification with his audience by meeting them at their point of interest and addressing their felt needs in order to lure them to feel a new but comparable type of need. But there is a more important identification going on between God's ways of the spirit and man's ways of the world. Donne thereby effects a Miltonic purpose of justifying the ways of God to men, bringing the spiritual order in line with the temporal, in order to bring his audience's temporal experience in line with the spiritual.

---

[487] Edward P. J. Corbett and Robert J. Connors, *Classical Rhetoric for the Modern Student*, 4th ed. (New York: Oxford University Press, 1999), 72.

CHAPTER FIVE

Courting Death: Symbolic Purification in Donne's Sermon "Preached to the Lords upon Easter-day," 1619[488]

Psalm 89:48
WHAT MAN IS HE THAT LIVETH,
AND SHALL NOT SEE DEATH?

O eloquent, just, and mighty Death! whom none could advise, thou hast persuaded; what none hath dared, thou hast done.

— Sir Walter Ralegh[489]

DEATH IS ONE OF DONNE'S FAVOURITE THEMES in the sermons.[490] In addition to several sermons which directly address this subject, many more on other subjects draw upon themes of death. My interest here, however, is not that of Donne's psychologizers who read the sermons for his views and attitudes toward death to explain this apparent obsession.[491] I rather con-

---

[488] *Sermons*, 2:9.

[489] From *The History of the World* (1614) in Brian Vickers, ed., *Seventeenth-Century Prose* (London: Longman, 1969), 55.

[490] Potter and Simpson express the contrary view (*Sermons*, 2:27). Donne is by no means unique in his concentration on death. In his advice to the preachers in his charge, Bishop Jeremy Taylor says (quite traditionally), "In your sermons to the people, often speak of the four last things, of Death and Judgement, Heaven and Hell": *Whole Works*, ed. Heber, 1:109.

[491] Most notoriously, Carey, *John Donne*, chap. 7. Also Mark Allinson, "Re-Visioning the Death Wish: Donne and Suicide," *Mosaic* 24 (1991): 31–46. The most recent disaster in this method of mining

tend that Donne frequently turns to this theme in his writing because he finds it useful for suasive purposes. Whether or not Donne personally had a death wish, or a morbid fascination with death, he certainly found it rhetorically compelling. Death recurs in his sermons not simply as a subject, but also as a topic for deriving rhetorical matter that can be applied to a variety of subjects. Whereas for Lancelot Andrewes and Jeremy Taylor death is a doctrinal necessity to be preached upon, Donne much more frequently visits death as a courtship *topos*, as a means of evoking conditions of "estrangement" that can be used to move his audience toward identification with God.

Preaching to a culture saturated with the *ars moriendi*,[492] Donne faced the problem of investing his treatment of death with *ethos* and restoring these well-worn commonplaces with a new sense of urgency and relevance. Robert Watson describes another aspect to the rhetorical problem Donne may have faced as a preacher addressing issues of death in the early seventeenth century, when

> assurance about personal salvation was declining while attachment to both the external properties and internal subjectivities of the human individual were increasing. The resulting demands on the promise of afterlife became so great that the Christian denial of death threatened to become visible as a mere ideology, a manipulative illusion rather than an absolute truth.[493]

While Watson includes Donne as part of the problem of growing scepticism (which he somewhat overstates) regarding the afterlife, I argue that his sermons provide a solution to this rhetorical problem by appealing to the very "attachments" Watson describes, symbolically infusing his congregation's life experiences in the world with thoughts of death as a means of reinforcing traditional Christian consolation.

I do not mean to suggest that Donne creates something new out of the topic of death, but rather that he draws upon common resources and employs them in innovative and compelling ways: more precisely, Donne

---

the sermons for psychological data on Donne's attitudes toward death is Robert N. Watson's *The Rest is Silence: Death as Annihilation in the English Renaissance* (Berkeley: University of California Press, 1994), 156–252.

492 On the ubiquity of the *ars moriendi* see Arnold Stein, *The House of Death* (Baltimore: Johns Hopkins University Press, 1986), 11–16; Nancy Lee Beaty traces the history of the *ars moriendi* from its inception in the fifteenth century in *The Craft of Dying* (New Haven: Yale University Press, 1970).

493 Watson, *The Rest is Silence*, 2.

invests commonplace treatments of death with courtship motives.[494] In a culture that saw life as a journey-quest, routinely emblematized in images of ascent, it is not impossible to construe death as a courtship. But for death to work as a deliberative topic, Donne must effect its transformation.[495] He must make it an object of desire, a recognizable good. The notion that death might be seen as a "good" was expressed by St. Ambrose,[496] among others, but Donne's manner of transforming death into an end to be courted is distinctively his own.

Death, for Donne, is often associated with resurrection and potential reward, so that he can speak of death in overt courtship terms as a consummation at the apex of hierarchy, as when he tells his congregation at St. Paul's that "[t]he Resurrection then, being the Coronation of man, his Death, and lying downe in the grave, is his enthroning, his sitting downe in that chayre, where he is to receive that Crown" (6:13.387–389). This assertion derives its effect not from Donne's dubious logic but from the courtship motives it inspires by analogy. Moreover, for Donne there is a clear sense that death is life's ordering principle, the ultimate term which draws all things into proper relation: "'Tis the *end* that qualifies all," as he says in another sermon (4:6.301). He makes this statement about death in the context of explicit courtship motives: "If Mannor thrust Mannor, and title flow into title, and bags powre out into chests, if I have no anchor, (*faith in Christ*) if I have not a ship to carry to a haven, (a soule to save) what's my long cable to me?" (290–293).

Yet for Donne, that final moment is constituted by the life which leads up to it. Elsewhere, expanding on the occasion of Paul's farewell in Acts 20:25, Donne rounds out the form of the apostle's life with another courtship image of death. Previously, on the feast in the church calendar assigned to Paul's conversion (25 January), Donne must have preached on Paul's epiphany on the road to Damascus, for now, says Donne,

---

[494] Perhaps no subject was more widely treated in commonplaces than death (see for example Montaigne's essays on the subject). Many of the commonplaces I touch on in the next two chapters can be found in *An Exhortation against the feare of Death* from *Certain Sermons or Homilies*, or in Jeremy Taylor's *Holy Living and Holy Dying*. Bettie Anne Doebler's *The Quickening Seed* (Salzburg: Institut für Englische Sprache und Literatur, Universität Salzburg, 1974) and, more recently, her *"Rooted Sorrow": Dying in Early Modern England* (London and Toronto: Associated University Press, 1994) provide excellent overviews of Donne's handling of death within the tradition he inherited.

[495] Taylor expresses his duty as a priest "to direct your sorrows that they may turn into vertues and advantages": *Holy Living and Holy Dying*, ed. P. G. Stanwood, 2 vols. (Oxford: Clarendon Press, 1989), 2:6. As Stein describes, one way Donne achieves this transformation is through his *exempla* of good deaths (*The House of Death*, chap. 3).

[496] St. Ambrose, *De Bono Mortis*, in *Seven Exegetical Works*, trans. M. P. McHugh, Fathers of the Church 65 (Washington, DC: Catholic University of America Press), 70–113. Stein describes this commonplace (*The House of Death*, 8).

our Apostle, whom, in our former Exercise, for example of our
humiliation, we found faln to the Earth, in this, to the assistance
of our Exaltation, in his, we shall find, and leave, upon the last step
of *Iacobs* ladder, that is, entring into Heaven, by the gate of death
(8:6.105–109).

This sermon mini-series, touching on the termini of Paul's career in ministry
(a formal pattern of death-as-humiliation in the present and then death-as-
exaltation in eternity), brings the congregation through a parallel courtship
which culminates in (and leaves them thinking upon) death and the final
resurrection, the top rung of the ladder of their lives.

   Temporizing of essence is a central strategy in Donne's handling of that
culminating moment of death. Burke describes an effect of this strategy,
whereby the poet, functioning as homeopath, "immunize[s] us by stylistically infecting us with the disease." By attenuating a dosage, one can transform poison into medicine: and so with death.[497] This is part of Donne's
consolatio strategy of temporizing the final (essentializing) moment of death
into a narrative of deaths played out in the everyday events of life. In this
way, he makes something fresh out of the commonplace of the "always-
dying life" that was the focus of so much meditation on death.[498] Donne
uses it in this manner in a sermon at St. Paul's, where he says of poison (a
similitude for death) that

   If a man use himselfe to them, in small proportions at first, he may
   grow to take any quantity: He that takes a dram of Death to day,
   may take an ounce to morrow, and a pound after; He that begins
   with that mortification of denying himselfe his delights, (which is
   a dram of Death) shall be able to suffer the tribulations of this
   world, (which is a greater measure of death) and then Death it
   selfe, not onely patiently, but cheerefully (8:6.409–416).

---

[497] *PLF*, 65. For authority Burke cites Aristotle's notion of catharsis, *via* the preface to *Samson
Agonistes*, where Milton speaks of tragedy's function of "raising pity and fear, or terror, to purge the
mind of those and such like passions, that is to temper and reduce them to just measure with a kind
of delight, stirr'd up by reading or seeing those passions well imitated" (*Complete Poems*, 549). In
The Soul's Conflict, Richard Sibbes describes this process under the broader rubric of affliction (of
which death is chief): "When any thing is strange and sudden, and lights upon us unfurnished and
unfenced, it must needs put our spirits out of frame. It is good therefore to make all kind of troubles familiar to us, in our thoughts at least, and this will break the force of them": *Works of Richard
Sibbes*, ed. Alexander Grosart, 7 vols. (Edinburgh: James Nichol, 1862), 1:163.

[498] Doebler, *"Rooted Sorrow"*, 183. Stein traces this commonplace to its Stoic roots (*The House of
Death*, 8, 17–19), and cites Socrates's idea that the philosopher's life is a rehearsal for death (6).

This strategy of dying daily has a transforming effect on death. Death is no longer an estrangement, but a more complete union with the beloved:

And to such a man, death is not a dissolution, but a redintegration; not a divorce of body and soule, but a sending of both divers wayes, (the soule upward to Heaven, the body downeward to the earth) to an indissoluble marriage to him, who, for the salvation of both, assumed both, our Lord and Saviour Christ Jesus (416–420).

Moreover, an established pattern of death-in-this-life argues by *logos* a continuation into the next, so that final death becomes a consummation rather than a crisis.

Another tactical advantage for Donne in extending the final moment of death into the narrative of the present life is to bring that "undiscovered country" near and to put it into a space that is familiar and safe to his audience.[499] There is temporary discomfort involved in the immunization process, in infecting the present moment with death, however small the dosage. Yet it is this discomfort that sets his congregation "in the way" toward death, so that this life thus becomes, in a sense, a present participation in (or courtship of) death.

Relating another instance of temporized essence, Burke remarks that "the essence of a thing can be defined narratively in terms of its *fulfillment* or *fruition*"; he goes on to note "how the imagery of death could be a narrative equivalent of the Aristotelian entelechy."[500] Death epitomizes the entelechial motive in courtship of finding identity in the fulfilment of one's end. In 2:9, the sermon I will examine in this chapter, Donne models two such possible avenues of courtship. The first is the inexorable process of a life characterized at every step by its biological end in death, a process that functions as an actualization of his audience's identity with Adam in the Fall and ultimately with the Devil (implicitly in hell). The second is Christian death, the final and defining act of the Christian's life which brings life's journey to its destination of union with Christ. This second avenue of courtship, clearly the eulogistic alternative, is the one Donne

---

[499] Stein notes the traditional idea that to think of death continually is to control it; similarly, the *ars moriendi* enabled the subject to control death by putting it into a conventional form (*The House of Death*, 33 and chap. 2 *passim*).

[500] *RM*, 13, 14. Montaigne says of the moment of death, "It is the master day, the day that is judge of all the others": *The Complete Essays*, trans. Donald M. Frame (Stanford: Stanford University Press, 1976), 55.

promotes to his congregation. Accordingly, Doebler finds in Donne's sermons a developing sense of "longing for perfect integration into the ideal
societas: the ultimate loving communion with the divine"; conversely, for
Donne hell "is eternal absence [estrangement] from a loving God ... a relationship of deprivation rather than a place of physical torment."[501] To
Donne, then, death is the ultimate courtship.

In this chapter, however, I will again expand my discussion of
courtship to emphasize its purgative aspect with reference to Donne's
related forensic strategy. As Donne makes clear early in his sermon, death
(here configured as execution) is also an ultimate defining moment in the
juridical process (the determination of guilt). In this sermon on Psalm
89:48, Donne uses forensic strategies to capitalize on the Bible's legal
encoding of spiritual guilt. He also uses legal discourse as a veneer for
strategies of temporizing essence which enable him to talk about evidence
of religious guilt without having to adhere to rigorous juridical demands of
evidential proof. In religious matters, and particularly in death, the very
problem Donne addresses is his congregation's lack of concrete proof. I am
thus interested in the way his legal fiction engenders a mode of thought
and feeling in his audience as a means of proof: that is, Donne uses law, like
economics, as a similitude, an analogical way of configuring his audience's
religious experience in a manner (i.e. courtship) that will induce a responsiveness toward their spiritual needs. Again Donne combines *logos* and
pathos to compel his audience to a new way of thinking and feeling about
themselves in relation to the divine. But as is made clear in the *peroratio*,
logos becomes this sermon's dominant mode of proof as Donne seeks to
infuse his congregation's thinking about this life of deaths with a new spiritual significance.

◡· II ·◡

This is Donne's first extensive treatment of death in a sermon, and he uses
his theme to full rhetorical advantage as he takes his audience through a
juridical purgation of guilt, from their implication in God's judgement of
Adam and Eve in the Fall to their identification with Christ in the New
Covenant where Donne finds satisfaction for God's Edenic penalty.
Concomitantly, he effects a purification of death itself from its connotations of imprisonment to its new signification of rapture and release for
those in contemplation of the Saviour. To borrow a few more terms from

---

[501] *"Rooted Sorrow"*, 199, 195. Cf. 5:13.779–780: "but to fall out of the hands of the living God, is a
horror beyond our expression, beyond our imagination." The contrast is with Hebrews 10:31.

Burke, Donne's sermon takes his audience the "Upward Way," giving them a new perspective and an adequate idea of future death to equip them better for living in the present.

Donne's introduction, comprised of *exordium* and *divisio*, establishes the rhetorical situation of his sermon and the dynamic of its rhetorical process. In his *exordium* Donne speaks in a forensic mode as he proves the guilt of his audience. He begins with a three-part statement that sounds like a *divisio* (and is indeed a stripped-down version of it) but rather serves a preparatory function:

> AT FIRST, God gave the judgement of death upon man, when he should transgresse, absolutely, *Morte morieris*, Thou shalt surely dye: The woman in her Dialogue with the Serpent, she mollifies it, *Ne fortè moriamur*, perchance, if we eate, we may die; and then the Devill is as peremptory on the other side, *Nequaquam moriemini*, do what you will, surely you shall not die (2:9.1–6).

This opening statement prepares the audience by enacting their universal fall from God, through Eve, to the Devil. Donne uses temporal indicators to give a sense of movement: "At first," when God speaks, man is in a state of right relation to God; next, Eve questions God's decree; "and then," the Devil brings his temptation. Next in the narrative sequence is, of course, the Fall, but here it is only implied. Donne continues his temporal progression: "And now God in this Text comes to his [the Devil's] reply, *Quis est homo*, shall they not die?" (6–8). Here, in Donne's text of Psalm 89:48, God's absolute position in Genesis is reformulated as a rhetorical question. He puts this question to his congregation as a means of involving them in the deliberation even while forcing them to acknowledge what they know to be the answer: yes.

The sermon begins, then, with a clear sense of opposition between two absolute positions. God is absolute on one side and the Devil "peremptory on the other side," with Eve "mollifying" in the middle. Now Donne adds to this alignment by identifying himself with God's interrogative position — "Give me but one instance, but one exception to this rule" (8) —, implying that his audience, to whom he addresses the challenge, is on the other side leaning toward the Devil. Donne confirms this implication by association as he continues,

> Let no man, no woman, no devill offer a *Ne fortè*, (perchance we may dye) much lesse a *Nequaquam*, (surely we shall not dye) except he be provided of an answer to this question, except he can

give an instance against this generall, except he can produce that
mans name, and history, that hath lived, and shall not see death
(9–14).

Here he takes the stance of a prosecuting lawyer, asserting God's case for
general guilt against those of the Devil's party and demanding from them
exemplary evidence to the contrary. He concludes his introduction by
hypothesizing his audience's defense — "I may live as well, as another, and
why should I dye, rather then another?" — and then challenging it by
retorting, "but awake, and tell me, sayes this Text, *Quis homo?* who is that
other that thou talkest of?" (23–25).

Donne's transplanting of his text into the context of the Edenic conflict is significant. First, this opening progression establishes a hierarchy
through which the audience will move to find redemption. At the top (in
the beginning) and in a position of right(eous)ness is God, and at the anti-
thetical apex, in a position of error, the Devil. In the middle of this *agon* is
the yet undetermined Eve (and by implication the audience) who can move
either way. As we have noted, Donne leaves the Fall implicit so that,
chronologically, the audience is left to identify with Eve at her point of will-
ful uncertainty, a position he will exploit in the amplification of the second
point of his *divisio*. Yet once the events leading up to the Fall are evoked,
Eve is guilty already in the memory of the audience, so that Donne is able
to assert a universal identification of his audience with Adam and Eve's
original sin: "Wee are all conceived in close Prison" (14–15), which calls to
mind Psalm 51:5, "Behold, I was shapen in iniquity; and in sin did my
mother conceive me."

Furthermore, by framing the issue of guilt in the biblical narrative of
beginnings, Donne is able to capitalize rhetorically on the theological logic
(or as Burke would have it, logological logic) of the Fall. His use of the
Genesis story of origins is important to the way in which he constructs his
audience's identity of guilt. It allows for a strategy of temporizing essence,
which derives from "puns of logical and temporal priority whereby the *logical* idea of a thing's essence can be translated into a temporal or narrative
equivalent by statement in terms of the thing's source or beginnings" or,
Burke adds, in terms of its fulfilment or fruition.[502] For example, "you state
a man's timeless essence in temporal terms if, instead of calling him 'by
nature a criminal,' you say, 'he will end on the gallows'." Donne characterizes his audience's essential nature by both their origin and their fulfilment:

---

[502] *RM*, 13.

Wee are all conceived in close Prison; in our Mothers wombes, we are close Prisoners all; when we are borne, we are borne but to the liberty of the house; Prisoners still, though within larger walls; and then all our life is but a going out to the place of Execution, to death. Now was there ever any man seen to sleep in the Cart, between New-gate, and Tyborne? (14–19).[503]

When he figures conception as imprisonment and life as "a going out to the place of Execution," it is but a narrative way of saying human life is essentially guilty. Moreover, in situating his audience in the conflict of the Fall, he finds them guilty already by virtue of their origins and the outcome of that conflict. Donne's temporizing of essence thus serves as a figure of proof, a sort of enthymeme by which he can devise visible evidence: because in Eden death is issued as the penalty for guilt, anyone who dies must be guilty. The benefit of this strategy is obvious the first time he refers to his text as a call for evidence: "*What man is he that liveth, and shall not see death?*" Death is a readily observable consequence of a less evident cause. In this forensic mode, Donne relies on death as hard evidence of his audience's guilt. As Donne asserts in the first partition, we can "*see*" and "*taste*" death (170–172).

Donne's forensic mode derives its decorum (and its authority) from his merger of theological and legal discourses. His enthymeme depends on the precedent of Christian theology's meta-narrative which enables him to argue a "legal" case with evidence that could never stand up in civil court (where punishment could never, or should never, stand as evidence for guilt). In *The Rhetoric of Religion*, Burke is interested in the first three chapters of Genesis as an account of temporal "firsts" that deals narratively with principles or logical "firsts." Specifically, he finds in the events surrounding the Fall a statement of the principles of governance which can be used as justification for socio-political order. But in logology, all processes are subject to reversal. Though there may be social motives at work in Donne's sermon, his primary purpose is to convince his audience of their breach of God's order. Here the socio-political (specifically, legal) analogy reinforces the biblical narrative of human nature, an instance such as Burke describes where "a vision of the natural order can become infused with the genius of the verbal and socio-political orders."[504] This infusion enables Donne to

---

[503] This would have been a vivid image in Donne's time, when public executions of Newgate prisoners were common at Tyborne.

[504] *RR*, 185.

represent the principles of the Fall, and therefore (according to Christian theology) human nature, in a contemporary narrative of juridical proceedings: characterized by original sin, human life begins as imprisonment, continues as house arrest, and ends at Tyburn, the place of execution. This strategy allows Donne to treat his audience's sin as a legal problem, without having to name sin directly.

Another effect of Donne's contextualizing of his text in the narrative of the Fall is the creation of a situation where he can move freely between what Burke calls "narrative" style and "cyclical" style. To take Burke's example, although the Fall precedes the need for redemption, "[l]ogologically, the 'fall' and the 'redemption' are but parts of the same cycle, with each implying the other."[505] Everyone knows, for example, that a story that ends at Tyburn has as steps in its process (proceeding backwards) judgement, guilt, transgression, and law, yet each step implies every other: there can be no transgression, for example, without law. Similarly, Donne treats his audience's guilt as a process that can be traced backwards chronologically through death, judgement, guilt, transgression, and implicitly back to covenant (because there can be no transgression without an agreement). From his audience's situation in the story of beginnings, Donne derives a logic of implication which he uses throughout the sermon, so that he can talk about his audience's guilt in terms of death, "our generall humiliation," in the first partition, and in terms of judgement in the second (27). Having established his audience's guilt in the narrative of the Fall, Donne can then go on to characterize their life as an ongoing cycle of judgement and death.

One more point in Donne's introduction warrants mention before we proceed. While establishing his audience's guilt in the narrative of the Fall, Donne initiates a process which will ultimately culminate in their "Transfusion, a Transplantation, a Transmigration, a Transmutation into [Christ]" (546–547). In Donne's *divisio*, a transformation is already taking place. Whereas the *exordium* moves from God's warning, by chronological implication, to man's fallen state, Donne will finally bring his reader from a state of assured guilt, "our generall humiliation," to identification with the exception to the rule, Jesus Christ. In his forensic mode, Donne enacts a variant of the rhetoric of rebirth which, according to Burke, characteristically moves through the three main archetypal clusters: pollution (hell), purification (purgatory), and redemption (heaven).[506] In the first partition,

---

[505] *RR*, 218. In a detailed reading of the first three chapters of Genesis, Burke derives a cycle of terms that he finds clustering implicitly in the idea of "order." I would not presume to encapsulate in brief what Burke takes a hundred pages to develop and what others far more qualified than I have found daunting. My best recourse is simply to refer the reader to Burke's chart (Figure 11).

[506] Rueckert, *Kenneth Burke*, 104.

184   The Rhetoric of Religion

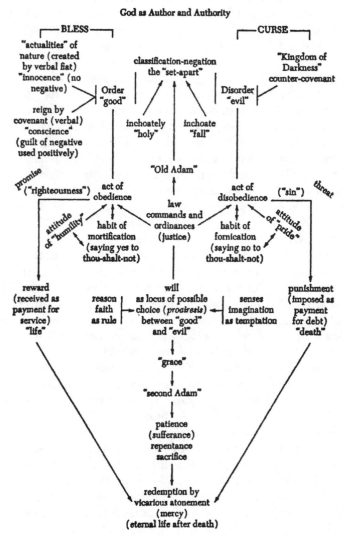

Fig. 11.
"Cycle of Terms Implicit in the Idea of 'Order',"
from Kenneth Burke's A Rhetoric of Religion
Copyright 1970, *The Regents of the Univeristy of California*

Donne proves his audience's guilt (pollution), which associates them with the Devil's error (his "peremptory" obduracy before God) and hence hell. In the second partition, his audience is placed in a judicial balance and confronted with a decision to purify themselves from sin in preparation (purgatory — of course applied figuratively here, not doctrinally) for imminent final judgement. Finally, in his third section Donne proves the validity of a contract between Christ and God which provides for his audience an escape from death (to heaven).

Donne begins his section on general guilt by asserting that the punishments meted out in Eden "are many wayes extended" in the recurring activities of human life (hunger, thirst, weariness, sickness, and desire), which is another way of saying that life spins out into narrative the logic of the Fall: if punishment, then guilt (60). Since the punishments of Genesis 3 follow from general sin, these same recurrent events are but a continuation of the story of man's guilt. Or, said another way, the hardships of life are *exempla* of the *logos* of guilt. Donne's strategy here is to identify death in the cycles of daily life and thereby emphasize the readily visible proof of death in life, and therefore guilt. Focusing on the final phrase of his text, Donne suggests, "this *Videbunt, They shall see*, implies also a *Viderunt*, they have seene, that is, they have used to see death, to observe a death in the decay of themselves, and of every creature, and of the whole World" (189–192). Donne sees evidence of death "in many of those steps" of life (202). A man's life is made of a series of temporal transformations (from infancy to youth for example), beginnings and ends, each of which is a death. Man has seen and studied death "in every Booke" (the book of man, of nature and of creatures), and "they doe presently see death in every object" (213–215). Moreover, this evidence of decay argues a continuation of this "seeing" of death, implying also a continuation of this sequence toward their own future death.

In this first partition, Donne clearly has his particular congregation in mind. As the sermon's header states, he preached this sermon "*to the Lords upon Easter-day, at the Communion, The King being then dangerously sick at New-Market.*" He allows that he knows many a man "that hungers and thirsts not, that labours not, that sickens not," and if any can claim such exception, his privileged audience of lords is likely to include them (67–68). "[B]ut contract the question to that one of death," continues Donne, "And I know none" (69–70).[507] Death's universality ensures his sermon's applicability to each member of his exceptional congregation. Furthermore, Donne knows that sickness at this time would be a particu-

---

[507] Donne deliberately ignores, for rhetorical purposes, the traditional Old Testament counterexamples of Enoch and Elijah, who did not die but "were taken up" (to heaven).

larly poignant sign of mortality even to those who could as yet claim exception from it. Potter and Simpson note that there was considerable anxiety among the court of lords as the king in his sickness seemed for a time to be in imminent danger of death.[508]

A few paragraphs later, Donne again tailors his point to his audience's status as he plays on the Hebrew words for "man" in a sort of lexical *auxesis* that evokes courtship motives. In his sermon's text, the word is

> Not *Ishe*, not *Adam*, not *Enos*; but it is *Mi Gheber*, *Quis vir*, which is the word alwayes signifying a man accomplished in all excellencies, a man accompanied with all advantages; fame, and good opinion justly conceived, keepes him from being *Ishe*, a meere sound, standing onely upon popular acclamation; Innocency and integrity keepes him from being *Adam*, red earth, from bleeding, or blushing at any thing hee hath done; That holy and Religious Art of Arts, which S. *Paul* professed, *That he knew how to want, and how to abound*, keepes him from being *Enos*, miserable or wretched in any fortune; Hee is *Gheber*, a great Man, and a good Man, a happy Man, and a holy Man, and yet *Mi Gheber*, *Quis homo*, this man must see death (129–140).

Donne's hierarchy of terms for man, from the least in dignity, "a meere sound," to the highest, "*Gheber*, a great Man," builds his audience up for a universal fall (Fall): "and yet, *Mi Gheber*, *Quis Homo*, this man must see death." Donne enacts the same rising and falling motion as he "carr[ies] this question a little higher" (141). He says, "Aske it of those, who are Gods by participation of Gods power, of those of whom God saies, *Ego dixi, dii estis*, and God answers for them, and of them, and to them, *You shall dye like men*" (143–145). The gods of the passage Donne alludes to (Psalm 82) are socio-political gods, "the congregation of the mighty" (v.1) — in this case, Donne's congregation of lords. Again, even the king is implied in the continuation of the passage Donne omits: "But ye shall die like men, and fall like one of the princes." Donne's manipulation of hierarchy asserts a universal human condition. If even the king and the most privileged of men are susceptible to death, so must everyone else be. One more time he "carr[ies] this question higher then so, from this *Quis homo*, to *quid homo*, what is there in the nature and essence of Man, free from death?"

(157–159). And once more, he brings his audience back to origins, back to the principle of universal guilt.

The first partition ends appropriately with an emphasis on judgement, whereby Donne reads back from death into its cause. Again he is concerned with evidence. From the "testimony" of death we can deduce "that our Heavenly King is angry" (231–232). Juridical imagery continues as he asserts that "this death ... if ye weigh it in the Divine Balance, it is a seale of Gods anger against sin" (233–236). This allusion to "a seale" sends us back to the opening line of the sermon where God speaks the prohibition of his covenant relationship with Adam and Eve. Death is a seal, a testimony that this covenant has been broken and replaced, as Donne later suggests, by a new "*Covenant with death*" (516). It is on the basis of covenant (or rather contract, its legal counterpart) that Donne will argue his audience's defense in the third point, while the image of the balance of judgement figures prominently in the second partition.

Donne often finds room in his sermons for a digression on issues of doctrine or polity, but he typically does so for rhetorical effect. Here he begins his second section by distinguishing between dogmatical and problematical points of doctrine and setting out policy regarding the latter, suggesting "we are to weigh them in two balances, in the balance of Analogy, and in the balance of scandall ... wee must weigh them with faith, for our own strength, and we must weigh them with charity, for others weaknesse" (249–255). This digression serves his rhetorical purpose by introducing the final judgement, one such problematical point of doctrine, as well as the judicial uncertainty represented in the balance. The certainty of death now affects any sense of future final judgement. The completion of the death cycle begun at the Fall necessarily leads to the uncertainty of one's standing before God. Donne introduces his second point by echoing Eve's words in the opening sequence ("perchance we shall dye"), which places his audience, by association, at a place of decision (240–241). Doctrinal uncertainty thus provides an occasion for him to address his audience's conscience.

Donne takes his text as one such problematical point: "It may be that those Men, whom Christ shal find upon the earth alive, at his returne to Judge the World, shall dye then, and it may be they shall but be changed, and not dye" (264–267). Acts 10:42, "*Hee shall judge the quick and the dead*," does not solve the problem because "the quick" may experience an instantaneous death and resurrection (269–270). He turns to other passages which pertain to this issue, a strategy which only adds confusion to the matter. Whether Paul signifies that "we shall not die" or that "we shall not be buried" when he says "*We shall not all sleep*" in I Corinthians 15.51, "that may be a mystery still" (281–285). Whether those "*which are alive*," as Paul says in I Thessalonians 4:17, will experience "An instant and sudden dis-union, and re-union of body and soul," as Augustine suggests,[509] and thus in essence die, "who can tell?" (286–291). Consider the Scriptures and Authority, continues Donne in the next paragraph, "and we shall be absolutely concluded neither way" (299–300). He goes on to show that tradition is split between the Fathers and "the Schoole," and that currently the Catholic and Reformed churches are split even among themselves: "*Take later men*, and all those in the Romane Church," where Cajetan comes down on one side and Catherinus on the other; "*Take later men*, and all those in the reformed Church," where Calvin leans one way and Luther the other (301–307, italics mine). It all ends up being very confusing, as Donne intends it to be. This strategic use of *aporia* (or *dubitatio*) leaves his audience grasping for certainty, thereby enhancing the impact of that which *is* certain.[510] He completes the *anaphora*: "Take then that which is certain; It is certain, a judgement thou must passe" (316–317).

Yet the certainty of judgement only translates the audience's doctrinal uncertainty into personal uncertainty. Before they can recover from his doctrinal vertigo, Donne introduces a long periodic sentence with two unsettling conditionals that list frightening realities of the day:

If thy close and cautelous proceeding have saved thee from all informations in the Exchequer, thy clearnesse of thy title from all Courts at Common Law, thy moderation from the Chancery, and Star-Chamber, If heighth of thy place, and Authority, have saved thee, even from the tongues of men, so that ill men dare not slander thy actions, nor good men dare not discover thy actions, no not to thy self, All those judgements, and all the judgements of the world, are but interlocutory judgements; There is a finall judgement, *In judicantes & judicatos*, against Prisoners and Judges too, where all shalbe judged again (317–326).

---

[509] Augustine, *City of God* 20.20 [PL 41.689].

[510] The effect of this figure of *aporia* is described by Puttenham: "oftentimes we will seeme to cast perils, and make doubt of things when by a plaine manner of speech wee might affirme or deny him" (*Arte of English Poesie*, 234). Specifically, Donne uses the figure of *dialogismo*, a species of *aporia* which involves questioning and answering (Smith, *Mystery of Rhetoric*, 8–9, [B4v]–B5). Shuger describes this strategy as a device of absolutist theology, whereby Donne riddles his congregation with doubt and uncertainty in order to force their dependency on his priestly power and position as a representative of divine authority (*Habits of Thought*, 207). Shuger's habit of lifting passages out of context allows the misapprehension that Donne is vainly exercising personal power; but read in the larger rhetorical context, as I demonstrate here and in the next chapter, instances of *aporia* bear a much more subtle and productive rhetorical purpose.

Here Donne embeds the Boethian *topos* of fortune's variability[511] to enhance his congregation's sense of uncertainty. Although the fact of this judgement is sure and without exception, its outcome is not. As Donne says a few lines later, "judgement is certain, and the uncertainty of this judgment is certain too" (328–329). Though the fact of judgement is indisputable, its particulars, when and how it will come about, are problematical and therefore call for a response of "sobriety" in respect to both personal morality and doctrine (243).

In this second section, forensic judgment is used as a substitute for death and serves much the same purpose, and there is a similar evidential significance to Donne's socio-political analogue. As sickness, hunger, and thirst are perennial signs of death, so civic judgements point to the final judgement. Again Donne has his privileged audience in mind when he acknowledges that the "heighth of th[eir] place, and Authority" may have saved them from civic judgement (320). Yet he asserts there is one judgement which, like death, none will escape. Donne's cycle of terms works to advantage here. Although final judgement does not have the empirical force that final death does, because of the logical implication of guilt, death, and judgement in the biblical story of human origins, judgement shares (in a sense, borrows) the logical inevitability of death. At the same time, his congregation's thoughts on final judgement are invested with a sense of immediacy drawn from its analogy to social juridical procedure.

Donne ends this section by situating his audience at Eve's point of decision to move either upward in a hierarchy of obedience toward God or downward in obduracy toward the Devil. He uses the same sentence structure that characterizes the uncertainty of his doctrinal controversy — "whether *A*, or whether *B*" —, but here he calls for a personal rather than a doctrinal decision. He asks each individual to determine

> whether God in his mercy, do put off this judgement, till these good motions which his blessed Spirit inspires into thee now, may take roote, and receive growth, and bring forth fruit, or whether he put it off, for a heavier judgement, to let thee see, by thy departing from these good motions, and returning to thy former sins, after a remorse conceived against those sins, that thou art inexcusable even to thy self, and thy condemnation is just, even to thine own conscience (330–337).

---

[511] Boethius, *Consolation of Philosophy*, 2 pr. 1, pr. 4.

Donne again employs a variant of temporized essence, whereby God's timing in death coincides with the fulfilment of a person's nature. A man's essential nature is signified by his state at death. Donne therefore encourages his audience to let the ordinance of preaching "work some tendernesse in thee" and let the "good motions" of the Spirit take root so that at death they may be found growing and bearing fruit (340). Once more we get a sense of a movement or "motion" in Donne's sermon as it urges the congregation to "grow" toward God and away from condemnation with the Devil.

The way upward, however, requires some legal manoeuvring, as Donne still has not found an assured loophole from the general doctrine of death. Following the forensic process, he effects a negotiation of a new covenant in the third partition of the sermon. But before getting into the legalities, Donne presents Augustine's interpretation of his text[512] to spur his audience on in their final movement toward identification with Christ: "this question is moved, to move thee to seek out, and to have thy recourse to that man which is the Lord of Life ... in whom, for all us, there is Redemption from death" (370–373). In rituals of purification, there is usually a transfer of guilt from the polluted to a scapegoat, of which Christ is the obvious exemplar. Though the scapegoat is a commonplace of biblical theology, Donne's representation of this concept is interesting for his heightening of the pollutant element. In his first partition, Donne notes that "[a]s we could not be cloathed at first, in Paradise, till some Creatures were dead, (for we were cloathed in beasts skins) so we cannot be cloathed in Heaven, but in his garment who dyed for us" (208–211). As man's pollution is figured in Adam and Eve's wearing of dead animal remains, so Christ takes on man's pollution in the third partition by being "clothed in mans flesh" (392).

Donne also figures this transfer of guilt as a legal payment. He finds in the Gospels a "contract between him [Christ], and his Father" requiring Christ's death; in the prophets he finds "ratification of that contract" (399–402). And again in the Gospels, he finds "testification" of Christ's death (406). And so he proves "[h]ow stands the validity of that contract" (408). That "contract" is of course the New Covenant by which his audience is able to identify with the "Lord of Life," who is the exception to the "generall doctrine" of death. Donne concludes his examination of the contract by noting that "though Christ Jesus did truly die, so as was contracted ... yet hee did not die so, as was intended in this question, so as other naturall men do die" (411–414).

---

512 Augustine, *Enarr. in Ps.* 88.2.10 (PL 37.1138). Donne made extensive use of this passage in inventing matter for his sermon.

Significantly, Donne has been using "contracted" throughout the sermon to describe how God's Edenic judgements are epitomized, summa-
rized, and condensed in death, saying in effect that death is of the essence
of human nature. But death is also contracted in the sense of being assured
by way of contract. That is, like guilt, God's contract or covenant is implicit
in God's judgement of death on humankind. Jesus, however, was contracted to death under different conditions. Because of his place in the narrative of origins, his death is of a different kind, "the penalty of death
appertaining only to them, who were derived from *Adam* by carnall, and
sinfull generation" (429–430). Conceived of a virgin, he "was not subject
to the Law of death" and was "not included in the generall penalty" (432,
436–437). Jesus entered his contract willingly rather than by compulsion
of his own guilt.

In his *peroratio*, Donne's forensic purification of his audience is made
complete with reference to the *exordium*'s opening opposition between the
Devil and God. Using himself as an *exemplum*, he explains,

> though *I have made a Covenant with death, and have been at an
> agreement with hell,* and in a vain confidence have said to my self,
> *that when the overflowing scourge shall passe through, it shall not
> come to me,* yet God shall annull that covenant, he shall bring that
> scourge, that is, some medicinall correction upon me, and so give
> me a participation of all the stripes of his son (516–521).[513]

Donne's talk of contracts is now translated into the biblical idiom of
covenants. Through his identification with Christ, Donne is able to participate in the Son's contract or covenant of death with the Father.
Significantly, his participation in this judicial payment ("the stripes of his
son")[514] is charged with curative significance as "medicinall correction."
Also in the *peroratio*, the general movement of the sermon from imprisonment to release finds resolution in a new death of contemplative
"rapture, of extasie" (545).

---

[513] Here Donne amplifies an identification principle set down by St. Paul, who expresses his wish "that
I may know him, and the power of his resurrection, and the fellowship of his sufferings, being made
conformable unto his death" (Philippians 3:10).

[514] Isaiah 53:5

⤻· III ·⤻

Donne's "death of the Contemplation of [his] interest in [his] Saviour" in the *peroratio* alerts us to another process that has been at work throughout the sermon, a "terministic transformation" of death itself by which he moves his audience in what Burke calls "the Upward Way" (504–505). The upward way typically

> begins with the pure soul and impure body joined; then, due to an often indeterminate cause, the ecstasy, or Way Up, begins, where the pure soul is separated from the impure body and ascends; the separated and pure soul then has a revelation or vision of some kind, usually of God, absolute purity, or absolute truth.[515]

Donne's sermon begins in kind with the commonplace Platonic image of the body as prison[516] ("we are borne but to the liberty of the house"), which implies an inmate soul. The cause of the soul's release, however, is not indeterminate. Donne makes clear that release comes through an awareness of one's guilt and need for identification with Christ, which he attempts to foster in his audience.

The upward way, for both Burke and Donne, is a dialectical process, "a heaping of perspective upon perspective in a logological quest for the adequate idea."[517] We see this process at work as Donne takes his audience from an idea of death as imprisonment to an idea of death as contemplative rapture or release. An adequate idea of death is important for his purposes because, as we have seen, death is the essence of his audience's identity, so that to transform the term "death" is symbolically to transform his congregation: if his audience is so characterized by death, Donne can symbolically cleanse them by reforming their idea of death. Thus in terministically transforming death, Donne at the same time transforms his audience's sense of themselves and the essence of their lives.

In his quest for the adequate idea, Donne takes death through a "terministic catharsis," which Burke describes as

> another word for 'rebirth,' transcendence, transubstantiation, or simply for 'transformation' in the sense of the technically developmental, as when a major term is found somehow to have

---

[515] Rueckert, *Kenneth Burke*, 109.

[516] The famous sōma (body)/sēma (tomb) pun; see for example, Plato *Cratylus* 400B–402C.

[517] Henderson, *Kenneth Burke*, 129.

moved on, and thus to have in effect changed its nature either by adding new meanings to its old nature, or by yielding place to some other term that henceforth takes over its functions wholly or in part.[518]

We have already seen Donne transforming death's definition from its general, "natural" sense to a possible different sense (sudden disunion and reunion of body and spirit at the final judgement) and then to a positively different sense in application to Jesus who did not die "so as other naturall men." And there is a discernible change in the nature of death from its original association with sin and the Devil to its new function in the purging of sin through Christ.

In this sermon, death is also defined and redefined dialectically: it has meaning only in so far as it relates to its counterpart, life, and *vice versa*. In a life figured as progressive stages of punishment, the fullness of life becomes tantamount to death. Donne's dialectic begins in his *exordium* where "all our life is but a going out to the place of Execution." In his first partition, he alerts his reader to the idea that life is properly considered a narrative of deaths. Following Seneca, he observes that in the many steps of life,[519] "Wee have seene *Mortem infantiæ, pueritiam*, The death of infancy in youth; and *Pueritiæ, adolescentiam*, and the death of youth in our middle age; And at last we shall see *Mortem senectutis, mortem ipsam*, the death of age in death it selfe" (203–206). Donne's addition of a schematic arrangement of *parison*, along with a loose form of *climax*, emphasizes the integrity of the process. For those caught in the natural course of life, this dialectic offers little hope of release from the cycle of death, and little improvement in perspective. At best they might

> see the death of some prophane thoughts in themselves, by the entrance of some Religious thought of compunction, and conversion to God; and then they see the death of that Religious thought, by an inundation of new prophane thoughts, that overflow those (216–219).

However, Donne goes a step beyond his source to provide the key to an upward transformation of death itself: "We shall see the death of Death it self in the death of Christ" (208). The way of transcendence requires an awareness of general guilt and judgement on the one hand, and contempla-

---

[518] *LASA*, 367.
[519] Loosely based on Seneca, *Ep.* 24.20, 49.3, 70.2.

tion of Christ, the exception to the general rule, on the other. As Donne draws the sermon to a conclusion, he takes Solomon's statement that "Death and life are in the power of the tongue" to suggest that death is a matter of perspective, so that

> If my tongue, suggested by my heart, and by my heart rooted in faith ... can say, That the blood of my Saviour runs in my veines, That the breath of his Spirit quickens all my purposes, that all my deaths have their Resurrection, all my sins their remorses, all my rebellions their reconciliations, I will harken no more after this question, as it is intended *de morte naturali*, of a naturall death (489–497).

From such a perspective, the daily parade of death he describes in his first partition takes on a whole new significance. For the contemplative Christian, each occasion figuring the Edenic punishment of death — eating, for example — involves a process of correspondence: "Christ sayes, that as often as wee eate the Sacramentall Bread, we should remember his Death, so as often, as we eate ordinary bread, we may remember our death" (218–222).

Donne's upward way of contemplation operates on this principle of dialectical correspondence between physical and spiritual experience. This dialectic, I suggest, is figured in his analogy of concentric circles, which occurs midway through his first partition. I will approach this analogy by way of Burke. To review, Burke's fifth analogy states that "'Time' is to 'eternity' as the particulars in the unfolding of a sentence are to the sentence's unitary meaning."[520] That is, "the *meaning* of the sentence is an *essence*, a kind of fixed significance or definition that is not confined to any of the sentence's parts, but rather pervades or inspirits the sentence as a whole."[521] Donne's use of death works the same way. Death is a person's essence spelled out in the narrative of his life. Each step, each occasion in a man's life, from birth to eating, must be understood as a partial expression of the whole of his identity in death. In this sense, the life of natural man has its "meaning" in death.

A similar relation between time and eternity figures prominently in Donne's use of the circle as a transformational image.[522] Noting the custom

---

[520] *RR*, 33.

[521] *RR*, 27.

[522] See Michael L. Hall for a good introduction to the meaning of circle imagery in Donne and for references to earlier studies on the subject. Hall argues that this circular imagery corresponds to a

wherein the early church considered the martyr's day of death a birthday, he comments,

> Their death was a birth to them into another life, into the glory of God; It ended one Circle, and created another; for immortality, and eternity is a Circle too; not a Circle where two points meet, but a Circle made at once; This life is a Circle, made with a Compasse, that passes from point to point; That life is a Circle stamped with a print, an endlesse, and perfect Circle, as soone as it begins. Of this Circle, the Mathematician is our great and good God; The other Circle we make up our selves; we bring the Cradle, and Grave together by a course of nature (106–114).

This is similar to Donne's strategy of temporizing election, where this life is seen as a temporal enactment of an essential state of being. The compass-drawn circle is a person's natural life *in time* as represented elsewhere in the sermon, a narrative of death from beginning to end; however, for the saint, not only is birth a death, but death is a birth as well into another circle, eternity. The final way upward is through the point of physical death where the two circles meet; however, Donne gives this image significance for *this* life in his *peroratio*, where he posits a corresponding grave and another death: "The contemplation of God, and heaven [eternity], is a kinde of buriall,"[523] and therefore also a point of access to transcendent meaning (502–503). Here we get a picture of how the upward way effects the ter-ministic transformation of death *in time*. The second circle, eternity, is all essence, a fixed meaning that is printed, not drawn, so that when the Christian gains access to it in a rapture of contemplation, a new meaning or essence infuses the whole of his temporal, earthly existence.

This circular imagery is also relevant to Donne's representation of covenants and contracts. Adam's violation of the first Edenic agreement began the cycle of mortal time by bringing the judgment of death, so that each person's birth is a death. Theologically, the new contract introduces a way of escape from this general condition by the death of death in Christ, so that final death becomes a new birth; linguistically, the oxymoron accepts the logical binary it describes. Furthermore, in this life a person

---

circular methodology in the structure of Donne's sermons: "Circles and Circumvention in Donne's Sermons," *JEGP* 82 (1983): 201–14.

523 Perhaps taken from Gregory the Great, *Moralia in Job* 5.6.9 (PL 75.684B), altered from "sepulcrum mentis est quo absconditur anima."

identified with Christ bears the stamp of a new contract, a new nature and with it a new perspective. The new contract, the printed circle, gives a new significance and meaning to the sequence of events which figure death. For example, while under the old *"Covenant with death,"* Donne hoped to evade *"the overflowing scourge"* (516–518), but under the new covenant with Christ, he welcomes the scourge as a participation in his Saviour and a "medicinall correction" (520).

The purifying process of Donne's upward way with death might be best illustrated in death's association with images involving bodily expulsion. Another of Burke's peculiarities is his emphasis on his "Demonic Trinity" — urinating, elimination of feces, and sexual orgasm — which invariably point to sin and guilt in want of purging. According to Burke, the "fecal motive" must be expressed before any purgation and redemption can be complete.[524] Such expression usually involves the unloading, unburdening or expelling of something undesirable, filthy, or abhorrent.[525] However, in his upward way of purification, Donne's reference to bodily functions tends toward a vision of assimilation of experience rather than elimination.

As might be expected of a sermon, Donne keeps any sexual implications vague, yet they are significant to his argument. Death in its association with the sex act, a Renaissance commonplace, could be considered a sort of pollution by expulsion. At the beginning of the sermon, death is associated with the womb (which is usually an image of life) by force of analogy. The womb which encloses the unborn child is like the prison holding a prisoner. Theologically, the womb belongs to a cluster of images associated with guilt because "the penalty of death" is "derived from *Adam* by carnall, and sinfull generation" (429–430). Conception is therefore an act of pollution, a transmission of sin. In the first partition, death is characterized by "wantonnesse, and sportfulnesse" in the way it "playes with us" — all terms with strong sexual overtones associated with erotic narrative (79). In her wooing of Adonis, for example, Shakespeare's Venus describes her influence on Mars who, she says, "for my sake hath learned to sport and dance, / To toy, to wanton, dally, smile, and jest" (105–106).[526] In one of Spenser's versions of the same myth in *The Faerie Qveene*, Venus "reape[s] sweet pleasure of the wanton boy" (Adonis), while Cupid "with faire *Adonis*

---

[524] Rueckert, *Kenneth Burke*, 92–3. See also idem, "Kenneth Burke's 'Symbolic of Motives' and 'Poetics, Dramatistically Considered'," in *Unending Conversations: New Writings By and About Kenneth Burke*, eds. Greig Henderson and David Cratis Williams (Carbondale: Southern Illinios University Press, 2001), 99–124, here 110–11.

[525] Rueckert, *Kenneth Burke*, 97.

[526] *Venus and Adonis* in *William Shakespeare: The Complete Works*, gen. ed. Alfred Harbage (New York: Penguin, 1969), 1406–1418, here 1407.

playes his wanton parts" (III.vi.46, 49).[527] Interestingly, A. C. Hamilton glosses stanza 46 by noting that "[Adonis's] state suggests (sexual) death," which Hamilton cross-references with Donne's notorious play upon the sexual connotations of dying in his "First Anniversary" where he says, "Wee kill our selves to propagate our kinde" (110). This pun is particularly appropriate to the procreation imagery of this sermon.

This is not to say that sex is dirty, for Donne describes his contemplating of his Saviour in similar terms. Rather, there is good sex and bad sex corresponding to good death and bad death. Death and sexual imagery are further conflated when Donne says that Jesus's death as attested in the Gospels is a "consummation" (as well as a "testification") of his contract with God — a fitting term considering this contract is in payment for man's penalty of death which begins with conception (405). The "rapture" and "extasie" of contemplation of Christ also carry sexual implications, albeit vague. In usage contemporary to Donne, rapture meant not only transport of mind, but the act of carrying off a woman, as well as rape, while the "extasie" in Donne's poem of the same name clearly plays on the ambiguity between sexual and spiritual delight. In Thomas Carew's erotic lyric "A Rapture," a seducer describes to a woman in quasi-spiritual terms the rapture of their potential love-making:

> ... til a soft murmure, sent
> From soules entranc'd in amorous languishment
> Rowze us, and shoot into our veines fresh fire,
> Till we, in their sweet extasie expire (51–54).[528]

Again ecstasy, both sexual and spiritual, reaches consummation in a type of death as the lovers "expire."

Also in connection with contemplation of the Saviour, Donne refers to his audience's "*Covenant with death*" specifically as a marriage contract with hell which "God shall annull" (516–519). In this contract with the Devil, the Christian is a widow who has lost her true husband, Christ. If we compile a few images, we see on the one hand the death of Christ, who is the Church's husband, as a "consummation" of death, so that contemplation of him is figured as a "rapture" and "extasie." On the other hand, for those still under contract with hell, death is figured as sexual conception which perpetuates the curse of the Fall, making corporeal life an imprisonment. Sexual release, then, seems a fitting metaphor for spiritual release.

[527] *The Faerie Qveene*, ed. A. C. Hamilton, 364.

[528] Carew, *The Poems*, ed. Rhodes Dunlap (Oxford: Clarendon Press, 1947, repr. 1957), 49–53, here 50.

There are also some distant cousins to the "Demonic Trinity" in Donne's presentation of himself in ecstatic contemplation. Describing God's medicinal correction, Donne suggests, "he shall give me a sweat, that is, some horrour, and religious feare, and so give me a participation of his Agony; he shall give me a diet, perchance want, and penury, and so a participation of his fasting" (521–524). As a sign of the curse of death, sweating brings a religious fear, but it also brings a participation in its counterpart in Christ's Passion at Gethsemane. In this way, expulsion of sweat can signify a purifying moment, not simply through an expulsion of pollution but through identification with Christ as scapegoat. Similarly, hunger is portrayed as a "diet," a variant of expulsion which has its counterpart in Christ's fasting. Donne finally gives a proper completion to the "fecal motive" as he rounds out his ingestion imagery by figuring his transformation in Christ as a perfect bowel movement: "for good digestion brings alwaies assimilation, certainly, if I come to a true meditation upon Christ, I come to a conformity with Christ" (547–549).

In this dialectic of purification, the Christian's signs of contagion are perfectly assimilated and sanctified. Donne transforms the daily earthly experience of his audience into spiritual significance by taking them on the upward way, where he leaves them at the end of the sermon in meditation upon the Saviour, who is the answer to the question posed by the sermon's text. As his audience turns from the sermon back to daily life, they will thus leave better equipped for living. The upward way, this withdrawal, culminates in a new vision followed by the downward way "whereupon the visionary can once again resume his commerce with the world, which he now sees in a new light, in terms of the vision earned during his stage of exile."[529] When the contemplator descends back into this quotidian world, something of that perspective remains and inspirits the events of life with a new meaning, as argued in Donne's image of the circles. The "Downward Way" then reaches completion "when the soul, with the new knowledge gained from its vision, attempts to effect changes at an earthly level, attempts, that is, to make its complete self and the world in which it lives approach the perfection perceived in the vision."[530]

---

[529] *RM*, 95.
[530] Rueckert, *Kenneth Burke*, 109.

Expanding on Donne's comment that "The art of *salvation*, is but the art of *memory*" (2:2.52), Joan Webber adds that "the preacher's office is not that of a teacher, but that of an arouser, a reminder, an official conscience."[531] Donne fulfils all three roles in this sermon. He arouses his audience from sleep and complacency; he convinces them of their guilt through the evidence of death in the events of their daily lives; and he offers these events not only as memorials of mortality, but as reminders of the upward way. Ideally, then, as his audience leaves his sermon they should be ever-stimulated in a dialectic of purification, ever reaching from this life of death to the death of contemplation in their interest in the Saviour, and ever bringing back to life a new and purified perspective. Although death comes loaded with Christian commonplaces, it is to Donne's credit that he makes in this sermon something fresh and compelling of it.

---

[531] Webber, *Contrary Music*, 145.

CHAPTER SIX

Form as Proof in Deaths Duell

Psalm 68:20
AND UNTO GOD THE LORD BELONG
THE ISSUES OF DEATH. i.e. FROM DEATH.

[T]he lyfe in this world is resembled to a pilgrimage in a
straunge countrie far frome God and that death, delive-
rynge us from our bodyes, doth sende us straight home into
our awne countrey and maketh us to dwell presently with
God for ever in perpetuall rest and quietnesse. So that to
dye is no losse, but profite and winnynge to all true
Christen people.
Certain Sermons or Homilies (1547)[532]

THE BURDEN OF THIS CHAPTER IS TWOFOLD: to broaden the
scope of this discussion of Donne's rhetorical treatment of death-as-
courtship, and to answer the question of decorum raised by certain critics
of Sermons 2:9 and *Deaths Duell.* The latter will be achieved at the conclusion of the chapter with reference to commentary provided in the printed
preface to *Deaths Duell* and to Donne's elegy on Prince Henry. But first, I
should like to account for the unique quality of *Deaths Duell,* which

---

[532] *Certain Sermons or Homilies (1547) and A Homily against Disobedience and Wilful Rebellion (1570):*
A Critical Edition, ed. Ronald A. Bond (Toronto: University of Toronto Press, 1987), 151.

nonetheless bears so many similarities to Donne's first extant sermon on death, as described in the previous chapter.

In his final sermon on death, preached on the first Friday in Lent in 1630/1, Donne revisits many *topoi* from his first (2:9), to the point that it is not unlikely that he had the earlier sermon beside him while composing this one. Despite these similarities, *Deaths Duell* is a very different sermon because it adopts a different principle of *inventio*. This difference can be discerned in the functions of the key images of each sermon. The governing image of 2:9 is that of concentric circles, which function discursively, by *logos*; whereas the central images of *Deaths Duell* — corruption (signifying agitation) and architecture (signifying comfort) — function affectively, by *pathos*. Donne uses the latter, affective appeal as he does in his sermon on prodigality (1:1): to engender and frustrate desire in his audience as he directs them toward identity with Christ in the *peroratio*. Of course no discourse relies exclusively on one mode of proof. The difference is one of emphasis. While the previous sermon on death features *logos*, this one subordinates *logos* to *pathos*.

This choice of proof is an issue of decorum. In *Deaths Duell*, Donne's principle of decorum derives from the formal operations of his *dispositio*. In the first half of the sermon, Donne agitates his audience with repulsive images of corruption in death to induce a certain restlessness and desire for rest signified in the static imagery of the *divisio*. He then channels and directs their desire throughout the remainder of the sermon, keeping them in a state of restlessness until half-way through (at the end of the first partition) where he offers the theoretical means for satisfying their desire: faith (or rest) in the authority (or architecture) of the text. But the congregation's agitated emotions are not finally brought to rest until the long *peroratio*, which takes up most of the third partition, where Donne draws on meditative practice to infuse in them a new affective pattern of experience. Here Donne uses formal devices to bring his congregation into identification with Christ, in whom there is reassurance regarding the issues of death.

Briefly stated, Donne's *dispositio* in *Deaths Duell* is formal, rather than exegetical as his *divisio* seems to suggest. Thus although courtship imagery is less prominent in this sermon than in many others, the courtship *topos* is nonetheless fundamental to its *inventio*. Donne brings his audience to court assurance in a providential God by goading them with conditions of estrangement (a sense of unease and distance from their object of desire, a "good issue" of death) in preparation for their identification with Christ in the *peroratio*, who is their means of a good issue. This ritual of identification is in turn their means of consolation and relief from the agitation Donne so carefully amplifies throughout the bulk of the sermon.

⌣· II ·⌣

The sermon begins with an architectural image that is evocative of solidity and security. This effect is complemented by the brick-laying effect of Donne's grammatical arrangement of *isocolon*:

BUILDINGS stand by the benefit of their *foundations* that susteine and *support* them, and of their *butteresses* that comprehend and *embrace* them, and of their *contignations* that knit and *unite* them: The *foundations* suffer them not to *sinke*, the *butteresses* suffer them not to *swerve*, and the *contignation* and knitting suffers them not to *cleave* (10:11.1–6).

Donne goes on to explain that the first part of the verse — "hee that *is our God* is the *God of salvation*" (7) — is the body of our building and that the former part, the text of the sermon, is in a sense the structure of that body laid bare. Even though the sermon was preached at Whitehall, St. Paul's Cathedral must have occurred to Donne's audience. It was the most imposing building in London with its flying buttresses without (Figure 12) and its vaulted ceiling within (Figure 13: although no contignation [the joining of wooden floor joists] was visible, the ribs and joints of the vaults would have provided a similar impression of being "knit" together). Notwithstanding the fire which destroyed its steeple in 1561, this specific correspondence between Donne's *divisio* and the architecture of St. Paul's would have provided the congregant a ready and accessible emblem of the security offered in this text.

In addition to its connotations of solidity and rest, this building imagery serves as a mnemonic device, a framework around which the congregation could visualize the text for later recall.[533] Donne frequently conceives of his *divisio* as a memory-aid and almost as frequently uses images of buildings to guide and organize his congregation's thoughts.[534] Sir Philip Sidney evokes the traditional notion of memory as an arrangement of storage places (*topoi* or *loci*) to explain the mnemonic quality of poetry. He says,

---

[533] Such a system was laid out in the treatise *Ad Herennium*, but perhaps the most accessible example of this in Donne's culture would have been Robert Fludd's memory theatre: Frances A. Yates, *The Art of Memory* (London: Routledge, 1966), 327–41.

[534] For examples of Donne's use of building structures see 3:8.91–93; 3:15.13–14; 4:3.121–122; 4:10.83–84; 5:12.20–31; 7:5.125–128; 8:15.80–83.

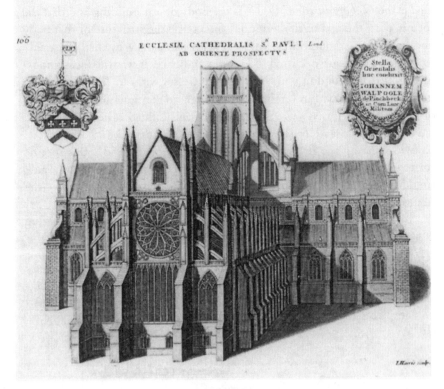

Fig. 12.
Old St. Paul's Cathedral with the flying buttresses,
from an engraving by Wenceslaus Hollar
University of Waterloo

Fig. 13.
The east side interior of the old St. Paul's from
an engraving by Wenceslaus Hollar
University of Waterloo

even they that have taught the art of memory have showed nothing so apt for it as a certain room divided into many places well
and thoroughly known. Now, that hath the verse in effect perfectly, every word having his natural seat, which seat must needs
make the word remembered.[535]

Sidney could just as easily have been speaking of Donne's *divisio*. Donne's
contemporaries, especially those at court who would have had occasion to
travel on the continent, would have been familiar with buildings used as
mnemonic devices. William E. Engel discusses the Scrovegni Chapel in the
Arena at Padua, Italy, as an example of mnemonically organized pictorial
space (Figure 14). In the painted panels of the interior one can read "a
mnemonic path to salvation."[536] Here in this sermon, in keeping with the
theme of his text, Donne uses the structural form of the building rather
than the spaces it contains. Later, in his *peroratio*, Donne will fill this architectural space (i.e. the grammar of the text) with a redemptive sequence of
verbal pictures, not unlike the scenes at Padua, as he describes the scenes of
Christ's twenty-four hours before his crucifixion. This architectural image
of biblical text would have been a familiar one to Donne's audience. Title-
pages of this period frequently depicted architectural structures. A very
notable example is the King James Bible, one of the most commonly accessible books at the time, which, like the Scrovegni Chapel, depicts biblical
scenes within an architectonic structure (see Figure 15).[537]

Donne's *divisio* does not, however, serve as "an analogy upon which to
build the structure of his whole discourse," as Potter and Simpson suggest.[538] In many respects this emblematic framework does not reflect the
dispositio of the sermon's argument at all, as one might expect of a *divisio*.
The image of the building, static and conceptual (therefore, logical), does
not accord with the *dispositio* of the rest of the sermon, which is dynamic
and experiential. It is experiential form, not hermeneutic division (which
the building represents), that determines the *dispositio* of this sermon. The

[535] Sidney, *Defence of Poetry*, 51.

[536] William E. Engel, *Mapping Mortality* (Amherst: University of Massachusetts Press, 1995), 13–23.
Engel describes such other pictorial sequences as the one in Lady Drury's Oratory, which I discuss
in chap. 1 (n. 112) in the context of emblematic art.

[537] cf. Margery Corbett and Ronald Lightbown, *The Comely Frontispiece* (London: Routledge & Kegan
Paul, 1979).

[538] *Sermons*, 1:28.

opening image must be understood in its place within the sermon's argument, where Donne moves his audience through a redemptive process by
first troubling them with life as a restless peregrination through death and
then delivering them, bringing them to rest, by faith, in the architecture of
the text (which Donne has ensured they will remember) through identification with Christ.[539]

Although the *divisio* seems designed to comfort, any hope in death is,
for the moment, short-lived. Donne begins his first partition by asserting
that "with *God*, the *Lord* are the *issues of death*, and therefore in all our
deaths, and deadly calamities of this life, wee may justly *hope* of a good *issue*
from him." But he takes a turn in mid-sentence that determines the direction of the whole first partition as he continues: "and all our *periods* and
transitions in this life, are so many passages *from death* to *death*" (64–67).
At this point, Donne aims not to deliver assurance of a good issue (as his
divisio seems to promise), but to agitate his audience about each "issuing"
through death. He outlines three stages of death — the prison of the
womb, life as a series of deaths, and putrefaction in the grave — and develops each in turn, taking his audience, as in the previous sermon, through a
process of seeing death in life from the cradle to the grave. Here, however,
this process serves not to win his audience's intellectual assent regarding
their essence as fallen (as in 2:9) but to repel them from the idea of death
figured in these two terminal events of life.

Although discussion of beginnings and endings always implies essence,
here, in contrast to 2:9, Donne deflects attention from the logic of origins
by focusing on grotesque details of the womb's deathliness. As I have suggested, the movement of this sermon derives from the formal operations of
pathos, an arousal of desire and promise of fulfilment. Donne moves his
audience by appealing to their affections with repulsive images of death,
again making effective use of *hypotyposis*. These images cause his audience
to feel the necessity (a sort of pathetic cause) of an issue *from, in*, and finally
(in the third partition) *by* death. This movement is established early as
Donne transforms death from a state to a process, from a static condition
to a dynamic one, from imprisonment to escape. He reiterates from the
earlier sermon the idea that

---

[539] Terry Sherwood describes the sermon's *dispositio* somewhat differently as moving from fear to
conformity with Christ, from death of the body to the resurrection of hope. In this process he sees
a redemption of fallen time (enacted in the bulk of the sermon) through its identification with
Christ in the events of his Passion so that "[g]radually, the sermon conforms time itself to Christ":
Fulfilling the Circle, 196. While Sherwood's analysis is complementary to my own (especially in
relation to Donne's temporizing of essence in the second and third partition), my aim is to move
from the "what" of the sermon to the "how" — that is, to emphasize the rhetorical *activity* of the
sermon upon its audience rather than its conceptual framework.

Fig. 14.
Nave of Scrovegni Chapel
William E. Engel, *Mapping Mortality* (Amherst: University of Massachusetts Press, 1995), p. 15

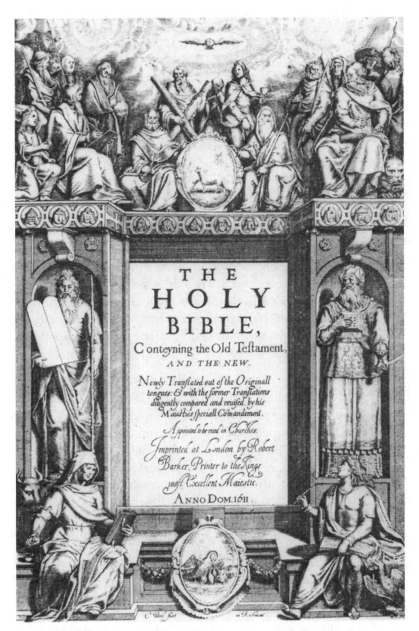

Fig. 15.
Title page of the King James Bible *(1611)*
Glasgow University Library, Department of Special Collections, University of Glasgow

Our very *birth* and entrance into this life, is *exitus à morte,* an *issue from death,* for in our mothers *wombe* wee are *dead so,* as that wee doe *not know* wee *live,* not so much as wee doe in our *sleepe,* neither is there any *grave* so close, or so *putrid* a *prison,* as the *wombe* would be unto us, if we stayed in it *beyond* our time, or dyed there *before* our time (67–72).

To be born is a type of death, but one which is, paradoxically, a deliverance into life, while to refuse to be delivered through this process of death is to die indeed.

The necessity of this exit is underscored by the disturbing image of an undeliverable child. The womb-as-grave similitude is amplified so that the undelivered fetus becomes a focal image of repulsion for Donne's audience; the fetus is an unnatural murderer likened to parasitic worms as Donne continues,

In the *grave* the *wormes* doe not kill us, wee *breed* and *feed,* and then *kill* those wormes which wee our selves produc'd. In the wombe the dead *child* kills the *Mother* that conceived it, and is a murtherer, nay a *parricide,* even after it is dead. ... And there in the *wombe* wee are taught *cruelty,* by being *fed with blood,* and may be *damned,* though we be *never borne* (72–76, 81–82).

The womb and the grave reciprocate repulsiveness such that it is unclear whether the womb amplifies the horror of the grave or *vice versa.* This ambiguity creates an emotional dilemma. By force of analogy, this life becomes an existential imprisonment if we remain in it beyond our time. Yet death, the only available exit, is no less despicable. We are made to feel at once the necessity and the repulsiveness of death.

Next follows a jarring juxtaposition which finally brings the sermon to what is ostensibly the first point of the *divisio,* the ability of God to deliver. But again the *dispositio* of the sermon fails to correspond to the *divisio.* In Psalm 139:14, "*I am wonderfully and fearefully made,*" a biblical commonplace of comfort in God's providence is undone by the immediately preceding images of still-birth and by the ensuing qualification by Job (10:8), "*thou hast taken paines about me,* and *yet,* sayes he, *thou doest destroy me*" (83–84; 88–89). God's theoretical providence in conception is for naught to his audience if not matched by his providence in delivery. The stillbirth image evokes anxiety over a safe delivery from death, notwithstanding God's ability. To a culture where the death of a mother and/or child at birth was all too common,[540] these images would carry great pathetic force. Moreover, the still-birth experience exemplifies "the *exaltation* of *misery*, to *fall* from a *neare hope* of *happines*,"[541] which mirrors a pattern of experience the sermon will now replicate, where desire builds to anticipation only to be frustrated (99).

The affective pattern Donne relentlessly asserts undermines that which his congregation knows, or should know, to be true. The desire for deliverance engendered here is, for a time, deliberately dissociated from any assurance that God will deliver as Donne focuses instead on the necessity of death. Here again the *logos* of the Aristotelian topic of *necessitas* contributes to the primary appeal of *pathos*. Emblematic of this frustration is the umbilical image which launches the section on the "manifold deathes of this *world*" where

> Wee have a winding sheete in our Mothers wombe, which growes
> with us from our conception, and wee come into the world,
> wound up in that *winding sheete*, for wee come to *seeke a grave*;
> And as prisoners discharg'd of actions may lye for fees; so when the
> *wombe* hath discharg'd us, yet we are bound to it by *cordes* of flesh,
> by such a *string*, as wee cannot goe thence, nor stay there
> (126–131).

This image contributes to the deathliness of the womb (the umbilical cord being, of course, a common cause of stillbirth), while its association with "the winding sheete" reminds us that we carry the promise of death from birth. Readers of the first two editions of *Deaths Duell* would be reminded of this association by the engraving of Donne in his winding sheet that faced the title page: an image that was later translated into the effigy that would mark his tomb in St.Paul's (fig. 16).[542] If Donne was half as calculating in his own approach to death as John Carey makes him out to be, it is not unlikely that the imagery of the sermon (which Donne apparently prepared for publication) and his portraits were designed to work in tan-

---

[540] See Lawrence Stone, *The Family, Sex and Marriage in England 1500–1800*, abr. and rev. ed. (London: Penguin, 1977), 54–65.

[541] This recalls Boethius, *Consolation of Philosophy*, 2 pr. 4. Cf. chap. 5, n. 511, above.

[542] Donne already knew when he commissioned his monument that a space had been set aside in St. Paul's for his tomb (Bald, *John Donne*, 528–29).

Fig. 16.
Effigy of Donne in his shroud in St. Paul's Cathedral,
from an engraving by Wenceslaus Hollar
University of Waterloo

dem on the memory of the Londoners who survived him.[543] In both cases, Donne identifies life with the inevitability of death.

At this point, Donne reintroduces the building imagery: more precisely, a "house" image which carries added connotations of home and rest promised in the *divisio*. But here it serves the contrary purpose of amplifying the sense of death-related restlessness Donne so carefully cultivates in the first partition. He continues to goad his audience's feelings of unrest and discomfort as he surveys the various sorts of "mansions" (John 14:2) available in heaven ("a *virgins* house" [141], "a *matrons* house" [142], and so on) to augment his assertion that "*Here wee have no continuing citty*" (150). He takes St. Jerome to task for calling the Israelites' journeys in the wilderness "Mansions" when the Hebrew word more properly "signifies but a *journey*, but a peregrination" (153–154). Now halfway through the sermon, Donne aims to convince that there is no house of rest in this life of wandering, this "*pilgrimage*" through "an *universall church-yard*" (159–161). This present house of death is a long way from the promise of rest engendered in the static but solid structure of the *divisio*.

Nor does Donne's temporizing of death bring comfort. Once again he figures his audience's life as a series of deaths, but with a significant difference. In 2:9 he uses the analogy of daily life to provide *exempla* of death and induce a way of seeing and thinking about life. In *Deaths Duell* death bears an abstract, non-particularized relation to daily life, temporized as "but *Hebdomada mortium, a week of deaths,* seaven dayes, seaven periods of our life spent in dying, *a dying seaven times over,* and there is an end" (164–166). Here images of death are less quotidian and more sensational, even fabulous. Donne repeats from 2:9 the Senecan image of aging as a progressive series of deaths (166–168), but he expands on this image with a decidedly affective purpose as he continues: "Nor doe all these, youth out of infancy, or age out of youth arise so, as a *Phœnix* out of the *ashes* of another *Phœnix* formerly *dead,* but as a *waspe* or a *serpent* out of a *caryon,* or as a *Snake* out of *dung*" (168–171). Donne's striking contrast of images again evokes a hope of deliverance signified in an image of rebirth (the Phoenix), only to dash all hope by asserting instead an image that is parallel in structure but opposite in tone (the serpent). This dyslogistic image of the snake generated out of dung argues that each life-stage is rather worse than the previous, further sinking any prospect of hope in the sermon.

---

[543] John Carey sees Donne's management of his last days as "[t]ypical of [his] determination to turn death into a drama of the will." For Carey, Donne's effigy signifies Donne obsessive desire to control death: "He was stage-managing his own demise. In this way he attained that command of death that the suicide aspires to. He made it appear that, like his 'Heroique' suicidal Christ, he chose how and when to die" (*John Donne,* 214).

Rounding out his depiction of this present life of deaths, Donne uses the testimonies of Elijah's and Jonah's despair as *confirmatio* to press his audience for agreement: "How much worse a death then death, is this life, which so good men would so often change for death?" (192–193).

Having felt the weight of this life of deaths for over a hundred lines of text, Donne's audience is ready to accept that "the *final dissolution* of body and soule" is indeed a deliverance:

> And if no other deliverance conduce more to his glory and my good, yet he hath the *keys of death*, and hee can let me out at that dore, that is, deliver me from the manifold deaths of this world, the *omni die* and the *tota die*, the *every dayes death* and *every houres death*, by that *one death*, the *final dissolution* of body and soule, the end of all (205–210).

Death seems to have undergone a blessed transformation, albeit only by becoming the lesser of two evils. This is not the typical message of a glorious deliverance through resurrection, but of a deliverance by a death that is "the end of all." Donne nonetheless has made the first point of his *divisio*, if he would care to press it: if final death is a deliverance from the continuous and burdensome deaths of this life (as his audience must now feel it is), and every man dies, according to God's decree, then it follows that indeed "it is in his [God's] power to give us an *issue* and deliverance" (15–16). But Donne's point in his first partition has nothing to do with his *divisio* at all. He does not, as he promised, assure us of how the "*Almighty Father* rescues his servants from the jawes of death" (50). Nor is Donne interested in pursing a syllogistic, logical argument. He aims rather to press on in building his audience's repulsion at this life of deaths and to augment their longing for deliverance even as he defers it, while at the same time amplifying the horrible aspects of the only available means of deliverance (biological death), again putting his audience in the impossible situation of both longing and loathing figured in the umbilical image.

As Donne rounds out his first partition, he dwells on the biology of death to render detestable the very means of deliverance. The final "issue" from this prolonged life of deaths is an issue *from* but also *into* another prolonged death, "an *entrance* into the *death of corruption* and *putrefaction* and *vermiculation* and *incineration*, and dispersion in and from the *grave*, in which every dead man dyes over againe" (215–217). This impressive string of rhyming, multi-syllabic Latinate words argues that this process of final death is no less tedious and burdensome than this life of deaths. But rather than launch another assault of troubling grave images, Donne offers his audience a brief promise of relief in Christ's exception from corruption in the grave. Donne again teases his agitated audience with a brief glimmer of hope. Any catechized schoolboy would have recognized this doctrine as a signal that a *confirmatio* of the assertion that "unto God belong the issues *from* death" was afoot, but Donne instead uses this doctrine to give his audience's agitation a new form in the uncertain (from the standpoint of human reason) cause of Christ's exception. This uncertainty is formulated in a deliberative series of questions, answers, and refutations (lines 219–257) as Donne seeks to determine "What gave him this priviledge?" The pattern is as follows: question-refutation; question-question-answer-refutation; question-question-answer-refutation. In each case an explanation is offered only to be rejected. As in 2:9, Donne's doctrinal *aporia* leaves his audience wavering and ready for a solid solution, even the difficult one which closes the cycle. Simply put, it was God's will that Christ not see corruption, from which Donne makes application to his audience, adding that "[t]he humble soule (and onely the humble soule is the religious soule) rests himselfe upon *Gods* purposes, and his decrees" (261–263). Donne thus effectively points the audience back to the text, to God's purposes and decrees, for "*unto God the Lord belong the issues of death.*"

Having been humbled by Donne's enactment of the failure of human reasoning and the (perverse) effectiveness of human emotion, his audience is ready to rely, in faith, on divine fiat. His strategy has been to use *pathos* in the worst that death can offer and in the staged failure of reason to drive his audience to take refuge in the *ethos* of God's decree in the testimony of Scripture: it is so because God says it is so. He might as well have said it is so because his audience wishes it so, for, in a sense, the basis of Donne's argument — desire — is the flip-side of faith. As the writer of Hebrews says, "faith is the substance of things hoped for."[544] But to his audience's emotional receptivity, Donne adds *confirmatio* in the *ethos* of demonstration. Paul and Peter base the doctrinal authority of Christ's exception from death not only on God's decree but on the "manifestation" of God's decree in the prophets and in its "reall execution" in history (266–275). From this Donne extracts the principle that "[a]ll *manifestation* is either in the *word* of *God*, or in the *execution* of the *decree*; And when these two concur and meete, it is the strongest *demonstration* that can be" (279–281). Donne then applies this principle of doctrine to the more personal issue of election, framing the issue of assurance as a rhetorical problem of proof as he continues,

---

[544] Hebrews 11:1 (KJV). Interestingly, the Revised Version substitutes "assurance" for "substance," which gives faith the significance of a "proof."

when therefore I finde those *markes* of *adoption* and *spirituall filia-*
tion, which are delivered in the *word* of *God*, to be upon me, when
I finde that reall *execution* of his *good purpose* upon me, as that *actu-*
ally I doe *live* under the *obedience*, and under the *conditions* which
are *evidences* of *adoption* and *spirituall filiation*; then, and so long as
I see these *markes* and live so, I may safely comfort my selfe in a *holy*
certitude and a *modest infallibility* of my *adoption* (281–288).

Not only must one believe God's decree of his ability to deliver, but one
must be able to feel that this deliverance has personal application.[545]

At this point in the sermon, this theoretical answer of assurance comes
as a somewhat perplexing miscue; it seems premature as Donne promptly
drops this argument of comfort and picks up again his audience's insecu-
rity *vis à vis* death. As in 2:9, Donne moves from the one exception from
the death of corruption, Christ, to the exception of the few who are alive
at his second coming (according to 1 Corinthians 15:51), but here he uses
this point of doctrine differently. He creates no theological *aporia*, but
directly sides with Augustine's theory of the "sudden dissolution and
reunion."[546] Instead of inviting his audience into a theological deliberation
as he does in the previous sermon, he presses his audience's present condition and continues to develop the repulsion of that final death of deaths —
corruption — with his famous image of worms and incest. Donne continues the image begun earlier, where life is a progressive series of deaths generating worse corruption, signified in carrion, dung, wasps, and snakes.
This time *aporia*[547] is spun out of a genealogy of grave worms in an amplification of Job 17.14:

Miserable riddle, when the *same worme* must bee *my mother*, and
my sister, and *my selfe*. *Miserable incest*, when I must bee *maried* to
my *mother* and my *sister*, and bee both *father* and *mother* to my
owne mother and *sister*, *beget*, and *beare* that *worme* which is all that
miserable penury (311–315).

---

[545] Richard Bernard emphasizes the importance of application, dividing it from the second part of the
traditional doctrine-use sermon structure: application "bringeth the Vses to their proper places, as
salues clapt to the sores of such Patients, as Ministers then haue in hand" (*The Faithfull Shepherd*,
328, [P10v]).

[546] As discussed above in chap. 5.

[547] The rhetorician John Smith includes *aporia* as one of the "Figures of a sentence" which are pathetical
figures, "or such as move affection and passion" (*Mystery of Rhetoric Unveiled*, 8–9).

Donne's images double up on each other as he incorporates the earlier image of stillbirth with the later images of continuing corruption. Any attempt to untangle these befuddled relations sends the auditor-reader into vertigo, adding to his or her agitation regarding the issues of death.

Finally, the decay of death reaches its climax in the irony of corruption where the greatest men suffer the worst indignity. As for the spiritual elite, "[e]ven those bodies that were *the temples of the holy Ghost,* come to this *dilapidation,* to ruine, to rubbidge, to dust" (327–329). Again building imagery works contrary to the *divisio's* connotations of rest and security. Far from resting in a secure building of comfort, the audience is made to feel dilapidated. And for Donne's politically privileged congregation at court, even "that *Monarch,* who spred over many nations alive" will "bee mingled in his dust, with the dust of every high way, and of every dunghill, and swallowed in every puddle and pond." "This," adds Donne, "is the most inglorious and contemptible *vilification,* the most deadly and peremptory *nullification* of man, that wee can consider" (336–345).

The challenge posed to God's power in bringing an issue from such a thorough death is heightened and then made to seem impossible, and even more so as Donne evokes as an *exemplum* Ezekiel's valley of dry bones where, in putting flesh to dry bones, "*God* seemes to have caried the declaration of his *power* to a great height" (345–346). But is God's power sufficient for the sort of death Donne has described? He sows seeds of doubt with two "buts" and a series of conditionals:

> But in that case there were *bones* to bee *seene,* something visible, of which it might be sayd, can this thing live? But in this death of *incineration,* and dispersion of dust, wee see *nothing* that wee can call *that mans*; If we say, can this dust live? perchance it *cannot,* it may bee the meere *dust* of the *earth,* which never did live, nor never shall. It may be the dust of that mans worms which did live, but shall no more. It may bee the dust of *another* man, that concernes not him of whom it is askt (350–357).

Once more Donne eschews reason and brings his audience back to the shelter of the text: "This death of *incineration* and dispersion, is, to naturall *reason,* the most *irrecoverable death* of all, and yet *Domini Domini sunt exitus mortis, unto God the Lord belong the issues of death*" (357–360). Again Donne answers his audience's desire with a call to faith in the *ethos* of God's decree. Here the promise of the *divisio* is finally answered.

I have noted an apparent discrepancy between the first part of the *divisio* which promises an issue from death and the corresponding first parti-

tion which proceeds to sink its audience into despair at death's inexorabil-
ity. Similarly, the static building metaphor of the *divisio* seems indecorous
to the rest of the sermon which presents a dynamic but restless experience
of the issues of death, figured first as homeless peregrinations and then as
the crumbling temple of this decaying corpse. The decorum of the opening architectural image is to be found in its relation to the argument of the
whole sermon: its *inventio* and *dispositio*. It is not the text that Donne expli-
cates; it is allowed to speak for itself. Rather, it is his audience's experience
of death that he expounds in preparation for receiving the claim of the text.
Having agitated his audience into restlessness, Donne brings them home to
the architecture of the text — "unto the Lord" etc. — in his call to faith in
God's decrees. As a counter-point to this formal operation of *pathos* is a
concomitant repetitive form which has been reinforcing the *ethos* of the
text by force of sheer accumulation. As Judith H. Anderson notes, the text
recurs as a refrain more incessantly than is usual even for Donne.[548] Even
as Donne is troubling his audience over death, he is persistently reminding
them where to go for shelter.

What I see as a persistent counterpoint, a refuge of faith in the *ethos* of
the text, Stanley Fish sees as "bald repetition" acting as an obstacle to the
audience's expectation of reason (*logos*).[549] For Fish, the promise of the text
is that "its point will be made discursively, and the making of the point will
take the form of a demonstrative argument, thesis and proposition, followed by a conclusion," a promise that is kept unfulfilled at every turn.[550]
But Fish overstates the sermon's promise to proceed discursively, taking the
divisio as a procedural statement. He derives this reading in part from the
logical implication of the "because" in lines 60–62: "he that is our *God*, is
the *God of all salvation*, because *unto* this *God the Lord belong the issues of
death*."[551] On the contrary, I suggest this "because" asserts that the sermon
will finally rest on the *ethos* of God's decree (subsequently stated) which
invites faith. Moreover, Fish works too hard to establish as a special case a
feature that is common to all of the sermons: Donne rarely begins without
a *divisio* of some sort stating the discursive procedure (order) of his sermon.
In the process, Fish fails to recognize what is *un*common: Donne's special
attention to pathetic proof. The promise of the *divisio* is not of a discursive
dispositio, but is itself a contributing factor to a *dispositio* that largely operates

[548] Judith H. Anderson, "Life Lived and Life Written: Donne's Final Word or Last Character," *HLQ*
51 (1988): 247–59, here 248.
[549] Stanley Fish, *Self-Consuming Artifacts* (Berkeley: University of California Press, 1972), 51.
[550] Fish, *Self-Consuming Artifacts*, 43.
[551] Fish, *Self-Consuming Artifacts*, 52.

by a manipulation of *pathos*. Judith Anderson similarly sees Donne's building image as a metaphor for the explanatory process of the sermon, which
includes Donne's refrain.[552] I am arguing rather that Donne's *dispositio* is
not expository at all (though it appears to be), but formal in its activity of
producing and satisfying desire.

Furthermore, any churched audience would recognize that *theologically*, Christ's victory over death is the cause of salvation, even though in
eternity God is the God of salvation and Lord of death all at once. Christ's
death and resurrection, in other words, are the implicit causes of the consolation the sermon will ultimately provide. From the outset, however, this
promise is forced into the recesses of memory as Donne's agitation process
takes over. Similarly, the sermon's confounding of reason is not so pervasive
as Fish suggests, but rather is a sub-strategy to this principally pathetic
mode of *inventio* in the sermon.[553] Symptomatic of Fish's misplaced
emphasis, I think, is his failure to account for the overpowering presence of
Donne's imagery of corruption in the first half of the sermon.

⁓· III ·⁓

Bereft of all other recourse, then, the congregation is forced by their own
desire for deliverance to admit the imperative of faith in the decree of the
text. But this is only a conceptual answer to his sermon's problem, one which
begs the question, "what assurance do we have of deliverance from Death?"
Faith in the authority of Scripture is fine for matters of doctrine, which
require intellectual assent; but faith is not enough for the matter of personal
assurance, especially when the residual effects of Donne's pathetic assault still
have his audience agitated regarding their own issues from death.

In matters of personal election, the *ethos* of divine decree must be
matched with a positive feeling of assurance. Donne must settle his trou-
bled souls with affective evidence, something they can grasp, because reason will not do, and the essence of faith is hard to apprehend. This is where
Donne finally turns to those "*markes*" and "*evidences* of *adoption* and *spir-*

---

[552] Anderson, "Life Lived and Life Written," 251–52.

[553] On one point Fish and I agree: the sermon sets frustrating conditions as a means of preparing its
audience to receive the message of the *peroratio*. But whereas Fish sees this frustration as a function
of failed *logos* leading the congregation to intuit a truth that is beyond reason, I see it as a function
of successful *pathos* that moves the congregation to rely upon the authority of the sermon's text.
Gregory Kneidel contends with Fish on this same point but argues that Donne's solution is to
model Pauline *paraklêsis*, preparing his auditory for an exhortation to mutual consolation and
encouragement within the community of believers ("John Donne's *Via Pauli*," *JEGP* 100 (2001):
231, 236).

ituall filiation" whereby "I may safely comfort my selfe in a *holy certitude* and a *modest infallibility* of my *adoption*" (281–288). In this we again have the basis for viewing election as an essence or meaning (recalling Burke's fifth logological analogy) figured in an unfolding series of marks culminating in the moment of death.[554] This relation serves a dual purpose of giving a palpable *confirmatio* of one's status regarding election and of implying an opportunity to change one's essence by adjusting the grammar of one's life, which is Donne's next order of business.

The second partition, "in death," is concerned with the manner or circumstances attending death, commonly taken as deathbed evidence. Donne typically concludes that no one should be judged on the circumstances of one's death. On this point, Christ serves as an adequate *exemplum*. Donne revisits the entelechial *topos* to "immunize" his audience against the final moment of death by temporizing the soul's essence (at the authenticating moment of death) into the whole course of life: "The *tree lyes as it falles*; 'Tis true, but yet it is *not* the *last stroake* that *fells* the *tree*, nor the *last word* nor *gaspe* that *qualifies* the *soule*" (410–412). And again, building upon an implicit criticism of death-bed repentance, Donne continues, "Our *criticall* day is *not* the *very day* of our *death*: but the whole course of our life. I thanke him that *prayes* for me when my bell tolles, but I thank him much more that *Catechises* mee, or *preaches* to mee, or *instructs mee how to live*" (422–425). The marks of election (and therefore assurances of a deliverance *from* and *in* death) are here figured as strokes of an axe, which imply human agency. Of course theologically this emphasis challenges the question of election, but logologically it effectively shifts the focus from that unsure future moment to the assurable now, while at the same time making the present and the future death consubstantial as instances in a continuing process. This sense of continuity between life and death argues a smooth continuation into the next life. It demystifies death, making it not a moment of crisis, but rather the final step in a process into which we are born. Death, in this way, is made to seem familiar.

Furthermore, the logic of sequence, once established as a principle of one's life, brings a sort of assurance by momentum. Donne expresses this idea in a grammar of the temporal-eternal: "As the first part of a sentence peeces wel with the last, and never respects, never hearkens after the *parenthesis* that comes betweene, so doth a *good life* here flowe into an *eternall life*, without any consideration, what *manner* of *death* wee dye" (431–435). The

---

[554] "'Time' is to 'eternity' as the particulars in the unfolding of a sentence are to the sentence's unitary meaning" (*RR*, 33).

final point of death is a temporary interruption rather than the sole determinant of meaning. Conversely, the grammar of the present life has a significant part to play in one's ultimate meaning. From another angle, in the same way that a subject implies a verb, life implies after-life.[555] The course of one's life gives an indication of what follows. In this way, Donne again shifts focus from those circumstances of death which are beyond human control to this life which is within human determination. The effect is to give the subject control and influence of his or her essence and a new focus on the present as a determinant of the future. A problem remains, however: this life has been characterized by a syntax of death and increasing corruption. Something of that pathetic urgency remains to be answered in the final partition.

In the final partition of this Lenten sermon, the grammar of life is brought into conformity with the paradigm of Christ's Passion so that the decree of the text is confirmed experientially. As Christ's death and resurrection ("the reall execution of the decree" as Donne puts it earlier) manifests the text, so the audience's ritual identification with Christ's Passion, which they would practice in Lent and the Holy Week, manifests a personal assurance that the grammar of one's life will signify an issue by death into eternity. In taking the Passion event by event, Donne temporizes the essence of salvation in a meditative process. As with Donne's audience, Christ's death is figured as the events leading up to and including it, and by insinuating his audience into those steps, Donne insinuates their salvation through Christ's sacrifice.

Whereas Donne at first enlarges our disgust with death by means of imagery, in the final section of the sermon he enlarges our admiration of Christ's death as he vividly describes it; we are repulsed from our own death (in so far as it is considered by natural reason and affection) but gravitated toward Christ's (in so far as it is apprehended from the perspective of faith). Donne uses a loose form of *auxesis* to describe Christ's sacrificial death. First, in regard to its miraculousness, Donne marvels,

> That the *Sun* could *stand still,* That an *Oven* could be *seaven times heat* and *not burne,* That *Lions* could be *hungry* and *not bite,* is strange, *miraculously strange,* but *supermiraculous* that *God could dye*; but that *God would dye* is an *exaltation* of that. But even of that also it is a *superexaltation,* that *God shold dye, must dye,* and *non exitus* (said *S. Augustin*)[556] *God* the *Lord had no issue but by*

---

[555] As I note in chap. 3, Burke cites this grammatical logic as an species of form (*CS,* 140).
[556] Augustine, *Ennarr. in Ps.* 67.29 (PL 36.831).

death, and *oportuit pati* (says *Christ* himself) all this *Christ ought to suffer,* was bound to suffer (487–495).

From miraculous, to supermiraculous, to a further exaltation, then a super-exaltation, Donne is at pains to enlarge the capacity of Christ's act until it far surpasses the height of impossibility we felt at God's task of bringing scattered dust together in the final resurrection (329–357). And the height of this wonder is that God *will* deliver, a point that was left in question in the earlier part of the sermon.

There follows a similar amplification of Christ's unquenchable love, which also suggests his willingness, such that

> He was *Baptized* out of his *love,* and his love determined not there; He wept over *Jerusalem* out of his love, and his love determined not there; He *mingled blood* with *water* in his *agony* and that determined not his love; hee *wept pure blood,* all his blood at all his eyes, at all his pores, in his *flagellation* and *thornes* (*to the Lord our God belong'd the issues of blood*) and these *expressed,* but these did *not quench his love* (503–510).

Here the more precise repetition of parallel structures through increasing intensity wins the assent of the reader-auditor by the sheer persuasiveness of form. This form, incidentally, follows the chronology of Christ's life so that his (fully human) life matches ours in its progressive quality.

Having built up the weight of Christ's death on our human under-standing, Donne changes direction to diminish the act as perceived by the Godhead: God calls it "but *a bruise,* and but a *bruising of his heele*" (524); Christ himself calls it "but a *Baptisme to be Baptized with*" (527–528); and the "*holy Ghost* calls it *Ioy*" (529). Although these issues of death seem inexorable to us, they are indeed well within God's ability. But now, unlike in the first partition, we are enabled to feel it is true. In continuing the third point, Donne recalls the second partition where future hope is extended back into the continuous present, noting that Christ's joy was "not a *joy* of his reward after his passion, but a joy that filled him even in the middest of those torments, and arose from them" (530–532). One final image, the "*Cuppe*" of his passion as Christ called it, renders death not detestable nor odious, in contrast to the images of the first half of the sermon (533–534). In Christ we finally receive satisfaction regarding the doctrinal basis, earlier frustrated, of God's providence in death. This attitude toward death exemplified by Christ is where Donne now takes his audience by means of a process of identification, urging them to "take it, that *Cup of salvation,* his *passion,* if not into your *present imitation,* yet into your *present contempla-*

tion" (537–539). A reformulation of the earlier *auxesis* of wonder closes off this section in relation to Donne's audience, confirming that Christ "*could dye, would dye, must dye,* for your *salvation*" (540).

As in 2:9, the essence of death changes through the sermon's meditative procedure of identifying the audience with Christ, but here the means of identification is pathetic, achieved in the vivid depiction and experience of the events of Christ's last twenty-four hours (as the congregation would experience them liturgically), unlike the logical, conceptual operation of the meditation (governed by his images of concentric circles) in the previous sermon. Donne notes that the pivotal word of the present text is one which marks our shared experience with Christ. At the mount of transfiguration, Jesus's conversation with Moses and Elijah was "of his *Exodus,* the very word of our Text, *exitus,* his *issue by death*" (545). Here Christ's exit is presented as a counterpoint to the horrifying exit Donne depicted earlier.

In Christ's transfiguration we also get an illustration of how Donne's rhetoric works affectively. Referring to Moses's passing through the Red Sea and Elijah's translation into heaven, Donne urges that they "had no doubt a great satisfaction in *talking* with our *blessed Lord de excessu eius,* of the *full consummation* of *all this* in *his death*" (550–552). Donne implies a similar typological connection for his congregation, except that "Our *meditation* of his *death* should be more *viscerall* and affect us more because it is of a thing already done" (553–554). It should be more visceral and affective because it is typology in reverse, where the fullness of the antetype is repeated in detail (rather than foreshadowed) by the type, i.e. the congregant in meditation. This coincidence of experience is more affective because it argues by precedence rather than by mere promise. The congregant no longer needs to hope for deliverance but can be assured of it because Christ, the antetype, has won possession of the issues of death.

And what of our own daily deaths so forcefully rendered in the first half of the sermon?: "To us that speake dayly of the *death* of *Christ,* (he was *crucified, dead and buried*) can the memory or the mention of our owne *death* bee yrkesome or bitter?" (559–561). Just as in 2:9 the concentric circles argue a new logic, a new way of understanding life, these experiences mirrored in meditation (Christ's experience imprinted on ours) transform our apprehension of death. Ironically, the very cause (agitation) provokes us toward its cure (Christ), and the two become one. Therefore, says Donne, "*It is good to dwell here,* in this *consideration* of his *death,* and therefore *transferre* wee our *tabernacle* (our *devotions*) through some of those *steps* which *God* the *Lord* made to his *issue of death* that *day*" (575–578). That "tabernacle" (which I take to be the text of the sermon, thus "our *devotions*") is incarnated, temporized into this "dwelling" (i.e. both the participle and the noun) in the ensuing meditation of the Passion. We are finally enabled in the *peroratio* to find refuge in the architecture of the text.

~· **IV** ·~

Before turning to Donne's completion of his audience's consolation in the sermon's *peroratio*, I should like to say something about the larger process of purification that is achieved in the formal structure (*dispositio*) of the sermon as a whole. In the first half of the sermon, human life becomes polluted with death and with the various dyslogistic images and circumstances associated with it, even as, theologically, death is polluted with its origins in sin. But more importantly to the argument of the sermon, Donne's audience becomes polluted emotionally by the pathetic effects of these images of life and death. Connotations of pollution abound: as children we are in "so *putrid* a *prison*, as the *wombe*" (71), where we become potential agents "fitted for *workes of darkenese*" (80), "*fed with blood*" and consequently "*damned*, though we be *never borne*" (82).

From these associations, a successful birth becomes a welcomed cleansing for the child and for the mother as well (together representing the congregation) who expels this threat of death. Jeremiah 1:5 reminds us of this need for natal cleansing, where God says to the prophet, "*Before I formed thee I knew thee, and before thou camest out of the wombe I sanctified thee*" (107–108). And then allusions to Noah and to Moses's bulrush ark associate escape from a putrid prison and a putrid life with the ritual cleansing of baptism which these patriarchs typologically represent (108–114). Upon entering the world, we signify this need for cleansing as "[w]e begge one Baptism with another, a sacrament of tears" (134–135). The crying mother and child are made emblems of fallen humanity.[557] Along the lines of Burke's demonic trinity, this life of death is associated with wasps, serpents, carrion, dung, and dirt, which bespeak the sins and "deadly calamities [which] accompany every condition, and every period of this life" (176–177). The high point (or rather, low point) of this pollution is the final "*death of corruption* and *putrefaction* and *vermiculation*" of the grave (215–216). Our incestuous worms, the "rubbidge" of our dilapidated bodies, and our grave dust mingled with dung all contrast with Christ whose prerogative it was "not to dy this death, *not to see corruption*" owing to his "*exemption* from *originall sin*" (218, 254). Christ is thus able to endure a substitutionary death without being blighted by it.

---

557 See Genesis 3:16.

The second partition lays the groundwork for the sermon's ritual of cleansing by characterizing all of life as a temporal preparation for death. This commonplace of the *ars moriendi* tradition puts the audience in mind of the sort of processes prescribed by such handbooks, in anticipation of the sermon's *peroratio*. Because to Christ belong the issues of death, death is no longer associated with images of pollution, but instead becomes the "*gate* of *my prison*" (435). This motion of process together with Christ's purity by exception sets the stage for a ritual identification with Christ the scapegoat in the final partition.

This transformation of death is supported by another imagery pattern which reveals the courtship motive implicit in this purification process. James R. Keller sees in this ritual of purification an alchemical subtext in which Donne "translates death, resurrection, and man's relationship to the Christ sacrifice into an allegory of the fashioning of the 'philosopher's stone'."[558] Keller notes that early alchemists were concerned not so much with literally changing base metal into gold as with transforming their true subject, man, so that "by the transmutation of metals, they signify the conversion of man from a lower to a higher form of existence, from the life natural to life spiritual."[559] Alchemy, then, with its obvious connection to Christian soteriology, functions as a mode of courtship in the Burkeian sense of talking about perfection in one order (religion) by means of another (pseudo-science). Keller continues, "The philosopher's stone in its relationship to base metal corresponds to Christ's salvation of humanity, each having the capacity to transform that which is inferior to itself to spiritual perfection." Christ's spirit is the "noble tincture," or the philosopher's stone, and his blood is a healing balm related to alchemical quintessence. The *peroratio* of the sermon, then, models

[t]he 'hypostatic union,' which is the objective of the alchemical process [and] constitutes a synthesis of God and man or of physical and spiritual substance. The philosopher's stone is considered a fusion of physical and refined spiritual elements, and humanity, the corresponding subject of the experiment, through conformity with the Christ paradigm, can achieve a similar state.[560]

---

[558] James R. Keller, "The Science of Salvation: Spiritual Alchemy in Donne's Final Sermon," *SCJ* 23 (1992): 486–93, here 486. Cf. also above (193) on alchemical terminology.

[559] Keller, "The Science of Salvation," 487. Keller is quoting here from Arthur Edward Waite.

[560] Keller, "The Science of Salvation, 488.

To show how Donne's meditation mirrors steps in the alchemical process, Keller relies on various terms in *Deaths Duell* which are admittedly coincident in alchemy and Christian theology; in other cases, Donne's terms are merely suggestive of alchemical resemblants (Donne's "incineration," for example, suggests the stage of "calcination" which involves an application of heat to base metal). These terms are not, as Keller seems to suggest, "highly technical" in only an alchemical sense, exclusive of theology, or of common experience for that matter (Christ's "embalming" could simply refer to common funerary practice). Keller asserts that this imagery "is intentionally technical so as to delineate the precise fate of humanity after death," this being symptomatic of Donne's supposed felt need to gain personal assurance in the face of his own death.[561] But at no time does Donne presume to define the precise fate of anyone, either at death or after. Rather, in *Deaths Duell* Donne's focus is much less on confirming the after life than on preparation leading up to that final moment. Finally, Donne does not "attemp[t] to justify the grotesque horror of death by transforming it into a deliberate and exacting process [i.e. alchemy]."[562] The horror of death is not a given to which Donne reacts, but is an aspect of his own *inventio*, serving as part of the larger *dispositio* of the sermon which has the transformation of its audience as its ultimate goal. One should not, therefore, press the particulars of the alchemical connection too far, as Keller does. It is enough to note that a familiar mode of experience, alchemy, has enough presence here to be recognized by a court audience and to impress them with the transfiguring significance of this meditation. Further, Donne's meditation is able to borrow from alchemy an order of motives (courtship, purification, and in its most perverse form, avarice) that can be translated into the religious experience of the *peroratio*.

Beyond the alchemical allusion, Donne's *peroratio* makes use of a repetitive form which draws the audience into this process of ritual cleansing.[563] Not much needs to be said about these concluding lines except to note that they match the events of the congregation's twenty-four hours to those of Christ's Passion in a very formalized manner: "Make *this* present *day* that *day* in thy *devotion*, and consider what *hee did*, and remember what *you have done*" (581–582). The first point, for instance, concerns Christ's preparation for the passover, "that *act* of *humility*" in washing his disciples' feet (584). Significantly, Donne's sermon to this point has mimicked this

---

561 Keller, "The Science of Salvation, 492.
562 Keller, "The Science of Salvation, 493.
563 On repetitive form refer back to chap. 4.

preparation in humiliating his audience both emotionally and rationally and has thus already initiated this process, which he now enacts. This and the next five points of identification follow the same pattern. First comes a recounting of an event in Christ's Passion introduced by a temporal indicator — "Before" (582), "After" (590), "*At night*" (595), "About midnight" (609), "*Betimes*" (623) — except in the final instance (630). Then follows an application to the congregation in the form of a direct question variously formulated — "hast thou with a sincere *humility* sought a *reconciliation* with all the *world* ...?" (586–587). Finally, a concluding statement implies a logical connection, usually introduced with "if" or "then," that confirms identification with Christ: "If so ... thou hast spent that *first part* of this his *last day*, in a *conformity* with him" (589–590). Individually, these instances provide an almost syllogistic (or perhaps more appropriately, an enthymatic) progression: one which serves to enforce an identification of Donne's audience with an emotional pattern of experience in Christ's Passion.[564] Together, these instances comprise a conventional form recognizable to any churchgoer as the Passion-story, reenacted in the liturgy of the Holy Week.

The final two events of the Passion introduce variations to the form. The first provides doctrinal satisfaction to Donne's Arminian equivocation in the second partition, where he suggested that one's daily acts of devotion could stand in as representations (if not causes) of one's spiritual essence. In response to Christ's scourging, Donne asks, "Hast thou gone about to *redeeme thy sinne*, by *fasting*, by *Almes*, by *disciplines* and *mortifications*, in the way of *satisfaction* to the *Iustice* of *God?*" (647–649). By the formal operation of repetition established in the five previous Passion events, Donne's audience is inclined to assent. But Donne chastises them if they do, altering his third term into a rebuke: "that will not serve, that's not the right way, *wee presse* an utter *Crucifying* of that *sinne* that governes thee; and that *conformes* thee to *Christ*" (649–651). This utter crucifixion is found not in acts of devotion (temporal marks of election) but in a dependency on Christ's crucifixion.

The final instance of identification marks a temporal change where the noon of the Passion (Christ on the cross) becomes the experiential now of the sermon: "There now hangs that *sacred Body* upon the *Crosse* ..." (653–654). This is the essential moment, the eternal now to which all that has come before is preparation and signpost-markers. And it is here that Donne leaves his congregation, in a perpetual present of identification with Christ:

---

[564] It is enthymatic in the sense of arguing by a logic of probability rather than by the certainty of a syllogism.

There wee leave you in that *blessed dependancy*, to *hang* upon *him* that *hangs* upon the *Crosse*, there *bath* in his *teares*, there *suck* at his *woundes*, and *lye downe in peace* in his *grave*, till hee vouchsafe you a *resurrection*, and an *ascension* into that *Kingdome*, which hee *hath purchas'd for you*, with the *inestimable price* of his *incorruptible blood*. AMEN (668–673).

In this redemptive sequence of verbal pictures, Donne completes his mnemonic chapel, furnishing it with emblems of the Passion. These scenes operate much as the mnemonic sequence at Padua described by Engel: "These plaques are designed, literally and metaphorically, to indoctrinate, to put doctrine into the person using this emblem and by making it part of his daily regime."[565] The text and the meditation thus come together: the ethical assurance of the text is logically inseparable from its cause, Christ's Passion. The proof of the text is therefore in the individual's identification with Christ achieved in the fusion of the Passion with the congregant's daily regime. In this way, through the symbolic activity of the sermon, the congregation's life in the world again becomes a temporal courtship of eternal essence.

~· **V** ·~

It remains to answer the question of decorum in Donne's handling of death in these two sermons. While Potter and Simpson admit that 2:9 "is a particularly clear, simply expressed discourse" whose "construction is neat, almost though not quite to the point of being artificially ingenious," they fault this sermon for its incomplete expression of ideas which would be more "potently" developed in later sermons, most notably *Deaths Duell*.[566] This judgement is in part owing to a failure to appreciate these passages within the context of each sermon's unique rhetorical strategies. The decorum (appropriateness) of these passages is found in the way they fit with the *dispositio* and contribute to the *inventio* of the whole. Conversely, Potter and Simpson reserve their praise for the *peroratio* of 2:9 describing death as a rapture, where Donne rises "to a greater height of eloquence than in most parts of it."[567] Rather, I have suggested that the brilliance of this passage is

---

[565] Engel, *Mapping Mortality*, 23.
[566] *Sermons*, 2:27.
[567] *Sermons*, 2:29.

best appreciated in light of its function in the logical development of the whole sermon, to which Donne's circular image is key. In short, Potter and Simpson's introduction exemplifies the too common tendency to hunt for purple passages and poetic images and to evaluate a sermon based on their number and relative quality without a full appreciation of their context in the whole argument of the sermon.

One instance of Donne's incomplete expression cited in their introduction is his handling of the building metaphor: in 2:9, "it appears merely as an unimportant and briefly suggested comparison" (*Sermons*, 2:28). On the contrary, in 2:9 the metaphor contributes to Donne's rhetorical strategy as it unfolds in his ensuing lines where he deliberately shakes his audience off their foundations regarding "collateral" doctrine, where they are allowed no position of assurance. Far from being mere ornamentation, the image emblematically mirrors the effect of this passage. As noted in the previous chapter, Donne uses this doctrinal controversy to put his audience in a state of *aporia*, to replicate their identification with the mollifying Eve in order to engender their desire for certainty, for foundation. That foundation is the certainty that "a judgement thou must pass"; it is also Christ who is the cornerstone and the final resting point of the sermon. Donne's employment of this image is not extensive, but even in its brevity it contributes fittingly to his *inventio* as it develops in the sermon.

This same strategy is writ large in the *dispositio* of *Deaths Duell*. In this sermon, Donne uses similar imagery to construct an *exordium-divisio* which is indeed very close to being "artificially ingenious," to recall the Potter-Simpson criticism of 2:9, but only if one takes it in isolation. While the three aspects of foundations, buttresses, and contignations that Donne sets out here work nicely to suggest the integrity and stability that his text can bring to the audience's attitude toward death, there is no apparent congruity between them and the prepositions they represent — "from," "in" and "by" death — which suggest a rather more dynamic *dispositio* than this building imagery would seem to allow. This is not to say that this imagery is gratuitous, only that taken in isolation it seems merely ornamental and bears no logical relation to Donne's exposition. But as I have demonstrated, Donne's building metaphor does real pathetical work in the *inventio* and especially the *dispositio* of the sermon.

Michael Stanford also raises questions regarding Donne's decorum (albeit in a contradictory manner), this time with respect to *Deaths Duell*. Stanford describes the closing passage of Sir Thomas Browne's *Hydriotaphia* as both admonition and confession, while

> *Death's Duell* is never anything but a sermon; wasted, heroic,
> dying, Donne hectors his audience. Behind the adjurations to
> humility we feel his contempt for weaker, more fearful people; we
> sense the arrogance of the younger Donne. But Browne makes one
> with his readers in their frailty and fear.[568]

Stanford's assessment is contradictory because he dismisses *Deaths Duell* as
a mere sermon, one which he characterizes as "hectoring," a quality which
does not fit any definition of a sermon Donne would have recognized.
More perplexing is Stanford's denial of the proper sermonic qualities of
admonition and confession to this sermon. The whole sermon is about the
business of admonishing or moving its audience into identity with Christ.
Furthermore, Donne (himself a personification of death in the pulpit)
expresses a visual confession of his own mortality, while his *peroratio* testifies to his complete dependency on Christ. But more to the point of decorum, Donne's passages on death's corruption may seem like a gloating
performance characteristic of a younger Donne (if Donne himself, as distinct from his poetic *personae*, was ever gloating), but only if taken in isolation. In the whole of the sermon, these passages serve the precise purpose
Stanford sees in Browne: to convince of man's fearful frailty.

Decorum is an issue of *dispositio* but also of *inventio*. That is, one's
rhetorical strategy must be fit to the subject matter and occasion at hand
and to the end to which it moves. I earlier suggested a difference which may
account for the respective principles of *inventio* in these two sermons. In
2:9 Donne's treatment of death is concerned with adjusting his audience's
attitude toward the present circumstances of life. In *Deaths Duell*, himself
near his deathbed, Donne's concern is chiefly to reconcile his audience
(and, some have suggested, himself) to that terrible moment itself, and
thus his sustained focus on the issues or circumstances of death. Although
he is not remiss in making clear the relevance of death to his audience *now*
— "Make *this* present *day* that *day* in thy *devotion*" (581) — here it is with
a view to preparation against that final day of actual death. It is for this reason that *Deaths Duell* appropriately relies on *pathos* with a consistency that
is not evident in any of Donne's other sermons on death.

The preface to the first edition of *Deaths Duell* gives a contemporary
perspective on this issue of decorum. Richard Redmer, the apparent author
of the preface, provides an insightful if brief commentary on Donne's ser-

---

568 Michael Stanford, "The Terrible Thresholds: Sir Thomas Browne on Sex and Death," *ELR* 18
(1988): 413–23, here 423.

mon.[569] Redmer judges the sermon to be styled "*Most fitly: whether wee respect the time, or the matter.*"[570] As to time, the circumstances lend authority to the sermon. As the sermon itself points out, the issues of death belong to God, so that there was a certain "*Sacred Authoritie*" added to the preacher who thus, as Redmer states, "*stiled [his] owne funeral Sermon*" upon his imminent death. Redmer also notes that "*A dying Mans words, if they concerne our selves; doe usually make the deepest impression, as being spoken most feelingly, and with least affectation.*" Such circumstances seem tailor-made for the combination of *pathos* and *ethos* that we find in *Deaths Duell*.

As to the matter of death itself, Redmer notes its double nature as enemy and benefit and implies the sermon's transforming activity in adding that "*Death is every mans enemy, and intends hurt to all; though to many, hee be occasion of greatest goods.*" To illustrate, he observes that "*living [Donne] did almost conquer; having discovered the utmost of his [Death's] power, the utmost of his crueltie.*" To one observer, then, the preacher stood in the pulpit as an *exemplum* of the sermon he preached, where death is "discovered" in its utmost cruelty, anatomized, and thereby to some degree controlled and finally transformed.

Another useful commentary on the decorum of Donne's handling of death is his "*ELEGIE* On the vntimely Death of the incomparable Prince, HENRY."[571] Donne uses this poem as an occasion to explore both epistemological and rhetorical issues related to death. In *Deaths Duell*, Donne implies his principle of decorum in arguing by *pathos* and *ethos* rather than *logos* when he urges that, "the *Mysteries* of our *Religion*, are *not* the *objects* of *our reason*, but *by faith we rest* on *Gods decree* and purpose, (It is so, ô God, because it is *thy will*, it should be so)" (10:11.276–279). Similarly, in the Prince Henry elegy, reason (associated here with *logos*) operates within the province of temporal experience in the world, while matters which are beyond this scope, including the circumstances or issues of death, require faith which, in the poem, is associated with emotion and desire, that is, *pathos*. The poem begins,

---

[569] Redmer, a bookseller in St. Paul's churchyard from 1610 to 1632, is cited on the title-page as co-publisher of the first edition (R. B. McKerrow, gen. ed., *A Dictionary of Printers and Booksellers* [Oxford: Bibliographical Society, 1968], 225). The preface is signed simply "R," seeming to indicate Redmer, and indeed it was common practice for publishers to write prefaces. Such seems to be the case here.

[570] "To the Reader" in *Death's Duel* (1632).

[571] For this poem I am using *The Variorum Edition*, gen. ed. Gary A. Stringer, vol. 6 (Bloomington: Indiana University Press, 1995), 160–62.

Look to Me, *Faith*; and look to my *Faith*, G O D:
For, both my *Centres* feel This *Period*.
Of *Waight*, one *Centre*; one, of *Greatness* is:
And R E A S O N is That *Centre*; F A I T H is This
(1–4).

Thus there are two means by which one comes to terms with death, reason
and faith, but from the outset the speaker is inclined to the latter as he
addresses issues related to the actual moment of death.

The ensuing lines offer a possible explanation for Donne's differing
modes of *inventio* in 2:9 and *Deaths Duell*. Sermon 2:9 is concerned with
death as it relates to the concerns of the congregation's present lives with the
aim of changing their thinking regarding these concerns, and so it functions
discursively. Donne continues,

For, into our *Reason* flowe, and there doe end,
All that this naturall World doth comprehend;
Quotidian things, and Equi-distant hence,
Shut-in for Men in one *Circumference* (5–8).

In contrast to 2:9, *Deaths Duell* deals primarily with the moment of death
itself, and beyond, which is the province of faith, and so it operates affectively, much as Donne goes on to describe:

But, for th'enormous *Greatnesses*, which are
So disproportion'd and so angulare,
As is G O D ' S *Essence, Place*, and *Prouidence*,
Where, How, When, What, Soules do departed hence:
These *Things* (*Eccentrique* else) on *Faith* do strike (9–13).

Donne's affective response to these issues of faith in lines 43–62 is implicitly associated with *pathos* when, in line 63, he turns to "th'other *Centre*,
R E A S O N" and finds that logical discourse of "*Causes*," "*Substances*,"
and "*Accident*" is futile when the object of consideration (Prince Henry) is
so far removed (66–70). *Deaths Duell*, like no other of Donne's sermons,
similarly touches upon God's providence in the unknown circumstances of
death — "to God the Lord belong the issues of death"; consequently, this sermon fittingly operates in the province of faith, and therefore warrants proof
by *pathos*. Thus in Donne's first and last sermons on death, the courtship
topos proves to be a flexible resource not only for variety of matter, but for
varying demands of proof.

❧ Conclusion

The last half of this book has addressed two central features in scholarly caricatures of Donne — his ambition and his interest in death — in order to demonstrate that a great deal of what seems to be of personal relevance to Donne must be regarded as rhetorically contingent upon a more public purpose. Far from being simple indications of his raging ambition, Donne's abundant references to courtship concerns are reflections of rhetorical strategies functioning deep within the structures of his sermons, strategies that are as much indicators of the needs of Donne's audience (as he conceives them) as they are of the preacher himself. In fact, Donne's courtship references point to a preacher who is fully conscious of his own propensities and those of his congregation, but who turns these inclinations to good use for their spiritual benefit.

This study thus also adds to the growing evidence of continuity in Donne's literary career from poet to preacher.[572] Donne, who so thoroughly played the courtier for much of his life, finally turned his energies and skills to drawing his congregations into a courtship of the Divine. In a sermon preached at St. Paul's Cathedral, Donne describes himself as "Gods Ambassadour" who has come to reconcile his congregation to his heavenly Prince (10:5.431). And so he pleads,

> Let naturall reason, let affections, let the profits or the pleasures of the world be the *Councell Table*, and can they tell you, that you are able to maintaine a warre against God, and subsist so, without being reconciled to him? Deceive not your selves, no man hath so much pleasure in this life, as he that is at peace with God (447–452).

Throughout his sermons, Donne uses this "councell table" of worldly desires to good advantage, to tell his congregations that reconciliation is necessary to true fulfilment of "profit" and "pleasure," for these find their final end only in God. Donne goes on to describe the purifying effect of bringing motives in line with a proper courtship:

---

[572] Terry Sherwood in *Fulfilling the Circle*, for example. Lindsay Mann also demonstrates Donne's consistent advocacy of mutuality in love and marriage in both the *Songs and Sonnets* and the sermons: "Misogyny and Libertinism: Donne's Marriage Sermons," *JDJ* 11 (1992): 111–32. Similarly, I demonstrate that Donne's facility with courtship strategies was by no means lost when he turned from poet to preacher.

What an Organe hath that man tuned, how hath he brought all
things in the world to a Consort, and what a blessed Anthem doth
he sing to that Organe, that is at peace with God? His Rye-bread
is *Manna*, and his Beefe is *Quailes*, his day-labours are thrustings
at the narrow gate into Heaven, and his night-watchings are
extasies and evocations of his soule into the presence and communion of Saints, his sweat is *Pearls*, and his bloud is *Rubies*, it is
at peace with God (453–459).

It is in Donne's handling of various courtship strategies that this central,
transformative function in his sermons is accomplished.

My emphasis has been primarily on the textual rather than the *contex-
tual* aspects of Donne's rhetoric. Current interest in Donne's sermons has
been fuelled by scholarship that has drawn our attention to Donne's sophisticated responsiveness to the socio-political conditions in which he
preached. Future consideration of Donne's handling of cultural matter,
both in his sermons and elsewhere, would similarly benefit from a more
consistent attentiveness to his rhetorical purposes, especially with respect to
his devotional aims for his audience. What I have posed here is a manner
of seeing politics, economics, law, alchemy, and any other cultural discourse available to Donne not as topical ends in themselves, but as potential material for inducing a "holy ambition" in a congregation of hearers
and readers. The sermons, as texts, thus reward close reading much as
Donne's poems do, not simply for their political, cultural, or theological
content, but for their artfulness. This study will have finally succeeded if it
has equipped the reader with a set of interpretive tools that will facilitate
and enrich further reading of Donne's sermons as complete rhetorical and
literary texts.

Glossary of Rhetorical Terms

ad clerum	to the clergy, commonly used to refer to learned sermons
ad populum	to a popular audience
agon	a relationship of opposition or conflict between two elements
anadiplosis	the repetition of the last word of a clause at the beginning of the next
anaphora	the repetition of the same word or phrase at the beginning of successive phrases, clauses or lines
antistasis	repetition of a word in a different or contrary sense
aporia or *dubitatio*	an expression of doubt (often feigned) or deliberation by which a speaker appears uncertain as to what he or she should think, say, or do
auxesis or *incrementum*	words or phrases arranged in order of ascending intensity or importance
causa	the use of a narrative, myth, or history of origins to account for present conditions
circumstances	the key elements that comprise a narration: who, what, when, where, how, why
climax	see *gradatio*
commonplace	a general argument, idea, or statement that could be memorized and employed in composition for a variety of purposes or occasions (see also *topos*)
confirmatio	the part of an argument or oration dedicated to supporting, confirming, or asserting a proposition
congeries or *sinathrismus*	a heap or accumulation of words run together
consolatio	a rhetorical gesture of consolation or comfort for a cause or occasion of grief
copia	richness, abundance, or fullness in expression
diacope	repetition of words, phrases, or clauses with one or a few words in between
dialogismo	a species of *aporia* which involves questioning and answering
dispositio	the arrangement or order of material in a document or oration
divisio	a statement of the main points to follow in a document or oration
dubitatio	see *aporia*
elocutio	the quality and manner of one's use of words in expression, also referred to as style or ornamentation

epizeuxis	emphatic repetition of a word with no other words in between
ethos	the good character, credibility, and authority of a speaker, source, or argument
exemplum (*exempla* pl.)	an example used to illustrate or to serve as a model or paradigm
exordium	an introduction designed to catch an audience's attention
gradatio, or *climax*	linked words, phrases, or clauses (often by anadiplosis) in order of ascending power or degree
hypotyposis	a vivid, powerful depiction
incrementum	see *auxesis*
inventio	the activity of finding and developing material for composition
isocolon	see *parison*
locus (*loci* pl.)	see *topos*
logos	the rational, logical, intellectual quality of an argument
narratio	a narrative summary or history of a problem, case, or situation
parison	successive phrases or clauses of parallel structure and approximately equal length
pathos	the emotional quality of an argument
peroratio	a poignant conclusion
phronēsis	Aristotle's first species of *ethos*: practical wisdom
polyptoton	repetition of a word in a different form but from the same root
pronuntiatio	the speaking, articulation, or delivery of a speech or oration
propositio	a summary introduction of the proposition, assertion, or general gist of an argument
refutatio	the part of an argument or oration dedicated to debunking and refuting opposition to one's argument, either anticipated or actual
rhetor	a person who composes a document or delivers an oration
sinathrismus	see *congeries*
synecdoche	substitution of part for whole, or vice versa
topos (*topoi* pl.) or *locus* (*loci* pl.)	the "seat" of an argument, or a place where one goes to find an idea or strategy for argument (see also "commonplace," also known as *locus communis*)
translatio	metaphor

~ *Bibliography* ~

Primary Sources

Alighieri, Dante. *The Divine Comedy*, trans. Charles S. Singleton. 3 vols. Princeton: Princeton University Press, 1970.

[Allot, Robert]. *Englands Parnassus.* 1600. Menston, Eng.: Scolar Press, 1970. (STC 378)

Ames, William. *Conscience with the Power and Cases Thereof.* 1639. The English Experience 708. Amsterdam: Theatrum Orbis Terrarum; Norwood, NJ: Walter J. Johnson, 1975. (STC 552)

――――. *The Marrow of Theology*, ed. and trans. (from 3rd Latin ed.) John D. Eusden. Durham, NC: Labyrinth Press, 1983.

Andrewes, Lancelot. *The Works of Lancelot Andrewes.* Oxford: J. H. Parker, 1854; repr. New York: AMS Press, 1967.

Aphthonius. *Aphthonii Sophistæ Progymnasmata.* London, 1572. (STC 700)

Aristotle. *The Art of Rhetoric*, ed. and trans. H. C. Lawson-Tancred. New York: Penguin, 1991.

――――. *The Rhetoric and the Poetics of Aristotle*, intro. P. J. Corbett, trans. W. Rhys Roberts and Ingram Bywater. New York: Modern Library, 1954.

――――. *Topics: Books I and VIII*, trans. and comm. Robin Smith. Oxford: Clarendon Press, 1997.

Ascham, Roger. *The English Works*, ed. William Aldis Wright. Cambridge: Cambridge University Press, 1904.

Augustine. *De Doctrina Christiana*, ed. and trans. R. P. H. Green. Oxford: Clarendon Press, 1995.

――――. *On Christian Doctrine*, trans. and intro. D. W. Robertson Jr. New York: Macmillan, 1958.

――――. *Confessions*, trans. Henry Chadwick. Oxford: Oxford University Press, 1991.

Bacon, Francis. *Essays*, intro. Michael J. Hawkins. London: J. M. Dent & Sons, 1972.

————. *The Works of Francis Bacon*, ed. James Spedding, Robert Leslie Ellis, and Douglas Denon Heath. 14 vols. London: Longman, 1868; repr. Stuttgart: Friedrich Frommann Verlag Gunther Holzboog, 1963.

Baker, Augustine. *Sancta Sophia. Or Directions for the Prayer of Contemplation.* Douai, 1657. (STC B480)

Baxter, Richard. *The Practical Works of the Rev. Richard Baxter*, ed. William Orme. 24 vols. London: James Duncan, 1830.

————. *The Saints' Everlasting Rest.* ed. Benjamin Fawcett. Christian Classics Ethereal Library.
http://ccel.wheaton.edu/b/baxter/everlasting_rest/saints_rest.html

Becon, Thomas. *The Diversity Between God's Word and Man's Invention. Prayers and Other Pieces of Thomas Becon*, ed. John Ayre. Parker Society. Cambridge: Cambridge University Press, 1844; repr. New York: Johnson Reprint, 1968.

Bernard, Richard. *The Faithfvll Shepherd: Wholy in a manner transposed, and made anew, and very much inlarged both with precepts and examples, to further young Diuines in the studie of Diuinitie. With The Shepherds Practise in the end.* 3rd ed. London, 1621. (STC 1941)

————. *The Isle of Man: Or, The Legall Proceeding in Man-shire against Sinne.* 4th ed. London, 1627. (STC 1946.3)

Blackstone, William. *Commentaries on the Laws of England.* 3 vols. Oxford and London: printed for W. Strahan and T. Cadell, and D. Prince, 1783; repr. New York: Garland, 1978.

Blount, Thomas. *The Academy of Eloquence*, ed. R. C. Alston. 1654. English Linguistics 1500–1800 296. Menston, Eng.: Scolar Press, 1971. (STC B3321)

————. *Νομο-λεζικον: A Law-Dictionary.* London, 1670. (STC B3340)

Bocchi, Achille. *Symbolicarum Quaestionum de Universo Genere*, intro. Stephen Orgel. 1574. New York: Garland, 1979.

Boethius. *Boethius's de topicis differentiis*, trans. and notes Eleonore Stump. Ithaca: Cornell University Press, 1978.

Brinsley, John. *Ludus Literarius*, ed. R. C. Alston. 1612. English Linguistics 1500–1800 62. Menston, Eng.: Scolar Press, 1968. (STC 3768)

Bunyan, John. *The Pilgrim's Progress*, ed. Grace Latimer Jones. New York: American Book Co., 1914.

Burton, Robert. *The Anatomy of Melancholy*, intro. Holbrook Jackson. 3 vols. London: Dent, 1932.

Carew, Thomas. *The Poems of Thomas Carew with his Masque* Coelum Britannicum, ed. and intro. Rhodes Dunlap. Oxford: Clarendon Press, 1949, repr. 1957.

Carr, John. *The Ruinous fal of Prodigalitie: with the notable examples of the best aprooued aucthours.* London, 1573. (STC 4685)

Castiglione, Baldassare. *The Book of the Courtier*, trans. Thomas Hoby, intro. W. H. D. Rouse. New York: Dutton, 1928.

Cawdrey, Robert. *A Treasury or Store-house of Similies*, ed. R. C. Alston. 1600. English Linguistics 1500–1800 191. Menston, Eng.: Scolar Press, 1969. (STC 4887)

Ps.-Cebes. *Cebes' Tablet: Facsimiles of the Greek Text, and of Selected Latin, French, English, Spanish, Italian, German, Dutch, and Polish Translations*, intro. Sandra Sider. New York: The Renaissance Society of America, 1979.

Certain Sermons or Homilies *(1547) and* A Homily against Disobedience and Wilful Rebellion *(1570): A Critical Edition*, ed. Ronald A. Bond. Toronto: University Toronto Press, 1987.

Chappell, William. *The Preacher*, ed. R. C. Alston. 1656. English Linguistics 1500–1800 295. Menston, Eng.: Scolar Press, 1971. (STC C1957)

Church of England. *The Book of Common Prayer* (1559). (STC 16291)

Cicero. *De Inventione; De Optimo Genere Oratorum; Topica*, trans. H. M. Hubbell. Loeb Classical Library. Cambridge, MA: Harvard University Press, 1960.

Coke, Edward. *The First Part of the Institutes of the Lawes of England.* 1628. 2 vols. New York: Garland, 1979. (STC 15784)

The Contention Between Liberality and Prodigality, ed. W. W. Greg. Malone Society Reprints. Oxford: Oxford University Press, 1913.

Coote, Edmund. *The English Schoole-Maister*, gen. ed. Ian Lancashire, co-eds. Linda Hutjens, Brent Nelson, Robert Whalen, and Tanya Wood. Renaissance English Texts 2.1. http://www.library.utoronto.ca/utel/ret/coote/ret2.html

Cox, Leonard. *The Arte or Crafte of Rhethoryke*, ed. and intro. Frederic Ives Carpenter. Chicago: University of Chicago Press, 1899.

Cullum, John. *The History and Antiquities of Hawstead, in the County of Suffolk.* London, 1784.

Dalton, Michael. *The Countrey Iustice.* 1618. The English Experience 725. Amsterdam: Theatrum Orbis Terrarum; Norwood, NJ: Walter J. Johnson, 1975. (STC 6205)

Daniel, Samuel. *The Civil Wars*, ed. Laurence Michel. New Haven: Yale University Press, 1958.

Day, Angel. *The English Secretary*, intro. Robert O. Evans. 1599. Gainesville, FL: Scholars' Facsimiles & Reprints, 1967. (STC 6404)

Ps.-Dionysius. *Pseudo-Dionysius: The Complete Works*, trans. Colm Luibheid. Mahwah, NJ: Paulist Press, 1987.

Doddridge, John. *The English Lawyer. Describing A Method for the Managing of the Lawes of this Land*. 1631. The English Experience 503. Amsterdam: Theatrum Orbis Terrarum; New York: Da Capo Press, 1973. (STC 6981)

Donne, John. *Biathanatos*, ed. Michael Rudick and M. Pabst Battin. New York: Garland, 1982.

———. *The Complete Poems of John Donne*, ed. John T. Shawcross. New York: Doubleday, 1967.

———. *Death's Duel*. 1632. Menston, Eng.: Scolar Press, 1969. (STC 7031)

———. *Devotions Upon Emergent Occasions*, ed. Anthony Raspa. Montreal and London: McGill-Queen's University Press, 1975.

———. *The Divine Poems*, ed. Helen Gardner. Oxford University Press, 1952.

———. *Donne's Sermons: Selected Passages*, 1919, ed. Logan Pearsall Smith. Oxford: Clarendon Press, 1919, repr. 1968.

———. *Essays in Divinity*, ed. Evelyn M. Simpson. Oxford: Oxford University Press, 1952.

———. *John Donne's 1622 Gunpowder Plot Sermon: A Parallel-Text Edition*, ed. Jeanne Shami. Pittsburgh: Duquesne University Press, 1996.

———. *Letters to Severall Persons of Honour*, ed. Charles Edmund Merrill, Jr. New York: Sturgis & Walton, 1910.

———. *Paradoxes and Problems*, ed. Helen Peters. Oxford: Oxford University Press, 1980.

———. *The Poems of John Donne*, ed. Herbert J. C. Grierson. 2 vols. Oxford: Oxford University Press, 1912.

———. *Pseudo-Martyr*, ed. Anthony Raspa. Montreal & Kingston: McGill-Queen's University Press, 1993.

———. *The Satires, Epigrams and Verse Letters*, ed. W. Milgate. Oxford: Clarendon Press, 1967.

———. *Selected Prose*, selected by Evelyn Simpson, ed. Helen Gardner and Timothy Healy. Oxford: Oxford University Press, 1967.

———. *The Sermons of John Donne*, ed. and intro. George R. Potter and Evelyn M. Simpson. 10 vols. Berkeley: University of California Press, 1953–1962.

———. *The Songs and Sonets of John Donne*, ed. Theodore Redpath. 2nd ed. London: Methuen, 1983.

———. *The Variorum Edition of the Poetry of John Donne: The Anniversaries and the Epicedes and Obsequies*, vol. 6. Gen. ed. Gary A. Stringer. Bloomington: Indiana University Press, 1995.

Downame, John. *The Christian Warfare*. 1604. The English Experience 653. Amsterdam: Theatrum Orbis Terrarum; Norwood, NJ: Walter J. Johnson, 1974. (STC 7133)

Dugdale, William. *The History of St Paul's Cathedral in London, From its Foundation*. 2nd ed. London, 1716.

Dunbar, William. *The Poems of William Dunbar*, ed. James Kinsley. Oxford: Oxford University Press, 1979.

The Elizabethan Homilies (1623), ed. Ian Lancashire. Renaissance English Texts 1.2. (1997). http://www.library.utoronto.ca/utel/ret/homilies/elizhom.html

Elyot, Thomas. *The Book named The Governor*, ed. S. E. Lehmberg. London: Dent, 1962.

Erasmus. *De Copia*, ed. Craig R. Thompson. *The Collected Works of Erasmus*, vol. 24. Toronto: University of Toronto Press, 1978.

Fenner, Dudley. *The Artes of Logike and Rethorike*, intro. Robert D. Pepper. 1584. *Four Tudor Books on Education*. Gainesville, FL: Scholars' Facsimiles & Reprints, 1966.

Ferne, John. *The Blazon of Gentrie*. 1586. The English Experience 513. Amsterdam: Theatrum Orbis Terrarum; New York: Da Capo Press, 1973. (STC 10824)

Gainsford, Thomas. *The Rich Cabinet Furnished with varietie Of Excellent discriptions, exquisite Characters, witty discourses, and delightfull Histories, Deuine and Morrall. Together With Inuectiues against many abuses of the time: digested Alphabetically into common places*. London, 1616. (STC 11522)

Giovio, Paolo. *The Worthy Tract of Paulus Iovius* (1585) Translated by Samuel Daniel together with Giovio's *Dialogo dell 'Imprese Militari et Amorose*, intro. Norman K. Farmer, Jr. Delmar, NY: Scholars' Facsimiles & Reprints, 1976. (STC 11900)

Granger, Thomas. *Syntagma Logicvm. Or, The Divine Logicke. Seruing especially for the vse of Diuines in the practise of preaching, and for the further helpe of iudicious Hearers, and generally for all*. London, 1620. (STC 12184)

Greville, Fulke. *Certaine Learned and Elegant Workes*, intro. A. D. Cousins. 1633. Delmar, NY: Scholars' Facsimiles & Reprints, 1990.

Guazzo, Stefano. *The Civile Conversation of M. Steeven Guazzo*, trans. George Pettie and Barth Young, intro. Edward Sullivan. 2 vols. London: Constable; New York: Knopf, 1925.

Hall, Joseph. *The Works of the Right Reverend Joseph Hall*, rev. ed. by Philip Wynter. 10 vols. 1863. New York: AMS Press, 1969.

Hall, Thomas. *Vindiciæ Literarum, The Schools Guarded: Or, The excellency and usefulnesse of Arts, Sciences, Languages, History, and all sorts of humane Learning, in subordination to Divinity, & Preparation for the Mynistry.* 2nd ed. London, 1655. (STC H442)

Harvey, Gabriel. *Gabriel Harvey's Ciceronianus*, intro. and notes Harold S. Wilson, trans. Clarence A. Forbes. Lincoln: University of Nebraska Press, 1945.

Hemmingsen, Niels. *The Preacher*, trans. John Horsfall, ed. R. C. Alston. 1574. English Linguistics 1500–1800 325. Menston, Eng.: Scolar Press, 1972. (STC 13065)

Herbert, George. *George Herbert and Henry Vaughan*, ed. Louis Martz. Oxford: Oxford University Press, 1986.

———. *Works of George Herbert*, ed. F. E. Hutchinson. Corr. ed. Oxford: Clarendon Press, 1959.

Holy Bible. Geneva and KJV.

Hooker, Richard. *The Folger Library Edition of the Works of Richard Hooker*, ed. W. Speed Hill. 3 vols. Cambridge, MA: Belknap Press of Harvard University, 1977.

Hoskins, John. *Directions for Speech and Style*, ed. and intro. Hoyt H. Hudson. Princeton: Princeton University Press, 1935.

Hugo, Herman. *Pia Desideria*, intro. Hester M. Black. 1624. Continental Emblem Books 11. Menston, Eng.: Scolar Press, 1971.

———. *Pia Desideria: Or, Divine Addresses*, trans. Edmund Arwaker. London, 1686. (STC H3350)

Hyperius, G. Andreas. *The practise of preaching, otherwise called the Pathway to the Pulpet*, trans. John Ludham. London, 1577. (STC 11758)

The Institucion of a Gentleman. 1555. The English Experience 672. Amsterdam: Theatrum Orbis Terrarum; Norwood, NJ: Walter J. Johnson, 1974. (STC 14104)

Jonson, Ben. *Entertainment at Highgate*. In *Ben Jonson*, ed. C. H. Hereford and Evelyn Simpson, vol. 7: 136–44. Oxford: Clarendon Press, 1941.

Junius, Hadrianus. *Emblemata*, intro. Hester M. Black. 1565. Continental Emblem Books 12. Menston, Eng.: Scolar Press, 1972.

Justinian. *Justinian's Institutes*, trans. Peter Birks and Grant McLeod. Ithaca, NY: Cornell University Press, 1987.

MacDonald, George. *Unspoken Sermons: Third Series*. London: Longmans, 1891.

MacIlmaine, Roland, trans. *The Logike of The Moste Excellent Philosopher P. Ramus Martyr (1574)*, ed. Catherine M. Dunn. Northridge, CA: San Fernando Valley State College, 1969.

Milton, John. *Complete Poems and Major Prose*, ed. Merrit Y. Hughes. New York: Macmillan, 1957.

Montaigne, Michel de. *The Complete Essays of Montaigne*, trans. Donald M. Frame. Stanford: Stanford University Press, 1976.

Montenay, Georgette de. *Emblemes ou Devises Christiennes*, intro. C. N. Smith. 1571. Continental Emblem Books 15. Menston, Eng.: Scolar Press, 1973.

Paradin, Claude. *Devises Heroïques*, intro. C. N. Smith. 1557. Continental Emblem Books 16. Menston, Eng.: Scolar Press, 1971.

Peacham, Henry, the elder. *The Garden of Eloquence Conteyning the Figures of Grammar and Rhetorick*, ed. R. C. Alston. 1577. English Linguistics 1500–1800 267. Menston, Eng.: Scolar Press, 1971. (STC 19497)

Peacham, Henry, the younger. *Minerva Britanna*, intro. John Horden. 1612. English Emblem Books 5. Menston, Eng.: Scolar Press, 1969. (STC 19511)

Peele, George. *The Araygnment of Paris*, ed. R. Mark Benbow in *The Dramatic Works*, gen. ed. R. Charles Tyler Prouty. 3:3–131. New Haven: Yale University Press, 1970.

Perkins, William. *The Arte of Prophecying: Or, A Treatise Concerning the sacred and onely true manner and methode of Preaching*, trans. Thomas Tuke. London, 1607. (STC 19735.4)

Phillips, Edward. *The Mysteries of Love & Eloquence, Or, the Arts of Wooing and Complementing*, ed. R. C. Alston. 1658. English Linguistics 1500–1800 321. Menston, Eng.: Scolar Press, 1972. (STC P2066)

———. *Theatrum Poetarum or A Compleat Collection of the Poets*. 1675. Hildesheim: Georg Olms Verlag, 1970. (STC P2075)

Plato. *Complete Works*, ed. John M. Cooper. Indianapolis: Hackett, 1997.

[P. S.] *The Heroicall Devises of M. Claudius Paradin*, intro. John Doebler. 1591. Delmar, NY: Scholars' Facsimiles & Reprints, 1984.

Puttenham, George. *The Arte of English Poesie*, ed. Edward Arber, intro. Baxter Hathaway. London: A. Constable, 1906; repr. Kent, OH: Kent State University Press, 1970.

Quarles, Francis. *Emblemes*, intro. A. D. Cousins. 1635. Delmar, NY: Scholars' Facsimiles & Reprints, 1991. (STC Q20540)

Rainolde, Richard. *The Foundation of Rhetoric*, ed. R. C. Alston. 1563. English Linguistics 1500–1800 347. Menston, Eng.: Scolar Press, 1972. (STC 20604)

Ralegh, Walter. *The Poems of Sir Walter Ralegh*, ed. A. M. C. Latham. London: Routledge and Kegan Paul, 1951.

Richardson, Alexander. *The Logicians School-Master*. 2nd ed. London, 1657. (STC R1378)

Romei, Annibale. *The Courtiers Academie*. 1598. The English Experience 129. Amsterdam: Theatrum Orbis Terrarum; New York: Da Capo Press, 1969. (STC 21311).

Shakespeare, William. *Shakespeare's Sonnets*, ed. and comm. Stephen Booth. New Haven: Yale University Press, 1977.

———. *William Shakespeare: The Complete Works*, gen. ed. Alfred Harbage. New York: Penguin Books, 1969.

Sibbes, Richard. *The Soul's Conflict with Itself, and Victory Over Itself by Faith*. In *Works of Richard Sibbes*, ed. Alexander Grosart. Vol. 1. Edinburgh: James Nichol, 1862.

Sidney, Philip. *A Defence of Poetry*, ed. Jan Van Dorsten. Corr. ed. Oxford: Oxford University Press, 1975.

———. *The Poems of Sir Philip Sidney*, ed. William A. Ringler, Jr. Oxford: Clarendon Press, 1962.

Smith, John. *The Mystery of Rhetoric Unveiled*, ed. R. C. Alston. 1657. English Linguistics 1500–1800 205. Menston, Eng.: Scolar Press, 1969. (STC S4116A)

Southwell, Robert. *Marie Magdalens Funeral Teares*, intro. Vincent B. Leitch. 1591. Delmar, NY: Scholars' Facsimiles & Reprints, 1975.

Spencer, Thomas. *The Art of Logic*, ed. R. C. Alston. 1628. English Linguistics 1500–1800 245. Menston, Eng.: Scolar Press, 1970. (STC 23072)

Spenser, Edmund. *The Faerie Qveene*, ed. A. C. Hamilton. London: Longman, 1980.

The Statutes of the Realm. Vol. 4. repr. London: Dawsons of Pall Mall, 1963.

Stoughton, John. *Baruch's Sore Gently Opened: God's Salve Skilfully Applied.* London, 1640. (STC 23300)

Taylor, Jeremy. *Holy Living and Holy Dying*, ed. P. G. Stanwood. 2 vols. Oxford: Clarendon Press, 1989.

———. *The Whole Works*, ed. Reginald Heber, rev. ed. Charles Page Eden. 10 vols. London: Longman, 1847–1854; repr. Hildesheim: Georg Olms Verlag, 1969.

Traherne, Thomas. *Commentaries of Heaven, The Poems*, ed. D. D. C. Chambers. Elizabethan & Renaissance Studies 92:22. Gen. ed. James Hogg. Salzburg: Institüt für Anglistik und Amerikanistik, Universität Salzburg, 1989.

Vaughan, Henry. *Henry Vaughan: The Complete Poems*, ed. Alan Rudrum. New Haven: Yale University Press, 1976.

Vaughan, William. *The Golden-groue, moralized in three Bookes: A worke very necessary for all such, as would know how to gouerne themselues, their houses, or their countrey.* London, 1600. (STC 24610)

Visscher, C. J. *London Before the Fire: A Grand Panorama.* London: Sidgwick & Jackson, 1973.

Walker, Obadiah. *Some instrvctions concerning the Art of oratory.* London, 1659. (STC W410)

Walton, Izaak. *The Lives of John Donne, Sir Henry Wotton, Richard Hooker, George Herbert, and Robert Sanderson*, intro. George Saintsbury. London: Oxford University Press, 1927.

Whitney, Geoffrey. *A Choice of Emblemes*, intro. John Horden. 1586. English Emblem Books 3. Menston, Eng.: Scolar Press, 1969. (STC 25438)

Wilson, Thomas. *The Art of Rhetoric*, ed. Peter E. Medine. University Park, PA: Pennsylvania State University Press, 1994.

———. *The Rvle of Reason.* 1551. The English Experience 261. Amsterdam: Theatrum Orbis Terrarum; New York: Da Capo Press, 1970. (STC 25809)

Wither, George. *A Collection of Emblemes, Ancient and Moderne*, intro. Rosemary Freeman. 1635. Columbia, SC: University of South Carolina Press, 1975. (STC 25900)

Wright, Leonard. *A Svmmons for Sleepers.* London, 1596. (STC 26035)

Wright, Thomas. *The Passions of the Mind in General*, ed. William Webster Newbold. New York: Garland, 1986.

———. *the Passions of the Minde in Generall*, intro. Thomas O. Sloan. 1604. Urbana: University of Illinois Press, 1971. (STC 26040)

Wroth, Lady Mary. *The Countesse of Mountgomeries Urania*. London, 1621. (STC 26051)

———. *The First Part of The Countess of Montgomery's Urania*, ed. Josephine A. Roberts. MRTS 140. Binghamton, NY: Medieval & Renaissance Texts & Studies, 1995.

Secondary Sources

Abrams, M. H. *A Glossary of Literary Terms*. 3rd ed. New York: Holt, Rinehart and Winston, 1971.

Allinson, Mark. "Re-Visioning the Death Wish: Donne and Suicide." *Mosaic* 24 (1991): 31–46.

Anderson, Judith H. "Life Lived and Life Written: Donne's Final Word or Last Character." *HLQ* 51 (1988): 247–59.

———. "Patterns Proposed Beforehand: Donne's Second Prebend Sermon." *PS* 11 (1988): 37–48.

Anselment, Raymond A. *The Realms of Apollo: Literature and Healing in Seventeenth-Century England*. Newark, DE: University of Delaware Press, 1995.

Auksi, Peter. *Christian Plain Style*. Montreal and Kingston: McGill-Queen's University Press, 1995.

Bald, R. C. *Donne and the Drurys*. Cambridge: Cambridge University Press, 1959; repr. Westport, CT: Greenwood Press, 1986.

———. *John Donne: A Life*. Oxford: Clarendon Press, 1970.

Bates, Catherine. "'Of Court it seemes': A Semantic Analysis of Courtship and To Court." *JMRS* 20 (1990): 21–55.

———. *The Rhetoric of Courtship in Elizabethan Language and Literature*. Cambridge: Cambridge University Press, 1992.

Bath, Michael. *Speaking Pictures: English Emblem Books and Renaissance Culture*. London: Longman, 1994.

Beaty, Nancy Lee. *The Craft of Dying: A Study in the Literary Tradition of the Ars Moriendi in England*. New Haven: Yale University Press, 1970.

Beck, Ervin. "Terence Improved: The Paradigm of the Prodigal Son in English Renaissance Comedy." *RD* n.s. 6 (1973): 107–22.

Bertlesen, Dale A. "Kenneth Burke's Concept of Reality: The Process of Transformation and Its Implication for Rhetorical Criticism." In *Extensions of the Burkeian System*, ed. James W. Chesebro, 230–47. Tuscaloosa, AL: University of Alabama Press, 1993.

Bevan, Jonquil. "*Hebdomada Mortium:* The Structure of Donne's Last Sermon." *RES* n.s. 45 (1994): 185–203.

Bieman, Elizabeth. *Plato Baptized: Towards the Interpretation of Spenser's Mimetic Fictions.* Toronto: University of Toronto Press, 1988.

Blench, J. W. *Preaching in England in the Late Fifteenth and Sixteenth Centuries: A Study of English Sermons 1450–c.1600.* New York: Barnes & Noble, 1964.

Boenig, Robert. "George Herbert and John Climicus: A Note on 'Prayer (1)'." *N&Q* n.s. 37 (1990): 209–211.

Boston, Rosemary. "The Variable Heart in Donne's Sermons." *CSR* 1 (1971): 36–41.

Brown, Meg Lota. "'Though it be not according to the Law': Donne's Politics and the Sermon on Esther." *JDJ* 11 (1992): 71–84.

Bullough, Geoffrey. "Donne the Man of Law." In *Just So Much Honor*, ed. Peter Amadeus Fiore, 57–94. University Park: Pennsylvania State University Press, 1972.

Burke, Kenneth. *Counter-Statement.* Berkeley: University of California Press, 1968.

———. "The Five Master Terms: Their Place in a 'Dramatistic' Grammar of Motives." In *Landmark Essays on Rhetorical Invention in Writing*, ed. Richard E. Young and Yameng Liu, 1–12. Davis, CA: Hermagoras Press, 1994.

———. *A Grammar of Motives.* Berkeley: University of California Press, 1969.

———. *Language as Symbolic Action.* Berkeley: University of California Press, 1966.

———. *Permanence and Change: An Anatomy of Purpose.* 3rd ed. Berkeley: University of California Press, 1984.

———. *The Philosophy of Literary Form.* Berkeley: University of California Press, 1973.

———. *A Rhetoric of Motives.* Berkeley: University of California Press, 1969.

———. *The Rhetoric of Religion: Studies in Logology.* Berkeley: University of California Press, 1970.

———. "Thanatopsis for Critics: A Brief Thesaurus of Deaths and Dying." *EC* 2 (1952): 369–75.

———. "Theology and Logology." *KR* n.s. 1 (1979): 151–85.

———— and Stanley Romaine Hopper. "Mysticism as a Solution to the Poet's Dilemma." In *Spiritual Problems in Contemporary Literature*, ed. Stanley Romaine Hopper, 95–115. Gloucester, MA: Peter Smith, 1969.

Cameron, Allen Barry. "Donne's Deliberative Verse Epistles." *ELR* 6 (1976): 369–403.

Carey, John. *John Donne: Life, Mind, Art.* New York: Oxford University Press, 1981.

Carrithers, Gale H., Jr. *Donne at Sermons: A Christian Existential World.* Albany, NY: State University of New York Press, 1972.

Carrithers, Gale H. Jr. and James D. Hardy, Jr. "Love, Power, Dust Royall, Gavelkinde: Donne's Politics." *JDJ* 11.1,2 (1992): 39–58.

Carter, C. Allen. *Kenneth Burke and the Scapegoat Process.* Norman, OK: University Oklahoma Press, 1996.

Chamberlin, John S. *Increase and Multiply: Arts-of-Discourse Procedure in the Preaching of Donne.* Chapel Hill, NC: University of North Carolina Press, 1976.

Chambers, D[ouglas]. D. C. "Lancelot Andrewes and the Topical Structure of Thought." Ph.D. Diss., Princeton University, 1968.

————. *The Reinvention of the World: English Writing 1650–1750.* London: Arnold, 1996.

Cogan, Marc. "Rhetoric and Action in Francis Bacon." *PR* 14 (1981): 212–33.

Cohen, Kathleen. *Metamorphosis of a Death Symbol: The Transi Tomb in the Late Middle Ages and the Renaissance.* Berkeley: University of California Press, 1973.

Corbett, Edward P. J. and Robert J. Connors. *Classical Rhetoric for the Modern Student.* 4th ed. New York: Oxford University Press, 1999.

Corbett, Margery, and Ronald Lightbown. *The Comely Frontispiece: The Emblematic Title-Page in England 1550–1660.* London: Routledge & Kegan Paul, 1979.

Crane, R. S. *The Languages of Criticism and the Structure of Poetry.* Toronto: University Toronto Press, 1953.

Crockett, Bryan. *The Play of Paradox: Stage and Sermon in Renaissance England.* Philadelphia: University of Pennsylvania Press, 1995.

Crusius, Timothy W. *Kenneth Burke and the Conversation After Philosophy.* Carbondale and Edwardsville: Southern Illinois University Press, 1999.

Davies, Horton. *Like Angels From a Cloud: The English Metaphysical Preachers, 1588–1645.* San Marino, CA: Huntington Library, 1986.

Davies, J. T., J. Dutton, and C. Grey Morgan. *Electricity and Electrons.* Harmondsworth, Eng.: Penguin, 1973.

Davis, Walter R. "Meditation, Typology, and the Structure of John Donne's Sermons." In *The Eagle and the Dove,* eds. Claude J. Summers and Ted-Larry Pebworth, 166–88. Columbia, MO: University of Missouri Press, 1986.

Dean, William. "The Law of Criminal Procedure in *The Contention Between Liberality and Prodigality.*" *Ren&R* n. s. 1 (1977): 59–71.

Dees, Jerome S. "Logic and Paradox in the Structure of Donne's Sermons." *SCR* 4 (1987): 78–92.

Demaray, John G. "Donne's Three Steps to Death." *The Personalist* 46 (1965): 366–81.

DeStefano, Barbara L. "Evolution of Extravagant Praise in Donne's Verse Epistles." *SP* 81 (1984): 75–93.

Dixon, Michael F. N. *The Polliticke Courtier: Spenser's* The Faerie Queene *as a Rhetoric of Justice.* Montreal & Kingston: McGill-Queen's University Press, 1996.

Doebler, Bettie Anne. "Donne's Debt to the Great Tradition: Old and New in his Treatment of Death." *Anglia* 85 (1967): 15–33.

———. *The Quickening Seed: Death in the Sermons of John Donne.* Elizabethan & Renaissance Studies 30. Gen. ed. James Hogg. Salzburg: Institut für Englische Sprache und Literatur, Universität Salzburg, 1974.

———. *"Rooted Sorrow": Dying in Early Modern England.* London and Toronto: Associated University Press, 1994.

——— and Retha M. Warnicke. "Magdalen Herbert Danvers and Donne's Vision of Comfort." *GHJ* 10 (1986–1987): 5–22.

Doerksen, Daniel W. *Conforming to the Word: Herbert, Donne, and the English Church before Laud.* Lewisburg, PA: Bucknell University Press, 1997.

Dupriez, Bernard. *A Dictionary of Literary Devices: Gradus, A–Z,* trans. and adapted by Albert W. Halsall. Toronto: University of Toronto Press, 1991.

Engel, William E. *Mapping Mortality: The Persistence of Memory and Melancholy in Early Modern England.* Amherst: University of Massachusetts Press, 1995.

Esler, Anthony. *The Aspiring Mind of the Elizabethan Younger Generation.* Durham, NC: Duke University Press, 1966.

Faust, Joan. "John Donne's Verse Letters to the Countess of Bedford: Mediators in a Poet-Patroness Relationship." *JDJ* 12 (1993): 79–99.

Ferrell, Lori Anne. "Donne and his Master's Voice, 1615–1625." *JDJ* 11 (1992): 59–70.

Fish, Stanley E. *Self-Consuming Artifacts: The Experience of Seventeenth-Century Literature.* Berkeley: University of California Press, 1972.

Fitzgerald, John T., and L. Michael White. *The Tabula of Cebes.* Chico, CA: Scholars Press, 1983.

Foucault, Michel. *Discipline and Punish: The Birth of the Prison,* trans. Alan Sheridan. New York: Pantheon, 1977.

Frank, Armin Paul. *Kenneth Burke.* New York: Twayne, 1969.

Freeman, Rosemary. *English Emblem Books.* London: Chatto & Windus, 1948.

Freer, Coburn. "John Donne and Elizabethan Economic Theory." *Criticism* 38 (1996): 497–520.

Friedman, Donald M. "Donne, Herbert, and Vocation." *GHJ* 18 (1994): 135–58.

Fitzgerald, Allan D., ed. *Augustine Through the Ages.* Grand Rapids, MI: Eerdmans, 1999.

Frye, Northrop. *Anatomy of Criticism.* Princeton: Princeton University Press, 1957.

——. *The Great Code: The Bible as Literature.* New York: Harcourt, Brace, Jovanovich, 1982.

Gifford, William. "Time and Place in Donne's Sermons." *PMLA* 82 (1967): 388–98.

Goodblatt, Chanita. "An Intertextual Discourse on Sin and Salvation: John Donne's Sermon on Psalm 51." *Ren&R* n.s. 20 (1996): 23–40.

Guibbory, Achsah. "Donne's Religion: Montagu, Arminianism and Donne's Sermons, 1624–1630." *ELR* 31 (2001): 412–439.

Halewood, William H. *The Poetry of Grace: Reformation Themes and Structures in English Seventeenth-Century Poetry.* New Haven: Yale University Press, 1970.

Hall, Michael L. "Circles and Circumvention in Donne's Sermons." *JEGP* 82 (1983): 201–14.

Harland, Paul W. "Donne's Political Intervention in the Parliament of 1629." *JDJ* 11 (1992): 21–37.

——. "Dramatic Technique and Personae in Donne's Sermons." *ELH* 53 (1986): 709–26.

——. "Imagination and Affections in John Donne's Preaching." *JDJ* 6 (1987): 33–50.

Heatherington, Madelon E. "'Decency' and 'Zeal' in the Sermons of John Donne." *TSLL* 9 (1967): 307–16.

Henderson, Greig E. *Kenneth Burke: Literature and Language as Symbolic Action.* Athens, GA: University of Georgia Press, 1988.

Henricksen, Bruce. "The Unity of Reason and Faith in Donne's Sermons." *PLL* 11 (1975): 18–30.

Hester, M. Thomas. "John Donne's 'Hill of Truth'." *ELN* 14 (1976): 100–5.

Hickey, Robert L. "Donne's Art of Preaching." *TSL* 1 (1956): 65–74.

———. "Donne's Delivery." *TSL* 9 (1964): 39–47.

Hill, Christopher. *Liberty Against the Law: Some Seventeenth-Century Controversies.* London: Penguin Press, 1996.

Hodgson, Elizabeth M. A. *Gender and the Sacred Self in John Donne.* Newark, DE: University of Delaware Press, 1999.

Hoeniger, F. David. *Medicine and Shakespeare in the English Renaissance.* Newark, DE: University of Delaware Press, 1992.

Holdsworth, William. *A History of English Law.* 7th ed. 14 vols. London: Methuen, 1956.

Holland, L. Virginia. *Counterpoint: Kenneth Burke and Aristotle's Theories of Rhetoric.* New York: Philosophical Library, 1959.

Harmon, William and C. Hugh Holman. *A Handbook to Literature.* 8th ed. Upper Saddle River, NJ: Prentice Hall, 2000.

Howell, Wilbur Samuel. *Logic and Rhetoric in England, 1500–1700.* New York: Russell & Russell, 1961.

Howison, Patricia M. "Donne's Sermons and the Rhetoric of Prophecy." *ESC* 15 (1989): 134–48.

Huntley, Frank Livingstone. *Bishop Joseph Hall and Protestant Meditation in Seventeenth-Century England: A Study With the Texts of* The Art of Divine Meditation (1606) *and* Occasional Meditations (1633). MRTS 1. Binghamton, NY: Medieval & Renaissance Texts & Studies, 1981.

Jackson, Robert S. *John Donne's Christian Vocation.* Evanston, IL: Northwestern University Press, 1970.

Javitch, Daniel. *Poetry and Courtliness in Renaissance England.* Princeton: Princeton University Press, 1978.

Jayne, Sears. *Plato in Renaissance England.* International Archives of the History of Ideas 141. Dordrecht, Netherlands: Kluwer Academic Publ., 1995.

Johnson, Francis R. *Astronomical Thought in Renaissance England: A Study of English Scientific Writings from 1500–1645.* Baltimore: Johns Hopkins University Press, 1937; repr. New York: Octagon, 1968.

Johnson, Jeffrey. *The Theology of John Donne.* Studies in Renaissance Literature 1. Woodbridge, Suffolk: D. S. Brewer, 1999.

Johnson, Jeffrey. "Recovering the Curse of Eve: John Donne's Churching Sermons." *Ren&R* n.s. 23.2 (1999): 61–71.

Jones, Norman. *God and the Moneylenders: Usury and Law in Early Modern England.* London: Basil Blackwell, 1989.

Keller, James R. "The Science of Salvation: Spiritual Alchemy in Donne's Final Sermon." *SCJ* 23 (1992): 486–93.

Kinney, Arthur F., ed. *Rogues, Vagabonds, & Sturdy Beggars.* 2nd ed. Amherst: University of Massachusetts Press, 1990.

Kiralfy, A. K. R. *Potter's Historical Introduction to English Law and its Institutions.* 4th ed. London: Sweet & Maxwell, 1958.

Kneidel, Gregory. "John Donne's *Via Pauli.*" *JEGP* 100 (2001): 224–246.

Knox, George. *Critical Moments: Kenneth Burke's Categories and Critiques.* Seattle: University of Washington Press, 1957.

Krueger, Robert. "The Publication of John Donne's Sermons." *RES* 15 (1964): 151–60.

Lederer, Josef. "John Donne and the Emblematic Practice." *RES* o. s. 22 (1946): 182–200.

Leisher, John F. *Geoffrey Whitney's A Choice of Emblemes and its Relation to the Emblematic Vogue in Tudor England.* New York: Garland, 1987.

Lewalski, Barbara Kiefer. *Donne's Anniversaries and the Poetry of Praise: The Creation of a Symbolic Mode.* Princeton: Princeton University Press, 1973.

———. *Protestant Poetics and the Seventeenth-Century Religious Lyric.* Princeton: Princeton University Press, 1979.

Lindheim, Nancy. *The Structures of Sidney's Arcadia.* Toronto: University of Toronto Press, 1982.

Lottes, Wolfgang. "Henry Hawkins and *Partheneia Sacra* (concluded)." *RES* n. s. 26 (1975): 271–86.

Lovejoy, Arthur O. *The Great Chain of Being: A Study in the History of an Idea.* Cambridge, MA: Harvard University Press, 1957.

Low, Anthony. *Love's Architecture: Devotional Modes in Seventeenth-Century English Poetry.* New York: New York University Press, 1978.

Lowe, Irving. "John Donne: The Middle Way: The Reason-Faith Equation in Donne's Sermons." *JHI* 22 (1961): 389–97.

McCullough, Peter E. "Donne as Preacher at Court: Precarious 'Inthronization'." In *John Donne's Professional Lives*, ed. David Colclough, 179–204. Studies in Renaissance Literature 10. Cambridge: D. S. Brewer, 2003.

———. "Preaching to a Court Papist? Donne's Sermon Before Queen Anne, December 1917." *JDJ* 14 (1995): 59–81.

———. *Sermons at Court: Politics and Religion in Elizabethan and Jacobean Preaching.* Cambridge: Cambridge University Press, 1998.

MacKenzie, Clayton G. *Emblem and Icon in John Donne's Poetry and Prose.* New York: Peter Lang, 2001.

McKerrow, R. B., gen. ed. *A Dictionary of Printers and Booksellers in England, Scotland and Ireland, and of Foreign Printers of English Books 1557–1640.* Oxford: Bibliographical Society, 1968.

MacLure, Millar. *The Paul's Cross Sermons, 1534–1642.* Toronto: University of Toronto Press, 1958.

McGrath, Alister E. *A Life of John Calvin: A Study in the Shaping of Western Culture.* Oxford: Basil Blackwell, 1990.

McKevlin, Dennis J. *A Lecture in Love's Philosophy: Donne's Vision of the World of Human Love in the Songs and Sonets.* Lanham, MD: University Press of America, 1984.

McNees, Eleanor. "John Donne and the Anglican Doctrine of the Eucharist." *TSL* 29 (1987): 94–114.

Mann, Lindsay A. "Misogyny and Libertinism: Donne's Marriage Sermons." *JDJ* 11 (1992): 111–32.

Marotti, Arthur F. "Donne as Social Exile and Jacobean Courtier." In *Critical Essays on John Donne*, ed. Arthur F. Marotti, 77–102. New York: G. K. Hall, 1994.

Martz, Louis. *The Poetry of Meditation: A Study in English Religious Literature of the Seventeenth Century.* New Haven: Yale University Press; London: Oxford University Press, 1954.

Masselink, Noralyn. "A Matter of Interpretation: Example and Donne's Role as Preacher and as Poet." *JDJ* 11 (1992): 85–98.

May, Steven W. *Sir Walter Ralegh.* Boston: Twayne, 1989.

Merchant, W. Moelwyn. "Donne's Sermon to the Virginia Company." In *John Donne: Essays in Celebration*, ed. A. J. Smith, 433–52. New York: Barnes & Noble, 1972.

Metzger, Ernest, ed. *A Companion to Justinian's Institutes.* Ithaca, NY: Cornell University Press, 1998.

Merrill, Thomas F. "John Donne and the Word of God." *NM* 69 (1968): 597–616.

Millar, Oliver. *The Queen's Pictures*. London: Weidenfeld & Nicolson, 1977.

Milosh, Joseph E. *The Scale of Perfection and the English Mystical Tradition*. Madison, WI: University of Wisconsin Press, 1966.

Mitchell, W. Fraser. *English Pulpit Oratory from Andrewes to Tillotson: A Study of its Literary Aspects*. New York: Russell & Russell, 1962.

Monfasani, John. "The *De Doctrina Christiana* and Renaissance Rhetoric." In *Reading and Wisdom:* The De Doctrina Christiana *of Augutine in the Middle Ages*, ed. Edward D. English, 172–88, Notre Dame Conferences in Medieval Studies 6. Notre Dame, IN: University of Notre Dame Press, 1995.

Montrose, Louis Adrian. "Gifts and Reasons: The Contexts of Peele's *Araygnement of Paris*." *ELH* 47 (1980): 433–61.

Morrissey, Mary. "John Donne as a Conventional Paul's Cross Preacher." In *John Donne's Professional Lives*, ed. David Colclough, 159–178. Studies in Renaissance Literature 10. Cambridge: D. S. Brewer, 2003.

Mueller, William R. *John Donne: Preacher*. Oxford: Oxford University Press; Princeton: Princeton University Press, 1962.

Murphy, James J. *Rhetoric in the Middle Ages: A History of Rhetorical Theory from St. Augustine to the Renaissance*. Berkeley: University of California Press, 1974.

Neill, Michael. *Issues of Death: Mortality and Identity in English Renaissance Tragedy*. Oxford: Clarendon Press, 1997.

Nelson, T. G. A. "Death, Dung, the Devil, and Worldly Delights: A Metaphysical Conceit in Harington, Donne, and Herbert." *SP* 76 (1979): 272–87.

Ní Chuilleanáin, Eiléan. "Time, Place and the Congregation in Donne's Sermons." In *Literature and Learning in Medieval and Renaissance England: Essays Presented to Fitzroy Pyle*, ed. John Scattergood, 197–216. Dublin: Irish Academic Press, 1984.

Nicholls, George. *A History of the English Poor Law*, rev. ed. 2 vols. London: P. S. King & Sons, 1898; repr. New York: Augustus M. Kelley, 1967.

Oakeshott, Walter. *The Queen and the Poet*. New York: Barnes & Noble, 1961.

Ochs, Donovan J. "Cicero's *Topica*: A Process View of Invention." In *Explorations in Rhetoric: Studies in Honor of Douglas Ehninger*, ed. Ray E. McKerrow, 107–18. Glenview, IL: Scott, Foresman & Co., 1982.

Oliver, P. M. *Donne's Religious Writing: A Discourse of Feigned Devotion*. London: Longman, 1997.

Ong, Walter J. "Introduction" to John Milton. *A Fuller Course in the Art of Logic.* In *Complete Prose Works of John Milton*, vol. 8:144–205. New Haven: Yale University Press, 1953.

———. *Ramus: Method, and the Decay of Dialogue.* Cambridge, MA: Harvard University Press, 1958.

———. *Rhetoric, Romance, and Technology: Studies in the Interaction of Expression and Culture.* Ithaca: Cornell University Press, 1971.

Orgel, Stephen. *Cebes in England.* New York and London: Garland, 1980.

Parfitt, George. *John Donne: A Literary Life.* New York: St. Martin's Press, 1989.

Partridge, A. C. *John Donne: Language and Style.* London: Andre Deutsch, 1978.

Praz, Mario. *Studies in Seventeenth-Century Imagery.* 2nd ed. Rome: Edizioni di Storia e Letteratura, 1964.

Prest, Wilfrid R. *The Inns of Court under Elizabeth I and the Early Stuarts, 1590–1640.* Totowa, NJ: Rowman and Littlefield, 1972.

Quinn, Dennis. "Donne's Christian Eloquence." In *Seventeenth-Century Prose: Modern Essays in Criticism*, ed. Stanley E. Fish, 353–74. New York: Oxford University Press, 1971.

———. "John Donne's Principles of Biblical Exegesis." *JEGP* 61 (1962): 313–29.

Radin, Max. *Handbook of Anglo-American Legal History.* St. Paul, MN: West, 1936.

Ray, Robert H. "Another Perspective on Donne in the Seventeenth Century: Nehemiah Rogers's Allusions to the Sermons and 'A Hymne to God the Father'." *JDJ* 6 (1987): 51–54.

Reeves, Troy Dale. "*Sana Me Domine*: Bodily Sickness as a Means of Grace in Donne's Sermons and Devotions." *ABR* 33 (1982): 270–75.

Rooney, William J. J. "John Donne's 'Second Prebend Sermon' — A Stylistic Analysis." In *Seventeenth-Century Prose: Modern Essays in Criticism*, ed. Stanley E. Fish, 375–87. New York: Oxford University Press, 1971.

Rueckert, William H. *Kenneth Burke and the Drama of Human Relations.* 2nd ed. Berkeley: University of California Press, 1982.

———. "Kenneth Burke's 'Symbolic of Motives' and 'Poetics, Dramatistically Considered'." In *Unending Conversations: New Writings By and About Kenneth Burke*, eds. Greig Henderson and David Cratis Williams, 99–124. Carbondale: Southern Illinios University Press, 2001.

Sawday, Jonathan. *The Body Emblazoned: Dissection and the Human Body in Renaissance Culture.* London: Routledge, 1995.

Schleier, Reinhold. *Tabula Cebetis*. Berlin: Mann, 1973.

Schleiner, Winfried. "Donne's Coterie Sermon." *JDJ* 8.1 (1989): 125–32.

————. *The Imagery of John Donne's Sermons*. Providence, RI: Brown University Press, 1970.

Schoenfeldt, Michael C. *Prayer and Power: George Herbert and Renaissance Courtship*. Chicago and London: University of Chicago Press, 1991.

Sellin, Paul R. *So Doth, So Is Religion: John Donne and Diplomatic Contexts in the Reformed Netherlands, 1619–1620*. Columbia, MO: University of Missouri Press, 1988.

Shami, Jeanne. "Anatomy and Progress: The Drama of Conversion in Donne's Men of a 'Middle Nature'." *UTQ* 53 (1984): 221–235.

————. "Donne on Discretion." *ELH* 47 (1980): 48–66.

————. "Donne's Protestant Casuistry: Cases of Conscience in the *Sermons*." *SP* 80 (1983): 53–66.

————. "Donne's Sermons and the Absolutist Politics of Quotation." In *John Donne's Religious Imagination: Essays in Honor of John T. Shawcross*, ed. R.-J. Frontain and F. M. Malpezzi, 380–412. Conway, AR: University of Central Arkansas Press, 1995.

————. "Introduction: Reading Donne's Sermons." *JDJ* 11 (1992): 1–20.

————. *John Donne and Conformity in Crisis in the Late Jacobean Pulpit*. Studies in Renaissance Literature 13. Cambridge: D. S. Brewer, 2003.

————. "Kings and Desperate Men: John Donne Preaches at Court." *JDJ* 6 (1987): 9–23.

————. "Labels, Controversy, and the Language of Inclusion in Donne's Sermons." In *John Donne's Professional Lives*, ed. David Colclough, 135–157. Studies in Renaissance Literature 10. Cambridge: D. S. Brewer, 2003.

————. "'The Stars in their Order Fought Against Sisera': John Donne and the Pulpit Crisis of 1622." *JDJ* 14 (1995): 1–58.

Shawcross, John T. "The Concept of Sermo in Donne and Herbert." *JDJ* 6 (1987): 203–12.

Sherwood, Terry G. *Fulfilling the Circle: A Study of John Donne's Thought*. Toronto: University of Toronto Press, 1984.

————. "Reason in Donne's Sermons." *ELH* 39 (1972): 353–74.

Shuger, Debora Kuller. *Habits of Thought in the English Renaissance: Religion, Politics, and the Dominant Culture*. Berkeley: University of California Press, 1990; repr. Toronto: University of Toronto Press, 1997.

————. *Sacred Rhetoric: the Christian Grand Style in the English Renaissance.* Princeton: Princeton University Press, 1988.

Simpson, Evelyn M. *A Study of the Prose Works of John Donne.* 2nd ed. Oxford: Clarendon Press, 1948.

Slack, Paul. *Poverty and Policy in Tudor and Stuart England.* London: Longman, 1988.

Slights, Camille Wells. *The Casuistical Tradition in Shakespeare, Donne, Herbert, and Milton.* Princeton: Princeton University Press, 1981.

Sloan, Thomas O. "Rhetoric and Meditation: Three Case Studies." *JMRS* 1 (1971): 45–58.

Sloane, Mary Cole. *The Visual in Metaphysical Poetry.* Atlantic Highlands, NJ: Humanities Press, 1981.

Smith, Gregory G., ed. *Elizabethan Critical Essays.* 2 vols. Oxford: Oxford University Press, 1904.

Smith, Julia J. "Moments of Being and Not-Being in Donne's Sermons." *PS* 8 (1985): 3–20.

Stanford, Michael. "The Terrible Thresholds: Sir Thomas Browne on Sex and Death." *ELR* 18 (1988): 413–23.

Stanwood, P. G. "Donne's Art of Preaching and the Reconstruction of Tertullian." *JDJ* 15 (1996): 153–69.

————. "Donne's Reinvention of the Fathers: Sacred Truths Spiritually Expressed." In *Sacred and Profane: Secular and Devotional Interplay in Early Modern British Literature*, eds. Helen Wilcox et al., 195–201. Amsterdam: VU University Press, 1996.

————. "John Donne's Sermon Notes." *RES* 29 (1978): 313–20.

———— and Heather Ross Asals, eds. *John Donne and the Theology of Language.* Columbia: University of Missouri Press, 1986.

Stapleton, Laurence. "John Donne: The Moment of the Sermon." In idem. *The Elected Circle: Studies in the Art of Prose*, 17–41. Princeton: Princeton University Press, 1973.

Steadman, John M. *The Hill and the Labyrinth: Discourse and Certitude in Milton and His Near-Contemporaries.* Berkeley: University of California Press, 1984.

Stein, Arnold. "Handling Death: John Donne in Public Meditation." *ELH* 48 (1981): 496–515.

————. *The House of Death: Messages from the English Renaissance.* Baltimore, MD: Johns Hopkins University Press, 1986.

Stone, Lawrence. *The Family, Sex and Marriage in England 1500–1800*, abr. and rev. ed. London: Penguin, 1977.

———. "Social Mobility in England, 1500–1700." *P&P* 33 (1966): 16–55.

Strong, Roy. *The Renaissance Garden in England*. London: Thames and Hudson, 1979.

Sturt, Mary. *Francis Bacon: A Biography*. London: Kegan Paul, Trench, Trubner, 1932.

Sullivan, Ceri. *Dismembered Rhetoric: English Recusant Writing, 1580–1603*. Madison, NJ: Fairleigh Dickinson University Press, 1995.

Swift, Carolyn Ruth. "Feminine Identity in Lady Mary Wroth's Romance *Urania*." In *Women in the Renaissance: Selections From* English Literary Renaissance, eds. Kirby Farrell, Elizabeth H. Hageman, and Arthur F. Kinney, 154–74. Amherst: University of Massachusetts Press, 1990.

Tawney, R. H. "Introduction." In Thomas Wilson. *A Discourse Upon Usury ... [1572]*, 1–172. London: G. Bell and Sons, 1925.

Thompson, Geraldine. "'Writs Canonicall': The High Word and the Humble in the Sermons of John Donne." In *Familiar Colloquy: Essays Presented to Arthur Barker*, ed. Patricia Bruckmann, 55–67. Toronto: Oberon Press, 1978.

Tillyard, E. M. W. *The Elizabethan World Picture*. New York: Vintage Books, n.d.

Tippens, Darryl. "Shakespeare and the Prodigal Son Tradition." *ERC* 14 (1988): 57–77.

Trousdale, Marion. "Rhetoric." In *A Companion to English Renaissance Literature and Culture*, ed. Michael Hattaway, 623–33. Oxford: Blackwell, 2000.

Tuve, Rosemond. *Elizabethan and Metaphysical Imagery*. Chicago: University of Chicago Press, 1947.

Umbach, Herbert H. "The Merit of Metaphysical Style in Donne's Easter Sermons." *ELH* 12 (1945): 108–29.

———. "The Rhetoric of Donne's Sermons." *PMLA* 52 (1937): 354–58.

Underhill, Evelyn. *Mysticism: The Nature and Development of Spiritual Consciousness*. Oxford: Oneworld, 1993.

Veen, Otto van. *Amorum Emblemata*, intro. Stephen Orgel. 1608. New York: Garland, 1979.

Vessey, Mark. "Consulting the Fathers: Invention and Meditation in Donne's Sermon on Psalm 51:7 ('Purge me with hyssope')." *JDJ* 11 (1992): 99–110.

Vickers, Brian. *Classical Rhetoric in English Poetry*. 2nd ed. Carbondale, IL: Southern Illinois University Press, 1989.

————. *Seventeenth-Century Prose*. London: Longman, 1969.

Wall, John N., Jr., and Terry Bunce Burgin. "'This sermon … upon the Gun-powder day': The Book of Homilies of 1547 and Donne's Sermon in Commemoration of Guy Fawkes' Day, 1622." *SAR* 49 (1984): 19–30.

Wallace, Dewey D., Jr. *Puritans and Predestination: Grace in English Protestant Theology, 1525–1695*. Chapel Hill, NC: University of North Carolina Press, 1982.

Waller, Gary. *The Sidney Family Romance: Mary Wroth, William Herbert, and the Early Modern Construction of Gender*. Detroit: Wayne State University Press, 1993.

Ware, Tracy. "Donne and Augustine: A Qualification." *N&Q* 228 (1983): 425–27.

Watson, Robert N. *The Rest is Silence: Death as Annihilation in the English Renaissance*. Berkeley: University of California Press, 1994.

Webber, Joan. *Contrary Music: The Prose Style of John Donne*. Madison: University of Wisconsin Press, 1963; repr. Westport, CT: Greenwood Press, 1986.

Wells-Cole, Anthony. *Art and Decoration in Elizabethan and Jacobean England: The Influence of Continental Prints, 1558–1625*. New Haven: Yale University Press, 1997.

Wess, Robert. *Kenneth Burke: Rhetoric, Subjectivity, Postmodernism*. Cambridge: Cambridge University Press, 1996.

Whalen, Robert. *The Poetry of Immanence: Sacrament in Donne and Herbert*. Toronto: University of Toronto Press, 2002.

Whigham, Frank. *Ambition and Privilege: The Social Tropes of Elizabethan Courtesy Theory*. Berkeley: University of California Press, 1984.

White, Hayden V., and Margaret Brose, eds. *Representing Kenneth Burke*. Baltimore: Johns Hopkins University Press, 1982.

White, Helen C. *The Metaphysical Poets: A Study in Religious Experience*. New York: Macmillan, 1936.

Williamson, George. "The Convention of *The Extasie*." In *Seventeenth-Century English Poetry: Modern Essays in Criticism*, ed. William R. Keast, 132–43. Oxford: Oxford University Press, 1962.

————. *The Senecan Amble: A Study in Prose Form from Bacon to Collier*. Chicago: University of Chicago Press, 1966.

Wiltenburg, Robert. "Donne's Dialogue of One: The Self and the Soul." In *Reconsidering the Renaissance: Papers from the Twenty-First Annual Conference*, ed. Mario Di Cesare, 413–27. MRTS 93. Binghamton, NY: Medieval & Renaissance Texts & Studies, 1992.

Wolin, Ross. *The Rhetorical Imagination of Kenneth Burke.* Columbia, SC: University of South Carolina Press, 2001.

Woodbridge, Linda. *Vagrancy, Homelessness, and English Renaissance Literature.* Urbana: University of Illinois Press, 2001.

Wright, Nancy E. "The Figura of the Martyr in John Donne's Sermons." *ELH* 56 (1989): 293–309; repr. in *John Donne,* ed. Andrew Mousley, 182–97. New Casebooks. London: Macmillan, 1999.

Yates, Frances A. *The Art of Memory.* London: Routledge and Kegan Paul, 1966.

~ Index ~